Carriers in Combat

CARRIERS IN COMBAT

The Air War at Sea

Chester G. Hearn

PRAEGER SECURITY INTERNATIONAL
Westport, Connecticut • London

Library of Congress Cataloging-in-Publication Data

Hearn, Chester G.
    Carriers in combat : the air war at sea / Chester G. Hearn.
        p.   cm.
    Includes bibliographical references and index.
    ISBN 0-275-98557-1 (alk. paper)
    1. Aircraft carriers.   2. Naval battles.   I. Title.
    V874.H43 2005
    359.9'435—dc22   2005017478

British Library Cataloguing in Publication Data is available.

Library of Congress Catalog Card Number: 2005017478
ISBN: 0-275-98557-1

First published in 2005

Praeger Security International, 88 Post Road West, Westport, CT 06881
An imprint of Greenwood Publishing Group, Inc.
www.praeger.com

Printed in the United States of America

The paper used in this book complies with the
Permanent Paper Standard issued by the National
Information Standards Organization (Z39.48-1984).

10 9 8 7 6 5 4 3 2 1

To my wife, Ann, who puts up with my many hours of self-imposed isolation.

Contents

List of Illustrations   ix
Preface   xiii
Acknowledgments   xv
Abbreviations   xvii

Part I. The Dawn of Naval Air Power   1

1. From Dreadnoughts to Flight Decks   3
2. Mobilizing for War   19
3. Flattops in the Atlantic   27
4. The Rising Sun   41

Part II. Carriers at War   55

5. Fighting for Time   57
6. Coral Sea: Battle of Errors   73
7. Midway: The Turning Point   87

Part III. Evolution of Combat Tactics   105

8. The Eastern Solomons   107
9. The Battle for Guadalcanal   119

10. Refining Carrier Tactics   133
11. Island-Hopping in the Pacific   145
12. The Marianas Turkey Shoot   157

Part IV. Ascent of the Air Admirals   175

13. The New Air Navy   177
14. Prelude to the Philippines   187
15. Leyte Gulf   197
16. The Setting Sun   213

Part V. Command of the Seas   229

17. Korea: Carriers and Politics   231
18. Vietnam: President Johnson's War   243
19. Cold Wars and Brush Fires   261
20. The Desert Wars   273

Conclusion   285
Notes   289
Bibliography   297
Index   303

Illustrations

Figures

Eugene B. Ely discusses the operation of his pusher with the designer, Glenn Curtiss 6

Eugene B. Ely prepares to fly his Curtiss pusher from Presidio Army Air Field to the USS *Pennsylvania* 7

The HMS *Furious* in transition to a carrier 12

British Sopwith Camel takes off from the deck of HMS *Pegasus* 13

USS *Langley*, America's first carrier 21

A Martin T4M-1 flies over the USS *Saratoga* 23

A Vought O2U-2 flies over the USS *Saratoga* 24

HMS *Ark Royal* launching and receiving Fairey Albacores 28

British Martlet 35

Grumman F4F-4 Wildcats on the deck of the USS *Ranger* 39

Admiral Isoruko Yamamoto 45

Vice Admiral Chuichi Nagumo 46

Admiral Ernest J. King 58

Admiral Chester W. Nimitz 60

Admiral William F. "Bull" Halsey, Jr. 61

Lieutenant Edward H. "Butch" O'Hare 67

Vice Admiral Frank Jack Fletcher 74

Sinking of the USS *Lexington* 85

Vice Admiral Raymond A. Spruance   89

USS *Yorktown* struck by dive-bombers   102

Abandonment of the USS *Yorktown*   104

Bridge scene on the USS *Wasp* during marine landing at
    Guadalcanal   110

Landing accident on the USS *Long Island*   113

USS *Wasp* is hit by Japanese torpedoes   120

Quad-mounted 40-mm antiaircraft guns   121

Japanese fighters prepare to launch from a Japanese carrier   123

USS *Hornet* under attack by Japanese dive-bombers off
    Santa Cruz Islands   126

Rear Admiral Arthur W. Radford   147

Hellcat fighter prepares to take off from the new
    USS *Yorktown*   148

Rear Admiral Alfred E. Montgomery   151

Vice Admiral Frederick C. "Ted" Sherman   152

Vice Admiral Jisaburo Ozawa   159

Vice Admiral Marc A. Mitscher   162

USS *Enterprise* in the Marianas   164

Hellcat prepares to takeoff from USS *Yorktown*   166

U.S. fast carrier fleet underway, USS *Essex* in the foreground   188

Admiral Halsey during operations off the Philippines   198

Vice Admiral Takeo Kurita   200

Rear Admiral Gerald F. Bogan   204

Avenger catapulted from USS *Makin Island*   218

U.S.-built Corsairs interspersed with British Barracudas on the
    HMS *Illustrious*   220

Vice Admiral Philip L. Vian   222

USS *Belleau Wood* struck by a kamikaze   223

F4-U Corsair taking off from USS *Boxer* off Korea   235

HMS *Triumph* joining the U.S. Pacific Fleet   238

HRS helicopters fly off the USS *Sicily* off Korea   241

Skyraider preparing for takeoff on the USS *Intrepid*   247

USS *Independence* off Yankee Station   251
Vought A-7E Corsairs   252
Vought Crusaders in formation over the USS *Forrestal*   256
The nuclear-powered USS *Enterprise*   264
Russia's first modern carrier, the *Admiral Kuznetsov*   266
USS *John F. Kennedy, Saratoga*, and *America* steaming toward
   the Persian Gulf   275
Intruders refuel in flight from a KC-135E Stratotanker   276

Maps

Air Cover by Escort Carriers   37
Route of Admiral Nagumo's Pearl Harbor Strike Force   52
First Carrier Strikes: Marshall and Gilbert Islands   65
Battle of the Coral Sea, May 7–8, 1942   83
Battle of Midway: Movement of Forces to June 3, 1942   92
Battle of Midway: June 4–5, 1942   98
Division of the Pacific into Sectors of Command   108
Battle of the Eastern Solomons, August 24, 1942   116
Battle of the Santa Cruz Islands, October 26, 1942   124
Rabaul Carrier Strike, November 5, 1943   139
Rabaul Carrier Strike, November 11, 1943   143
Marianas Turkey Shoot and Battle of the Philippine Sea   168
Task Force 38 Movements, October 6–24, 1944   191
Leyte Gulf Naval Air Battle, October 24–25, 1944   199
The Korean Theater: Carrier Operations   236
Vietnam: Carrier Operations   246

Preface

Lieutenant William H. Hessler, USN, wrote in the November 1945 issue of *Proceedings*: "The Fast Carrier Task Force has appeared so often in news dispatches, has become so commonplace in this war of unnumbered innovations, that its uniqueness tends to escape notice. It represents in fact a revolution in naval war, and more completely than did the invention of the submarine and torpedo. To an extent almost beyond belief, today's naval war is different from that of World War I." Had Hessler written his conclusion in 2005 instead of 1945, he would have closed by saying, "Today's naval war is different *from that of any other war.*" Referring to the oceanic vastness, Hessler added, "The United States has built a fleet unlike any previous in history. It has devised its own stratagems—consistent, to be sure, with the unchanging principles of strategy—and has shaped its own tactics." The marriage of aircraft and technology to carriers, and the restructuring of tactics, is perhaps the greatest naval achievement of the 20th century.

In 1914, when war broke out in Europe, the most powerful weapon on earth was the dreadnought, otherwise known as the battleship. The big gunships served as the keystone of every navy. For a while, some of them carried floatplanes. The first true aircraft carrier never made an appearance until the very end of World War I. Nobody in 1918 would have predicted that by 1943 battleships would be playing second fiddle to aircraft carriers. Today, the grand old battlewagons have become a venerable vestige of the past, replaced by missiles and mind-boggling technology compacted into 90-plane, 35-knot, 92,000-ton, nuclear-powered aircraft carriers manned by 6,300 men and women.

Unlike battleship, cruiser, and destroyer actions, there has never been a war in which a fleet aircraft carrier came face-to-face in battle with an enemy surface ship. Air power and surveillance made the difference. Since World War II, there has never been an engagement between carrier air groups, but flattops have been prominent and essential in every war, skirmish, or terrorist act that could be struck by planes from sea. Carriers have no political boundaries. They range at will with planes that can be refueled in the air to strike targets thousand of miles inland.

More than 90 years has passed since the first rickety plane, stitched together with wood, wire, and canvas, took off from a wooden platform built over the bow of an American cruiser. That act, performed by a civilian barnstormer, spawned naval aviation and nourished the development of seaborne aircraft. Naval air came out of the incubator in the 1930s with America's first two fast carriers, *Lexington* and *Saratoga*, and has matured into the most flexible and powerful weapon afloat.

Tracing the combat history of aircraft carriers cannot be done without tracing the development of carrier aircraft, admirals, airmen, tactics, and technology together. To cover the subject in full detail would require several volumes. Those books already exist, and many of them can be found in the bibliography. Samuel Eliot Morison wrote a 15-volume *History of United States Naval Operations in World War II* and scratched the surface.

This book is not for experts who are interested in the detailed development of airborne radar or the propulsion characteristics of the quadruple screw-geared turbines on the USS *Enterprise* (CVAN-65), for which steam is supplied by eight nuclear reactors. This book is about the history of the development of aircraft carriers through combat and defense requirements and the complementary development of aircraft and air tactics from World War I to the present. Moreover, it is a history of carriers in combat and air power at sea that includes naval powers of the world. It is not a book filled with laborious facts and figures. It is a book of action.

Acknowledgments

I have many to thank for their help. Mary Goodrich pulled dozens of selected documents from the National Archives, including actions reports, excerpts from the U.S. Strategic Bombing Survey, a few Ship and Unit War diaries, along with material applying to the Korean and Vietnam wars.

Gordon Keiser at the U.S. Naval Institute supplied me with a stack of *Proceedings* back copies from which current events and analysis could be gleaned.

Timothy Wooldridge, also of the U.S. Naval Institute, provided me with dozens of articles on carrier and naval activities dating back to World War I.

Captain Kelly Frushour at Cencom led me to many Web sites that carry mountains of information pertaining to past, present, and future activities of the navy as it applies to carriers and carrier aircraft.

Glenn Helm at the U.S. Naval Historical Center led me to boxes of information that the navy has over the years transferred to the National Archives.

Karen Stafford and the staff at the Erie County Public Library has once again done a superb job of locating the primary and secondary sources I needed to fill gaps in my research.

I owe the greatest debt to Michael G. Marino, who has not only made the book's 16 maps but also has worked assiduously on preparing, reprocessing, and electronically digitizing all the photographs and illustrations for publication. Most maps I have seen on carrier actions are either too busy to be read or too inadequate to depict the action. Mike takes the middle of the road and marries simplicity with thoroughness.

To those I may have overlooked, I apologize. Never meaning to offend anyone who has helped with this project, I did not retain all the names of those I contacted and who may have provided assistance along the way. To those unnamed contributors, I also give my thanks.

Abbreviations

AA	antiaircraft
AAA	antiaircraft artillery
AAF	Army Air Forces
ABDA	American, British, Dutch, and Australian
Anzac	Australia-New Zealand Area Command
ARM	antiradiation missiles
ASW	antisubmarine warfare
CAP	combat air patrol
CCF	Chinese Communist Forces
CinC	Commander in Chief
CincPac	Commander in Chief Pacific
CNO	Chief of Naval Operations
CominCh	Commander in Chief, United States Fleet
CV	aircraft carrier (Fleet)
CVA	attack aircraft carrier
CVAN	attack aircraft carrier, nuclear powered
CVB	aircraft carrier, large
CVE	aircraft escort carrier
CVHA	assault helicopter aircraft carrier
CVL	light aircraft carrier
CVN	(replaced CVAN)
DMZ	demilitarized zone
HARM	high-speed antiradiation missile
IGH	Imperial General Headquarters
IGS	Imperial General Staff
IJA	Imperial Japanese Army
IJN	Imperial Japanese Navy

JCS	Joint Chiefs of Staff
LANTIRN	low-altitude navigation and targeting infrared system for night
LHA	amphibious assault ship (general purpose)
LHD	amphibious assault ship
LPH	amphibious assault ship
MEU(SOC)	Marine Expeditionary Unit (Special Operations Capable)
NATO	North Atlantic Treaty Organization
NKPA	North Korea People's Army
NTDS	Naval Tactical Data System
NVA	North Vietnam Army
POL	petroleum, oil, and lubricants
POW	prisoner of war
PRC	People's Republic of China
RAF	Royal Air Force
RN	Royal Navy
ROK	Republic of Korea
SAM	surface-to-air missile
SAR	search and rescue
SEAL	sea, land, air (teams)
SCAP	Supreme Commander Allied Powers
SLAM	stand-off land attack missile
TARPS	tactical air reconnaissance pod systems
TEZ	total exclusion zone
TF	task force
TG	task group
TLAM	Tomahawk land attack missile
USA	United States Army
USAF	United States Air Force
USMC	United States Marine Corps
USN	United States Navy
USSBS	United States Strategic Bombing Survey
VC	Viet Cong

PART I

The Dawn of Naval Air Power

It is all a question as to whether the airplane carrier, equipped with 80 planes, is not the capital ship of the future.

(Admiral William S. Sims, February 14, 1921)

CHAPTER 1

From Dreadnoughts to Flight Decks

On September 14, 1901, Teddy Roosevelt became the twenty-sixth president of the United States. He was a navy man, having held the post of assistant secretary of the navy in 1897–98 before volunteering for the Spanish-American War. He had watched the navy slowly grow but was never satisfied with its progress. His impatience intensified as European nations colonized the world and expanded their navies to protect their holdings. "I have a great horror of words that cannot be backed, or will not be backed, by deeds. The American people must either build and maintain an adequate navy, or else make up their minds definitely to accept a secondary position in international affairs."[1]

The United States entered the race for colonization late, the major spoils of war—Cuba, Puerto Rico, Guam, and the Philippines—coming at the expense of Spain. Midway had been annexed in 1867, Hawaii in 1898. The acquisition of the Philippines became unpopular because four years of insurrection followed, taking the lives of 4,200 Americans and 20,000 Filipinos. The Japanese viewed the intrusion of Americans and Europeans into their sphere of influence with suspicion, and a new race began for control of the islands of the Pacific. Senator George Gray of Delaware predicted that taking the Philippines would "make necessary a navy equal to that of the largest powers; a greatly increased military establishment; immense sums for fortifications and harbors; [multiple] occasions for dangerous complications with other countries, and increased burdens of taxation."[2] Gray could not convince the president, although every word he said was true.

In December 1902, Germany, Great Britain, and Italy defied the Monroe Doctrine by blockading Venezuelan ports because the Venezuelan government had defaulted on payment of $12.5 million in bonds. When German warships began firing shells at Venezuela's forts, Roosevelt dispatched a naval force to the area and convinced the Europeans to settle the case in the International Court of Justice at The Hague. Roosevelt assessed the situation for what it portended, and in his 1904 annual message to Congress, said, "If we are willing to let Germany or England act as the policeman for the Caribbean, then we can afford not to intervene when gross wrongdoing occurs. But if we intend to say

'Hands off' to the powers of Europe, then sooner or later we must keep order ourselves."[3]

In 1894–95, Roosevelt had watched with interest as Japan astonished the world when its navy, so long ignored, defeated China in a conflict over Korea. Eight years later, Japan signed a pact with Great Britain, and the agreement affected the world's naval equilibrium as much as the Spanish-American War. The move checked the Russo-Franco-German expansion of their spheres of influence and reduced the need for Great Britain to keep so many ships in the Far East—exactly what Japan wanted. Germany refused to take a back seat, and under the professional guidance of Admiral Alfred von Tirpitz another major navy took shape. Soon five navies dominated the world—those of Great Britain, Japan, Germany, Russia, and the United States.

In his Fourth Annual Message, delivered December 6, 1904, Roosevelt said, "Chronic wrongdoing . . . in the Western Hemisphere . . . may force the United States . . . to the exercise of an international police power."[4] Roosevelt's Corollary, as this was called, led to America's temporary occupation of Haiti, the Dominican Republic, Nicaragua, and the authorization of 250,000 tons of new naval construction, including 10 first-class battleships. The navy asked for 48 battleships to keep pace with Great Britain, but Roosevelt balked. Instead, he became interested in heavier-than-air technology and pressured the War Department into investigating "a Wright flying machine." In 1909, Orville Wright gave birth to army aviation by producing a flyable contraption, but the Navy Department remained circumspect.[5]

In the meantime, following one of his own best-remembered presidential phrases—" Speak softly and carry a big stick"—Roosevelt decided in 1907 to send his Great White Fleet on an extended tour of the world. From his yacht *Mayflower*, he watched as the long column passed in review. He already knew that his navy was obsolete, even the battleships *Vermont*, *Minnesota*, *Kansas*, and *Nebraska*, all commissioned that year. Never had the world seen such a demonstration of steam-powered steel battleships, and never had so many—16 in all—circumnavigated the world. They sailed on December 17, heavily coated with white paint, and began a two-year tour that spanned 46,000 miles.

Great Britain rained on Roosevelt's parade. In 1906, the Royal Navy put the 17,900-ton HMS *Dreadnought* to sea, an omen of things to come. She mounted 10 guns in her main battery, compared with 4 in American battleships, and naval experts called her the "all-big-gun ship" of the future. She introduced a revolution in marine propulsion, powered by steam turbines rather than cranky reciprocating engines prone to breakdowns. She could show her heels to any battleship afloat. Roosevelt realized that it was imperative to keep pace with Europe, so the navy began work on four American dreadnoughts. Roosevelt was no longer in office on January 4, 1910, when the USS *Michigan* (BB-27) went into commission.

Neither Roosevelt nor his successor, William Howard Taft, watched the development of aircraft. Secretary of the Navy George Meyer, however, became curious after the army obtained its first airplane from the Wrights. His interest increased in 1909 after Commander F. L. Chapin, having attended the first great international aviation meet at Reims, France, not only recommended naval aviation "but suggested the possibilities of the aircraft carrier."[6] Meyer detached Captain Washington I. Chambers from the battleship *Louisiana* to report on the progress of aviation. At the time, the United States ranked 14th in the world on expenditures for naval aviation.

On October 20, 1910, Chambers, then in his mid-50s, acted as the navy's official observer at the International Air Meet at Belmont Park, New York. What he saw amazed him. He witnessed a French Blériot fly at 69 miles per hour, and he watched as Ralph Johnstone, flying a "baby" Wright pusher, climbed to a new record of 9,714 feet.

Two days later, Chambers met 24-year-old Eugene B. Ely, a member of Glenn Curtiss's flying team and a civilian barnstormer who had already survived several crashes. On hearing that Chambers was looking for someone to fly off a ship, Ely volunteered to use his own plane if Chambers would supply the vessel.

At the Norfolk Navy Yard (Norfolk, Virginia), John Barry Ryan, head of the U.S. Aeronautical Reserve, provided money for building an 83-foot wooden platform over the foredeck of the scout cruiser *Birmingham*. The platform sloped about five degrees from the bridge to the bow to provide a gravity-assisted 57-foot takeoff run for Ely's Hudson-Fulton Flyer.

On the morning of November 14, a crane deposited the plane on *Birmingham*'s deck. Ely installed his four-cylinder pusher engine behind the pilot's seat. At noon, the cruiser steamed down the Elizabeth River and into the Hampton Roads waterway on the lower James River (Virginia) for Ely's test flight. The destroyers *Terry* and *Roe* followed, acting as "planeguards" to retrieve Ely should he plunge into the sea.[7] Squalls delayed the experiment until mid-afternoon. At 3:16 P.M., Ely gunned the engine and the rickety biplane bumped down the ramp. With wheels skimming the water and splashing spray into Ely's goggles, the propeller cracked but the plane still lurched into the air. Five minutes later, after climbing to 500 feet, Ely landed on the beach. During the discussion that followed, Ely assured Chambers that "an aviator could alight on a ship (as well as takeoff) with little difficulty."[8]

Earning the distinction of becoming the first pilot to fly off a ship brought a small reward. At Chambers's suggestion, Ryan awarded Ely $500 and made him a lieutenant in the Aeronautical Reserve. Ely reciprocated and gave Ryan his damaged propeller.[9]

Fifteen days later, aviation pioneer Glenn Curtiss offered to instruct a naval officer in the operation and construction of his aircraft. Secretary Meyer accepted the proposal and allotted $25,000 for further experiments. On December 23, he detailed Lieutenant Theodore G. Ellyson, a volunteer from the submarine service, to attend a course of instruction at Glenn Curtiss Aviation Center in Los Angeles. Meyer, although a skeptic, funded the program because it cost so little.

Eugene B. Ely (*l*) discusses the operation of his pusher with the designer, Glenn Curtiss (*r*). Ely later flew the pusher off the USS *Birmingham*. (U.S. Navy photo)

On January 18, 1911, Ely barnstormed again, this time while performing stunts at San Francisco. After becoming the first man to fly an airplane off a ship, he became the first man to land on one, bringing his Curtiss pusher down on a 127-foot-long wooden platform jury-rigged on the armored cruiser *Pennsylvania*. Hugh A. Robbins, an experienced circus performer, fitted three hooks to the undercarriage of Ely's 1,000-pound pusher-aircraft and stretched 22 ropes attached to sandbags across the platform to catch the plane as it landed. The

On January 18, 1911, Eugene B. Ely prepares to fly his Curtiss pusher from Presidio Army Air Field to the USS *Pennsylvania*. Floats have been attached under the lower wing for buoyancy if Ely is forced to ditch. (U.S. Navy photo)

arresting mechanism worked and eventually became the methodology for landing aircraft on flight decks.

Pennsylvania's skipper, Captain Charles F. Pond, extolled Ely's feat as "the most important landing of a bird since the dove flew back to the ark." The *San Francisco Examiner* added, "Eugene Ely Revises World's Naval Tactics." *Aero*, a British publication disagreed: "This partakes rather too much of the nature of trick flying to be of much practical value. A naval aeroplane would be of more use if it landed on the water and could then be hauled on board."[10] Captain Pond countered, and speaking for the future, said, "I desire to place myself on record as positively assured of the importance of the aeroplane in future naval warfare." He went on to suggest that the navy "construct new vessels to serve as floating airfields from which land-type aircraft [can] take off and land."[11] Captain Chambers disagreed because he believed that long platforms to carry planes would interfere with the placement of gun turrets. This marked the beginning of a debate over flight decks versus gun turrets that spanned the next two decades.

Ely set the standard and pocketed another $500 for his successful landing, but later that year he crashed and died. In 1933, although he never joined the navy, he received the Distinguished Service Cross posthumously. During his short career as a flyer, he pioneered naval aviation long before an aircraft carrier became a matter of serious discussion.

Secretary Meyer could not visualize the future quite as clearly as men like Chambers. Despite his concerns about special ships with flight decks, Chambers became the "father of naval aviation." He believed that "aircraft could not only supply information about the location of enemy fleets but could destroy enemy mines, submarines, shore installations, provide communications between fleet and army commanders, and operate as part of an expeditionary force. Chambers designed the steam catapult, and then lobbied for automatic controls, safety devices, more dependable engines, and a national aerodynamic laboratory devoted to testing aircraft parts and systems and to experimental research best carried out in a wind tunnel."[12]

In 1910, navy men could not shift their sight away from battleships, and Meyer, who was among them, expressed his skepticism in a challenging letter to Chambers: "When you show me that it is feasible for an aeroplane to alight on the water alongside a battleship and be hoisted aboard without any false deck to receive it, I shall believe the airship of practical value to the Navy."[13] Chambers accepted the challenge, knowing that M. Henri Fabre of France had already taken off and alighted on water in a four-pontoon hydroplane and became the first to do so.

Three weeks later, Chambers completed contract specifications for the first two naval aircraft and handed them to Glenn Curtiss. In 1910, planes were cobbled together with wooden frames, canvas, and cable. Curtiss decided to put the engine and propeller in front of the pilot's seat, thereby changing the hydroplane to a pulling rather than a pusher-type aircraft.

On February 17, 1911, Curtiss taxied his hydroplane to the cruiser *Pennsylvania* off San Diego and sailors hoisted it on deck. Curtiss offered a short speech before being lowered back into the water. He made a successful takeoff, flew back to his dock at North Island, and fulfilled the terms of Secretary Meyer's challenge.

The exercise convinced Meyer that a naval air wing might have value. In September, he authorized the formation of the first naval air station at Annapolis, Maryland, across the Severn River from the Naval Academy. On April 12, 1911, Lieutenant Ellyson completed his flight training with Curtiss and became the navy's first pilot. The Marine Corps instantly recognized the potential of an air wing, and on May 22, 1912, Second Lieutenant Alfred A. Cunningham qualified as the first Marine aviator at the navy's new air station.

Curtiss disliked the strong blast of the propeller blowing in his face and converted the hydroplane back to a pusher-type. During the changeover, Chambers suggested adding wheels so that the hydroplane could be amphibious. A week later, the first Triad "hydroaeroplane" rolled out of Curtiss's workshop. On February 26, 1911, Curtiss lifted off water and alighted on land, and then rose from the ground and alighted on water. The trials convinced Meyer, who asked Curtiss to bring the Traid east.

At Chambers's request, Curtiss continued making refinements. He transported the 80-horsepower A-1 Triad to Hammondsport, New York, and on July 1,

1911, Lieutenant Ellyson flew it from shore and landed it on the waters of Lake Keuka. The navy's first pilot had now flown the navy's first airplane. Meyer asked Chambers how much money he needed to begin a naval aeronautics program. Chambers said $25,000 but soon discovered he should have asked for much more.

With the seeds of air power planted in the minds of naval thinkers, Rear Admiral Bradley A. Fiske, one of the navy's most ingenious innovators, began looking for ways to make aircraft fighting machines, and on July 16 he patented the first aerial torpedo.

Chambers recommended at least two planes for every scout cruiser, or, as an alternative, one two-seater, and he wanted more planes for pilot training. He also wanted more money and an independent Office of Aeronautics organized under the secretary of the navy. His demands drew a reaction from Rear Admiral Richard Wainwright, who believed that "aerial warfare would soon be outlawed by international agreement." Wainwright said establishing an Office of Aeronautics would be superfluous and denounced the request.[14]

Despite opposition, Chambers continued to press his demands and advance his experiments. He replaced his steam catapult with one using compressed air, and on July 31, 1912, Ellyson tested the system. The A-1 Triad cartwheeled into the Severn River because mechanics failed to secure the aircraft to its launching tracks. Undeterred by his dunking, Ellyson made his next attempt in November. The compressed air catapult boosted Ellyson and his hydroaeroplane into the air from a barge anchored off the Washington Navy Yard. Observer Glenn Curtiss wrote, "It is now possible and practicable to have the large ships of the Navy equipped with aeroplanes."[15] Ellyson then traveled to Lake Keuka at Hammondsport and on November 30 tested the Curtiss C-1, the navy's first flying boat. Although still in the experimental stage, the successful trial entitled navy pilots to participate in annual fleet maneuvers. On January 6, 1913, the collier *Sterling* arrived at Guantánamo Bay with a pair of planes, marking the first time that aircraft other than dirigibles participated in naval exercises.

Chambers continued to experiment with aircraft, and Wilbur Wright developed the B-2, a two-man hydroaeroplane. On June 20, 1913, Ensign W. D. Billingsley (naval aviator no. 9) flew the plane into a violent downdraft. At 1,600 feet over Chesapeake Bay, the wind tossed him into the air. Lieutenant John H. Towers (naval aviator no. 3) clung to the plane, survived with injuries, and 30 years later became an admiral. Nobody thought to give flyers safety belts. Billingsley became the first casualty of navy aviation, but it was not enough to deter Civil War veteran Admiral George Dewey, who headed the General Board of the Navy, from demanding, on August 30, 1913, the formal establishment of an official Naval Air Station. Despite the efforts of Chambers, Fiske, and Dewey, the United States still ranked 14th in the world on the basis of aviation expenditures, and the Navy Aviation Corps consisted of only 14 pilots and 4 aircraft. The historians Frank Owsley and Wesley Newton noted that, "Faith in aviation in general, and the money to back it up, lagged in the land of its origin."[16] By then, even Russia had entered the flying boat business and was adopting ways to put them on ships.

Josephus Daniels, the new secretary of the navy, gave Captain Mark L. Bristol the task of developing aerial tactics. Daniels put the Naval Aeronautical Station at the Pensacola Navy Yard and detached the old battleship *Mississippi* so Bristol and his team could learn how aircraft could work with ships at sea. Lieutenant Towers brought 9 officers and 23 men from Annapolis and by the beginning of February 1914 had the flight school staffed and running. Daniels sent another officer abroad to learn more about Europe's aircraft programs and then asked Congress for funds for 50 airplanes, 75 officers, and 250 men.[17]

The move to Pensacola proved timely. Dissidents in Mexico revolted, forcing Daniels to send Rear Admiral Frank F. Fletcher's First Division, Atlantic Fleet, to Veracruz. On April 24, 1914, two Aero Sections of two aircraft each, one unit commanded by Towers and the other by Lieutenant Patrick N. L. Bellinger (naval aviator no. 8), arrived off Veracruz on the cruiser *Birmingham* and the battleship *Mississippi*. The following day, Bellinger lifted off *Mississippi* in a Curtiss A-3 (rated at 60 mph with a 75-hp V-block water-cooled engine) to search for mines in the harbor, marking the first navy flight into a combat zone. Eleven days later, Bellinger set another mark when he and his reconnaissance observer, Lieutenant (jg) Richard C. Saufley, became the first flyers to have their aircraft damaged by ground fire.

When World War I began on August 5, 1914, no nation had envisaged a ship such as an aircraft carrier. The slow and clumsy biplanes needed little takeoff space, but they were getting faster, and the U.S. Navy had only evaluated float-planes that could be catapulted from the decks of gunships and recovered with cranes.

On November 23, Captain Bristol became the new director of naval aeronautics and continued the work begun by Chambers. Because a plane had never been launched from a moving vessel, Bristol experimented with catapults. A year later, Lieutenant Commander Henry C. Mustin catapulted a Curtiss AB-2 flying boat from the cruiser *North Carolina* when underway in Pensacola Bay. The feat went unnoticed in the next hefty navy appropriation. The $500 million Naval Act of 1916 provided for 10 battleships, 6 battlecruisers, 10 scout cruisers, 50 destroyers, 9 fleet submarines, 58 coastal submarines, and 16 auxiliary vessels. Naval air was barely mentioned, but not for long. World War I induced advancements in aviation that would affect every navy of the world for generations to come.

The need for a seaborne airfield occurred in 1916 when lightly armored British battlecruisers failed to fulfill reconnaissance and attack missions during the Battle of Jutland. The Royal Navy sought a solution and built an aircraft carrier.

Like Eugene Ely and Ted Ellyson, British aviators had been flying floatplanes off battleships ever since 1912. France, Germany, and Japan got into the act in 1914, followed by Russia and Italy in 1915. Russia called their seaplane carriers "hydrocruisers," and used them effectively in the Black Sea.[18] A few countries were beginning to understand the potential of air power.

The British led the world in developing naval aviation because in 1912 Winston Churchhill, First Lord of the Admiralty, took an interest in the Royal Naval Air Service and promoted its development. For the next three years, the Royal Navy ran numerous trials on experimental flight decks built on battleships and cruisers without deciding on a final ship design.

On May 7, 1913, the cruiser *Hermes* became the first parent ship for seaplanes. Modifications included a two-track launching platform over the forecastle for seaplanes on trolleys, a canvas seaplane shelter on the quarterdeck, and a long aircraft-recovery boom fitted to the lower mainmast. When *Hermes* went on maneuvers in 1913, she carried two innovative aircraft: a French Caudron G.111 with wheels recessed into its twin floats, and a new Short S.64 twin-float biplane with folding wings. The folding-wing concept eventually became a standard feature on carrier aircraft.

During 1913 maneuvers, *Hermes* performed the longest sustained test of shipboard aviation before World War I. Six more seaplane carriers followed, some converted from packet ships. They carried three to six planes, and all saw service during the war. Trials on *Hermes* shaped the Royal Navy's interest in designing a ship to carry fighters, bombers, and torpedo-planes. There was still much to learn. A Russian hydrocruiser could launch seven planes in 14 minutes. A British seaplane carrier required 20 minutes to launch one.[19]

The first two carriers to evolve during the war were crude conversions. The 19,513-ton *Furious* began life as a light battle cruiser but during construction was modified to a carrier with an 18-inch gun aft and a 228-foot aircraft-launching platform forward. She went into service on June 6, 1917, as a fast seaplane carrier with 10 aircraft. The Royal Navy decided this was not what they wanted and in November 1917 began modifying the flight deck to accept Sopwith Pups, some with wheels and some with skids. By 1918, the reconfigured *Furious* began taking the shape of a modern carrier. Her deck stretched from one end of the ship to the other. She had an island offset amidships, hangar storage below deck with lifts fore and aft, improved arresting wires, 20 planes, and 175 of her 932 men dedicated to aviation. As aircraft changed so did *Furious*. Probably no ship ever received so many changes, and she became the only carrier to see action in World War I. World War II finally wore her out, and in 1948 she was sold for scrap.

The second British carrier, the 16,000-ton *Argus*, began life in 1914 as an Italian cargo-liner, but after the war began the Admiralty halted construction and converted her into the world's first flight-deck carrier. When launched on December 2, 1917, the Admiralty could not decide whether to make her a seaplane carrier or a landplane carrier. After trying Sopwith 1½ Strutters, they finally decided to equip her with 20 Sopwith T.1 Cuckoo single-seat torpedo planes with wheel undercarriages. On September 14, 1918, when she went into service, the only structures projecting above her 550-foot flight deck were a retractable pilothouse and masts. *Argus* went into service too late to see action but was used

The HMS *Furious* in 1918, after she had been fitted with a landing deck aft and before an island replaced her original superstructure. (U.S. Navy photo)

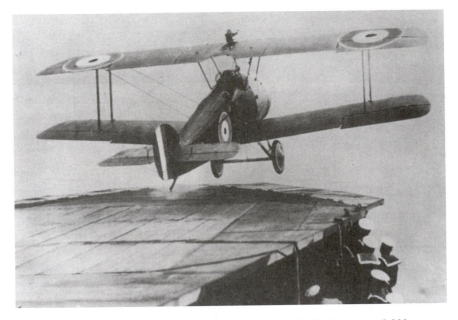

In 1918, a Sopwith Camel takes off from the deck of the HMS *Pegasus*, a 3,300-ton experimental aircraft carrier converted from a mail steamer. (British Air Ministry)

extensively during the next two decades to train pilots and develop carrier techniques. Before ending her career in 1944, *Argus* experimented with "44 different types of aircraft—probably a record for any carrier of any nationality," and contributed new standards for flight-deck carriers of the future.[20]

In 1918, Great Britain had two aircraft carriers; no other nation of the world had one. The Japanese, however, moved swiftly with the 7,600-ton *Hosho*, the first flight-deck carrier in the world built from the keel up. Over time, Japan developed carrier air tactics, whereas Great Britain lost its advantage by unifying naval aviation under the RAF. The British gave little thought to carrier tactics until the rise of Nazi Germany.

World War I brought the U.S. Navy's 1st Aeronautical Detachment to Europe in what became an enormous buildup of naval air power, growing to 16,000 officers and men, 500 aircraft, and 26 naval air stations. Most flyers joined the hunt for German U-boats. Some served under British command and flew better aircraft—Sopwith Camels and Dehavilland DH-4s—from shore-based airfields. Ensign Stephen Potter became the first American pilot to shoot down an enemy plane in the North Sea when on a long-range patrol with the RAF. A month later, he lost his life battling seven German aircraft over the English Channel.

Great Britain did not need aircraft carriers to engage in war on continental Europe. Planes could fly across the English Channel and settle comfortably on grassy French airfields. For Americans, short-deck carriers would have come in handy escorting convoys across the North Atlantic, but such vessels remained in the future. Instead, the U.S. Navy continued to develop seaplanes, and even Fiske's innovative aircraft-launched torpedo changed few minds. But after 19-year-old Lieutenant David S. Ingalls, on temporary duty with the RAF, scored his fifth victory flying a Sopwith Camel and became the navy's first and only World War I ace, the navy began showing interest in other types of aircraft.

American flyers preferred the faster and more maneuverable British aircraft to their own sluggish floatplanes. They joined the Northern Bombing Group in France, settled into DeHavilland DH-4s, and formed the Marine Day Wing and the Navy Night Wing. On October 14, 1918, Captain Douglas B. Robin's marines flew their first raid, an eight-plane strike against Belgian rail yards at Thielt. Twelve German planes attacked. Second Lieutenant Ralph Talbot and Gunnery Sergeant Robert G. Robinson shot two down and became the first marine flyers to earn the Medal of Honor.

Four weeks later the war ended, leaving the United States with the largest navy in the world. Although wartime construction concentrated on destroyers and submarine chasers, the air arm obtained important exposure to European aircraft. The Marine Corps incorporated Curtiss JN6 "Jennies" into their ground forces, and Lieutenant Commander E. O. McDonnell, who in 1917 was the first to launch Admiral Fiske's torpedo from a floatplane, became the first to fly a Sopwith Camel off a turret platform on the battleship *Texas*. With the advent of *Furious* and *Argus* in Great Britain, the U.S. Navy began to consider a ship dedicated to carrying aircraft.

Meanwhile, marines, looking for ways to establish their role in future wars, used the Cacos uprising in Haiti to experiment with ground support techniques. In the first coordinated air-ground action which eventually became a Marine Corps specialty, pilots in a Curtiss Jenny and a DeHavilland DH-4 flew air support for a surprise ground attack on a Cacos encampment that wiped out 200 bandits.

In 1920, Brigadier General "Billy" Mitchell, the controversial chief of the U.S. Army Air Service, also gave navy aviation an unexpected boost when he began testing tactics for bombing ships. Mitchell believed that air power would eventually diminish the importance of gunships, and he set out to prove his hypothesis. The general was right in one respect: airplanes were economically cheaper than building battleships, but he could not convince his listeners that the old tools of war were changing.

The navy caught wind of Mitchell's plans and quietly put the principle to test. Using the best aircraft and ordnance available, pilots spent the week of October 28, 1920, dropping bombs on the USS *Indiana*. The old battleship, although severely damaged, survived the bombing. The navy concealed the experiment from Mitchell, who was lobbying the House Appropriations Committee for an opportunity to prove that airplanes could sink any ship afloat.

Mitchell got his chance after the navy received its apportionment of German warships from the war. He became as determined to prove himself right as the navy, with equal determination, intended to prove him wrong. Mitchell agreed that all tests would be under the control of the Commander in Chief (CinC) of the Atlantic Fleet, but he stumbled into a problem when the navy invoked rules of engagement, limited the number of hits allowed, and stipulated the size and weight of the bombs.

Without conferring with the navy, Mitchell prodded the Army Ordnance Corps to develop a 2,000-pound bomb, twice as heavy as any bomb in the army's arsenal. He then attached the 2,000-pounders to the only aircraft that could carry them, the new Martin MB-2 heavy bomber. Mitchell wanted no mistakes. He brought experienced flyers up from Kelly Field, Texas, and began dropping live ordnance on two discarded battleships.

On June 21, 1921, official trials began when three navy flyers dropped 100-pounders on a U-boat and sent it to the bottom. Three weeks later, the navy used a squadron of Austin SE-5 pursuit planes to strafe and bomb a drifting German destroyer. The SE-5s carried 25-pound bombs for the first run; DH-4s followed with 100-pounders. Mitchell waved the DH-4s off and sent in 16 Martins, each carrying six 300-pound bombs. On the 44th hit, the destroyer sank. The navy, miffed by Mitchell's interference, condemned the amount of ordnance required to sink a destroyer.

Tests continued, the next target being the German light cruiser *Frankfort*. Once again the navy made the first strike, this time using 250- and 300-pound bombs. After five more efforts, the navy gave up. Mitchell sent in six Martins armed with 600-pound bombs and sank her.

The toughest test came when the navy hauled out the heavy German battleship *Ostfriesland*. Fifty-two bombs, including a number of 1,000-pounders dropped by Martins, failed to sink the battleship. The navy ruled the tests complete and unsuccessful. Mitchell demanded one more strike. He already had seven aircraft in the air armed with 2,000-pounders. The navy finally gave the go-ahead, unaware of the heavier ordnance, and the Martins sank the *Ostfriesland* with four bombs. Mitchell felt vindicated but others remained unconvinced and continued to regard air power as just another adjunct to help gunships win battles.

The tests, however, stimulated discussion within the navy. If aircraft could sink heavy warships, and because warships could be anywhere at sea, there might be advantages to having ships capable of carrying more than seaplanes. The discussions led to "Plan Orange."

In 1919, Woodrow Wilson predicted "with absolute certainty that within another generation there will be another war if the nations of the world do not concert the method by which to prevent it."[21] Not everyone agreed with Wilson, but the statement raised questions of where the next war might be fought. Lieutenant Commander Earl H. "Pete" Ellis of the Marine Corps pointed to Micronesia. Rear Admiral Montgomery M. Taylor, CinC of the American Asiatic Fleet, confirmed that relations between the United States and Japan were backsliding and becoming more contentious.

Ellis, working at the Naval War College, masterminded the strategy for "Plan Orange," a code name for responding to war with Japan if U.S. possessions in the Pacific were attacked. In this remarkable document, written in 1921, Ellis called for the development of an amphibious capability the navy and Marine Corps eventually adopted and effectively deployed two decades later. He also accurately forecast the general course of the Pacific campaigns to come. The navy thought so much of Ellis's ideas that they sent him on a secret mission to the Far East to reconnoiter Japan's newly acquired island possessions. Whether the Japanese learned of Ellis's mission or whether he died of alcoholism when in the Pacific remains a mystery. To this day, Ellis has not been found.

The word "aircraft carrier" entered into discussions during the First International Conference on Limitation of Naval Armaments held on November 11, 1921, in Washington. Japan's 7,600-ton *Hosho* was nearing completion. Britain's *Hermes* was still under construction. The U.S. Navy's *Langley* (CV-1), in the process of being converted from the collier *Jupiter*, was still in the shipyard.

Eight foreign nations attended the Washington Conference—Great Britain, Japan, France, Italy, The Netherlands, Belgium, Portugal, and China—most with vast colonial empires to protect. It required a congressional resolution to urge Warren Harding, the new president, to sponsor the conference.

Weaker nations took a back seat when on February 6, 1922, the United States, Great Britain, Japan, France, and Italy hammered out a Five-Power Treaty on naval arms limitations, establishing a ratio on capital ships (battleships and aircraft carriers) on a 5:5:3:1¾:1¾ basis. This marked the first time in history that Great Britain, the traditional ruler of the seas, conceded parity to another naval power.

To meet treaty limitations, which allowed the United States 525,000 tons for battleships and 181,000 tons for aircraft carriers, the three principal powers (the United States, Great Britain, and Japan) agreed to scrap more than 60 capital ships. Other articles of the treaty created a 10-year moratorium on laying down new capital ships, and limited all battleships to 35,000 tons and carriers to 33,000 tons. The terms played into the hands of Japan. They were allowed to fortify their home islands and their Pacific possessions, whereas Great Britain pledged not to improve the defenses of its possessions.

The carrier clause in the treaty worked against the interest of the United States but caught the attention of Congress. Other nations were already moving construction programs ahead while America languished in the experimental stage. The new tonnage limitations created another problem. Aircraft were becoming heavier and faster, adding length to landing platforms. British carriers set the early design standards for the United States and Japan. America could not watch and do nothing. Rear Admiral William A. Moffet, Director of Naval Aviation, made it clear that "Naval aviation cannot take the offensive from shore; it must go to sea on the back of the fleet."[22]

On March 20, 1922, the U.S. Navy commissioned the long-awaited 11,500-ton USS *Langley* (CV-1). During her conversion from *Jupiter*, Lieutenant Frederick W. Pennoyer improved the aircraft arresting system, adding axle hooks and fore- and aft-wires for guiding the arresting hook. For training, the naval air station at Hampton Roads anchored a large circular wooden platform offshore with a landing surface scaled to the size of *Langley*'s flight deck.

On October 17, *Langley* participated in fleet exercises in Chesapeake Bay, and navy pilots began doing what British pilots had done for years. Flying a Vought VE-7SF, Lieutenant Commander Virgil C. Griffin became the first man to take off from *Langley*'s flight deck. Nine days later, Lieutenant Commander Godfrey Chevalier, flying an Aeromarine 39B, became the first pilot to land on her. On November 18, another landmark event took place when Commander Kenneth Whiting, *Langley*'s commanding officer, made the first catapult launching. After that, takeoffs and landings became routine.

In 1923, *Langley* received the first Curtiss TS-1 fighters and Vought UO-1 scoutplanes. The TS-1 became the navy's first built-for-the-purpose carrier plane. A year later, *Langley* received Douglas DT-2 torpedo-bombers. She now had a full complement of carrier aircraft and began participating in fleet battle-problem exercises.

It soon became apparent to navy flyers that *Langley*'s nonaviator commanding officer, Captain H. R. Doyle, did not understand aviation. Commander Whiting, the executive officer, used political friends to convey the problem to Assistant Secretary of the Navy Franklin D. Roosevelt. After the same problem occurred during World War II, Roosevelt remembered Whiting's warning and issued orders that he wanted only naval aviators commanding carrier task groups.

In 1925, the old "Covered Wagon," as *Langley* was called, shed her "experimental" status and went into the Pacific. It was there that Captain Joseph Reeves began training pilots and developing air combat tactics.

The navy took immediate steps to build more carriers. A great number of ships, started in yards in response to World War I, lay about in various stages of construction. On July 1, 1922, Congress authorized the use of two unfinished battlecruiser hulls for building the 33,000-ton fleet carriers *Lexington* (CV-2) and *Saratoga* (CV-3).

Delays in designing the ships worked to the navy's advantage. Little had been learned about carrier construction or the flattop's role in combat. In 1922, navy flyers numbered only 314, and none of them were trained as carrier pilots. To fully man two carriers required eight new squadrons, and the types of naval aircraft available could not measure up to army pursuit planes.

While waiting for *Lexington* and *Saratoga* to be commissioned, carrier aviation continued to be represented by "constructive carriers"—battleships and cruisers with catapults or hoists to lower seaplanes over the side for takeoff and recovery from the water. But the carrier race had begun. After *Hosho*, Japan moved with alacrity and began building two heavy carriers—*Akagi* and *Kaga*—patterned after *Lexington* and *Saratoga*. Design technology had a curious way of bridging two oceans.

For the maritime powers of the world, the 1920s marked a new era in shipbuilding and the beginning of a new age in naval air tactics. Five ships led the way—*Lexington*, *Saratoga*, *Akagi*, *Kaga*, and HMS *Furious*.

CHAPTER 2

Mobilizing for War

In December 1927, after five years in construction, *Lexington* (CV-2) and *Saratoga* (CV-3) went into commission. According to the 1922 Washington Naval Treaty, the carriers could not exceed 33,000 tons, but on completion they displaced 36,000 tons. A provision in the treaty gave the builders an out, allowing that the standard displacement of 33,000 tons "does not include weight for providing means against air and submarine attack."[1] The clause opened the door for a multitude of construction exceptions.

For years to come, *Lexington* and *Saratoga* were the largest aircraft carriers in the world. Converted from battlecruisers, they were built with flight decks 901 feet long and 100 feet wide. The navy fitted them with lowerable crash barriers, a significant yet simple innovation that enabled American carriers to quadruple the landing rate of aircraft, making it possible for *Lexington* and *Saratoga* to operate 86 planes, whereas the new British carrier *Courageous* operated half that number. Powered by diesel-fueled turbines with electric motors, the two carriers could generate a speed of 34 knots. They each carried sixteen 5"/38 guns and, somewhat as a shock to the navy, a complement of 3,373 men.[2]

While the carriers were being built, congressional debates over appropriations caused delays. Design changes also interrupted work as engineers discovered better methods and devices for equipping and operating the ships. In 1923, Calvin Coolidge became president and could never decide how many ships he wanted for the navy. When in 1925 the five signatories of the Washington Naval Treaty all reported that they had scrapped the tonnages necessary to comply with the document's terms, a surge of new construction began. By imposing limits, the Washington Naval Treaty, which was intended to reduce and control the size of the world's navies, actually created a condition in which the participants disposed of their obsolete ships and replaced them with modern vessels equipped with better technology. Carriers, however, remained low on the list of construction priorities because the concept, unlike battleships, cruisers, and submarines, had not been tested in combat.

Improvements in aircraft boosted interest in carriers. New air-cooled engines reduced the weight per horsepower of the engine, used less fuel, and lessened maintenance costs. Roger Heller, who studied the era, reported that "by 1926, [aircraft] were 400 percent more dependable than those of World War I."[3] At Pratt and Whitney, 500-horsepower engines began replacing 200-horsepower engines. In 1927 Charles Lindbergh crossed the Atlantic Ocean nonstop, and Secretary of the Navy Curtis D. Wilbur used the publicity to persuade Congress to appropriate more funds for aviation. The connection between air power and carriers had not completely registered with politicians because *Lexington* and *Saratoga* were still labeled experimental.

The union between carriers and aircraft got a boost during fleet exercises off San Pedro, California. On October 22, 1926, a squadron of aircraft delivered the first simulated surprise and highly successful dive-bombing attack against the Pacific Fleet. Although the planes came from shore, they could have come from a carrier. The Japanese, with increasing suspicion, took notes as they watched Pacific Fleet exercises.

On July 16, 1927, during the outbreak of civil war in Nicaragua, Major Ross E. Rowell, commander of Marine Observation Squadron 1, led the first live dive-bombing attack in history when his five DH-4s killed about 300 rebels surrounding a detachment of marines at Ocotal. Naval tacticians began considering whether, in the absence of land bases, such attacks could also be delivered from carriers. When *Lexington* and *Saratoga* went into commission five months later, the navy had formed a better idea of how to use the ships.

In January 1929, both flattops participated in fleet maneuvers. For the exercise, the navy divided the fleet in two: one for defense, the other for offense. *Lexington* became the defender, *Saratoga* the attacker. The target was the Panama Canal. Anyone in December 1941 looking back at this exercise might detect similarities to the Japanese strike on Pearl Harbor. *Saratoga*'s planes made an end run around the defending fleet, launched a simulated air strike against the Panama Canal, and "destroyed" it.

In 1930, the United States felt compelled to reexamine the Washington Naval Treaty's construction restrictions. Battleships and battlecruisers still dominated discussions, but the treaty signed on February 6, 1922, needed changes. Aircraft carrier tonnage had been limited to 135,000 tons for the United States and Great Britain, 81,000 tons for Japan, and 60,000 tons for France and Italy. The United States already had 77,500 tons afloat (*Langley, Lexington*, and *Saratoga*), the smaller 14,500-ton *Ranger* (CV-4) under construction, and two more carriers on the drawing board. The United States and Japan wanted the freedom to build more capital ships but had to settle for a few more cruisers. Japan intended to build eight more carriers and eventually ignored the agreement. Their plans for Far East expansion required more carriers. On September 18, 1931, the Japanese army invaded Chinese Manchuria—the first major international act of aggression since World War I.

On June 16, 1933, newly elected President Franklin Delano Roosevelt began bolstering the U.S. Navy by allocating $238 million from the National Industrial

Modifications to the USS *Langley* (CV-1) included two hinged smokestacks. Curtiss TS-1 fighters line her deck. (U.S. Navy photo)

Recovery Act for 32 vessels to be laid down over a three-year program. The mix included two carriers, *Yorktown* (CV-5) and *Enterprise* (CV-6).

Twelve months later, *Ranger* (CV-4) went into commission at Newport News, Virginia, the first American carrier built from the keel up. Although rated as a heavy carrier at 14,500 tons, *Ranger* displaced less than half the tonnage of *Lexington* or *Saratoga.* She had a 769-foot deck, a 109-foot beam, a draft of 24 feet 6 inches, and a speed of 27 knots. She carried eight 5"/25 guns, 72 planes, and a complement of 2,461 men.[4] *Ranger* operated an improved catapult that could launch a 9,000-pound plane at 55 knots, but the navy considered her too slow and her construction too light. The same mistakes would not be repeated with *Enterprise* and *Yorktown.*

It was important to the navy that carrier and aircraft technology kept pace with each other. Those who quibbled about expenditures could not predict the future, so in 1934 Carl Vinson, Chairman of the House Naval Affairs Committee, declared that the navy must be built up to the treaty limits allowed and that it must be done within eight years. Vinson used Japan's invasion of Manchuria to make his point, and Congress approved funds for construction of the carrier *Wasp* (CV-7).

Designers at Northrop began making strides to match aircraft with carrier capabilities. During November 1934, the company received a contract to manufacture the first BT-1s, a dive-bomber that eventually evolved into a favorite among carrier pilots, the Douglas Dauntless.

As aircraft improved, deck-handling problems increased. For solutions, the navy ran experiments using the old *Langley.* How to make a blind landing on a flattop became a hotly discussed topic. On July 30, 1935, Lieutenant Frank Akers, flying an OJ-2 observation plane, said he could do it and did. An enormous difference existed, however, between flying a light OJ-2 biplane and the heavy and faster monoplanes coming off America's aircraft assembly lines, but blind landings soon became part of every naval aviator's training.

In 1935, Japan's invasion of Manchuria and Germany's military mobilization caught the attention of the American public. In an effort to reduce the prospect of another world war, Congress passed legislation outlawing the sale of arms and ammunition to belligerent nations. A second naval disarmament conference followed. The United States, Great Britain, Japan, France, and Italy sent envoys to London to hammer out their differences. Japan demanded parity with the United States and Great Britain, and when denied withdrew from the conference. Italy refused to sign the agreement, leaving the United States, Great Britain, and France to finally conclude a pact that had so many contingency clauses that the document, when signed in March 1936, became meaningless. Fourteen years of arms limitations came to an abrupt end.

Japan waited 15 months before signaling its intentions. On July 7, 1937, the Imperial Japanese Army (IJA) invaded China proper, initiating a conflict that would sweep into World War II.

On September 30, 1937, the 19,800-ton carrier USS *Yorktown* (CV-5) went into commission at Newport News. She was the first of her class and was joined

In 1932, a Martin T4M-1 flies over the USS *Saratoga* (CV-3). The Martin served as one of the last of the fast carrier's biplane torpedo bombers. (National Archives)

in May 1938 by her sister, the USS *Enterprise* (CV-6). Both carriers were 827 feet 4 inches long with a beam of 114 feet, a draft of 28 feet 6 inches, and a speed of 34 knots. Each vessel carried eight 5"/38 guns, 85 planes, and a complement of 2,919 men.[5] In 1939 both flattops went from the Atlantic to the Pacific, and there they stayed.

In 1938, the navy conducted spring exercises off Hawaii. For Fleet Problem XIX training exercise, *Saratoga* carried a squadron of new Douglas TBD Devastators, the first torpedo-bomber to serve on flattops. *Saratoga* launched a sneak attack on Pearl Harbor and caught the base flat-footed. Three years later, the Japanese did the same, this time dropping live bombs and shallow-running torpedoes.

Until 1938, the navy appeared to be keeping current with naval arms expansion among the world powers. Japan, however, went into full production, giving a back seat to battleships in an effort to get carriers to sea. They had not commissioned a battleship since 1921 (*Mutsu*), having filled their shipyards with cruisers and six new carriers. The United States gave Japan's rapid mobilization close attention, and on May 17 Congress passed the Navy Expansion Act, authorizing a dramatic increase in the strength of the fleet by authorizing 10 *Essex*-class carriers and 3,000 aircraft. Carriers could not be built overnight, and *Essex* (CV-9) would not go into commission for 42 months.

Since the introduction of steamers in the mid-1800s, operations in the Pacific depended on having coaling and fueling stations. Hawaii, Guam, Midway, Wake,

The Vought O2U-2 became the *Saratoga*'s primary observation plane. (U.S. Navy photo)

the Philippines, Samoa, and numerous British and Dutch possessions in the Far East provided the service. By 1939, with the likelihood of war threatening, the navy began looking for other ways to refuel vessels. Instead of distant, widely scattered naval bases, ships needed a mobile force of oilers and gasoline tankers to keep ships and aircraft operational. On June 11, *Saratoga* ran trials with the navy's first oiler, *Kanawaha* (AO-1), and while underway off the west coast filled up with diesel fuel. The system proved invaluable. The navy commissioned 101 oilers during World War II.

On September 1, 1939, the world began tumbling into chaos when Germany invaded Poland. Two days later, Great Britain and France, tied to treaties with Poland, declared war on Germany.

On September 5, President Roosevelt issued a proclamation of American neutrality and ordered Admiral Harold R. Stark, Chief of Naval Operations (CNO), to establish a Neutrality Patrol using naval air units to prevent belligerent acts in American waters. Roosevelt then asked for an expansion of the 12-mile international limit. Congress authorized a "neutral zone" 300 miles from shore, stretched it from Maine to Trinidad, and authorized the navy to patrol it. On November 4, Congress passed the Neutrality Act of 1939, establishing "danger zones" into which American ships were not permitted to enter. Waters surrounding the British Isles became the foremost danger zone, requiring extra effort by the navy to patrol the perimeter.

The new neutrality laws highlighted the shortage of carriers: they were all in the Pacific. Too slow for Pacific combat, *Ranger* returned to duty in the Atlantic and there she remained until 1944.

On April 15, 1940, the USS *Wasp* (CV-7) went into commission. *Wasp*'s displacement of 14,700 tons made her similar to *Ranger*, but she was shorter in length (739 feet), narrower in beam (80 feet 9 inches), and shallower in draft (20 feet), but she carried more planes (84) and required a smaller number of men (1,800). At 30 knots, she exceeded the speed of *Ranger* but was slower than fast carriers. The navy wanted another flattop in the Atlantic, and *Wasp* served the purpose, eventually assisting the British Home Fleet during operations in the North Atlantic.

On June 14, the same day that France fell to Germany, Roosevelt signed the Naval Expansion Act of 1940, once again authorizing a substantial increase in the U.S. Fleet. For Admiral Stark the appropriation was too little too late. He appeared before Congress and asked for $4 billion in funds to build a two-ocean navy, enough to double the size of the existing combat fleet, and 15,000 aircraft to go with it. Congress amended the Naval Expansion Act and gave the admiral what he wanted.

When Japan learned of the bill, they acted fast and in September signed a tripartite pact aligning themselves with Germany and Italy. President Roosevelt responded with a "destroyer-for-bases" deal and shipped 50 World War I destroyers to Great Britain to help fight German U-boats in the Atlantic. Some called Roosevelt's alliance with Prime Minister Winston S. Churchill an unofficial declaration of war, but the president still hoped to keep the country out of war with Germany and Japan.

In February 1941, Admiral Stark divided the U.S. Fleet into the Atlantic and Pacific Fleets. He had no choice. American interests were being threatened in both oceans. Although the United States was still officially neutral, naval and military representatives got together with their counterparts in Great Britain and signed the ABC-1 Staff Agreement. The two powers agreed that if America were drawn into the war in Europe, both nations would concentrate their resources on defeating Germany. Roosevelt pledged to help defeat Hitler first, and if Japan attacked America, to employ a *defensive* strategy. This did not mean a "holding strategy," as some believed, but a series of tactical offensives. Japan was already involved in its own blitzkrieg of China. President Roosevelt informed Admiral Stark that "he wanted naval task forces 'popping up' at various places in the Western Pacific to keep the Japanese guessing," but Stark opposed dividing naval units and kept them based together at Pearl Harbor.[6] The debate abruptly ended on December 7, 1941.

Roosevelt agreed to help the Royal Navy escort convoys of arms and supplies across the North Atlantic. The new arrangement did not make it easy for Admiral Stark to put together a two-ocean navy. The escort service, however, did not require capital ships and freed three battleships, the carrier *Yorktown*, four light cruisers, and two destroyer squadrons. Stark sent them all to the Pacific.

On May 1, 1941, the United States had three carriers assigned to the Pacific, the Royal Navy one. The combined fleets of the U.S. Navy, the Royal Navy, and the Royal Netherlands Navy matched up well against the Japanese Navy in numbers but not in the quality of ships or in the number of carriers, of which Japan had 10. In May 1941, only the Japanese believed that carriers would become the centerpiece of the coming war in the Pacific.[7]

Roosevelt's hesitancy to declare war against Germany encouraged Japan to step up their occupation of the Far East. On July 24, 1941, the IJA moved into French Indochina. The action created a cycle that hastened World War II. Roosevelt froze Japanese assets and halted the sale of oil. Japan's commerce and war machine could not function without imported oil. Confronted by two alternatives, Japan could either bow to Roosevelt and withdraw from Indochina or stay the course and obtain oil by capturing British and Dutch possessions in Southeast Asia.

The Japanese deliberated for two months, stalling for time through diplomatic circles. Prime Minister Prince Fuminaro Konoye made gestures of peace and kept pestering Roosevelt for a summit conference. The president refused because Japan had not withdrawn from Indochina. Having reached an impasse, General Hideki Tojo replaced Konoye on October 2 and took a militant stance on the issues facing his nation. Tojo had a specific plan in mind, but two months and five days passed before that plan became clear to the rest of the world.

During the interlude, the 20,000-ton USS *Hornet* went into commission at Newport News. The 34-knot carrier was slightly bigger and faster than *Ranger* and *Wasp*. She carried 81 planes and a complement of 2,072 men. Her commander, Captain Marc A. Mitscher, would make her famous, but first she needed a shakedown cruise before steaming into the Pacific.

On November 20, 1941, Japanese Special Envoy Saburo Kurusu appeared before Secretary of State Cordell Hull with Japan's demands—a free hand in the Far East. Hull sent Kurusu away with a flat rejection, but six days later he handed a counterproposal to Japanese Ambassador Kichisaburo Nomura urging a settlement of issues in the Far East. Among other demands, Hull's counterproposal called for Japan to withdraw from China and Indochina. Neither Hull nor Roosevelt expected Nomura to accept the terms. Several days passed before Hull heard again from Nomura. December 7, 1941, had arrived.

A strike force under Vice Admiral Chuichi Nagumo had secretly sailed from the Kurile Islands in northern Japan. The force consisted of six carriers, two battleships, three cruisers, nine destroyers, three fleet submarines, and auxiliary support vessels. Nagumo's instructions were clear. Unless an agreement could be reached with the United States by December 5, he was to attack the U.S. Pacific Fleet at Pearl Harbor.

Naval intelligence knew that Nagumo's combat fleet had sailed without troop transports. On November 27, Admiral Stark issued an alert to American forces in the Pacific, but the message failed to pinpoint where the attack would fall. The Philippines went on full alert. On December 6, the Pacific Fleet and air bases at Pearl Harbor slumbered into the night. Come daylight, the United States would be at war.

CHAPTER 3

Flattops in the Atlantic

In September 1939, 26 months before Japan struck Pearl Harbor, Great Britain and France declared war on Germany. The Royal Navy operated seven carriers: France none. The British had shown little interest in naval aviation until the rise of Nazi Germany in the mid-1930s. France ignored naval aviation almost entirely. Despite having respectable battle fleets, such neglect rendered both nations unprepared for war at sea.

Of Britain's seven carriers one was modern, the 22,000-ton, 30-knot *Ark Royal*, which went into service in 1938. She had an 800-foot flight deck and eight lower decks. Manned by 1,575 officers and men, she carried five squadrons (60 aircraft) of Fairey Swordfish torpedo-bombers and Blackburn Skua fighter-bombers. *Courageous*, *Furious*, and *Glorious* suffered from age, having been designed for fewer, lighter, and smaller aircraft. The other carriers, *Argus*, *Eagle*, and *Hermes*, were relics of the past. In the late 1930s, the Admiralty authorized four 23,000-ton, 31-knot, 72-plane *Illustrious*-class carriers, which with *Ark Royal* and two modified versions that came later, represented Great Britain's World War II fast carrier fleet. The Admiralty armored the flight decks to withstand heavy bomb hits, an attribute that would have saved American lives had the United States done the same.

At the outbreak of war, the Royal Navy's Fleet Air Arm suffered from two decades of neglect. The only aircraft assigned to carriers were antiquated fabric-covered biplanes, inferior monoplanes, and modified land planes. Conditions remained unchanged until American Lend-Lease Grumman Wildcats (Martlets) and Douglas Dauntlesses arrived.

In 1939, the RAF's Gloster Sea Gladiator biplane became the carrier's slothful fighter, and the Fairey Swordfish biplane, a canvas-covered two-seater with World War I–style open cockpits and two machine guns, served as the torpedo-bomber. Swordfish carried one 18-inch torpedo or six 250-pound bombs.

In 1938, the first Skua single-wing fighter-bombers went into service and began replacing Gladiators. Armed with four front-firing machine guns and one rear gun, Skuas made 200 knots. Winston Churchill put Skuas on carriers to protect Atlantic sea-lanes. On September 14, 1939, *Ark Royal* received a distress call from a merchantman attacked by a U-boat. Three Skua pilots responded to the call and found the freighter sinking and *U-30* in plain sight. Lieutenant Commander Dennis Campbell led the attack. The bomb blast blew the tail off the second Skua, and the same thing happened to the third. Both planes crashed and *U-30* rescued the pilots. Campbell returned to *Ark Royal* and reported that his bomb was more dangerous to Skuas than the enemy. Thus ended the use of high-explosive bombs for low-level attacks.

Germany built several battleships and battlecruisers but concentrated mainly on producing U-boats. The Royal Navy responded to the U-boat threat by deploying carriers and destroyers equipped with ASDIC (sonar) equipment in convoy routes. On September 17, 1939, *U-29* spotted *Courageous* recovering aircraft from an antisubmarine sweep, fired a spread of torpedoes, sank her, and got away. *Courageous* earned dubious notoriety by becoming the first carrier in history to be sunk by enemy action.

Ark Royal also experienced a narrow escape. On September 14, *U-39* launched a spread of three torpedoes, but they all exploded in *Ark Royal*'s wake. The German skipper believed he had sunk the carrier and radioed his superior. Propaganda minister Dr. Josef Goebbels announced the feat to the public. *Ark Royal*'s escorting destroyers, however, hunted down *U-39* and sank her with depth charges.

The HMS *Ark Royal* launches and receives Fairey Albacores torpedo/reconnaissance aircraft. (U.S. Navy photo)

The Admiralty decided that antisubmarine work might not be the best use of fleet carriers and merged them into surface fleets. *Furious* joined the Home Fleet off Norway and on April 11, 1940, launched 18 Swordfish against German shipping in Trondheim harbor. All torpedoes exploded in the shallows. On April 12, the same air group tried bombs at Narvik and hit two merchant ships. A coordinated attack on April 13, with the battleship HMS *Warspite* netted better results—eight German destroyers—but lack of good fighter air cover made British ships vulnerable.

Six weeks later, *Ark Royal* and *Glorious* arrived with Skuas to relieve *Furious*, which had suffered damage from a near miss. Skua pilots discovered they could not compete with Messerschmitt Me-109s, so on June 9 the British withdrew from Norway. *Glorious* departed ahead of the fleet with two escorting destroyers but flew no combat air patrol (CAP). At 4:00 P.M., the German battlecruisers *Scharnhorst* and *Gneisenau* sighted smoke, attacked, and sank all three ships. The incident provoked the Admiralty into asking for more carriers and better planes.

The experience in Norway led to several changes. The Royal Navy discovered that high-performance aircraft could be operated from carriers and took over an order for Grumman Wildcats (Martlets) placed by France before her June 1940 surrender. The Norway campaign also underscored the need for coordination of fighter aircraft, and this led to the development of fighter direction control by ship's radar. The loss of *Glorious* further emphasized the need for CAP, especially where land-based air cover was unavailable. Although armored flight decks might stop a few bombs, air cover provided the best defense against air attack.

On June 10, 1940, Italy entered the war and added a substantial fleet to Axis operations in the Mediterranean. Four days later, France fell. Such swift success encouraged Adolf Hitler to launch his Mediterranean Plan, calling for the capture of Gibraltar and Suez and the elimination of British naval power in the Mediterranean. The plan included an alliance with General Francisco Franco of Spain, whose airfields the Luftwaffe wanted for expanding Mediterranean operations. Franco balked at any arrangement with Hitler until Germany proved it could defeat Great Britain. To this end, Hitler hoped to win Franco's support by pitting the Italian fleet, and perhaps the French fleet in North Africa, against the Royal Navy.

The British moved swiftly, sending Captain Cedric S. Holland's *Ark Royal* to Oran to urge Admiral Marcel Bruno Gensoul to surrender the French fleet. The two men were old acquaintances, but Gensoul refused to discuss the matter. Holland told him to either release the ships or watch them sink. Gensoul remained obdurate, so on July 3 *Ark Royal's* Swordfish acted as artillery spotters while Force H, the British Mediterranean fleet at Gibraltar, sank the battleship *Bretagne*, two destroyers, and ran the battleship *Dunkerque* aground. Skuas also participated by attempting to bottle up the French fleet by mining Oran's harbor.

On July 4, the new French battleship *Strasbourg* broke for sea. Swordfish pilots attacked, launched torpedoes from too far away, but miraculously scored one hit. *Strasbourg*, barely injured, disappeared in the dark.

On July 5, carrier reconnaissance pilots spied *Dunkerque* being repaired for sea. *Ark Royal* dispatched two squadrons of Swordfish. The first flight swung over the harbor at sunrise, dropped six torpedoes, and watched four strike the battleship. In three days the Royal Navy, using inferior carrier planes, immobilized most of the French fleet, and, having done so, began laying plans for operations against the Italian fleet. *Ark Royal* departed to obtain new planes because the Swordfish's fabric covering had corroded due to constant exposure to salt.

Admiral Andrew B. Cunningham, CinC Mediterranean, knew the Italian navy contained 6 battleships, two of which were among the newest in the world, 9 cruisers, and 17 destroyers. Having detached *Ark Royal*, Cunningham added the new carrier *Illustrious* and the old *Eagle* to the capital ships of Force H. *Illustrious* arrived with 15 new Fairey Fulmar fighter-bombers, 18 Swordfish, and the latest radar equipment. The lumbering Fulmars replaced Skuas without solving the problem of poor speed and maneuverability. *Illustrious*, however, was the first of Great Britain's modern carriers, and her operations against Italy's Taranto naval base would attract interest from afar.

On July 9, Force H struck the Italian fleet at sea, damaged the battleship *Cesare*, and compelled the enemy to withdraw. Admiral Cunningham took Force H to Alexandria and waited until photoreconnaissance confirmed that the Italian fleet had entered Taranto, located in the heel of Italy's boot. A fire on *Illustrious* and boiler failure on *Eagle* delayed Cunningham's plans. *Eagle*'s situation seemed hopeless, so he postponed the air strike and transferred some of her aircraft to *Illustrious*.

At 8:30 P.M., November 11, *Illustrious* approached Taranto and launched 12 Swordfish. The Italian battleships were moored in a semicircle and protected by torpedo nets, but this did not trouble Cunningham because the 18-inch torpedoes would pass under the netting and were fitted with Duplex Pistols, a magnetic device that detonated the warhead as it passed beneath the ship. Six planes carried torpedoes, four carried bombs, and two carried flares. The flare-droppers droned in at 5,000 feet and illuminated the harbor. While battleships, cruisers, and shore batteries fired at flares, Swordfish approached from different directions. Pilots swooped in under antiaircraft (AA) fire, diving so low that their wheels skimmed the water before releasing their torpedoes. Fulmars carrying 250-pound armor-piercing bombs flew high above the harbor, completely confusing the enemy's batteries.

A second strike followed, and more explosions occurred, lighting up the harbor with fire and smoke. Carrier pilots waited until morning to learn the results. Photoreconnaissance showed the old battleship *Cavour* aground where she sank, and two battleships, a cruiser, and several destroyers severely damaged. In one stroke, and at the cost of two Swordfish, the naval ratio in the Mediterranean reverted back to the British. Half the Italian battle fleet spent the next six months undergoing repairs at Naples. The attack demonstrated what could be achieved by the aggressive use of carrier aircraft against an enemy fleet, and Japanese observers did not miss the opportunity to study the tactics employed by Admiral Cunningham at Taranto. British officers, later visiting Pearl Harbor, "cautioned that the Taranto raid could be repeated there."[1]

The air strike convinced the Admiralty that more could be accomplished with better planes. In December 1940, the first Sea Hurricanes became available, but not soon enough for Cunningham. On January 10, German reconnaissance aircraft spotted *Illustrious* near the Italian coast and reported her position. Fulmars flying CAP successfully fought off two Italian SM79 torpedo-bombers, but when Luftwaffe Stukas appeared high overhead, the clumsy Fulmars could not climb fast enough to meet them. Six direct hits, three near misses, and one 1,100-pound bomb that penetrated *Illustrious*'s armored deck crippled the ship, but she stayed afloat. Cunningham sent her through the Suez Canal to the U.S. Navy Yard at Norfolk, Virginia, where she remained for several months. This left Force H with *Eagle* until March 1941 when *Formidable*, another *Illustrious*-class carrier, arrived in relief.

The greatest battle in the Atlantic occurred between the Royal Navy and Germany's 50,000-ton "pocket battleship" *Bismarck*, which on May 18, 1941, sailed from Gdynia with the heavy cruiser *Prinz Eugen* to attack British convoys. The Swedish destroyer *Gotland* spotted *Bismarck* going to sea and warned the British Admiralty.

Vice Admiral Sir John Cronyn Tovey, commander of the Home Fleet, reacted swiftly and sailed from Scapa Flow with the battleships *King George V, Prince of Wales*, and *Repulse*, the battlecruiser *Hood*, the carrier *Victorious*, and numerous escorts. *Victorious*, loaded with disassembled Hurricanes for Malta, carried only six Fulmars and nine Swordfish on her deck.

On May 23, the cruisers *Suffolk* and *Norfolk* sighted the German battle group in the Denmark Strait but lost contact when the ships disappeared into heavy fog to rendezvous with tankers above the Arctic Circle. At daybreak on May 24, *Suffolk* reported *Bismarck* coming down the strait. *Norfolk* took position off *Bismarck*'s other flank. Both cruisers used the navy's new tracking radar to shadow the battleship. To intercept *Bismarck* and *Prinz Eugen*, Tovey detached the unarmored *Hood*, commanded by Vice Admiral Lancelot E. Holland, and the battleship *Prince of Wales*. At 5:52 A.M., *Hood* and *Prince of Wales* began exchanging 15-inch shells with the German ships. Eight minutes later, a shell from *Bismarck*'s fifth salvo plunged into *Hood*'s four-inch magazine, caused an explosion that touched off the eight-inch magazine, and blew the ship apart. Only three men survived, a midshipman and two seamen. The new *Prince of Wales*, with untested equipment and an inadequately trained gun crew, turned away. *Bismarck* sustained a modest amount of damage but not enough to deter her jubilant commander, Admiral Gunther Lütjens, from continuing his mission.

At 10:00 P.M., Swordfish pilots from *Victorious* spotted *Bismarck* steaming south and struck her 15-inch armor belt amidships with a single 18-inch torpedo that did no damage. The air attack, however, troubled Lütjens. Under cover of darkness he headed for the Bay of Biscay and remained unseen until May 26, when an RAF Catalina from Coastal Command sighted *Bismarck* heading for Brest.

The old battlecruiser *Renown* and Admiral James Sommerville's *Ark Royal* sortied from Gibraltar and began searching the Bay of Biscay. Fourteen Swordfish pilots from *Ark Royal*, unaware that the light cruiser HMS *Sheffield* also was in the area, attacked her by mistake. Fortunately, the torpedoes were defective and detonated prematurely.

After discovering their mistake, embarrassed aircrews returned to *Ark Royal* to rearm and resume the search. Two hours later, the clumsy air group of 85-knot Swordfish torpedo-bombers stumbled on *Bismarck*, formed into small groups, and attacked from different angles. Eleven torpedoes missed, one struck *Bismarck* amidships but did no damage, and one "ripped a large hole in the stern structure beneath the steering gear room [and]. . .disabled the port and starboard rudders."[2] The ship's rudders, hard over at the time of contact, stuck fast, causing the ship to circle. Lütjens tried to steer by alternating propellers but could make no headway. He knew the ship was doomed. On the morning of May 27, the battleships *King George V* and *Rodney* closed in and pummeled *Bismarck* for five hours. Swordfish fired 75 torpedoes, and this time most of them hit home. British battleships ran low on fuel and were forced to leave the battle to cruisers. Finally, at 10:40 A.M., *Bismarck* rolled over and sank. Although gunships took credit for defeating her, one might speculate on the outcome of the battle had it not been for *Ark Royal*, her antiquated aircraft, and one 18-inch torpedo.

Ark Royal steamed for Gibraltar, an area becoming rapidly infested by U-boats. On November 13, 1941, two U-boats, operating independently, sighted the carrier and began tracking her. Destroyer sonar picked up occasional blips but nothing definitive. *U-205* followed *Ark Royal* through the night, and at 5:00 A.M. fired three torpedoes. Two of them exploded in the carrier's wake. Men on the starboard destroyer heard a noise, but as no damage occurred, they remained unconcerned. *U-205* withdrew and reported *Ark Royal* sunk.

On November 14, Admiral Somerville put search planes in the air, but pilots reported no U-boats in the area. They overlooked *U-81*, whose captain had been watching *Ark Royal*'s movements and noticing how the ship turned into the wind to recover aircraft. *U-81*'s skipper waited for the right moment and at 3:40 P.M. fired a spread of three torpedoes. One struck *Ark Royal* beneath the island, curled up a section of armored deck, and lifted five planes off the flight deck. The blast knocked out communications and the lower conning tower began filling with oil. The ship developed a list, which continued to worsen.

Those on board *Ark Royal* believed an internal explosion had occurred because no U-boats had been seen. Somerville soon discovered the extent of the damage and at 4:00 P.M. began moving 1,487 officers and men onto destroyers. He kept the engine room crew on board to run pumps and raise steam, but water began flooding the boiler rooms. At 5:00 P.M., engineers reported that without boilers steam could not be generated, and without electric power, pumps, lights, and ventilators would shut down.

Destroyers pulled alongside with pumps and 100 more volunteers to keep the crippled carrier afloat. The effort continued into the night. At 10:45, engineers got some of the engines working and partial power restored, and she began moving toward Gibraltar at five knots. The list improved and then inexplicably worsened. A fire started in one of the boiler rooms, shutting off steam. Lights went out, the steering gear quit, and men began dropping from exhaustion. Destroyers and tugs came alongside, pulling her ever so slowly toward Gibraltar. The list worsened to 25 degrees, then to 27. Once again Somerville removed men from the ship. The list increased, and as the last man came off the ship, she heeled over to 35 degrees.

Thousands of men watched as *Ark Royal* tipped to 45 degrees, and then slowly, degree by degree, buried her flight deck in the sea. Her island remained suspended above the water like a giant walkway when deep in her bowels the rumble of explosions began. At 6:13 A.M., she went down about 20 miles from Gibraltar. From her crew of 1,749, only one man was lost. The Royal Navy trained its seamen well, making the sinking of *Ark Royal* one of the most remarkable rescue accounts of the war.

The loss of *Ark Royal*, combined with Axis operations in Greece, Crete, and North Africa, put enormous pressure on Britain's lifelines to Gibraltar and Malta. The British relied on carriers for air power because they had lost so many Mediterranean bases. When the Germans began pummeling Malta, the only way to resupply the island with aircraft was to deliver them by carrier or merchant ship.

In August 1942, Malta hung by a thread. The Admiralty formed Operation Pedestal and dispatched four aircraft carriers—*Eagle*, *Furious*, *Indomitable*, and *Victorious*—loaded with planes and escorted by 2 battleships, 7 cruisers, and 24 destroyers. Once inside the Mediterranean, enemy air attacks became relentless.

U-boats tracked the convoy, looking for an opportunity to penetrate the destroyer screen and pick off a capital ship. On August 11, *U-73*, having stalked the convoy for several hours, slipped inside the destroyers during a refueling operation and came to periscope depth 500 yards from *Eagle*. At 1:15 P.M., a spread of four torpedoes struck *Eagle* and sent her to the bottom in eight minutes.

On August 12, near Malta, German planes struck *Indomitable* with three bombs and scored four near misses. Her armored deck saved her. She sent her planes to *Victorious* and began repairs.

Operation Pedestal was only one of 25 convoys that delivered 718 aircraft to Malta. Without Malta, and without aircraft carriers, the Allied invasion of French North Africa that led to the eventual defeat of Germany and Italy might never have happened.

In 1940, after France fell, the U-boat menace in the Atlantic became severe. Use of French ports extended the range of U-boats by thousands of miles. Aircraft protection for convoys, limited by range from land bases, left huge gaps in the Atlantic without air support. The shortage of carriers forced the British to install catapults on merchantmen for launching fighter-bombers. Having no deck on which to land, returning pilots tried to ditch beside a ship and be rescued. Too often pilots lost contact with the convoy, ran out of fuel, and vanished.

In 1939, Winston Churchill foresaw a need for small carriers to work with destroyers hunting U-boats, but Britain's overworked shipyards were full. The idea of small, special-purpose carriers made sense. Two years later, the Admiralty put the 10,000-ton *Audacity*, converted from a captured 6,000-ton German liner, into service, and the first British escort carrier went to sea. On September 20, *Audacity*'s Martlets scored their first victory by shooting down a Focke-Wulf Fw-200 Kondor tracking a convoy.

Audacity began escorting Gibraltar convoys soon after Admiral Dönitz put U-boats in the Mediterranean. In mid-December *Audacity*, with six Martlets, joined a 32-ship convoy escorted by 15 destroyers and corvettes. On several occasions, Martlets spotted and depth-bombed prowling U-boats, and finally on December 16 sank *U-131*.

Pilots, however, did not like landing on *Audacity*'s flight deck, which was half as long as an *Illustrious*-class deck. One pilot admitted, "Flying had to be kept to a minimum, as there was always a bigger risk than in other carriers."[3] By December 19, a combination of landing accidents and enemy action had reduced *Audacity*'s operational aircraft to three. The following morning, all three planes took to the air, fought off FW-200 attacks, and returned to report several submarines in the area.

On the night of December 21, the convoy escort commander foolishly decided to conduct a U-boat attack exercise and lit the sky with star shells. Although *Audacity* stood aside from the commotion, *U-751* caught sight of her silhouette, put two spreads of torpedoes into her, and the Royal Navy lost its first escort carrier.

Audacity proved the tactical value of escort carriers by forcing U-boats to submerge, thereby reducing a submarine's ability to shadow convoys or to communicate with other U-boats. *Audacity*'s six Martlets, although too few, did disrupt U-boat operations. World War II submarines could not stay underwater indefinitely. They had to surface once a day to charge batteries, and escort carriers disrupted the routine.

On November 17, 1941, the Royal Navy launched HMS *Archer*, the first escort carrier designed as such. Weeks later, *Archer*'s planes spotted *U-572* tracking a convoy and sank it. After that, escort carrier building in Great Britain accelerated. In April 1942, the first of 10 *Attacker*-class carriers built on merchant hulls and 20 *Ruler*-class carriers went into commission. By then, the United States had accepted the task of supplying Great Britain with escort carriers.

Between 1939 and the attack on Pearl Harbor the Atlantic became an area of grim struggle involving American ships. The navy announced that of 110

The Royal Navy could not settle on a carrier-based fighter and eventually obtained Grumman F4F-4s and changed their name to Martlets. (U.S. Navy photo)

decommissioned destroyers, 40 would be dedicated to neutrality patrol duty and that 8 would be lent to Great Britain. By September 3, 1940, the number of destroyers on loan to Britain jumped to 50. Then, on March 11, 1941, Congress passed the Lend-Lease Act, enabling the United States to supply Allied powers with war materials on credit or loan. Sixteen days later, military representatives from the United States and Great Britain signed the ABC-1 Staff Agreement, committing their resources to the defeat of Germany. The pact also provided for the immediate deployment of the Atlantic Fleet to assist the Royal Navy in escorting convoys. The two agreements marked the end of America's fictitious neutrality and the beginning of an undeclared war on Germany. It came as no surprise when on October 17, 1941, *U-586* fired a torpedo into the USS *Kearney* (DD-432), or two weeks later when a torpedo from *U-562* struck the USS *Reuben Jones* (DD-245) amidships and split her in half. On November 7, Admiral Stark glumly observed, "The Navy is already at war in the Atlantic, but the country does not seem to realize it."[4] The wake-up call came a month later when Japanese carrier planes, emulating the British attack on Taranto, struck Pearl Harbor.

Communications had steadily improved since the days of World War I, when U-boats operated independently. Admiral Karl Dönitz's wolf packs, numbering up to 20 submarines, positioned themselves to intercept convoys and waited until they received radioed instructions before moving. As the war progressed, convoy tracks became well known. Northern convoys ran from New York to Reykjavik, Iceland, and there they split. One group circled through the Denmark Strait to Murmansk and down the White Sea to Archangel, Russia. The other group sailed to Great Britain. From England, convoys made the Malta run, sometimes merging with U.S. convoys crossing the Atlantic from Norfolk, Virginia.

U-boats surfaced after dark, obtained coordinates, and set their courses, using faster surface speeds to intercept freighters. After attacking, they submerged to avoid surface detection but kept on the heels of the convoy, sometimes covering 1,000 miles during the chase. After the United States entered the war, U-boats enjoyed a new "shooting season" because American vessels off the eastern seaboard traveled without escorts.

The battle at sea became one of detection. The United States and Great Britain relied on two instruments, sonar and radar. Over time, both became vastly improved. Sonar bounced supersonic waves against hulls of submerged U-boats, and radar bounced radio waves off hulls of surfaced U-boats. Neither device worked at long range. Early in the war, the countermeasure to wolf packs were destroyers, destroyer escorts, and floatplanes. When the Royal Navy added the escort carrier *Archer* to the mix, the search area broadened by hundreds of miles. The idea caught fire and baby flattops became the solution to submarine detection in sections of the Atlantic that could not be covered by land-based aircraft.

On June 2, 1941, the U.S. Navy's first escort carrier, the 7,886-ton, diesel-propelled *Long Island* (CVE-1), went into commission. Built by Sun Shipbuilding on a C-3 merchantman hull, she had a 492-foot deck, a 102-foot beam, and could make 16 knots. She carried 21 planes, 3 antiaircraft guns, and 1,970 men. Sun built a sister ship from *Long Island*'s design, and the Maritime Commission transferred it to Great Britain under Lend-Lease.

Sun also built the 8,000-ton escort carrier *Charger* (CVE-30). On March 3, 1942, she went into commission and became the navy's training ship for pilots learning the techniques required for takeoff and landing on small, unstable flight decks. Four sister ships, also built on C-3 hulls, went to Great Britain and became the HMS *Avenger, Biter, Dasher,* and *Tracker.*

The navy's demand for more C-3 hulls led to the *Bogue*-class carriers, the first major class of escorts built during the early 1940s. The Seattle-Tacoma Shipbuilding Corporation took 37 C-3 hulls and converted them to 7,800-ton, 17-knot, 28-plane escort carriers 495-feet long. Twenty-six went to Great Britain.

During the same period, four oiler hulls were converted into 11,400-ton *Sangamon*-class carriers. At 553 feet, the 18-knot *Sangamon*s were faster and carried 30 planes. Escort carriers became so useful in the Atlantic and Pacific that the U.S. Navy commissioned 77 of them during the war and sent 30 more to Great Britain.[5]

On September 6, 1938, when CNO Admiral William D. Leahy formed the Atlantic Squadron, the words "escort carrier" had not been invented. Leahy increased the Atlantic Squadron in 1939 to four battleships, nine cruisers, and six destroyer divisions. Almost as an afterthought, he included the 14,500-ton USS *Ranger*. She carried 72 planes and could make 30 knots, but Leahy could not quite decide what to do with her.

Vice Admiral Royal E. Ingersoll solved the problem and added *Ranger* to the Atlantic Fleet. By August 1942, his group included *Ranger* and seven escort

Grumman F4F-4 Wildcats are parked on the deck of the USS *Ranger* on the way to French Morocco during November 1942. (U.S. Navy photo)

the *Santee* and her squadrons."[6] At 11:48 P.M., French Morocco capitulated, and two days later the Mediterranean task force under the command of Admiral Burroughs secured Oran and Algiers.

After North Africa, carriers played a minor role in European operations. British escort carriers provided most of the air support at Salerno and in southern France. Flattops were conspicuously missing during D-Day operations at Normandy because of the close proximity of British airfields to assault beaches. For the first time since the beginning of the war, the Royal Navy found little employment for fleet carriers and began sending them to the Pacific.

In 1942, Great Britain tried to leap into the carrier-building business. The Admiralty developed plans for 20 fleet carriers and 32 escort carriers. The program called for four 36,800-ton *Audacious*-class, ten 13,190-ton light *Colossus*-class, and six 14,000-ton light *Majestic*-class carriers. In 1943, the Admiralty added three large 45,000-ton *Gibraltar*-class and eight 18,300-ton *Hermes*-class light carriers to their plans.

When construction began, the Admiralty noticed that American flattops carried twice as many planes as British carriers of similar size. This was partly because of larger hangars and a permanent deck park for aircraft stored outside hangars. When *Illustrious* returned after extensive repairs at the Norfolk Navy Yard from damage sustained in the Mediterranean, the Admiralty noticed that she had been fitted with improved catapults for tail-down launching, which was four times faster than catapulting from old-style British trolleys. The Royal Navy asked for retrofits of the new catapults, but delays occurred because all their planes had been built for trolley launchings. By 1945, when British flattops began appearing in the Pacific, many of the problems had been corrected.

By late 1943, the British had 33 carriers under construction or on order, some with armored decks, some without, and all with modifications to allow for more planes and speedier launchings. With more plane carrying capacity, *Illustrious*-class commanders discovered that aviation gas storage had not been increased, thereby limiting flight operations to two or three days. The list of design changes, from catapults to height-finding radar and fighter-direction control, continued to grow, but for the Royal Navy it happened too late. Five *Colossus*-class carriers went into service before the end of the war but were never needed. Others languished in shipyards while the Admiralty decided which to finish. To the Royal Navy's credit, they never built another battleship.

During the summer months of 1942, fleet carriers in the Atlantic could find little employment, but in the Pacific they had become the most desperately needed weapon in the navy's arsenal. Without them, the war with Japan could not be aggressively prosecuted.

CHAPTER 4

The Rising Sun

Japanese culture, tracing back to earliest history, emanated from the primitive religious mythology of Shinto. The people believed they were ruled by a direct descendent of Jimmu, the ancient emperor who came to earth from the Plains of Heaven in 660 B.C. to rule the Japanese people, who themselves were descendents of lesser gods. For 25 centuries, little changed. Japan became and remained a feudal state that emphasized internal militarism and isolation from the outside world. The Japanese never lost a war, and foreign efforts to penetrate the islands never succeeded. During the 13th century, when the Mongols established a beachhead on Kyushu, a typhoon wrecked their fleet and forced them to withdraw. The Japanese called the typhoon *kamikaze*, meaning "divine wind." The timely storm substantiated Japan's belief in "Nihon Seishan," the mythical spirit who prevailed over all enemies. As the historian Paul S. Dull observed, "The influence of such beliefs was strongest among the military men, especially the junior officers whose limited education had not yet exposed them to the larger world. But it affected almost all of the Japanese people."[1]

The "coming out" for Japan began on July 8, 1853, when Commodore Matthew C. Perry, on a mission of peace, entered Edo (Tokyo) Bay with two side-wheel steamers and two 20-gun sloops. Perry hoped to establish relations with one of the most backward nations in the world. He approached the people by mixing courtesy with firmness and patience, but the marvel of his steamships made the deepest impression. The commodore gave the Japanese much to think about when three days later he sailed for China, promising to return in the spring to resume talks.

On March 8, 1854, Perry revisited Japan and after three weeks of negotiation concluded a treaty of peace that led to commercial relations. The opening of Japan to the Western world caused enormous internal turmoil. Japan's de facto ruler, the shogun, had signed the treaty with national interests and safety in mind, but the emperor, a conservative and xenophobic man, refused to ratify it. He had not seen the gun-bearing black steamships from across the sea and refused to believe that any power on earth could conquer the sacred islands. Civil disturbances followed, culminating in a 15-year civil war—the first gift of the West to the people of Japan.

In 1868, Emperor Meiji took the reigns of government and created a new maxim—"Enrich the country, strengthen the army."[2] The emperor's followers contemplated the future and decided that Japan must be militarily strong to remain independent, or become another Western colony in the Far East. The sea no longer provided a barrier that shielded the homeland from invasion. In 1872, the government made the Imperial Japanese Navy (IJN) a department of state, but Japan had no shipyards and for several years relied on the United States and Great Britain to provide their vessels.

In 1876, Great Britain made a survey of the world's navies and found only 15, including those of minor nations such as Brazil, Turkey, Greece, and Peru. Five years later, Japan appeared on the list. By 1911, the IJN amazed the world by defeating China and Russia and stood third among nations behind Great Britain and Germany. The revelation came as a shock to the United States. In 1912, Alfred Thayer Mahan, America's foremost authority on naval thinking, wrote, "The U.S. Navy should be second to only that of Great Britain."[3]

Relations between the United States and Japan remained friendly for more than 50 years, although their values, each derived from a long past, were markedly different. Americans accepted the peculiar virtues of the Japanese, who in turn regarded America as their best friend in the outside world. During the Russo-Japanese War, American opinion was predominantly anti-Russian, and Teddy Roosevelt probably averted the defeat of Japan through mediation with Russia. The United States and Japan were allies during World War I, and although they voiced differences at the Peace Conference of 1919, both made concessions. Japan asked for all the German colonies in the Pacific, including the Marianas (less Guam, an American possession), the Carolines, and the Marshalls. Japan agreed not to fortify the islands, and although she had done no fighting in World War I worth mentioning, received a mandate to all German possessions north of the equator. Three years later, the Washington Treaty of 1922, which limited naval construction, seemed sufficient to dispel any cause for concern. Commercial relations between the United States and Japan remained profitable as each produced what the other needed.

During the 1920s, there appeared to be no reason for any country to go to war against another, but within Japan internal conflicts brewed. Although in 1930, at the London Naval Conference, Japan agreed to live by the same naval armament ratios as in 1922, days of moderation were ending. Militant Japanese came to power, vowing to withdraw from the treaty. They sought to recover Japan's traditional primacy, which had been undermined by civilian preferences. So in 1931 militants provoked the "Mukden Incident" by setting off an explosion that lightly damaged a railroad in Japanese-controlled Manchuria. Using the incident as an excuse to invade and conquer Chinese-controlled Manchuria, the Japanese set up the puppet government of Manchukuo. The United States refused to recognize Manchukuo and condemned the invasion as the first major international act of aggression since World War I. Although the Japanese Diet (the legislative body) never authorized the attack, relations with the United States began to deteriorate.

Since time immemorial the Imperial Japanese Army represented a special place of trust and honor in the heart of the nation. The IJN had always taken a back seat to the army and in 1931 still did. Every young man growing up in Japan owed 20 years of military service to one of the services—at least two years of active service, the rest as a reservist. Officers entering the service in the 1930s were inculcated in Bushido, the traditional "way of the warrior." To serve in the armed forces was a privilege, and to die for the emperor an even greater privilege. Death brought eternal glory. The dead passed to a higher plane to join spirits forever guarding the native land.

In 1933, General Sadao Araki, the army's minister, defined Japan's destiny when he declared, "in order to have enough of the raw materials . . . which will be lacking in wartime, we should plan to acquire and use foreign resources existing in our expected sphere of influence, such as Sakhalim, China, and the Southern Pacific."[4]

Japan's military leaders did not agree with the London Naval Treaty of 1930. They did not want limitations on the construction of battleships, cruisers, and carriers. Restrictions deeply offended Japan's national pride, and the new crop of militarists became rebellious toward civilians serving on the Diet who allowed treaties to determine Japan's naval strength. The strategists understood that whereas treaties provided for Japan's safety, they also forced the government to shelve plans for expansion by conquest. To break the cycle of peace, the militarists launched a campaign to convince an easily deceived public that Western nations, and America in particular, were imposing inferiority upon the Japanese by keeping the naval arms limitation ratios in effect. The ruse worked. In 1935, after withdrawing from the League of Nations, the Japanese, represented by Vice Admiral Isoroku Yamamoto, withdrew from the Second London Conference on the grounds that the West rejected his demands for parity.

During the treaty years, Japan consistently built the maximum number of ships allowed. The United States lagged behind, and by 1934 the IJN attained 80 percent of the U.S. Navy's strength. Prince Hiroyasu Fushimi, who headed Imperial General Headquarters (IGH), declared that the U.S. Navy's presence in the Pacific hindered "the strategies of the Imperial Navy." Looking down the road to Pearl Harbor, he said that the Japanese fleet must "clear out the enemy's seaborne military power in the Orient and at the same time, in cooperation with the army, attack their bases, thereby controlling the western Pacific; then, while protecting the empire's trade, to harass the operations of the enemy fleet, and thereafter await the assault of the enemy's home fleet and defeat it through surprise attack."[5] Fushimi's outline for war against the United States matched the U.S. Navy's Plan Orange in reverse.

During 1937, Admiral Mitsumasa Yonai, Japan's navy minister, and Yamamoto, now vice minister of the navy, tried to calm international concerns by vocally opposing any suggestion of an American-Japanese war. Even as they spoke, Japan was secretly building midget submarines, four carriers, and superbattleships with 18.1-inch guns. The Japanese doubted they could out-produce the United States in the quantity of ships but believed they could build superior vessels.

On July 7, while Yonai and Yamamoto spoke publicly of Japan's non-aggression policy toward America, the IJA invaded China without taking the trouble to declare war. The invasion led to a mishap six months later when Japanese naval aircraft bombed five British ships on the Yangtze River and sank the USS *Panay*, a 450-ton shoal-draft river gunboat. Yamamoto promptly apologized to Joseph C. Grew, the American ambassador in Japan, who considered the act extremely reckless and wrote in his diary, "I cannot look into the future with any feeling of serenity."[6] The bombing, however, was no accident. Neither Yamamoto nor Grew knew that Colonel Hashimoto, who planned the attack, hoped to "provoke the United States into a declaration of war" to muffle dissention in Japan's Diet.[7]

In January 1938, the United States and Great Britain signed a secret agreement of mutual protection in the Far East. If Japan moved farther south, the U.S. fleet would concentrate at Pearl Harbor and the British fleet at Singapore. Intelligence flowed into Washington warning that Japan and Germany were arming but neither wanted to involve the United States in a war. Military buildup around the world, however, continued at a frenetic pace. On May 12, when the United States commissioned its sixth aircraft carrier, *Enterprise*, Japan already had five in operation, two scheduled for completion in 1939, and three more under construction. By 1941, the IJN would be more powerful than the combined Allied fleets in the Pacific.

The American naval attaché in Japan kept close watch on the IJN's activities. His messages to Washington were blunt. Unlike American ships, which operated with complements ranging from 90 to 95 percent, Japanese warships were fully manned, armed, and supplied. They cruised at high speed during the day and were darkened at night. Unseen in desolate areas of the ocean, Japanese ships performed blockade duty, fought mock battles using carrier aircraft, cooperated with the army in amphibious landings, and performed every other exercise consistent with warfare. Men went without sleep. One drill followed another. Officers pressed their men to achieve a superhuman degree of skill and fighting efficiency. The attaché summed up his report, writing: "[Japan] would not hesitate to undertake offensive operations but not beyond supporting distance of her strategically excellent geographical position. By this is meant that Hong Kong, Singapore, Dutch East Indies, Philippines, Borneo, Guam, Aleutian Islands and possibly the Hawaiian Islands would be in jeopardy."[8] The naval office agreed that the targets mentioned were likely but doubted that Japan would venture as far eastward as Hawaii.

Relations between Japan and the United States continued to deteriorate. In 1939, President Roosevelt considered invoking neutrality acts to prevent the export of scrap iron, aviation gas, and war munitions to Japan. Ambassador Grew replied that if Japan were denied access to petroleum and steel products from

Admiral Isoruko Yamamoto had grave concerns about going to war with
America and set his mind on winning it in six months. (U.S. Navy photo)

America, or to oil, rubber, and tin from the British and Netherlands East Indies,
she would send her armed forces down there to get them.[9]

Samuel Eliot Morison summed up the organization of the IJN in *The Rising
Sun in the Pacific*:

The Commander in Chief of the Navy, as of the Army, was the Emperor; but the
Supreme War Council formulated policy in his name. This council, over which the
Emperor presided, comprised the War and Navy Ministers, the chiefs of the General
Staff and of the Naval Staff, all field marshals of the Army and fleet admirals of the
Navy, as well as other high officers appointed by the Emperor. In time of war a
smaller council called Imperial [General] Headquarters [IGH] was created in order

to exercise supreme military command. Corresponding to our Joint Chiefs of Staff, it had the same membership as the Supreme War Council except that the field marshals and fleet admirals and some special appointees were excluded. While the Supreme War Council determined basic policies and objectives, and allotted men and material, Imperial Headquarters drew up strategic plans and coordinated the activities of both armed forces. It was the Supreme War Council that made the decision to go to war with the United States and Great Britain.[10]

Japan, like other naval powers, had many years earlier begun building battleships. Those they built were faster than any in the U.S. Navy. After World War I,

Vice Admiral Chuichi Nagumo, Commander in Chief of the First Air Fleet, led the December 7, 1941, Japanese carrier strike on Pearl Harbor. (U.S. Navy photo)

the IJN became intensely interested in ship-based air power and, in 1927, commissioned the 26,900-ton, 32.5-knot, 60-plane carrier *Akagi*, converted from a battlecruiser. In 1930, they added the 29,600-ton, 28.3-knot, 72-plane carrier *Kaga*, converted from a battleship. Prior to *Akagi*, Japan's only carrier had been the 7,470-ton *Hosho*, commissioned in 1922. Japan did not begin building fast carriers from the keel up until 1936.

In 1937, Japanese and American tactics for aircraft carriers were similar: to provide an air umbrella for a strike force of battleships. In April 1938, Japan observed the U.S. Navy's exercises off Hawaii and noted with more than casual interest the surprise mock attack on Pearl Harbor from carrier-based planes on *Saratoga*. The exercise demonstrated a better use for flattops. Air power from carriers could deliver devastating blows deeper into enemy territory than any ship afloat. Japan accelerated the building of two 30,000-ton, 34-knot carriers and designed planes ideally suited for seaborne operations.

On December 1, 1941, the IJN operated ten carriers, the U.S. Navy eight, but only three American carriers were in the Pacific. One of the most unpleasant surprises of the war for the U.S. Navy was the superior performance of Japanese carrier aircraft, especially "Zeke" (Zero) fighters and "Kate" torpedo-bombers, against which American planes could barely compete.

Another surprise came when the U.S. Navy discovered that Japan had developed a shallow-running, 49-knot, oxygen-fueled torpedo that could carry a 1,210-pound explosive charge 5,760 yards. Later torpedoes ran 22,000 yards. In the years leading up to the war, the Japanese fired torpedoes freely during maneuvers, using practice experiments to make improvements. The U.S. Navy economized, did little testing with warheads and exploders, and spent many months during the war disposing of duds.

In 1940, Japan's population numbered 70 million. Twenty million men had military training, but most were in the reserves. IGH began pulling men out of civilian occupations and reassigning them to the army or navy because in January 1941 Yamamoto and his staff began planning the Pearl Harbor attack. Admiral Nagano, Chief of the Naval General Staff, knew nothing of the secret meetings until Yamamoto summoned his commanders to Tokyo in August to reveal the plan. Using a game board to simulate the strike, the attack team lost two of its six carriers. Nagano's staff regarded the proposal as too risky and vetoed the strike. Yamamoto listened patiently to Nagano's objections and then overruled him. In September, the strike force assembled for exercises off the Kurile Islands. By then, Yamamoto's force consisted of six battle fleets, one carrier fleet, and the Combined Air Force, which contained a thousand squadrons on carriers and widely scattered naval air bases. Not since the War of 1812 had the U.S. Navy been up against such a powerful and well-trained fighting force.

After war erupted in Europe, the United States moved rapidly to increase its navy, authorizing in 1940 six 45,000-ton *Iowa*-class battleships, five 58,000-ton *Montana*-class battleships (which were never built), six 27,000-ton *Alaska*-class heavy cruisers, ten 27,000-ton *Essex*-class carriers, and more than a hundred light cruisers, destroyers, and submarines combined.

The appropriation forced Japan to reassess its military situation because the homeland did not have the shipbuilding capacity, the steel, or the oil resources to match such a program. If forced into war with the United States, Japan would deplete its oil reserves in two years. Already committed to a deepening involvement in China, Japanese militarists decided to obtain by conquest the essential natural resources it needed, although doing so could bring war with the United States, Great Britain, and the Netherlands. So in July 1941, Japan initiated the next step in their plan of expansion and captured French Indochina. The United States, Great Britain, and the Netherlands reacted with alacrity, halted the sale of oil to Japan, and froze Japanese assets.

Japan now faced a crisis. Moderates wanted the embargo issue settled by diplomacy. Militarists believed the only solution was war. The two factions reached a compromise: If the embargo were not lifted by September 3, Japan would go to war and occupy specific areas of the South Pacific for defense. Militarists knew that President Roosevelt would not lift the embargo unless Japan withdrew from China and Indochina. On October 3, General Hideki Tojo became prime minister, and any hope for a peaceful settlement vanished.

The seeds of Japan's eventual destruction lay within the peculiar structure of the civilian government's relationship with the military. The war and navy ministries, though part of the parliamentary branch of government, could function independently of each other and independently of the Diet. The situation worsened during the 1930s, when junior officers and staff members were permitted to override the recommendations of their admirals and generals. Admiral Yamamoto, commander in chief of the IJN, opposed war with the United States but was goaded into it by his fiery subordinates.

Admiral Osami Nagano fiercely supported expansion in the South Pacific and declared that Japan should not hesitate to engage in war with the United States and Great Britain. To withdraw from China would represent a dishonorable "loss of face." Nagano went directly to the emperor and said, "The government has decided that if there were no war, the fate of the nation was sealed. Even if there is war, the country may be ruined. Nevertheless a nation which does not fight in this plight has lost its spirit and is already a doomed nation."[11] Nagano knew the risks and stood ready to take them. He could not predict the reaction of the United States with certainty. Nor could he predict the fate of Great Britain should Germany conquer Europe, which could leave Japan with only one enemy, the United States. Nagano believed he had the solution for an early victory: destroy the U.S. Pacific Fleet before America could mobilize its industry, thereby forcing the United States to accept a peaceful settlement.

In the rush to war, IGH never prepared an alternative plan should either the attack on Pearl Harbor or the invasion of the South Pacific fail. The carrier strike on Pearl Harbor became the centerpiece of Japan's opening move. It represented an enormous gamble and must succeed. Every other operation—Guam, Wake

Island, the Philippines, Singapore, Dutch East Indies, Solomon Islands, New Guinea, and perhaps some day Australia and New Zealand—depended on success at Pearl Harbor. Tied to this strategy was the hope that Germany would prevail and defeat Great Britain.

The IJN, guided by Admiral Yamamoto, became the instrument of attack and the key factor in Japan's plans for domination of the Pacific. The admiral, now stoop-shouldered at five feet, three inches in height, and weighing no more than 125 pounds, understood the complexities of war better than most of his counterparts. Born in 1884, he had graduated from the Japanese Naval Academy in 1904, fought as a cadet in the 1905 Russo-Japanese War, and wore the scars to prove it. He later attended the U.S. Navy War College and studied at Harvard University. For three years, he served as a naval attaché to the United States and during the 1930s became one of the world's foremost authorities on naval aviation. Yamamoto understood the American culture and the temperament of the people. Being an extraordinarily skillful gambler gave him an opportunity to study the American mind. His weakness was an overactive sexual appetite that offended his wife but not the Japanese people who venerated him. Those who knew Yamamoto personally regarded him as "highly capable, intelligent, alert, aggressive, and dangerous," but he seldom gambled without first evaluating the odds.[12]

Gambling with war troubled Yamamoto. He warned IGH of the immense untapped industrial capacity of America. During the late 1930s, he risked assassination by junior officers because he stubbornly opposed war. When IGH gave him no choice, Yamamoto dropped his objections and resolved to strike the U.S. Fleet the most devastating blow possible. The general staff picked the right man to command the navy. Yamamoto was the first Japanese naval officer to foresee the potential of carrier-based air power.

Despite his distinguished title of Commander in Chief of the Combined Fleet, Yamamoto did not control Japanese military planning. Most of the officers at IGH were army men whose voices dominated matters concerning strategic planning. Yamamoto clearly understood the importance of destroying the U.S. Pacific Fleet at the outset of the campaign so the navy could transport the army unimpeded into the South Pacific. He believed a short war was the only way for Japan to win, and with the Pacific Fleet destroyed he believed the United States would be unable to wage a two-ocean war or have sufficient time to replace its fleet. For Japan to succeed, the carrier air strike on Pearl Harbor must be the decisive act of the war. Paul S. Dull observed: "It was a gambler's decision, but the gambler hoped to alter the odds with a bold plan and new naval concepts."[13]

Prime Minister Prince Konoye did not believe a war with America could be won. General Tojo disagreed. Differences led to the ousting of Konoye and the promotion of Tojo, who admired Hitler. During the war debates, Konoye distinctly remembered the words of Yamamoto, who said,

> If I am to fight regardless of the consequence, I shall run wild considerably for the first six months or a year, but I have utterly no confidence for the second or third

years. The Tripartite Pact [between Germany, Italy, and Japan] has been concluded and we cannot help it. Now that the situation has come to this pass I hope you will endeavor for avoidance of a Japanese-American war.[14]

Yamamoto's naval concepts involved fast carrier operations, ships fueled by oilers, and seaborne aircraft armed with heavy bombs and shallow-running torpedoes, the combination of which the world had never before seen. Such tactics were not new to the Japanese. Since the spring of 1940, the navy had been performing exercises to perfect the technique. In early 1941, Yamamoto knew his plan would work.

IGH understood the fundamentals of the U.S. Navy's Plan Orange and the five Rainbow strategies that followed during the 1930s. Plan Orange, conceived in 1921 and later modified by Rainbow, anticipated a war with Japan and projected an advance of American forces through the Marshall, Caroline, and Mariana Islands, and the eventual defeat of the Japanese navy near the home islands. Without the Pacific Fleet, the United States could not stop the advance of Japanese forces, thereby rendering the Orange/Rainbow plans useless.

Admiral James O. Richardson, Commander in Chief, United States Fleet (CominCh), no longer had confidence in Plan Orange and wrote Admiral Stark, CNO, that war with Japan could last more than five years. He objected to basing the fleet at Pearl Harbor for several reasons, among them ship congestion. He took his complaint directly to the president, and although he found some support among members of state department, impertinence cost him his job. On February 1, 1941, Stark divided the U.S. Fleet, giving command of the Pacific Fleet to Admiral Husband E. Kimmel, and the Atlantic Fleet to Admiral Ernest J. King.

Kimmel continued the practice of keeping the Pacific Fleet anchored at Pearl Harbor. The Japanese consulate in Honolulu sent coded messages each week to Tokyo reporting American ships in the harbor and those at sea. To Yamamoto, it appeared that Kimmel never moved his ships.

Yamamoto put Vice Admiral Chuichi Nagumo, CinC of the First Air Fleet, in charge of the Pearl Harbor Strike Force—six carriers, two battleships, two heavy cruisers, one light cruiser, three submarines, eleven destroyers, and eight tankers and supply vessels. Nagumo, a battleship man, had never been an airman. Now gray-haired and rotund, the 59-year-old admiral had graduated from the Japanese Naval Academy in 1908 and became a torpedo specialist. Although he had argued against the Pearl Harbor attack, he fully understood his mission and the responsibility it entailed. Gruff, taciturn, and not particularly liked by his subordinates, he was nonetheless Japan's top carrier commander. He worried about the vulnerability of his carriers because they were flimsier than battleships and heavy cruisers, and he feared that one or two well-placed bombs or torpedoes could cripple them. During the summer of 1941, after sharing his concerns with Yamamoto, he turned his attention to the Pearl Harbor strike fully determined to make it successful.

In September, Yamamoto sent the fleet to Kagoshima Bay in the Kurile Islands to train. He picked the site himself. Kagoshima resembled Oahu Island and Pearl Harbor—a perfect place to prepare his flyers.

On November 22, Nagumo's strike force rendezvoused at Tanken Bay and four days later steamed to sea. The six carriers formed two parallel columns of three, each followed by a battleship. Cruisers, destroyers, and submarines covered the flanks. Another squadron of destroyers steamed ahead. Helped by stormy weather, the fleet escaped detection, moving slowly through gales and fog to rendezvous with oilers. On December 2, the code-message "Niitaka yama nobore" (Climb Mount Niitaka) reached Nagumo on the flagship *Akagi*. Nagumo knew the meaning: "Proceed with Attack." Nothing could prevent the December 7 (December 8 in Japan) strike on Pearl Harbor but untimely detection by U.S. reconnaissance patrols.

Seaman Kuramoto reacted with astonishment and probably spoke for hundreds of others when he wrote, "An air attack on Hawaii! A dream come true! What will the people at home think when they hear the news? Won't they be excited! I can see them clapping their hands and shouting with joy! We would teach the Anglo-Saxon scoundrels a lesson!"[15]

Nagumo did not feel so ebullient. With each passing hour he worried that Pacific Fleet carriers and battleships might be at sea somewhere waiting along his route. He worried most about carriers, believing there could be as many as six flattops operating out of Pearl Harbor. He understood the long-range sting of carriers, placing them above battleships in importance. After sailing from Japan, Nagumo received good news: the heavy American carrier *Saratoga* was at San Diego, but he still did not know the whereabouts of *Lexington*, *Enterprise*, *Yorktown*, or others.

On the evening of December 6, as the Japanese fleet neared the Hawaiian Islands, Nagumo received worrisome intelligence from Tokyo—there were no American carriers at Pearl Harbor and nobody knew where they were. For Nagumo, the disheartening news caused a sleepless night. On the positive side, Nagumo believed his fleet had not been detected. There were 27 submarines in the area, some with small reconnaissance floatplanes, 5 with midget submarines on their decks, and they reported that the routes of American air patrols had not changed. The midgets had been training for such work for more than a year.[16]

Good news came when the Japanese consulate at Honolulu reported no signs of an alert, so at 9:00 P.M., 400 miles north of Oahu, Nagumo read Yamamoto's stirring battle order to the fleet. After the loud, emotional cheering ended, he ordered the strike force to turn south and proceed at 26 knots to a position 275 miles north of Oahu.

During the night, Nagumo received additional reports from Honolulu via Tokyo that most of the American fleet lay at anchor in the shallow waters of Pearl Harbor unprotected by torpedo nets. The one unanswered question that still tormented Nagumo was the location of the American carriers. Would they join

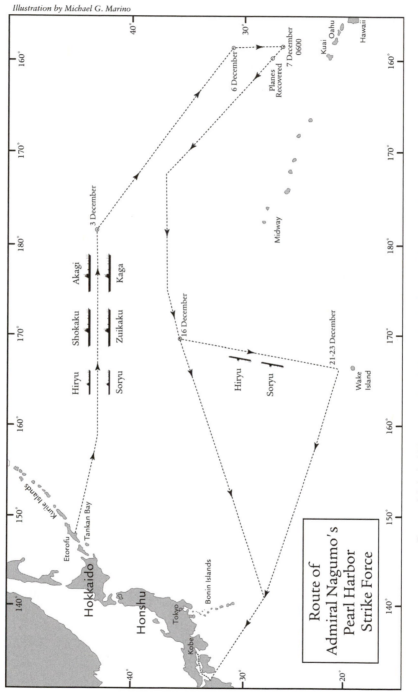

Route of Admiral Nagumo's Pearl Harbor Strike Force. (Michael G. Marino)

the main fleet during the night, or were they creeping through the early morning darkness of December 7 to pounce on his strike force at dawn? Once the fighters, bombers, and torpedo planes departed for Oahu, his carriers would become vulnerable to attack. Nagumo then received word that *Lexington* and *Enterprise* were definitely somewhere at sea, their location unknown.

At 1:30 A.M. on December 7, Nagumo spoke with Lieutenant Commander Mitsuo Fuchida, the flyer designated to lead the first air strike. "I have confidence in you," the admiral said, although the sentiment he expressed he did not feel. Nagumo still expected to lose half his carriers.[17]

Nagumo had jammed 423 aircraft onto his six flattops. He arranged to keep 30 planes available for CAP and 40 in reserve during the attack. The other 353 planes he hurled at Oahu, the pilots screaming "Banzai" as they waited for takeoff in the darkness before dawn. The strike force consisted of 100 Kates for high-level bombing, 40 specially equipped Kates for torpedo bombing, 131 dive-bombing "Vals," and 79 "Zeke" fighters. He retained 12 floatplanes, carried by battleships and cruisers, for combat and reconnaissance.

Americans gave Japanese aircraft the names of boys and girls. The standard carrier-borne two- or three-man Kates were Nakajima single-engine torpedo bombers with a 166-mph cruising speed and a range of 1,060 miles. Kates carried one 1,760-pound torpedo or the equivalent weight in bombs and were armed with three 7.7-mm machine guns.

The standard carrier-borne two-man Aichi Val dive-bombers cruised at 190-mph with a range fully loaded of 1,095 miles. Vals carried 1,078 pounds of bombs, two under each wing, and were fitted with three 7.7-mm machine guns.

The Mitsubishi Zero-Sen, or "Zeke" one-man fighter, worked from carriers or land bases. It had a normal cruising speed of 240 mph and a range of 790 miles. Zeros carried two 7.7-mm machine guns and two 20-mm machine guns. During the early stages of the war, the light, maneuverable Zero had no equal.

Japanese aircraft did have flaws. Designers and pilots had decided that self-sealing fuel tanks and protective armor plating added too much weight. This increased the range and payload but made the aircraft vulnerable. When on the morning of December 7 pilots revved their engines for take off, the Kates and Vals were so heavily loaded with ordnance that they staggered off the deck.

The Japanese air attack on Pearl Harbor came as a complete surprise. Based on information received from Washington, Admiral Kimmel believed that if Japan went to war, the Philippines would be struck. He took no measures at Pearl Harbor to widen air surveillance, send the fleet to sea, or put the base on alert. For those serving on ships in the harbor, the usual numbers went on shore leave that night and were still in the city at sunup. Personnel at Hickam, Wheeler, Kaneohe, Ewa, Bellows, and Ford Island airfields went to bed on Saturday night, and those who slept late were suddenly shaken awake at 7:55 A.M. when Kates and Zeroes bombed and strafed aircraft parked beside the runways.

The devastating Japanese carrier attack destroyed or damaged nine battleships, three light cruisers, three destroyers, three smaller vessels, and 347 aircraft.

American casualties tolled 2,403 killed and 1,178 wounded. The Japanese lost 29 planes and one *I*-class submarine, sunk by an American destroyer before the attack began.

Despite triumphant revelry on the Japanese carriers, Nagumo decided against additional strikes, although the planes, refueled and rearmed, stood ready. He had intercepted radio traffic and feared that at least 50 American land-based bombers—there were actually only 22—were still operational. Returning flyers reported the smoke so dense over Pearl Harbor that they could no longer see targets. But what worried Nagumo most was the location of American carriers. Neither his short-range air reconnaissance nor submarines in the area had sighted them. He still believed there were as many as five American carriers in the Pacific and that two of them might be within striking range. At top speed, he hastily withdrew toward Honshu. He did not want to diminish his brilliant victory by returning home with a damaged fleet. Along the way, he detached *Soryu* and *Hiryu* with two heavy cruisers and two destroyers to support landings on Wake Island.

Admiral Kimmel's lack of preparedness can be partly blamed on a number of conditions over which he had no control. The U.S. State Department had broken the Japanese diplomatic code and knew the U.S. peace plan would be rejected. Eight hours before the Pearl Harbor attack, Army Chief of Staff George C. Marshall's office began looking for him and found him horseback riding. Marshall appeared at his office at 10:30 A.M. and immediately ordered that a message be sent to Pacific commanders warning that war was imminent. The Japanese decrypted message did not say where the war would start, but Rainbow-5, conducted in 1940, pointed to the Philippines or Guam. Marshall rejected the navy's plea to relay the message through their communications network and ordered it sent through army channels with a copy to Kimmel. The army circuit to Hawaii was down for repairs and, not appreciating the gravity of the situation, the army routing clerk gave Kimmel's copy to the Western Union for commercial wireless transmission. The delivery boy did not arrive at army headquarters on Oahu until 3:00 P.M., eight hours after the Japanese attack.

Nagumo learned later that his Pearl Harbor strike had been made without a formal declaration of war. The Japanese ambassadors in Washington had been delayed by a lengthy decoding of the message from Tokyo and failed to deliver the declaration on time. The time set for message delivery was 20 minutes before the attack on Pearl Harbor. When the Japanese ambassadors appeared at the State Department, Cordell Hull already knew that Pearl Harbor had been attacked. Hull took the document and said that after 50 years of public service he had "never seen a document that was more crowded with infamous falsehoods and distortions."[18] The diplomatic failure provoked Yamamoto, who grumbled, "It does not do to cut a sleeping throat."[19]

In America, "Remember Pearl Harbor!" became the battle cry, and millions of young men went to war.

PART II

Carriers at War

"Scratch one flattop. Dixon to carrier, scratch one flattop."

Radioed message from Lieutenant Commander Robert E. Dixon to the carrier *Yorktown* on the sinking of *Shoho*.

CHAPTER 5

Fighting for Time

Sixty-three-year-old Admiral Ernest J. King knew something about carrier tactics. In April 1938, he had led the successful mock air strike against Pearl Harbor during Fleet Problem XIX. Three-and-a-half years later, Yamamoto adopted the same strategy. King had much in common with Yamamoto, good habits and bad. Both were caustic men, determined leaders, exceptional strategists, keen judges of men, and chronic womanizers. Yamamoto overcame a drinking problem, King never did.

For blunders at Pearl Harbor, King criticized his boss, CNO Admiral Harold R. Stark, and Pacific Fleet commander Admiral Kimmel for "faults of omission rather than faults of commission." In King's opinion, the "derelictions" of both men indicated a "lack of superior judgment necessary for exercising command . . . rather than culpable inefficiency. Appropriate administrative action would appear to be the relegation of both of these officers to positions in which lack of superior judgment may not result in future errors."[1] Had it not been for war, King's outspokenness may have cost him his career. Naval officers serving under King called him "rough, tough, and brilliant; some would say *mean*, tough, and brilliant."[2]

King's service stretched back to the Spanish-American War, after which he graduated in 1901 from the U.S. Naval Academy. During his career he commanded destroyers, submarines, and in 1927 earned his wings. In 1930, he became *Lexington*'s skipper, and three years later a rear admiral and Chief of the Bureau of Aeronautics. In January 1939, he became Commander Aircraft Battle Force, which included *Lexington*, *Saratoga*, *Ranger*, and later *Yorktown* and *Enterprise*. The exposure acquainted him with many of the men who in the days ahead would develop into top carrier commanders.

In 1941, King commanded the Atlantic Fleet, but the Pearl Harbor disaster brought him back to Washington. On December 20, he became Commander in Chief, U.S. Fleet (CominCh). His priorities included the destruction of the Japanese navy. In March 1942, he received a second hat, Chief of Naval Operations. Few officers in the U.S. Navy understood carrier air tactics better than King.

On December 20, 1941, Admiral Ernest J. King became Commander in Chief U.S. Fleet. (U.S. Navy photo)

Admiral Kimmel received most of the blame for the Pearl Harbor disaster, and on December 17, 1941, the navy relieved him as commander of the Pacific Fleet, much of which lay in ruins outside his office window. Three days later, King became CominCh and inherited the task of breaking in Kimmel's replacement. The president and the secretary of the navy chose 56-year-old Admiral Chester W. Nimitz, a man of exceptional ability.

Born in 1885 in Fredericksburg, Texas, Nimitz graduated from the U.S. Naval Academy in 1905 and spent the next four years with the Asiatic Fleet. After his initial tour of duty, he transferred to submarines and soon became an expert in undersea warfare. He studied diesel engine technology in Germany and put the knowledge to use converting some of the navy's coal-burners to oil. He spent 10 years with submarines before moving to the command of a cruiser division and eventually a battleship division.

King would have preferred a carrier man, and Nimitz would have preferred a seagoing command. Neither man got his way. Samuel Eliot Morison, who knew Nimitz personally, wrote, "He had an immense capacity for work, an equal talent for obtaining the best work from others, an almost impeccable judgment of men, and a genius for making prompt, firm decisions. Chester Nimitz was one of those rare men who grow as their responsibilities increase; but even at the end of the war, when his staff had expanded to 636 officers and he had almost 5,000 ships and over 16,000 planes under his command, he retained the simplicity of his Texas upbringing."[3] Nimitz arrived at Pearl Harbor on Christmas Day and a week later took command of the Pacific Fleet.

King drew a line on a chart from Midway to Samoa, Fiji, and Brisbane in northern Australia and told Nimitz to hold it "at all costs." From King's perspective, it was the only possible way for Nimitz to retain communications with his far-flung fleet.

Much had happened between December 7 and the day Nimitz arrived at Pearl Harbor. On December 10, Japan began exploiting the Pacific Fleet's weakness. Amphibious forces occupied Guam and landed on Luzon. Little Wake Island proved to be a tougher shell to crack. On December 11, a separate Japanese force failed in an attempt to assault the island. The Japanese lost the first ships of the war, two destroyers and a transport. The other ships withdrew, a light cruiser, two destroyers, and a freighter damaged.

Kimmel never understood carriers or carriermen, one of whom was Vice Admiral William F. "Bull" Halsey, Jr., a man with a decisive nature, a quick wit, a sharp tongue, and an abundance of stubborn determination. During World War I, Halsey earned the Navy Cross, and World War II would make him one of the most famous sea fighters in modern history. His biographer E. B. Potter said, "Halsey's fighting-cock stance, barrel chest, and beetle brows embodied the popular conception of an old sea dog. He could scowl fiercely and make strong men wince under the lash of his invective, but the wrinkles around his eyes were not from scowling. He was a genial, likeable man, known to his intimates as Bill and affectionately referred to by his subordinates as Admiral Bill," but his nickname "Bull" characterized him best.[4]

Born in 1882, Halsey graduated from the U.S. Naval Academy in 1904 and spent his early years in battleships, destroyers, and torpedo craft. During the 1930s, he studied at the Naval War College and took a keen interest in aviation. In 1938, after commanding the aircraft carrier *Saratoga*, Halsey received promotion to rear admiral and began commanding carrier divisions. In June 1940, he became a vice admiral and replaced Admiral King as Commander Aircraft Battle Force, which included all the carriers in the Pacific. He chose *Enterprise* (the "Big E") as his flagship and began developing some of the finest carrier-group commanders in the Pacific.

On December 31, 1941, Admiral Chester W. Nimitz became the
commander of the Pacific Fleet. (U.S. Navy photo)

Two prominent air admirals reported to Halsey. Rear Admiral Patrick N. L.
Bellinger, an airman since 1907, commanded all navy land-based and amphibian
aircraft at Pearl Harbor. Rear Admiral Aubrey W. "Jake" Fitch, an airman since
1906, acted as the local carrier division commander. Both men understood carriers and carrier air tactics. Because of their competency, Kimmel used them to
instruct senior officers whom he considered next in line for flag rank.

On December 7, by good luck rather than good information, Halsey had none
of his carriers at Pearl. At Kimmel's direction, Vice Admiral Wilson Brown had
taken a task force comprised of Rear Admiral John H. Newton's *Lexington*, three

Admiral William F. "Bull" Halsey, Jr., an airman, commanded carrier forces in the Pacific from the beginning to the end of World War II. (U.S. Navy photo)

heavy cruisers, and five destroyers west for the purpose of transporting Marine Scout Bombing Squadron 231 with 18 SB2U Vindicators to Midway. Newton planned to fly them off at noon, but during the morning he received word from Brown of the Pearl Harbor attack. The mission should have been completed, as Midway was in an excellent location to search for Nagumo's fleet, but Kimmel held the marine squadron on the carrier because he wanted *Lexington* to rendezvous with Halsey and search together for the enemy.

During the same period, Halsey had taken *Enterprise*, three cruisers, and nine destroyers 2,100 miles west and on December 4 delivered Marine Fighter Squadron 211 with Grumman F4F Wildcats to Wake Island. Three days later, from a position 150 miles west of Hawaii, he released 18 scout-bombers at dawn for a leisurely fly back to Pearl Harbor. The planes reached Oahu just as the Japanese were leaving. Five scout-bombers were shot down by a combination of nervous AA gunners on the ground and departing Zeroes.

When Halsey learned what had happened, he cursed his bad luck for releasing the planes. He might better have praised his good luck for avoiding the attack because a swarm of Kates would surely have pounced on *Enterprise*.

Kimmel expected Oahu to be invaded. He put every available ship under Halsey's command with instructions to search for the enemy's transports and destroy them. Scout planes from *Enterprise* went on a two-day wild-goose chase. A number of false sightings sent Halsey's task force wandering hither and yon while Nagumo rapidly withdrew to Japan. In the confusion, one of *Enterprise's* scout planes reported a squadron of warships southwest of Oahu. Halsey launched Dauntlesses and Devastators, only to discover at the last minute that the ships were Rear Admiral Milo F. Draemel's light cruisers and destroyers sent by Kimmel to join the hunt. Halsey entered Pearl Harbor at dusk on December 8 and after assessing the destruction uttered one of his memorable declarations: "Before we're through with 'em, the Japanese language will be spoken only in hell!"[5]

When Halsey reached headquarters, he found Kimmel, a longtime friend and classmate, in a state of frenzied confusion. He heard a staff officer tell Kimmel that Japanese gliders and paratroopers had just landed on Oahu's east coast. Observing that Kimmel was on the verge of a nervous breakdown, Halsey attempted to relieve the tension and laughed. Kimmel became furious, but Halsey merely shrugged and said, "The Japanese aren't going to waste their precious carrier decks on such nonsense."[6]

After the ships refueled, Kimmel sent *Lexington* back to Midway to deliver Marine Scout Bombing Squadron 231, and *Enterprise* went on a submarine-hunting errand. Halsey kept planes in the air for five days, growing more impatient every hour. Any suspicious ripple on the surface of the ocean caused an alert. "We were spying periscope feathers in every whitecap and torpedoes in every porpoise," Halsey grumbled.[7]

During the first day of the hunt, Lieutenant (jg) Edward L. Anderson, flying a Douglas scout-bomber (SBD), spotted the 2,000-ton *I-70* on the surface 200 miles northeast of Oahu. He dove on the sub and scored a near miss that prevented her from submerging. Another Dauntless flyer spotted the *I-70* on the surface and sank her. Meanwhile, *Enterprise* dodged two torpedoes fired from another submarine. On December 15, Halsey gave up the search and took the task force back to Oahu.

Kimmel had a number of nonaviator operational commanders at Pearl, among them Vice Admiral Wilson Brown and Rear Admirals Frank Jack Fletcher, Raymond A. Spruance, and Thomas C. Kinkaid. Although all capable officers, none had commanded a carrier. After the shooting started Kimmel had to decide whether to make Fletcher, a nonaviator, or Fitch, an aviator, a senior flag officer.

A nonaviator himself, Kimmel chose Fletcher. Fletcher did not know how to use carrier air effectively and eventually proved it, much to the annoyance of carrier men serving under him.

On December 15, Kimmel dispatched a Wake Island relief force commanded by Fletcher and built around the recently arrived *Saratoga*. The task force contained 3 heavy cruisers, 12 destroyers, and the 12-knot oiler *Neches*. Fletcher made two mistakes: he allowed *Neches* to dictate the pace and stopped frequently to top off fuel tanks. On December 22, he chose the worst time for doing it. Instead of making haste to Wake, he stopped to fuel. Had he pressed ahead, his task force would have intercepted the Japanese landing force, destroyed the squadron lying off shore, saved Wake Island, and given Americans something to cheer about. Instead, the enemy landed on the island on December 23 and captured it. Fletcher turned back, mission unaccomplished.

It became apparent to Kimmel that the attack on Pearl Harbor needed a scapegoat. That he had three undamaged carriers intensified the questions brewing in political circles regarding the admiral's perceived reluctance to use them. Kimmel knew he had to take action. He ordered *Lexington*'s task force to raid Jaluit Island and then move against Wake. Fletcher was already on his way to Wake with *Saratoga*. Halsey was also about to send *Enterprise* to Wake. Kimmel knew he did not need three carrier groups at Wake, so he considered leaving *Saratoga* at Wake and sending *Enterprise* and *Lexington* after Nagumo's fleet, which had already returned to Japan.

Before Kimmel could act, Vice Admiral William S. Pye relieved him on an interim basis. Pye showed even less willingness to risk the carriers. He abandoned Kimmel's efforts to save Wake Island, recalled *Lexington* and *Saratoga*, and immediately fell out of favor. The two carrier groups could have chopped up the cruisers and destroyers harassing the island, but they would have been assailed by daily air attacks from Japanese island-based bombers. Halsey never became involved because Pye kept the *Enterprise* on standby at Hawaii. Pye lost his one opportunity to achieve recognition, and eight days later Admiral Nimitz took command of the Pacific Fleet.

Admiral King expected Nimitz to be more aggressive, but neither he nor Nimitz could predict where the enemy would strike next. He sent Nimitz all the ships the navy could spare, but what Halsey wanted was more carriers and better planes.

During the early stages of the war, a task force consisted of a single fast carrier escorted by two or three cruisers, five or six destroyers, and an oiler. Even when two carriers acted together, they continued to function as two task forces.

Naval aircraft represented a sad testimony to America's unpreparedness for war. Grumman F4F Wildcat fighters were rugged but slow against the swift, maneuverable Japanese Zero. Douglas TBD Devastator torpedo planes were old, sluggish, unmaneuverable, and a sitting duck against AA fire and Zeros. Douglas SBD Dauntless dive-bombers, however, were durable, effective, and versatile enough to triple as a bomber, fighter, and scout plane. Each carrier air group consisted of 72 planes: 18 Wildcat fighters (VF), 18 Devastator torpedo planes (VT), and 36 Dauntless scout-dive-bombers (VSB). For the next seven months, carrier aircraft would not change.

The Japanese tipped their hand on January 6, when they began shelling Australia's air base on New Britain. On January 23, an enemy amphibious force, covered by Nagumo's carriers, landed at Rabaul and captured the airfield. The action telegraphed Japan's effort to establish a foothold in the Solomons, New Guinea, and the islands of the Coral Sea.

American carrier operations continued to encounter stumbling blocks. On January 9, 1942, *Saratoga*, under the command of Vice Admiral Herbert F. Leary, headed for the South Pacific. One day and 500 miles southwest of Hawaii, a deep-running torpedo from a Japanese submarine struck the carrier, killed six men, and flooded three firerooms. She limped back to Oahu under her own power and proceeded from there to the Puget Sound for repair and modernization.

A few days later, Nimitz sent Admiral Brown and the *Lexington* group on a bombing mission to Wake Island. A Japanese submarine sank the squadron's oiler and forced Brown to abort the mission. The act emphasized the ease by which an entire carrier group could be rendered useless by the loss of a single auxiliary vessel.

On January 11, a Japanese submarine shelled the U.S. naval station at Pago Pago, Samoa. The incident attracted Admiral King's attention because the island provided an essential link to the route stretching from Oahu to the Fijis, New Zealand, and Australia. Conscious of the weakness of the entire area and the importance of keeping seaborne communications open, King brought Admiral Fletcher to the States, put him in charge of a new task force built around the USS *Yorktown*, and sent the ships to the Pacific through the Panama Canal. With the group came four transports filled with marines. Halsey's *Enterprise* met them along the way to provide additional air cover. On January 23, the same day the Japanese invaded Rabaul, marines went ashore on Samoa.

Nimitz anticipated an attack on Samoa, and having two carrier groups available, he went on the offensive. On January 25, *Enterprise* (TG-8) and *Yorktown* (TG-17) sailed from Samoa. For the first time since the war began, Halsey warmed to the prospect of going on the offensive. Six days later, the two groups separated. Halsey headed for the Marshalls, Fletcher for the Gilberts, with island targets hundreds of miles apart.

Fifteen minutes before sunrise on February 1, Halsey launched what developed into a nine-hour attack. He sent cruisers, destroyers, and fighter planes to attack Wotje and Maloelap, while Dauntlesses and Devastators from *Enterprise* struck Kwajalein's Roi airfield and ships in the lagoon. Mist obscured Roi, causing pilots to fly aimlessly about. Zeros got off the ground and shot down four Dauntlesses. Despite the losses, the attack produced favorable results. The surviving Dauntlesses joined the torpedo-bombers and together destroyed or damaged

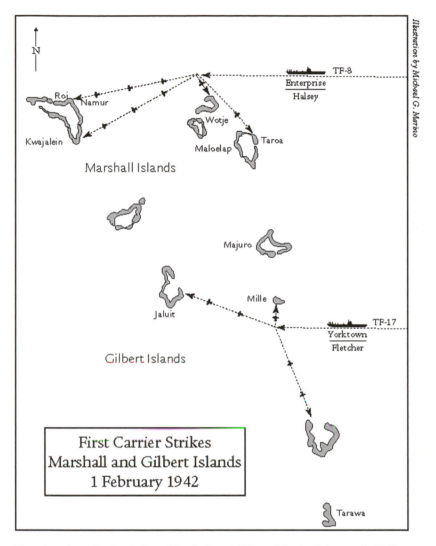

Illustration by Michael G. Marino

First American Carrier Strikes: Marshall and Gilbert Islands, February 1, 1942.
(Michael G. Marino)

10 ships and 18 planes. Japan reported the loss of 90 men, including area commander Rear Admiral Yashiro.

At 1:00 P.M. Halsey recalled his group, pulled away from the Marshalls, and
headed for Oahu. Forty minutes later a Mitsubishi "Betty" twin-engine bomber
spotted *Enterprise* and attempted a suicide crash on the carrier's deck. Bruno P.
Gaida, a young aviation mechanic, spotted the bomber's approach, jumped into

the rear seat of a parked Dauntless, and opened with the machinegun. "That," wrote Samuel Eliot Morison, "and a quick 'hard right' by the officer of the deck, caused the would-be kamikaze to strike the port edge of the flight deck and topple harmlessly over the side."[8]

Fletcher's TG-17 ran into bad weather at Jaluit and lost six planes. Strikes on Makin and Mili also failed. Fletcher decided against a second strike because it might entail a night recovery and withdrew. When compared with Halsey's determined effort, Fletcher made another poor showing. The *Yorktown* deserved better. In the final analysis, Halsey made headlines, having struck the Marshall Islands with audacity. Nimitz wrote off Fletcher's effort in the Gilberts as valuable combat experience. Fletcher's test lay in the future.

The Japanese capture of Rabaul caused great concern in Australia. The harbor could serve as a marshalling and supply center for carriers, cruisers, battleships, and troops, thereby putting the Solomons, New Guinea, New Hebrides, and New Caledonia in striking distance. King ordered Nimitz to send Rear Admiral Wilson Brown's *Lexington* force and all the planes and army bombers that could be spared to reinforce Vice Admiral Herbert F. Leary, who after being detached from the injured *Saratoga*, had taken command of Anzac (Australia-New Zealand) naval forces in the Fiji-New Caledonia area.

Any operation against Rabaul involved risks. Admiralty charts were old and unreliable, oilers would be needed at rendezvous points near Japanese-controlled waters, enemy aircraft patrolled a 600-mile perimeter, and Nimitz could not afford to waste a carrier.

Brown planned to creep within 125 miles of Rabaul at night and at 4:00 A.M. on February 21 launch his aircraft, but on the morning of the 20th, 350 miles east of Rabaul, *Lexington*'s radar picked up blips. Six Wildcats flew off and shot down a Kawanishi "Emily," a four-engine Japanese flying boat. Two more enemy planes appeared. American flyers downed one. The other got away. Knowing his task force had been reported, Brown prepared for trouble.

During the afternoon *Lexington*'s radar detected a flock of "bandits" coming in from the west. Brown sent up more Wildcats to reinforce his CAP. Minutes later, the first fight between Japanese and American carrier aircraft occurred in full view from *Lexington*'s deck. Every sailor came topside, yelling encouragement to the flyers overhead. Lieutenant Edward H. "Butch" O'Hare shot down five Kate torpedo-bombers, one of which attempted to crash on the carrier's deck. O'Hare became the first navy ace of World War II and received the Medal of Honor.

That afternoon "Lady Lex" demonstrated the power of an aircraft carrier. She lost two planes and one pilot, but the 18 Kates from Rabaul never made it back. *Lexington*'s flyers had single-handedly and so thoroughly fought off the attack that not a ship had been scratched. The action, in addition to doing wonders for morale, convinced Brown that F4F Wildcats could hold their own against Japanese planes. Yet he canceled the raid on Rabaul and withdrew.

Lieutenant Edward H. "Butch" O'Hare shot down five Kate torpedo-bombers and became the first navy ace of World War II, for which he received the Medal of Honor. (U.S. Navy photo)

King complained. He demanded unrelenting action, even if it meant small strikes here and there. He wanted the Japanese to begin worrying about the defense of their northern possessions, and he hoped such actions would discourage them from making further advances to the south.

Nimitz did not like his carriers wandering about the ocean with so little protection, but pressed by King, he sent Halsey and the *Enterprise* group to harass Wake and Little Marcus Island. The February 23 strike on Wake did little damage and was not worth the loss of a plane. A week later, *Enterprise* stood off Marcus Island, less than 1,000 miles southeast of Tokyo. The attack came as a surprise to the Japanese. No enemy aircraft got off the ground, but Halsey lost another plane to AA fire. Like the Wake attack, nothing of strategic importance resulted, and the Japanese continued their assault on the Solomons.

On February 27–28, far to the west in the Java Sea, the IJN cut to pieces Admiral Karel Doorman's ABDA (American, British, Dutch, and Australian) fleet. No carriers were involved, just old cruisers and destroyers. The forces were about equal, but the lack of spotter aircraft from Allied ships and the superiority of Japan's Long Lance torpedoes tipped the scales. Surviving ABDA ships withdrew into the Sunda Strait on the western end of Java and encountered Japanese transports landing troops in Banten Bay. Doorman's remnant force attacked and severely hampered the enemy's amphibious operation. The Japanese covering force, the same one Doorman had unsuccessfully fought the day before, arrived under Rear Admiral Takeo Kurita and destroyed the last of the ABDA fleet. During the two-day fight, the Japanese did not lose a ship. A single carrier may have turned the tide of battle, but Doorman had none.

Oddly enough, the old carrier USS *Langley* was in the area but had been reclassified as an aviation transport (AV-3). The 33-year-old ship was transporting 33 army pilots and 32 P-40 planes from Australia to Java. Vice Admiral Conrad E. L. Helfrich of the Royal Dutch Navy detached *Langley* and the freighter *Sea Witch*, which also was carrying planes and pilots, near the Javanese port of Tjilatjap because he wanted the aircraft to be based there. No Japanese force had been reported in the area, so after detaching the ships, Helfrich sailed away.

Commander R. P. McConnell, skipper of *Langley*, then received a number of mixed signals that caused him to slow down and backtrack to meet a pair of escorts. The delay proved fatal. Nine twin-engine Japanese bombers from nearby shore bases disabled the old carrier. *Langley* went down 75 miles south of Tjilatjap, and had she not been detained for escorts, she might have been useful during the Battle of Sunda Strait.

The virtual destruction of the ABDA fleet, although a few destroyers survived, convinced IGH that the Japanese army and navy could not be stopped. Admiral Brown's aborted raid on Rabaul and Halsey's strike on Marcus Island was no more than a pinprick in their plans. The surrender of Singapore on February 15 guaranteed Japanese possession of Malaya and soon led to the landing of forces on Lae and Salamaua in northeastern New Guinea. The last fighting remnants of American forces in the Philippines lay surrounded on the island of Corregidor, and fearing the loss of General Douglas MacArthur, President Roosevelt ordered him to escape to Darwin. In a letter written on March 7 to Winston Churchhill, Roosevelt said, "the Pacific situation is now very grave."[9] Three days later the Netherlands East Indies surrendered. The following day Admiral Nagumo shelled and bombed Port Moresby on New Guinea, Darwin on Australia's northern coast, and Tulagi in the Solomons. The Japanese seemed unstoppable.

Admiral Brown, after the aborted attack on Rabaul, told Nimitz that two carriers were required to conduct attacks on strong enemy bases. He also asked for extra tankers. Nimitz agreed and sent Brown the underemployed *Yorktown*, commanded by Admiral Fletcher.

Rabaul was becoming the most important enemy base south of the equator, and King wanted it smashed. In early March *Lexington* and *Yorktown* proceeded toward the island, but along the way Brown learned that the Japanese had landed on Lae and Salamaua. Both locations had airfields that could become equally as troublesome as Rabaul. Brown spent the night with his staff and decided to bypass Rabaul and strike Lae and Salamaua before the enemy had time to fortify the area. Instead of going through the uncharted Bismarck Sea, Brown jogged south through the New Hebrides and took both carriers, four cruisers, and nine destroyers into the Gulf of Papua.

To reach Lae and Salamaua, carrier air groups had to fly over New Guinea's 8000-foot Owen Stanley Mountains, which turned out to be a splendid idea. Brown turned air operations over to Captain Frederick C. "Ted" Sherman, *Lexington*'s skipper, who knew more about carrier air tactics than Brown and Fletcher combined. Sherman coordinated air attacks between the carriers and on March 10 launched 104 Dauntlesses and Devastators. The sudden appearance of carrier planes swooping down from the mountains surprised the Japanese. Not a single enemy plane got off the ground. The strike tore up the airfields and sank a light cruiser, a minesweeper, and a transport. Returning pilots wanted to rearm and launch a second attack because good targets had been left behind. Brown, however, worried about a counterattack, and Fletcher wanted to return to the auxiliaries and refuel. The attack did nothing to slow down the Japanese, and Rabaul remained unmolested. Brown lost none of his ships and only one plane. The hurried withdrawal did not satisfy the aggressive type of fighting Nimitz demanded. Captain Sherman, however, made an important observation on carrier tactics, noting that, "two or more carriers *could* work together in a combat team."[10]

In January 1942, Admiral King and his operations officer, Captain Francis S. Low, searched for a demonstrative way to show the Japanese that striking Pearl Harbor would have immediate repercussions. Pinprick attacks against small enemy-controlled islands would not do it. Something sensational and outrageous had to be done to make the Japanese feel vulnerable.

The report of Admiral Brown's air attack on Lae and Salamaua had barely been inked into the record books when on April 1, 16 modified B-25B "Mitchell" medium bombers under the command of Lieutenant Colonel James H. "Jimmy" Doolittle were hoisted onto the deck of the USS *Hornet* (CV-8). The dangerous mission had been worked out between King and Army Air Forces (AAF) General Henry H. "Hap" Arnold. Even Captain Marc Mitscher did not know why his carrier was to receive twin-engine army bombers until a few days before the loading began. The new 20,000-ton *Hornet* had been designed to carry 81 planes and a complement of 2,072 men. Mitchells had not been mentioned in the specifications. Their wide wingspan did not fit in *Hornet*'s elevators, so the bombers had to be stored on deck.

Until a few days before sailing, only six officers knew of the plan to bomb Tokyo. For so dangerous a task, Doolittle wanted only volunteers. Seventy officers and 130 enlisted men of the AAF volunteered to fly the mission. They were the same men who spent the last month modifying the B-25s and learning how to fly them off the ground, fully loaded, using special equipment designed for carrier launching. Not one pilot had ever flown off a flattop.

On April 2, *Hornet* put to sea from San Francisco Bay and headed west, escorted by two cruisers, four destroyers, and an oiler. Once underway, Doolittle opened his files and began discussing military targets in and around Tokyo. Each five-man crew received a primary and a secondary target. Once a bomber left the flight deck, there could be no turning back. Fuel had been carefully calculated. After the bomb drop, flyers were to cross the East China Sea and take refuge on specially designated airfields in China. Nobody knew what was happening in China or if the Chinese still controlled the fields.

On April 13, Halsey's *Enterprise* (TF-16) rendezvoused with *Hornet* to provide air cover. Mitscher could not have brought a Wildcat to *Hornet*'s deck without removing the bombers. Navy planes were all stored below with wings folded or dismantled. Without *Enterprise*, *Hornet* would have been defenseless, except for her eight AA guns.

Halsey estimated that to reach China, which was 1,093 nautical miles from Tokyo, the Mitchells, each carrying four 500-pound bombs and 1,141 gallons of gasoline, would have to fly off no less than 500 miles from Japan. He planned on launching the afternoon of April 18 for a night attack. When spotted for takeoff, the tail of the last Mitchell projected over the after edge of *Hornet*'s flight deck. During a final conference with his flyers, Doolittle said, "Well, if we ever get to Chungking, I'll throw the biggest Goddamn party you ever saw."[11]

Until 2:00 A.M. on April 18, everything went according to plan when radar picked up two ships dead ahead. Halsey altered course and at daylight launched search planes. At 7:00 A.M., pilots spotted three Japanese picket boats but sank only one. Halsey believed TF-16 had been sighted and reported, but *Hornet* was still 650 miles from Japan and 150 miles from the launch point. He could not risk losing the carriers. Doolittle said that by conserving fuel they could still carry out the mission and reach China. When 623 miles from the Japanese mainland, Halsey launched the Mitchells. One bomber nearly stalled on takeoff, but all 16 flew off and fell into formation. Halsey immediately turned TF-16 about and retired "at 25 knots."[12]

At noon, three-and-a-half hours later, Doolittle's Mitchells made a surprise appearance over Tokyo just as a practice air raid drill ended. Despite warnings from picket boats, Tokyo was unprepared. Pilots skimmed over the city at rooftop level and began engaging preassigned targets—sites engaged in the production of munitions, steel, chemicals, oil, electrical power, and shipbuilding. Three bombers assigned to Nagoya, Osaka, and Kobe carried only incendiary bombs.

Although damage to Japanese military targets was modest, face-saving Japanese authorities, fearing a reaction, attempted to suppress the news from the general public. The IGS suffered embarrassment in silence. Although some staff members believed the attack had come from Midway, Yamamoto knew better. He resolved to eliminate the possibility of another raid by the rapid destruction of America's carrier force. To accomplish the task, Yamamoto put his staff to work on a plan to capture Midway.

None of Doolittle's Mitchells made it to a Chinese airfield. One crew landed in Vladivostok, four planes crash landed in China, and eleven crews bailed out during the dead of night, landing in swamps, lakes, trees, and rocky ridges. The

Japanese captured several flyers and executed them. Seventy-one of the 80 flyers, including Jimmy Doolittle, survived the raid. Admiral Halsey, writing later, said, "In my opinion their flight was one of the most courageous deeds in military history."[13]

The Doolittle raid gave a tremendous lift to the American public. Bombing Tokyo created a powerful antidote to a nation trying to recover from Pearl Harbor. The Japanese remained puzzled about where the Mitchells came from and where they went. President Roosevelt humorously announced they came from "Shangri-La." Prime Minister General Tojo had never heard of James Hilton's novel *Lost Horizon*, and although Americans chuckled at the joke, the Chinese paid the price. Japanese poured through Chekiang Province and demolished every village believed to have sheltered Americans. Some 250,000 Chinese lost their lives over the raid.

Halsey and Mitscher never knew how close they came to colliding with Admiral Nagumo, whose powerful carrier force was returning to Japan after raiding Trincomalee. At the time, *Hornet's* deck was crammed wingtip to wingtip with B-25s. On April 25, TF-16 returned to Pearl Harbor hoping for a rest. Nimitz told Halsey to refuel. He was needed in the Coral Sea.

Meanwhile, on May 15, 1942, in Washington, Admiral King sent Secretary of the Navy Frank Knox a one-page "shopping list" for 1943—1.67 billion tons of new shipping. Such demands required President Roosevelt's approval, so King suggested that Knox take the request directly to the White House. Roosevelt looked at the document and told Knox, "I wish you and Admiral King would talk to me about this proposed new building program." King expected the summons.

Roosevelt had his own ideas about aircraft carriers. He wanted to discuss the "desirability of building 45,000-ton aircraft carriers, and the possibility of cutting the size of 27,000-ton aircraft carriers by four or five thousand tons and putting the saved tonnage into aircraft carriers of approximately 12–14,000 tons."[14] King talked Roosevelt out of 45,000-ton carriers and tried to do the same with escort carriers. During discussions, Henry J. Kaiser approached the Bureau of Ships and offered to mass-produce in six months 30 or more escort carriers of his own design. At first King did not like the idea, but Roosevelt accepted Kaiser's offer. King said he saw no immediate need for them but later changed his mind, admitting after the war, "When the Kaisers really got started, they did quite well."[15]

Kaiser Ship Building Company of Vancouver eventually built 50 *Casablanca*-class 7,800-ton escort carriers, all 512 feet 3 inches long with a 108-foot beam, a 22-foot, 4-inch draft, and a speed of 19 knots. They carried 28 planes and a complement of 860 officers and men. Roosevelt, however, never got his 45,000-ton carrier. Nor would he live to see one built.

CHAPTER 6

Coral Sea: Battle of Errors

On May 6, 1942, the Philippines fell, giving Japan virtually unmolested control of the Dutch East Indies' oil fields and paved the way for MO Operation, IGH's plan to extend conquests into the Southwest Pacific. Admiral Yamamoto argued that it was more important to bring about a decisive battle with the U.S. Pacific Fleet, and he believed that a decisive engagement would be fought if the IJN captured Midway. He also argued that deeper penetration to the south would weaken Japan's ability to concentrate its forces while the enemy gathered strength. Yamamoto yielded, however, to the demands of the army and agreed to support MO Operation—the capture of Port Moresby, southeastern New Guinea, and the Solomon Islands. From there, Japan could develop bases to attack Northern Queensland, Nauru, and the ocean islands of the South Pacific. Rabaul and Truk, untouched by American carrier efforts, became the launching points. Pacific Fleet code-breakers at Hawaii, however, picked up MO transmissions, and this induced Nimitz to send Halsey and Mitscher to the Coral Sea.

Because Yamamoto needed carriers for the Midway attack, he detached only Rear Admiral Tadaichi Hara's fast carrier division, *Shokaku* and *Zuikaku,* for MO operations and added the light carrier *Shoho* in Rear Admiral Aritomo Goto's covering group. He also provided cruisers, destroyers, and submarines from Rabaul and Truk, and 11 troop-carrying transports for the invasion of Port Moresby. Vice Admiral Takeo Takagi, fresh from victory in the Java Sea, commanded the carrier strike force. Vice Admiral Shigeyoshi Inouye, CinC Fourth Fleet, had overall command, which included a complex chain of coordinated operations. Neither Yamamoto nor Inouye expected American carriers to be in the area because *Enterprise* and *Hornet* had been reported west of Tokyo and *Saratoga* was still undergoing repairs at Puget Sound.

Even though Halsey and Mitscher came roaring down from Pearl Harbor, they could not reach the Coral Sea in time. The coming battle would have to be fought by air groups on *Lexington* and *Yorktown* and executed by the judgments of their officers. Fletcher still commanded TF-17 from the flagship *Yorktown,* but on April 3, Rear Admiral Aubrey W. Fitch had replaced Wilson Brown on

Vice Admiral Frank Jack Fletcher. (U.S. Navy photo)

Lexington. Ted Sherman, *Lexington*'s skipper, and Captain Elliott Buckmaster, *Yorktown*'s skipper, although among the best carrier captains in the business, had ever been tested in head-to-head battle with the enemy. Fitch was the most experienced carrier officer in the navy, and Sherman, who orchestrated the air strike on Lae and Salamaua was among the navy's outstanding authorities on air warfare. Fitch came under Fletcher's tactical command, and Fletcher was under orders to check further advances of the enemy in the New Guinea-Solomons area.

Earlier, King and Nimitz had met in San Francisco to discuss carrier strategy. They agreed that more must be learned about how the Japanese used carriers. During the meeting, King mentioned that he had lost confidence in Fletcher. Nimitz replied that he had no one else in the Pacific with more experience and argued for Fletcher's retention. King reluctantly agreed but reminded Nimitz, who needed no reminder, that as senior officer present Fletcher would be in command of any action in the South Pacific, and for this reason Nimitz tried to hurry Halsey into the area.

On May 1, *Lexington* and *Yorktown* rendezvoused to refuel west of New Hebrides. Rear Admiral J. G. Crace, Royal Australian Navy (RAN), was also on the way with an Allied support group of three cruisers and two destroyers. On May 2, Fletcher received a message from MacArthur that the Japanese could be moving on Tulagi. Fletcher broke off refueling *Yorktown* and on May 3 headed slowly west into the Coral Sea. He left Fitch behind with *Lexington* to finish fueling but with instructions to rejoin *Yorktown* in the morning. Fletcher and Fitch were seldom separated by more than 100 miles, but out of touch with each other and unsure of the enemy's movements.

Fletcher then learned from army intelligence that the Japanese had landed unopposed on Tulagi. Without waiting for Fitch, he headed north toward Guadalcanal. Early on May 4, shortly after *Yorktown* came within flying range of Tulagi, Admiral Takagi's carrier strike force off the eastern Solomons began approaching the Coral Sea. Takagi's job was to protect the Port Moresby Invasion Group, which was preparing to move into the Solomon Sea from Rabaul. Fletcher's last order to Fitch directed *Lexington* to a position southeast of *Yorktown*, but Fletcher then went north, leaving a gap of 250 miles between the two carriers.

At dawn on May 4, *Yorktown* launched 12 Devastators, 28 Dauntlesses, and 6 Wildcats. At 17,000 feet, the flight passed over scattered squalls and swung across Guadalcanal. Lieutenant Commander William O. Burch, leading the first wave of 13 Dauntlesses, spotted Japanese ships in off Tulagi. The Dauntlesses dropped to 10,000 feet, nosed over, and went into a steep 70-degree dive. At 2,500 feet, the pilots pulled back their joysticks and dropped 1,000-pounders on the surprised flotilla. Burch reported four ships hit and one probable before heading back to *Yorktown*. Lieutenant Commander Charles R. Fenton's Dauntlesses followed and damaged two more ships.

After the bombers cleared, Lieutenant Commander Joseph Taylor, fresh from the attack of Lae, came in low with 12 torpedo-bombers (TBDs). The Devastators leveled off at 50 feet above the water and dropped Mark-13s, an unreliable torpedo that could never be depended on to explode. Most of them missed or failed to detonate, but one struck and sank a minesweeper.

All planes returned safely, rearmed, and before the day ended made two more strikes without damaging a ship worth mention. The pilots, however, were euphoric. They reported sinking seven ships, claimed to have forced a light cruiser ashore, and believed three other ships had been damaged, including a seaplane tender that some flyers mistook for a heavy cruiser. What pilots needed most were two quick courses: one to improve bombing accuracy, the other to properly identify Japanese ships. Nimitz dourly spoke of the operation as "disappointing in terms of the ammunition expended," but useful "for target practice."[1]

Having alerted the Japanese to the presence of carrier aircraft, Fletcher withdrew on the afternoon of May 4 to rendezvous with *Lexington*. He found Fitch and Admiral Crace's cruiser squadron about 250 miles south of Guadalcanal and spent the next two days leisurely refueling. He kept scout planes in the air, but they never spotted Takagi's carrier force, which on May 4 was out of range east of Bougainville and covered by overcast. Fletcher rested on his laurels. Based on pilot reports, he mistakenly believed his flyers had single-handedly turned back a major part of Yamamoto's invasion force.

The Japanese were also in a tactical fog. On May 5, one of *Yorktown's* planes shot down a four-engine "Emily" from the naval base at Rabaul, but Admiral Inouye was too engrossed preparing for the invasion of Port Moresby to attach any significance to the snooper's disappearance.

On the evening of May 5, while Crace's cruisers steamed ahead, Fletcher moved slowly westward with Fitch's carrier group, following about 50 miles behind Crace and periodically slowing to top off his fuel tanks. As Fletcher steamed west, Admiral Takagi's strike force with Admiral Hara's carriers *Zuikaku* and *Shokaku* rounded San Cristobal, turned northwest, passed Rennell Island, and steamed toward Guadalcanal. During the same hours, Rear Admiral Aritomo Goto's covering group, composed of four heavy cruisers and the light carrier *Shoho*, began refueling in the Solomon Sea south of Bougainville. Neither Fletcher nor the Japanese squadrons converging toward Jomard Pass in the Louisiade Archipelago were aware of each other's presence.

On May 6, while cruising slowly westward across the Coral Sea, Fletcher decided to turn tactical air operations over to Fitch—an excellent idea because Fitch understood air operations. Fitch did not receive the message until two days later. Meanwhile, Fletcher began receiving reports from Brisbane and Pearl Harbor of large numbers of Japanese ships in the area, including three carriers, but his own search planes reported no sightings. Ignorant of Takagi's presence to the north, Fletcher resumed his westerly course and on May 7 reached a position within striking distance of Jomard Pass, through which he expected the Port Moresby invasion force to exit. Takagi also changed course and began moving directly down on Fletcher's route. When they were only 70 miles apart, Takagi stopped to fuel, and once again the distance widened between Fletcher and Takagi's groups.

Fletcher's orders were to destroy the Port Moresby invasion force, Takagi's orders were to support it, and both admirals began looking for it. The two groups were inevitably on a collision course. Samuel Eliot Morison observed, "The main action of the Battle of the Coral Sea should have been fought on 6 May, and would have been if each force had been aware of the other's presence."[2]

The confusion continued. Takagi did not hurry because he knew the exact hour to begin looking for the Port Moresby flotilla. Another Emily flying boat spotted the American squadron and reported its position to Rabaul before being shot down, but Takagi did not get the message until later. Meanwhile, four B-17 Flying Fortresses out of Port Moresby spotted the carrier *Shoho* and Goto's

Covering Group near the Jomard Pass and reported it to the AAF's 19th Bombardment Group, but no one advised Fletcher. Follow-up flights also sighted the Port Moresby bound force. Inouye now knew that Takagi with Hara's carrier group was waiting in the Coral Sea. With Goto's squadron protecting his left flank, Inouye began moving his 28-ship invasion force down the Solomon Sea toward Port Moresby.

On the morning of May 7, Hara suggested sending out aircraft to make a search to the south. Takagi knew American carrier planes had struck Tulagi on May 4, and although no intelligence had been reported since, he agreed. Two search planes sighted the oiler *Neosho* and the destroyer *Sims*, which had been left behind by Fletcher, but the pilots reported the ships as a carrier and a cruiser.

Hara reacted with alacrity and ordered an all-out attack. The Japanese were no more adept at identifying and destroying enemy ships than American flyers. Fifteen Vals flew over *Neosho* and *Sims*, missed with bombs, and disappeared. An hour later, 10 more dive-bombers attacked *Sims* and missed again. At noon, 36 Vals arrived. Sixteen dove on *Sims* and sank her. The other 20 went after *Neosho*. After being struck by six direct hits and once by a suicide plane, a section of *Neosho*'s deck burst into flames. Although severely damaged and her radio dead, Captain J. S. Phillips kept her afloat and drifted west. On May 11, the skipper of the destroyer *Henley* found *Neosho* 100 miles from where she had been attacked. He picked up 123 survivors, including 14 from *Sims*, and scuttled her. Hara's pilots never sank *Neosho* but thought they did. Takagi continued on course, no longer worried about American carriers in the Coral Sea.

During the night of May 6–7, Fletcher moved into position about 100 miles southeast of Jomard Pass. In the morning, after the sun rose, he turned north and looped about. Because he had sent Crace's cruisers ahead to watch the pass, he lost the protection of TF-44's AA fire. During the day, Crace never saw a Japanese ship, but three attacks by Japanese aircraft and another by three overzealous pilots flying AAF B-17s kept him busy. Crace performed a masterful job of evading bombs and torpedoes and fought off four attacks without suffering damage. His expertise would be sadly missed in the hours to come, but in the final analysis Crace drew off 50 enemy planes that might otherwise have been deployed against Fletcher.

Early on May 7, search planes from *Yorktown* reported ships on the move, but this was not the large force Fletcher expected. The flyers had stumbled on Rear Admiral K. Marumo's little squadron of two old light cruisers, a seaplane carrier, and three gunboats that were part of the Port Moresby invasion group. Later, another search plane reported two aircraft carriers and four heavy cruisers north of the Louisiades. What the pilot actually saw was Admiral Goto's covering force with the light carrier *Shoho*.

At almost the same hour, Goto's search planes spotted Fletcher's carriers and reported their position. Goto had most of his planes covering the Port Moresby invasion force and called them back to refuel and prepare for a fight. He also radioed Admiral Inouye to stay clear of Jomard Pass, causing the Port Moresby invasion force to turn away until Goto and Takagi disposed of the threat.

At 9:25 A.M., while Takagi's carrier planes were attacking *Neosho* and *Sims*, Admiral Fitch prepared to strike Goto's force. Air Group Commander William B. Ault launched from *Lexington*, followed five minutes later by a strike force from *Yorktown*. Ninety-two planes flew to the coordinates provided by search planes and found nothing but stormy weather. They orbited, listening in vain for radio chatter from the enemy.

At 10:50 A.M., Lieutenant Commander Weldon L. Hamilton, flying a *Lexington* Dauntless, passed over Tagula Island at 15,000 feet and spotted Goto's covering force: four heavy cruisers, one destroyer, and *Shoho*. Hamilton radioed Ault, who seven minutes later arrived with *Lexington*'s air group.

Seeing American aircraft aloft, Goto ordered evasive maneuvers. When Ault dove, he observed *Shoho* twisting snake-like in heavy seas. His bombs missed but one exploded close enough to knock five planes off *Shoho*'s deck.

At 11:10 A.M., Hamilton's 10 SBDs attacked, followed by *Lexington*'s torpedo squadron and *Yorktown*'s air group. With 92 planes converging on *Shoho*, she had no chance. Despite deplorable bombing accuracy, two 1,000-pounders dropped by Lieutenant Commander Robert E. Dixon's SBDs smashed through the rear elevator on *Shoho*'s flight deck and exploded. Fires on the hangar deck ignited aviation fuel and flames spread toward the torpedo storage room. Devastators moved in low, sending torpedoes into *Shoho*'s starboard side aft, wrecking the steering apparatus, tearing up the water mains, and knocking out the ship's electrical power. Ten minutes into the attack, smoke covered the vessel. Only her bow could be seen from the air. Now dead in the water, more bombs and torpedoes ripped into her from every direction. When water reached her gun deck, Captain Ishinosuke Izawa ordered the carrier abandoned, and at 11:36 A.M. she sank. *Shoho* went down quickly, taking 631 men. Only 132 of her crew survived.

In the first major battle between carrier planes, American and Japanese fighter pilots learned something about the performance of each other's aircraft. Zeros moved about with stunning speed and agility. Wildcat pilots had difficulty turning with the nimble Zeros, but Japanese planes had no armoring for the pilot, and a well-aimed volley could kill him. Nor were Japanese fuel tanks protected, and a single shot started them smoking. Japanese pilots found Americans hard to shoot down because their planes were armored and did not catch fire easily. The battle in the skies over *Shoho* was waged mainly between fighters, but one Dauntless pilot foolishly tried to engage a Zero in single combat and lost his life.

During the battle, nervous officers and enlisted men gathered outside the radio room on *Lexington* and listened to the chatter. Ted Sherman paced the bridge, waiting anxiously for positive news. The static on the speaker suddenly cleared and he heard the voice of Lieutenant Commander Dixon: "Scratch one flattop! Dixon to carrier, scratch one flattop!"[3]

After the cheering stopped, the waiting began. The rugged Dauntlesses winged in slowly, their bomb racks empty, wings shot up, holes in the fuselage, and some with wheels gone. Then came the old Devastators, which should have been replaced by better aircraft years ago, but on this day they served with distinction. Of 92 aircraft launched that morning, all but three returned.

At 3:00 P.M., with planes refueled and rearmed, the pilots wanted to go back and destroy Goto's heavy cruisers. Fletcher said no. *Yorktown*'s radio operators had intercepted communications from aircraft belonging to Admiral Takagi's carrier force. Fletcher had no intelligence on the position of *Shokaku* and *Zuikaku* but suspected that Takagi's scouts may have spotted *Yorktown* and *Lexington*. Because of storms, Fletcher did not put any search planes in the air and began backtracking.

While recovering planes from the *Neosho* and *Sims* attack, Takagi began receiving radio intercepts about the sinking of *Shoho*. He also found the weather worsening, but unlike Fletcher, he launched 15 Kates and 12 Vals to locate and attack the American carriers. Japanese pilots had the advantage of being trained in night flying, but they ran into rainsqualls and poor visibility. After searching to the limit of their range, Lieutenant Commander Shigekazu Shimazaki ordered the planes to jettison their ordnance and return to the carrier.

Toward evening, Shimazaki stumbled on TF-17. *Lexington*'s radar spotted them in time to launch fighters. The Japanese took a severe mauling, losing a Val and eight Kates at the cost of two Wildcats. The surviving Japanese planes formed up and at dusk flew over *Yorktown*. Three pilots thought they had located their own carrier and began to orbit, blinking their code on Aldis lamps for permission to land. *Yorktown*'s signalmen, equally puzzled, blinked back. As the enemy pilots lowered wheels and flaps to land on *Yorktown*'s deck, AA opened and drove them off. Twenty minutes later, three more Japanese pilots tried the same stunt. This time one paid the price. As the enemy sped away, Fitch used *Lexington*'s radar to track their heading. Thirty miles to the east the planes began orbiting, but they were lost. Only six planes made it back to Hara's carriers. The others ran out of fuel and ditched.

Fitch, thinking the enemy carriers were only 30 miles away, radioed Fletcher. *Yorktown*'s radar could not confirm, so Fletcher did nothing. Takagi's force was actually 90 miles to the north. Fletcher considered making a night attack with cruisers and destroyers and then talked himself out of it on the assumption that Hara's two carriers would by then be somewhere else. Fletcher later defended his decision when criticized by Admiral King, writing, "The best plan seemed to be to keep our force concentrated and prepare for a battle with the enemy carriers next morning."[4]

Admiral Inouye, who had withdrawn the Port Moresby invasion force, considered sending Admiral Goto's cruisers in a night attack on Fletcher's carriers but changed his mind. Admiral Takagi considered doing the same. The last-quarter moon shed too little light, a band of stormy weather covered the area, and Hara advised against a night attack. Takagi relented. He had only two heavy cruisers and six destroyers to protect him, and he did not know how many escorts Fletcher had.

In 1942, Japanese carriers had neither radar nor homing devices, and for night air operations Hara had to turn on lights to recover planes. American carriers also operated radio-jamming equipment that could disrupt frequencies used by Japanese planes, and this often prevented enemy scouts from reporting the position of U.S. ships. After debriefing pilots from the six planes recovered that night, Takagi decided that the American carriers were about 60 miles to the west, although the actual separation was closer to 100 miles. At midnight, both Takagi and Fletcher changed course. Takagi went north, and Fletcher jogged west, still undecided what course of action to take. Neither admiral knew what the other was doing, but not for long.

The carrier forces under Fletcher and Takagi matched up about evenly. Because Fletcher had detached Crace, he had less supports than the day before, but he still had five heavy cruisers and seven destroyers. Takagi had one fewer of each. Fletcher had 122 planes, Takagi 121, and the pilots from both groups had seen action. The types of aircraft, however, gave a distinct advantage to the Japanese. *Shokaku* and *Zuikaku* carried a greater number of torpedo planes, which were far superior to Devastators, and Hara's fighters were faster and more maneuverable than Fletcher's bulky Wildcats.

At 6:00 A.M. on May 8, Fletcher and Fitch launched 18 SBD scouts to locate *Skokaku* and *Zuikaku* before Japanese snoopers spotted them. Intelligence received during the night, combined with shipboard radio direction finders, indicated that Takagi's force was either to the west or the east. Hara's two carriers, however, were actually 175 miles to the north.

At 8:25 A.M., Admiral Hara launched an attack group of 90 planes to search for *Lexington* and *Yorktown*. Fitch and Fletcher's search planes were already in the air and some were returning.

Before launching, Fitch had drawn a 360-degree circle around *Lexington*'s position and assigned each search squadron a pie-shaped sector. The search east and west produced no sightings. At 8:15 A.M., 10 minutes before Hara's carrier planes launched, Lieutenant (jg) Joseph G. Smith spotted *Shokaku* and *Zuikaku* and radioed the position.

Warrant Officer Kenzo Kanno, flying a Kate, had the good fortune to notice a few American planes returning to *Lexington* and followed them back to the carrier. At 8:28 A.M. Fitch's radio-room intercepted a message from Kanno to Hara giving the course and speed of *Lexington*. Hara immediately radioed the coordinates to his air group. Fletcher promptly turned south to prepare for the attack.

At 9:30 A.M., because Smith needed to refuel, Lieutenant Commander Dixon moved into Smith's sector to keep watch on Takagi's force. More than an hour had passed since Smith's sighting and Dixon reported the Japanese position farther to the north, although the enemy had actually moved about 20 miles south. This discrepancy eventually caused immense confusion.

Twenty-five minutes after receiving Smith's initial report, Fletcher ordered both carriers to launch strikes. Overhead, the skies were blue and the sun sparkled on waves capped white by the trade winds. About 130 miles to the north, *Shokaku* and *Zuikaku* lay under a covering of squall clouds. At 9:15 A.M., *Yorktown* launched 30 Dauntlesses, 9 Devastators, and 14 Wildcats. Ten minutes later, 22 Dauntlesses, 12 Devastators, and 9 Wildcats roared off *Lexington*. The battle Fletcher hoped to win by surprise was now to be settled by skill, luck, and weather.

Admiral Hara's strike force was already in the air, and what American and Japanese admirals feared most was about to happen. Aside from planes, carriers also acted as repositories for high-octane fuel and tons of ammunition. With planes gone, carriers became vulnerable to simultaneous attack, and according to experts, the result could be mutual annihilation.

At 10:32, *Yorktown*'s SBDs sighted *Shokaku* and *Zuikaku* about eight miles apart and screened by escorts. For 20 minutes, the Dauntlesses orbited under a cloud waiting for the slower torpedo planes to get into position. The delay gave Hara time to elevator up fighter reserves and for *Zuikaku* to slip into a rainsquall. Even Hara's escorts shamelessly attempted to get out of the way.

At 10:57, Lieutenant Commander Joe Taylor of Torpedo Squadron 5 led the attack on *Shokaku* just as she turned into the wind to launch her fighters. *Zuikaku* had vanished behind a curtain of rain. Taylor failed to deploy his TBDs for an "anvil" attack. They approached *Shokaku* from the same side and dropped their torpedoes from too great a distance. The M-13s either missed or failed to explode. Commander Burch's SBDs dove from 17,000 feet. The sudden change in atmosphere fogged canopies and gunsights and created more trouble than the pestiferous Zeros. Only two bombs scored hits, but one damaged *Shokaku*'s flight deck, rendering her unable to recover planes, although she could still launch them. Gasoline caught fire and smothered the carrier in a tower of smoke. When *Zuikaku* emerged from the rainsquall, Admiral Hara took one look at the blazing *Shokaku* and thought she had been destroyed.

Lexington's planes, following Smith's earlier coordinates, did not find any ships in the area. By flying a box search, the torpedo squadron eventually located Hara's flattops, but some planes were short fuel and turned back.

The balance of *Lexington*'s strike force, led by Ault and now reduced to 11 TBDs, 4 SBDs, and 6 Wildcats, descended through a break in the clouds and targeted on the burning *Shokaku*. A swarm of Zeros foolishly pounced on the Wildcats instead of the Devastators and shot three down, losing two of their own.

Lieutenant Commander James H. Brett, Jr., led the Devastator attack, launched torpedoes from too great a distance, and missed. Brett flew away thinking his torpedo-bombers had sunk one carrier when in actuality they had narrowly missed the cruisers *Furutaka* and *Kinugasa*.

Only one bomb struck *Shokaku*, and the reports brought back by pilots stating that she was settling fast were false. *Shokaku* was never holed below the waterline, and the fires blossoming from gasoline tanks were soon extinguished. Officers on *Shokaku* later remarked that as long as American torpedo-bombers launched from such great distances, they would never hit a Japanese ship. Takagi sent *Shokaku* home, thinking that his attack planes had sunk both U.S. carriers. American admirals were not the only ones to get false reports.

Returning American planes found both *Lexington* and *Yorktown* hit. Sixty-nine planes from *Shokaku* and *Zuikaku* struck the carriers at the same time pilots from *Yorktown* and *Lexington* were striking them. The Japanese attack began at 11:13 A.M. and lasted 27 minutes. Fitch had earlier put eight fighters in the air for CAP, but when the Japanese strike force finally appeared, Wildcats were running out of fuel. Nor could they land because Fitch was putting nine more fighters in the air to meet the attack. Fitch also used 23 Dauntlesses to pick off Japanese torpedo planes, but the SBDs were too slow to double as fighters. They shot down four torpedo planes but lost the same number trying. After that, the duel became a battle between American AA fire and attacking enemy planes.

The Japanese came with a better-balanced force, better aircraft, and better trained pilots. Fitch began evasive maneuvers the moment the strike force became visible. A half-mile away a pair of Kates swung in low over the water on both of *Lexington*'s bows to drop torpedoes. Five-inch AA shells blew both of them up.

Captain Sherman observed a torpedo splashing into the water and ordered full right rudder, only to discover another torpedo bearing down on the opposite bow. To turn *Lexington* required a tactical diameter of about a mile. Swift Long Lance torpedoes were now swimming toward the carrier from every direction. Eleven "fish" passed either under, ahead, or alongside of her. Carrier juggling could last just so long, and two torpedoes finally tore into *Lexington*'s port side.

After Kates swung clear, Vals screamed down from 17,000 feet and dropped their payloads at 2,000 feet. Seven bombs hit *Lexington*, including a 1,000-pounder that demolished Admiral Fitch's cabin. Nineteen minutes later, the enemy formed up and vanished.

Yorktown also came under attack, but she had better maneuverability and a shorter turning circle. Eight Kates came at her from one direction, making it easier for Captain Buckmaster to evade the torpedoes. As soon as the Kates cleared, Vals roared down from above and dropped 800-pound armor-piercing bombs with delayed action fuses. Buckmaster dodged all but one. The bomb pierced *Yorktown*'s steel flight deck inboard from the island, tore through the hanger deck and the galley deck, then through the first, second, and third decks, and exploded in a storeroom 50 feet inside the ship, killing or injuring 66 men. A fire broke out below but was quickly extinguished. At 11:45, the 27-minute battle of the Coral Sea ended.

At first, the tally sheet looked like an American victory. The Japanese had lost the light carrier (*Shoho*), a destroyer, several minesweepers, and gunboats, and *Shokaku* could no longer fight and turned for home. Fletcher had lost an oiler and a destroyer, and although his two carriers had suffered damage, at midday they were still fully operational. Fletcher counted more than 50 planes ready for duty, Admiral Hara 39.

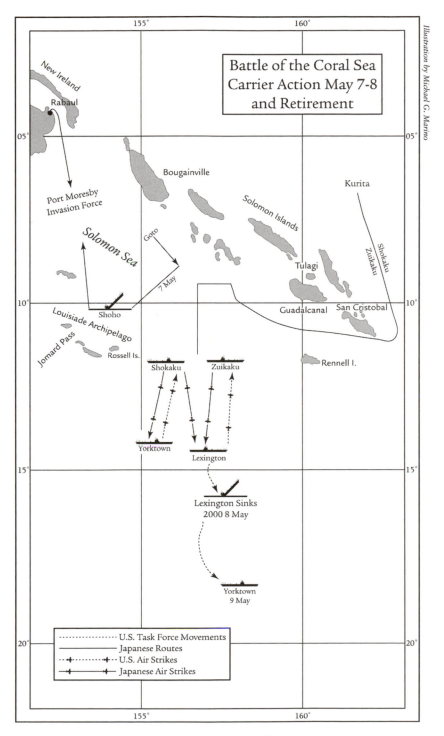

Battle of the Coral Sea: Carrier Action, May 7–8, and Retirement. (Michael G. Marino)

Although *Lexington* developed a seven-degree list and still had fires burning, firemen and water-tenders corrected the list by shifting oil ballast. Sherman had her deck cleared to launch and recover aircraft, and just about the time the ship's company began to relax, a running motor generator that somebody forgot to shut down ignited gasoline vapors in the bowels of the ship. The explosion started a chain reaction that knocked out part of the firefighting system. Despite the damage, *Lexington* continued steaming at 25 knots while men fought fires and recovered planes returning from the morning attack.

A mid-afternoon internal explosion knocked out the ship's engine room ventilators. Heat from fires threatened to detonate ordnance on the hanger deck and in the bomb storage area. Sherman reported the situation hopeless. He sent all serviceable planes to *Yorktown* and issued orders to remove the wounded. Surgeons and pharmacist's mates continued administering injections, blood plasma, and tannic acid to skin burns on about 150 wounded men being lowered in basket stretchers to whaleboats.

At 7:00 P.M., Admiral Fitch called down from his bridge to Captain Sherman, "Well, Ted, let's get the men off." Three hundred sailors began descending from lifelines, hand over hand until they reached the water. Rear Admiral Kinkaid, commanding the cruiser *Minneapolis*, came alongside with three destroyers and plucked men from the water. Not one was lost, not even the captain's dog.[5]

With everyone clear of the carrier, Fletcher ordered the destroyer *Phelps* to sink her. Four torpedoes smashed into her undamaged side. At 8:00 P.M., she slipped beneath the Coral Sea, stern first, all because someone failed to turn off a motor generator. An officer standing beside war correspondent Stanley Johnston said, "There she goes. She didn't turn over. She is going down with her head up. Dear old Lex. A lady to the last."[6]

Lexington was not a fragile ship, like so many battleship supporters thought. Enemy torpedoes and bombs could not break her back or sink her. She absorbed punishment far beyond what the experts expected of her. In the end, she had to be scuttled by her own escort. New carriers, soon on their way, would be even tougher.

Nimitz ordered Fletcher to retire, which the latter was already doing. What might be said about how an air battle between aircraft carriers should have been fought no longer mattered. Those who studied tactics called the engagement in the Coral Sea the "Battle of Naval Errors." Fletcher, however, thwarted the Port Moresby invasion and stopped the Japanese juggernaut in its tracks. That had been his assignment.

Takagi's strike force also retired. At midnight on May 8, Yamamoto ordered him to go back and finish off the American force. Takagi made a half-hearted try, but by then Fletcher was far to the south.

The Battle of the Coral Sea opened a new chapter in naval warfare: aircraft became the weapons and carriers the deliverers. The battle stands as the first carrier-to-carrier combat in which all losses occurred by air action. No ship on either side ever sighted a surface vessel. The results of the action pushed carrier

The USS *Lexington* is abandoned in the aftermath of the Battle of the Coral Sea and becomes the first American carrier lost in an air action during World War II. (U.S. Navy photo)

tacticians onto a new fast-track learning curve. Americans did not like losing *Lexington*, but on May 10, when the grim news reached the United States, no one could clearly appreciate the sorry condition of the Japanese carriers. *Shokaku* went out of service for two months, and *Zuikaku*'s plane losses put her out of action for five weeks. Neither would be ready by June 4. Whether or not they may have tipped the scales between victory and defeat at Midway will never be known.

CHAPTER 7

Midway: The Turning Point

Weeks before the setback in the Coral Sea, Admiral Yamamoto became fixated on drawing the Pacific Fleet out of Pearl Harbor to destroy it. To accomplish this objective, he planned dual operations: a diversionary invasion of Alaska's Aleutian Islands timed to a massive assault on Midway. He assured IGH that defeat of the Pacific Fleet would compel President Roosevelt to remove his forces, negotiate a peace, and concentrate on crushing Germany. Otherwise, Yamamoto cautioned, Japan would be defeated.

Not everyone agreed with Yamamoto. When *Shokaku* and *Zuikaku* limped home from the Coral Sea, Admiral Ryunosuke Kusaka suggested giving the fleet a two-month rest before mounting a major campaign. Ships needed repairs, he said, and carriers needed planes. Some of the best pilots had been lost, and others had been on constant duty since the Pearl Harbor attack. Kusaka suggested bringing battle-tested veterans ashore to teach carrier air tactics to men undergoing flight training. Kusaka's argument made sense. After the Coral Sea engagement, rotating veteran flyers to train new pilots was exactly the method adopted by the U.S. Navy. Yamamoto, however, discarded Kusaka's suggestions in favor of quick and decisive action.

Yamamoto listened to everyone's arguments, not because his mind had changed but out of courtesy. IGH worried that drawing out the Pacific Fleet involved risks, and they used the Coral Sea as an example. Some argued that Midway, if captured, would be difficult to hold and supply because American long-range bombers could strike the island from Hawaii. Yamamoto, however, remained adamant. America's fleet must be destroyed before it became stronger. The Doolittle raid had shocked Japan, and from Yamamoto's perspective the setback in the Coral Sea (which had not been accurately communicated to the public) must not be repeated. The admiral believed that Japan must stay on the offensive and that Midway, 1,150 miles northwest of Hawaii, must be captured. Successful occupation of Midway would open the way to capturing Hawaii, a scheme supported by Rear Admiral Matome Ugaki of IGH, giving Japan total domination of the Pacific.

During May, Admiral Nimitz suspected the Japanese were planning something larger than the Port Moresby invasion. Commander Joseph Rochefort's navy cryptanalysts at Pearl Harbor had intercepted a flurry of messages referring to "AF" and "AO" but could not interpret their meaning. Nimitz believed that Yamamoto had sharpened his sights on the Central Pacific and perhaps Midway. Rochefort suggested a way to find out: have Midway send a message in the clear that their distillation plant had shut down and the island was running out of fresh water. Within hours, the radio room picked up a message from Japanese intelligence to Admiral Nagumo that "AF" was short of water.

Nimitz acted quickly. He had only three carriers in the Pacific, Halsey's *Enterprise*, Mitscher's *Hornet*, and Fletcher's *Yorktown*, which had been damaged in the Coral Sea. In late April, he had sent Halsey to the South Pacific and hurriedly called him back. He wanted Halsey in charge of Midway's defense, but the admiral had developed shingles and could not get out of bed. *Yorktown* had not returned, so Nimitz put 55-year-old Vice Admiral Raymond A. Spruance in charge of TF-16, composed of Murray's *Enterprise*, Mitscher's *Hornet*, six cruisers, eleven destroyers, and two oilers.

Nimitz struggled over the decision to give carrier groups to Spruance, a gunship man currently in command of Halsey's cruiser division. But Spruance was also a highly qualified strategist and an excellent tactician with a reputation for making precise, intelligent decisions. He had never been an aviator, but he would have the assistance of Murray and Mitscher, two of the best aviation men in the navy, and Captain Miles Browning, an expert in carrier operations. Nimitz had no clear idea of the size of Yamamoto's force or how much of it Spruance would confront at Midway. He suspected that Yamamoto would come with at least the same number of carriers that struck Pearl Harbor, making the odds six to two.

On May 27, Fletcher reached Pearl Harbor with the injured *Yorktown*. Nimitz asked how long it would take for repairs, and Fitch replied three months. Nimitz said do it in three days. The crew put her into drydock and 1,400 workmen climbed on board. On May 28, Spruance sailed for Midway with two carriers. Two days later, the odds improved. *Yorktown* departed with Fletcher and Buckmaster.

On May 27, Yamamoto sailed from Bungo Strait in the battleship *Yamato* to oversee an operation as complicated as the Port Moresby fiasco.

The Advance Expeditionary Force, already at sea, consisted of 16 submarines in three groups to serve as lookouts and communicate any movement of the Pacific Fleet from Pearl Harbor. The subs arrived too late to see the carriers leave.

The Northern Area Force under Vice Admiral Boshiro Hosogaya consisted of the medium carrier *Junyo*, light carrier *Ryujo*, and three heavy cruisers. Hosogaya's assignment was to attack Kiska, Adak, and Attu in the Aleutians on June 3 in an effort to confuse Nimitz and draw the Pacific Fleet north. Yamamoto did not want America to build air bases in the Aleutians from which Japan could be bombed.

Vice Admiral Raymond A. Spruance's performance during the Battle of Midway led to his promotion to full admiral and commander of the Central Pacific Force. (U.S. Navy photo)

Because the Coral Sea battle had rendered *Shokaku* and *Zuikaku* unavailable, Admiral Nagumo's strike force contained four heavy carriers instead of six—*Akagi*, *Kaga*, *Soryu*, and *Hiryo*—but this did not curb his optimism for a quick and decisive victory. Two battleships, two cruisers, twelve destroyers, and five oilers composed the balance of his battle fleet. Nagumo carried the heaviest burden: to soften up Midway on June 4, and if the Pacific Fleet challenged from Pearl Harbor, to sink it. The success of the operation hinged on Nagumo's air tactics. He anticipated another easy victory, laconically declaring, "Although the enemy is lacking in fighting spirit, he will probably come out to attack as our invasion proceeds."[1] Pearl Harbor had been too easy. He believed so steadfastly in his advantage of surprise that it made him careless.

Vice Admiral Nobutake Kondo's Midway Occupation Force followed Nagumo with the light carrier *Zuiho*, 2 battleships, 8 cruisers, 21 destroyers, oilers, seaplane tenders, minesweepers, and 12 transports carrying more than 5,000 occupation troops.

Yamamoto led the Main Body, composed of the light carrier *Hosho*, 7 battleships, 2 light cruisers, 13 destroyers, 2 seaplane carriers, and 4 oilers. He placed his force between Midway and the Aleutians to intercept any American ships coming from Pearl Harbor. He hoped that Nimitz would react to the Aleutians attack and send the Pacific Fleet north, where it would be intercepted by his battleships and demolished by carrier aircraft. If Yamamoto needed support, he could call on Kondo's covering group. To make the strategy successful depended on surprise, an element lost when Rochefort's code-breakers fingered Midway as the principal target.

James H. Belote remarked that "the total acreage of . . . Midway Atoll was less than that occupied by the decks of [Yamamoto's] 140 warships, transports, and auxiliaries."[2] Inside a coral reef six miles in diameter lay Midway's two small islands. Sand Island held the communication center, a seaplane base, and a detachment of Marine defenders. Eastern Island's 5,300-foot airfield gave Spruance the equivalent of a fourth aircraft carrier.

Among the 121 assorted aircraft squeezed onto the island were 32 PBY Catalina patrol bombers and six new Grumman Avenger torpedo-bombers. Marine flyers were at a distinct disadvantage. Aside from 16 Dauntlesses and a few Wildcats, the other planes were obsolete SB2U Vindicator dive-bombers and F2A-3 Buffalo fighters that should have been replaced years ago. The army operated 19 B-17 Flying Fortresses and four B-26 Marauders, which had just arrived from Oahu after being fitted with torpedo hangers. The island came equipped with two efficient air-search radars, but old planes and inexperienced crews diminished the island's air defenses.

Aircraft on American carriers were of better quality, consisting of 79 Wildcats, 112 Dauntlesses, and 44 Devastators, bringing the all-Midway plane total to 356 planes. Nagumo's four flattops carried 272 aircraft; 86 Val dive-bombers, 93 Kate torpedo planes, and 93 Zeros. Although Spruance could claim an advantage in numbers, Nagumo held the advantage in trained carrier pilots and better torpedo-bombers. Tactics would determine the outcome.

Nimitz wisely remained at Pearl Harbor's communication center. He knew about Japan's planned diversionary attack in the Aleutians, and to make Yamamoto believe the ruse was working Nimitz detached five cruisers under Rear Admiral Robert A. Theobald and sent them north. He did not want to lose any carriers through sloppy tactics and told Spruance and Fletcher to take calculated risks but avoid becoming overwhelmed by superior forces. He tried to obtain *Saratoga*, which had been damaged by a torpedo in January, but she was at San

Diego training a new air group. He also could have pulled six old battleships from San Francisco Bay, but they would have slowed down the carriers.

At 9:00 A.M. on June 3, Ensign Jack Reid, flying a PBY, spotted Admiral Kondo's 60-ship Occupation Force 700 miles to the west. Fletcher radioed the information to Nimitz, who replied, "This is not, repeat not, the striking force."[3] That afternoon nine B-17s took off from Midway to bomb Kondo's group. Pilots flew at 20,000 feet, like they did when bombing stationary land targets, and never hit a ship. At 1:00 A.M. the following morning four night-flying PBYs equipped with torpedoes damaged the oiler *Akebono Maru*. When Yamamoto received word of the incident, he decided against breaking radio silence to remind Nagumo to increase and broaden reconnaissance. He expected Nagumo to think of taking such measures himself. Nagumo was not concerned. Thick, cloudy weather had covered his approach, but on June 4, as the first streaks of dawn ushered in the day, the sky cleared.

At 4:30 A.M., Air Officer Commander Shogo Masuda signaled "Go" to the pilots revving their engines on *Akagi*'s darkened flight deck. Moments later, the planes roared skyward. Aircraft from *Kaga*, *Hiryu*, and *Soryu* followed. Within minutes, 36 Zeros, 36 Vals, and 36 Kates disappeared into scattered cumulus clouds. They carried high-explosive bombs for use against land installations. A second wave of Nagumo's best planes and pilots began assembling on deck. This time Kates received "long-lance" Type-31 torpedoes and Vals armor-piercing bombs because Nagumo expected his search planes to find the Pacific Fleet.

Commander Mitsuo Fuchida, who led the attack on Pearl Harbor, became bedridden at Midway after surgeons performed an emergency appendectomy. Instead, Lieutenant Joichi Tomonaga, the aggressive air group commander from *Hiryu*, led the first strike group. Like many pilots, Tomonaga was a veteran but new to carrier combat.

Fuchida believed Nagumo made a serious error by not ordering a double-phase search of the ocean before launching the strike, but Nagumo said the American carriers were still at Pearl Harbor. He sent only seven planes in a single-phase north-to-south search east of Midway. Only one plane instead of two covered each of seven fan-shaped search sectors. Two cruiser floatplanes, one in particular from the cruiser *Tone*, got off late because of catapult trouble. Another plane experienced engine trouble. The search included sectors occupied by Fletcher and Spruance's carriers. Had the snoopers moved on schedule, they would have spotted the flattops. One eventually located *Yorktown*, but it was too late to influence the outcome of the battle.

During the evening of June 3, Fletcher expected Nagumo's carriers to approach Midway from the northwest. He changed course to put *Yorktown* about 200 miles north of Midway at daybreak and in good position to intercept Nagumo. He correctly assumed that *Yorktown* had not been sighted and he doubted whether Japanese planes attacking Midway in the morning would be able to see him. Had

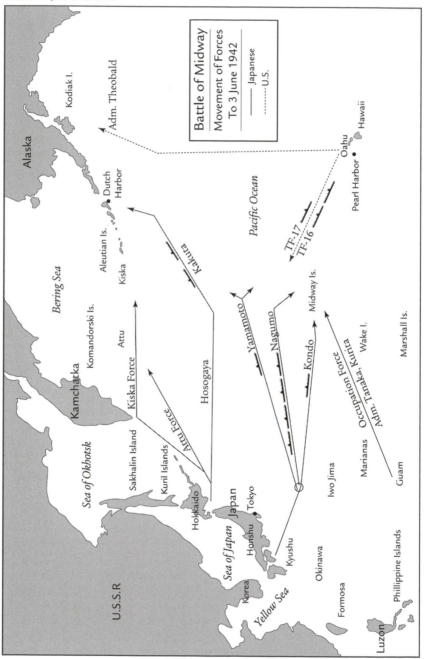

Illustration by Michael G. Marino

Battle of Midway: Movement of Forces to June 3, 1942. (Michael G. Marino)

the two carrier forces continued on their paths—Nagumo to the east, Spruance and Fletcher to the west—they would have collided a few miles northwest of Midway.

At 4:30 A.M. on June 4, *Yorktown* launched 10 SBDs to cover a search radius of 100 miles to the north. The pilots found nothing because Nagumo stood 215 miles to the west and was launching his first strike. Midway's PBYs, however, spotted the enemy carriers at 5:34 A.M. and 10 minutes later reported planes headed toward Midway. Fletcher and Midway now knew the approximate position of Nagumo's carriers. Midway launched everything that could fly, but Fletcher waited to recover his search planes. Fletcher should have launched immediately, but the delay proved to be a lucky stroke that shaped the outcome of the developing battle.

Thirty miles northwest of Midway, Marine Major Floyd Parks dove seven F2A-3 Buffaloes and five F4F Wildcats full throttle through Lieutenant Tomonaga's tight formation and shot down two Kates. Had Parks not made a second pass, most of his planes might have survived. Instead, Parks led the squadron back into the battle and were jumped by Zeros. Of 26 Midway fighters, 17 were lost, 7 suffered damage, and only 2 remained flyable. Fifteen marine pilots lost their lives, including Parks. The Japanese lost 11 planes, some from AA fire and others were damaged beyond repair.

Major Kirk Armistead, after leading a squadron of Buffaloes, admitted upon returning to Midway, "It seems useless to even try to make more than one pass." Captain Marion E. Carl, who shot down a Zero, added, "The [Buffalo] is not a combat plane. The Japanese Zero . . . can run circles around it. It is my belief that any commander who orders pilots out for combat in an F2A-3 should consider the pilot as lost before leaving the ground."[4]

If Spruance expected help from Midway, he did not get it. Two of the four torpedo-equipped B-26 medium bombers at Midway were shot down; the other two missed. Six Avenger torpedo-bombers attacked and hit nothing. Only one returned. American Mark-13 torpedoes traveled at 33 knots, the same speed as a destroyer. Even aircraft carriers had enough speed to evade them. Such miserable performance, combined with the absence of any American carrier aircraft, was more than enough to satiate Nagumo with steady doses of optimism. It must have looked to him like Pearl Harbor all over again.

As Lieutenant Tomonaga returned to *Hiryu*, he radioed ahead to *Akagi* and reported that another strike was needed to finish the job. His 10-minute attack had not destroyed Eastern Island's airstrip or the heavy AA emplacements on Midway's beaches. To pave the way for Admiral Kondo's invasion force, Nagumo considered removing torpedoes and armor-piercing bombs from planes waiting on the flight deck and change back to high-explosive bombs. The conversion would take an hour, and Nagumo disliked losing time. At 7:15, 10 minutes after the torpedo-laden B-26s and Avengers came roaring in from Midway but failed to hit any of his ships, he ordered the changeover.

At 7:28, after the exchange of bombs for torpedoes began, Nagumo received a radio message from *Tone*'s floatplane—the plane delayed because of catapult trouble: "what appears to be ten enemy surface ships, in position bearing 10°, distance 240 miles from Midway. Course 150° degrees, speed over 20 knots."[5] Nagumo now knew he might have to deal with enemy ships, but the radio communication mentioned no carriers. He had already sent the torpedo-bombers below to clear the flight decks for receiving Tomonaga's incoming planes and had to let them land. He still had a few Kates on deck, but for 16 minutes he could not decide whether to put them in the air or change their ordnance to bombs. At 7:45, after trying unsuccessfully to contact *Tone*'s floatplane, he decided that the 10 American ships heading his way could be dealt with later.

At 7:48, the same AAF B-17s that failed to do any damage to Admiral Kondo's group on June 3 appeared overhead at 20,000 feet and dropped their bombs on Nagumo's carriers. The 600-pounders created a neat pattern of geysers around *Akagi*, *Soryu*, and *Hiryu* but missed. Zeros at low altitude climbed to attack the big planes, but could not overtake them.

Nagumo enjoyed a refreshing spectacle at 7:55 when Major Lofton Henderson, leading 16 Marine Corps SBDs from Midway, appeared in the sky off *Akagi*. Henderson's pilots had never been fully trained on Dauntless tactics and none had dive-bombing experience. So instead of coming down from 17,000 feet, Henderson put the SBDs into an old-fashioned glide-bomb approach at 4,000 feet. The formation flew into a Zero CAP that shot Henderson down before he could drop his bombs. None of the pilots who followed scored better than a near miss. Only eight SBDs returned to Midway, six of them damaged beyond repair.

At 8:10, 15 more B-17s appeared at 20,000 feet and dropped 64 tons of bombs on Nagumo's strike force. Pilots reported several damaging near misses, but not one bomb came close to hitting a ship.

Ten minutes later, as Lieutenant Tomonaga's returning aircraft began to land, Major Benjamin W. Norris approached Nagumo's carriers with eleven old Marine Corps Vindicators. Norris found the air swarming with Zeros around the carriers, so he shifted the Vindicators to the nearest target, the battleship *Haruna*. Zero pilots, sensing easy marks, came quickly. Norris ordered bombs dropped, lost two planes, and returned to Midway with no hits.

During the turmoil Nagumo received a radio message from *Tone*'s other floatplane: "Enemy is composed of 5 cruisers and 5 destroyers," and when the admiral asked for additional verification, the pilot radioed ten minutes later that "The enemy is accompanied by what appears to be a carrier."[6] The carrier was Fletcher's *Yorktown*, but Nagumo possibly remembered that during the Coral Sea engagement Admiral Takagi's scout planes had mistaken an oiler for a carrier, and perhaps this was happening again.

Knowing that an American carrier might be in the area, Nagumo still showed patience, even though his flight decks were awash with incoming aircraft low on fuel and most of his torpedo planes had been sent below. It took 25 minutes to remove armor-piercing bombs from the Kates and rearm them with torpedoes. During the changeover Nagumo did not know that at 8:25 the submarine USS *Nautilus* had reported his position, fired a torpedo at the battleship *Haruna,* and missed.

Nagumo felt well satisfied with the morning's work. Although 40 planes had been lost, his aircraft had damaged Midway's installations, his fighting ships were all in top condition, and his fighters had destroyed almost every American plane attempting to penetrate his CAP. He decided to destroy the enemy ships reported by *Tone*'s floatplanes and return to Midway later to finish the job.

At 8:55, on the advice of Commander Genda, Nagumo issued orders to rearm and refuel Tomonaga's planes and send them with 93 Kates waiting on standby for orders. At 9:18, the last plane from Tomonaga's Midway strike force settled onto the deck of *Akagi.* Nagumo immediately turned the carriers north to engage the approaching American squadron. But he had a problem. None of his search planes had discovered the presence of *Enterprise* and *Hornet,* which were south of *Yorktown,* and Nagumo was obliviously setting himself up for a big surprise. What Nagumo needed was another carrier group so he could order a strike without waiting for returning planes to land, but Yamamoto had devoted four light carriers to his other operations.

At 6:00 A.M., Midway PBYs had already reported Nagumo's position. Admiral Spruance immediately turned *Enterprise* and *Hornet* toward the enemy's coordinates. Fletcher held back, waiting to recover search planes. Spruance intended to come within 100 miles of Nagumo's strike force before launching because his torpedo planes had a combat range of only 175 miles. Captain Miles Browning, Halsey's chief of staff and an airman, said the strike ought to be made immediately. According to his calculations, if planes launched quickly they might catch Nagumo's carriers recovering aircraft from the Midway attack. Spruance acted quickly on Browning's proposal. He knew Devastators and Wildcats might not have enough fuel to make it back to the carriers, but the Dauntlesses could.

At 7:02, *Enterprise* and *Hornet* launched every operational plane except fighters needed for CAP. From *Enterprise,* 14 Devastators, 35 Dauntlesses, and 10 Wildcats took to the air. *Hornet* launched 15 Devastators, 35 Dauntlesses, and 10 Wildcats. Fletcher still waited, perhaps remembering the Coral Sea when all his planes were attacking the Japanese carriers at the same time Kates and Vals were striking him. At 8:38, after no enemy planes appeared, he launched 12 Devastators, 17 Dauntlesses, and 6 Wildcats, but he kept a squadron of Dauntlesses spotted for takeoff just in case he needed them.

Pilots from *Enterprise* and *Hornet* followed coordinates provided by Spruance's air controllers, and they expected to intercept Nagumo's strike force on a track that led directly to Midway. The same controllers failed to communicate with Midway, whose spotter planes knew that Nagumo had made many stops to recover aircraft and at 9:30 had actually reversed course and headed north. As a consequence, Nagumo's ships were not at Point Option, the theoretical point of contact where Spruance's controllers had directed the planes.

Lieutenant Commander John C. Waldron's Torpedo 8 from *Hornet*, having kept more to the north, spotted Nagumo's carriers dead ahead. Waldron had no fighter protection, but his 15 Devastators paired up and bored in about 50 feet over the water. Zeros patrolling at high altitude spotted the clumsy TBDs and swooped down with nose and wing guns blazing. One after another, Devastators splashed into the sea. Not a single torpedo touched a Japanese ship. The only survivor, Ensign George H. Gay, crawled into a rubber raft and took a ringside seat for the battle that followed.

Commander Stanhope C. Ring, leading *Hornet*'s Wildcats and Dauntlesses, guessed wrong after he found no Japanese ships at Point Option. Believing they were closer to Midway, he flew toward the island and found an empty sea. Ring waited too long before returning to *Hornet*. He lost 3 Dauntlesses and all 10 Wildcats because they ran out of fuel and ditched.

At 9:30, *Enterprise*'s Torpedo 6, led by Commander Eugene E. Lindsey, and *Yorktown*'s Torpedo 3, led by Commander Lem Massey, spotted Nagumo's carriers about 30 minutes after Ensign Gay crawled onto his rubber raft. Lindsey's Devastators attacked like those from *Hornet* and suffered the same fate. Massey's TBDs barely got organized for the torpedo drop when Zeros tore them apart. Few pilots had time to aim their torpedoes, not that it made much difference. Massey's TBDs had twin-mounted guns in the rear seat, which gave Zero pilots something to think about. Commander James Thach's Wildcats provided a small amount of cover, but not enough. Massey and Lindsey each returned with four planes. Of 41 TBDs sent from three American carriers, all but eight were shot down. Nor did a single torpedo score a hit.

Nagumo now had even more reason to feel confident. Not one of his ships had been touched, but the Americans were learning. Thach had worked out a defensive tactic when fighting Zeros that became known as the "Thach weave." When Zeros dove on the Wildcats, Thach discovered that by turning his flyers sharply toward each other gave Zero pilots difficult deflection shots. But the maneuver also enabled Thach's flyers to shoot the Zero that had been on the other Wildcat's tail. Thach, after tallying two Zeroes at Midway, discovered that his pilots should never break out of their "weave" until the Zeros had given up. His two-pair, four-plane formation, or "finger four" became the standard used by the army and navy for the duration of the war, and he validated its efficacy on Nagumo's Zeros during the Battle of Midway.

After the first engagement with American Devastators, Nagumo's Zeros began running out of ammunition and fuel. At 10:20 A.M., they started landing at the same time Nagumo's Vals and Kates were preparing for a full-strength launch against Fletcher's task force. Before sending them off, Nagumo created another delay when he decided to add more fighter protection. The carrier *Hiryu* also needed extra time because many planes had been damaged at Midway and needed to be stored below before reserve aircraft could be brought to the deck and armed.

Nagumo had been lucky, seemingly invincible, and he became careless. High in the sky, 30 miles away, came another kind of hell.

At 9:55 A.M., Commander Wade McClusky, flying at 19,000 feet, looked down from his cockpit at the wrinkled blue ocean below and spotted a lone destroyer (*Arashi*) steaming north. He followed, hoping that *Arashi* would lead him to Nagumo. His hunch worked, for ahead he spotted the forms of three widely scattered carriers. Although he passed the safe limit for fuel consumption, he could not ignore the golden opportunity to strike the Japanese flattops.

Three Dauntlesses had returned to *Enterprise* because of engine trouble, but McClusky still had 30 dive-bombers armed with 1000-pounders. Further to the east, Lieutenant Commander Max Leslie approached with 17 Dauntlesses from *Yorktown*. With the exception of scattered cumulus clouds, McClusky and Leslie could see for 50 miles in every direction, but they did not see each other. They simultaneously spotted Nagumo's carriers grouped in box-like formation and surrounded by a protective screen of battleships, cruisers, and destroyers. Every Zero had either landed on one of the carriers to rearm or was orbiting to wait in turn to land.

The carriers had broken formation to evade torpedo attacks: *Akagi* to the west, *Kaga* to the east. *Soryu*, farther to the east, circled and faced south. *Hiryu* had separated from the main body and lay farther to the north. No carrier had been hit, and crews attributed all their marvelous luck to divine intervention. They were far too busy handling deck problems to notice dive-bombers forming overhead.

McClusky's SBDs, dangerously low on fuel, had been in the air a full hour longer than Leslie's group. McClusky split his group and concentrated on *Kaga*. Lieutenant Richard H. Best took five Dauntlesses and headed for *Akagi*. At 280 knots McClusky dove to 1,800 feet, dropped his 1,000-pounder, and missed. The next two planes also missed. Then came Lieutenant W. E. Gallaher. Commanding Scouting 6, he dropped a 500-pounder on *Kaga*'s deck just forward of the bridge. The explosion ignited aviation fuel and set the carrier on fire. The next three bombs landed on the flight deck, tearing it up. When Lieutenant Clarence Dickinson, flying ninth, approached the carrier, he observed internal explosions deep inside the ship were blasting her apart.

Lieutenant Best led Bombing 6 past the burning *Kaga* and tipped over above *Akagi*. Best missed, but Lieutenant Edward J. Kroeger, closely following, struck *Akagi* amidships with a 1,000-pounder that tore open the flight deck and ignited gasoline fires. Forty planes on the deck and in the hanger burst into flames. Inside *Akagi*, bombs and torpedoes exploded. Deck plates broke loose, curled upward, and thrust burning planes tail up. Water pressure on fire mains failed, and *Akagi* became engulfed in flames. Although most bombs missed, Kroeger's 1,000-pounder doomed Nagumo's flagship.

When Leslie observed Dauntlesses from *Enterprise* attacking *Kaga* and *Akagi*, he radioed *Yorktown*'s SBDs to attack the carrier standing east of the

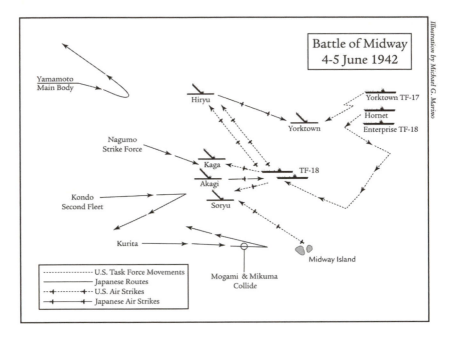

box-formation. Seventeen Dauntlesses dove on *Soryu*. Pilots encountered wind-shield and gunsight fogging, but three bombs smashed into *Soryu*'s flight deck, ignited barrels of aviation fuel, blew up the munitions storage area, and set fire to 18 torpedo-laden Kates waiting for takeoff. Twenty minutes later, Captain Ryusaku Yanagimoto ordered *Soryu* abandoned. Four of Leslie's pilots dropped their bombs on Nagumo's battleships and cruisers because *Akagi*, *Kaga*, and *Soryu* were dead in the water and engulfed in flames.

Had *Hornet*'s dive-bombers not made the error of taking the wrong direction when searching for Nagumo's strike force, *Hiryu* may not have escaped unde-tected and become the fourth fatality.

McClusky's *Enterprise* pilots, the first to attack, attracted all the Zeros that had been hunting for the last of Massey's Devastators. The Dauntlesses stuck together, dodging diving Zeroes by performing Thach's weave and using gunners in the rear seats to fend off attacks. Not one Dauntless was shot down, but most of them ran out of fuel when returning and ditched.

A few Zeros flew off the burning carriers, but those that did showed no aggressiveness. They had probably spent their ammunition on the Devastators and never rearmed.

At first, Nagumo refused to abandon *Akagi* and remained on the bridge. The captain and his bridge officers insisted that the admiral, as commander-in-chief, transfer to a safe ship. They finally dragged him from the bridge and through piles of burning debris to a waiting destroyer. Nagumo temporarily transferred tactical command of the strike force to Rear Admiral Hiroaki Abe, who commanded the battleship and cruiser screen, and he remained out of communication for an hour.

As a testament to the inferiority of American torpedoes, Commander Takahisa Amagai, flight officer of *Kaga*, was treading water when he saw a periscope pop up. Moments later, a torpedo sped toward *Kaga*. It hit the side of the carrier, caromed off, and circled about until the warhead dropped off. When the cylinder popped to the surface, sailors used it as a floatation device, which was all the torpedo was good for. The only American submarine known to be in the area was Commander Brockman's *Nautilus*. At 2:00 P.M., he fired three torpedoes into the burning *Soryu*, and they all exploded.

At 10:50, while Nagumo was transferring his flag to the light cruiser *Nagara*, Rear Admiral Tamon Yamaguchi launched *Hiryu*'s ready aircraft. Eighteen Vals and a small Zero escort knew just where to look because a Japanese search plane had located *Yorktown* and kept a close watch on her movements.

Yamaguchi also radioed Yamamoto that *Akagi*, *Kaga*, and *Soryu* were on fire, which must have come as one of life's grimmest shocks to the man responsible for planning the operation. Had Yamamoto been less stunned, he might have considered his losses and ordered Yamaguchi to withdraw *Hiryu*. But Yamamoto said nothing, and Yamaguchi, being an aggressive individual, began fishing about the deck for flyable planes that could be used for a second attack. He still had a few, many of them from burning carriers. The rest were gone.

At 11:00 A.M., Fletcher launched 10 SBDs on a scout. He still believed that somewhere in the vicinity lurked another enemy carrier waiting to pounce on *Yorktown* as soon as he launched a strike. He kept seven Dauntlesses fully armed and gassed below, but wisely sent Thach's 12 Wildcats on CAP to protect the ship. *Enterprise* and *Hornet* were some 20 miles to the southeast, prayerfully waiting to recover long overdue planes.

At noon, *Yorktown*'s radar picked up blips that registered as "bogies." Captain Buckmaster cleared the deck of inflammables and sealed doors and hatches as tightly as possible—the opposite of what the Japanese had done. After his Coral Sea experience, Buckmaster became a believer in precautions. He also sent Leslie's SBDs, which were returning after hammering *Soryu*, to *Enterprise*. On the way, two Dauntlesses ran out of gas and ditched.

Wildcats from *Hornet* and *Enterprise* joined Thach's "Fighting 3" and pounced on Yamaguchi's strike force. Only eight Vals got through. AA fire felled two, but the six survivors gave American flyers a lesson in dive-bombing. They pulled out at 500 feet and scored three hits on *Yorktown*. Navy pilots usually pulled out around 2,000 feet, which explained the high number of misses.

Had Buckmaster not taken precautions, *Yorktown* would have been ablaze. Instead, men quickly extinguished the flames and repaired a 10-foot hole blown in the deck that had temporarily stopped the launching and landing of aircraft. Eighty minutes after the attack, Buckmaster had the carrier steaming at 20 knots and aircraft refueling operations underway. Fletcher had shifted his flag to the cruiser *Astoria* and was pleasantly surprised to see *Yorktown* operational again.

Around 1:00 P.M., Admiral Yamaguchi salvaged 10 Kates and 6 Zeros from the jumble of damaged aircraft on *Hiryu*'s deck and told Lieutenant Tomonaga to finish off the American carrier. At 2:30, *Yorktown*'s radar operators reported "bogies" at 53 miles. Thach's 12 Wildcats, some with gas tanks near empty, met the approaching group about 12 miles out and shot down half the Kates. AA fire accounted for another, but four Kates survived. Skimming over the water at 50 feet and angling in from different directions, Kate pilots dropped four torpedoes. *Yorktown* avoided the first two, but the others tore open her hull, knocked out electric power, and jammed the rudder. The big carrier began listing, and when she reached 26 degrees, Buckmaster radioed Fletcher, reminding him that the hurried repairs made at Pearl Harbor left much undone, and if the ship capsized, hundreds of men would be lost. Fletcher concurred and Buckmaster issued the order to abandon ship.

Not realizing that *Hiryu*'s bombers had already hit *Yorktown,* Tomonaga believed his planes had struck a second American carrier. Yamaguchi accepted Tomonaga's report, but in the two attacks on *Yorktown* he had lost thirteen Vals, five Kates, and six Zeros. Counting repaired planes, he now had five Vals, four Kates, and six flyable fighters, and he resolutely armed them for one last strike. Believing his planes had crippled two American carriers, and having now located *Enterprise* and *Hornet*, Yamaguchi wanted to finish off the others in a twilight attack.

At 2:30 P.M., as Yamaguchi prepared his final strike, Lieutenant Samuel Adams spotted *Hiryu* with her escorts. He radioed the carrier's position, course, and speed with exceptional accuracy. At 3:30, *Enterprise* launched 24 Dauntlesses, 10 of which had come from *Yorktown*. Thirty minutes later, 16 more SBDs from *Hornet* joined the hunt.

At 4:45, Lieutenant Gallaher, acting as *Enterprise*'s Air Group Commander, spotted *Hiryu* preparing to launch Yamaguchi's final strike. Fuel hoses were draped across the deck with pools of gasoline collecting near the aircraft. Yamaguchi had only four Zeros in the air and apparently no lookouts on the carrier because at 5:01 Gallaher tipped over into his dive without being seen. Gallaher missed, but those who followed dropped four bombs on *Hiryu*. Gasoline fires ignited and swiftly spread, setting off ammunition that tore through the carrier apart.

When *Hornet*'s SBDs arrived there was little left to do but go after Nagumo's battleships and cruisers. Perhaps pilot fatigue contributed to so many misses. *Hornet*'s dive-bombers hit nothing. Of 40 SBDs sent to sink *Hiryu* and her escorts, only four bombs struck the carrier, but that was enough. Admiral Nagumo lost his last flattop when at midnight Admiral Yamaguchi shut down *Hiryu*'s engines and ordered her abandoned.

Most of *Hiryu*'s crew—some 416 officers and men—went down with the ship. Only 34 men survived. The IJN lost Admiral Yamaguchi, a brilliant flag officer, a fierce fighter, and a man slated as Yamamoto's successor.

Yamamoto, hundreds of miles from Midway, did not know the extent of damage to *Akagi*, *Kaga*, and *Soryu* until noon, June 4, when he received the first grim news from Admiral Yamaguchi. Instead of ordering the undamaged *Hiryu* out of the area, he ordered Admiral Kondo's covering group, which contained the light carrier *Zuiho*, to join Nagumo. He also recalled Rear Admiral Kakuji Kakuta from the Aleutian strike because Kakuta had two light carriers, *Ryujo* and *Junyo*. Yamamoto's main force contained the light carrier *Hosho*, and it appeared that the admiral intended to do what he should have done in the beginning and group all his carriers together. At 7:55 P.M., Yamamoto received word that *Hiryu* had been hit, and he now knew that Nagumo's four carriers were lost. He desperately needed to create victory from disaster and urged Nagumo to turn Kondo's invasion force back on Midway and use all his available gunships to destroy the enemy fleet.

Nagumo no longer felt like fighting. The unexpected defeat, so unlike the surprise attack on Pearl Harbor, turned tragic. Instead of following Yamamoto's orders, he ordered the group to withdraw from Midway. He also deluded himself into believing that the Americans had five carriers, not three. He could not believe *Yorktown* was one of them: it was supposed to have been sunk in the Coral Sea. Nor had he accurately reported the extent of his own losses, but from Yamaguchi's messages Yamamoto obtained a clear picture of the disaster. When he learned that Nagumo intended to withdraw, he relieved him and put Admiral Kondo in command of the Midway operation and gave him the same orders he had given Nagumo. Yamamoto clearly blamed Nagumo for the defeat after he learned the admiral had failed to take the usual precautions ordered by Japanese fleet procedures of doubling search planes. Had Nagumo done so, the American carriers would have been discovered and perhaps destroyed. On such small details are great battles won.

With *Yorktown* crippled and listing, Fletcher relinquished his command to Spruance and sent all his planes to *Enterprise* and *Hornet*. Spruance did not want to risk a night surface engagement with Nagumo's (now Kondo's) gunships and steamed eastward before doubling back on Pont Luck north of Midway. Spruance expected to find a fifth carrier with Kondo's force, and he was right, for the light carrier *Zuiho* was with Kondo's surface force. Spruance knew his battle group was inadequately trained for night action. Had he sailed west, he would have run into Kondo's battleships and cruisers about midnight. Kondo hoped for a night engagement and advanced at full speed, knowing that Yamamoto would also arrive the following day. When Kondo failed to locate Spruance, and after receiving confirmation that Nagumo's four heavy carriers had been lost, Yamamoto cancelled the Midway expedition and at 2:55 A.M. on June 5 ordered the entire force back to Japan.

Spruance swung back on a northwesterly course after reports from the submarine USS *Tambor* placed Kondo's retiring battle group 90 miles west of Midway. On June 6, search planes spotted two heavy cruisers, *Mogami* and *Mikuma*, which had been lightly damaged by colliding when attacked by *Tambor*. Spruance launched three strikes that severely damaged *Mogami* and sank *Mikuma* and the destroyer *Arashio*. Once again, bombing accuracy remained

Crews on the USS *Yorktown* work to keep the carrier afloat after being struck by Japanese
dive-bombers. (U.S. Navy photo)

deplorably poor. The pilots, however, made an important discovery. Their instantaneously fused 1,000-pound bombs worked well when striking flimsy carrier
flight decks but would not penetrate armored top-decks. Pilots requested and
eventually received armor-piercing bombs with delayed fuses for operations
against enemy battleships and cruisers.

Unlike Fletcher, Spruance continued the chase until his ships ran low on fuel.
Then he put the force about and rendezvoused with his oilers.

Spruance hoped to save the crippled *Yorktown* and bring her home for repairs. Captain Buckmaster still had a skeleton crew on board shaving top weight
to correct her list. A ring of destroyers circled the carrier, listening to sonar for
submarine activity. Somehow *I-168*, commanded by Lieutenant Commander
Yahachi Tanabe, slipped through the screen. Yamamoto had sent *I-168* specifically to sink the crippled carrier. Tanabe fired four torpedoes. One missed, two
hit *Yorktown*, and the fourth cut the destroyer *Hammann*, moored alongside, in
half. When morning came, the gallant but battered *Yorktown* sank. Apart from

Tanabe's 11th-hour torpedo attack, Yamamoto suffered a crushing defeat and Nimitz won a miraculous victory. Two weeks passed before the American press realized the scope of the victory. Then the jubilation began, but a closer look must be taken at a great victory that could easily have become a devastating defeat.

The Pacific Fleet had the advantage of intelligence, without which Nimitz would never have deciphered Yamamoto's plan and would have fallen into the wily admiral's carefully laid trap. Nagumo, although made arrogant by the successes of the past, may have prevailed had the carriers *Zuikaku* and *Shokaku* been available during the Midway strike. If so, Yamamoto might well have crippled the Pacific Fleet and captured Midway.

The Americans had the great good luck of attacking all four Japanese carriers when their crews were recovering aircraft or preparing them for take off. The navy's torpedo-bombers performed "a gallant by useless sacrifice."[7] All three squadrons were destroyed without scoring a single hit. Torpedoes were defective and slow and the tactics used to launch them from great distances eliminated most chances of a hit. Japanese torpedoes were far superior to U.S. Navy issue: two of them sank *Yorktown* and a third cut a destroyer in half.

Dauntless dive-bombers sank four enemy carriers, but targeting tactics were poor because pilots dropped payloads at 2,000–2,500 feet, while Vals dropped and pulled up at 500 feet. Because of the Midway success, bombing techniques remained substandard for much of the war.

American ships used radar. Japan had none. By being able to detect enemy aircraft 15–20 minutes before they arrived overhead enabled carrier commanders to launch more fighters. Vals and Kates were no match for Wildcats, but many slipped through when accompanied by fighters. The Thach weave, first tried at Midway, became the only defensive/offensive technique that worked well against Zeros.

Navy pilots had the good fortune of destroying most of Nagumo's aircraft while parked on the carriers. Pilots on *Enterprise*, *Hornet*, and *Yorktown* were among the very best in the navy, yet 147 planes were lost. Some ditched, but many were lost in battle.

Apart from aircraft losses, the Pacific Fleet lost one carrier and one destroyer. Of 547 casualties, 340 sailors and marines died. Compared with Japan's loss of four carriers, a cruiser, a destroyer, 332 planes, 400 flyers, and more than 3,000 sailors, America's loss seemed small. At first, neither Nimitz nor King could believe the Japanese losses at Midway or appreciate the great victory. For the second time in 30 days, the second of five great battles had been fought in the Pacific with aircraft doing all the hitting. Not one surface ship fired on another.

When Yamamoto returned home, the survivors were cautioned against talking. IGH withheld the defeat from the public. Not even Prime Minister General Tojo learned of the carrier losses until later. The lone communiqué simply said that one American carrier had been sunk, one had been damaged (which was untrue), that the Japanese had won a glorious battle by invading the Aleutians (which was neither glorious nor strategically important), and that a naval battle had been fought off Midway. Nothing was mentioned about the fact that Admiral Yamamoto's

Despite efforts on June 4, 1942, to keep the USS *Yorktown* afloat, she is abandoned after being struck by enemy torpedoes. (U.S. Navy photo)

plans for extending Japanese conquests in the Pacific suffered a permanent setback. Any plans to take the New Hebrides, New Caledonia, Fiji, and Samoa died on June 4 with the sinking of Nagumo's carriers. Japan now had two, *Shokaku* and *Zuikaku*, backed up by the medium carrier *Junyo* and three light carriers.

The United States remained as vulnerable as before. With only *Enterprise*, *Hornet*, and *Saratoga* in the Pacific, and *Wasp* and *Ranger* in the Atlantic, a few well-placed enemy torpedoes could shorten the odds. The smaller *Ranger* was not fit for duty in the Pacific, and the navy did not have much time to replace lost aircraft with better planes. But changes were coming, and for the first time since the beginning of the war, attrition began to favor the men in white ducks.

Admiral Spruance summed up the Battle of Midway in five words: "We were shot with luck."[8]

PART III

Evolution of Combat Tactics

Hitler's fate was sealed. Mussolini's fate was sealed. As for the Japanese, they would be ground to powder. All the rest was merely the application of overwhelming force.

(Winston Churchill, *The Second World War*, vol. 5, 539)

CHAPTER 8

The Eastern Solomons

The loss of *Lexington* in the Coral Sea induced caution on the part of Admiral King, so he advised Nimitz and Halsey to not operate beyond land-based airpower. Nimitz disagreed and continued to act without always consulting King on carrier deployment. A month later, victory at Midway changed King's mind and influenced the thinking of the Joint Chief of Staff (JCS) for the remainder of the war.

On March 30, 1942, the JCS divided the Pacific into two commands, the Southwest Pacific Area (Australia, New Guinea, and the Solomons) under General Douglas MacArthur, and the Pacific Ocean Area under Admiral Nimitz. The action, made with Roosevelt's blessing, ranked among the worst decisions of the war. Within months the consequences became manifest in the South Pacific and culminated in a complete breakdown of communications during the 1944 Leyte campaign.

King placed 59-year-old Vice Admiral Robert L. Ghormley in charge of the South Pacific Area, which included all the Pacific islands from the equator to the South Pole. King thought Ghormley was the right man for the job, and Nimitz agreed. Both were wrong. Ghormley, however, made an excellent decision when he selected Rear Admiral John S. McCain as Commander Aircraft South Pacific Area. McCain would later become a distinguished carrier task force commander, but for the present he exercised operational control over all land-based Allied planes.

On July 2, after discovering that Japan was building an airstrip on Guadalcanal, the JCS authorized Operation Watchtower. Guadalcanal, an island in the southern Solomons, lay just inside Nimitz's command sector. Major General Alexander A. Vandegrift's 1st Marine Division had been equipped and trained for amphibious landings and were handed the task of capturing Guadalcanal's airfield and the islands of Tulagi and Gavuto across the sound. Nimitz received his orders on July 10 with a month to launch the operation.

After Midway, Spruance became Nimitz's chief of staff, and because Halsey was still bedridden, Nimitz sent Fletcher into the South Pacific. During the same

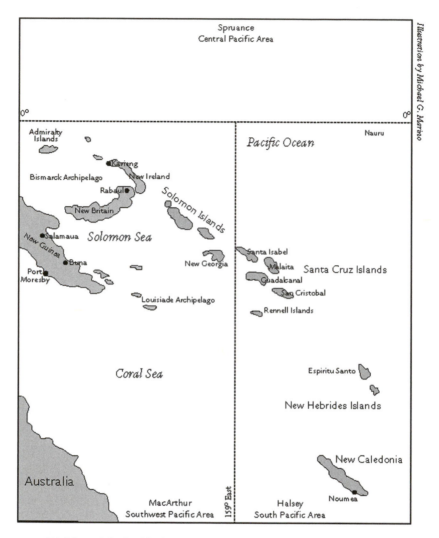

Illustration by Michael G. Marino

Division of the Pacific into Sectors of Command. (Michael G. Marino)

period, the navy began discarding the utterly useless TBD Devastators and replaced them with Grumman TBF-1 Avengers, a rugged torpedo-bomber long
overdue in joining the fleet.

Fletcher also picked up *Wasp*, which had come racing around the world from
Malta with the battleship *North Carolina*, heavy cruiser *Quincy*, light cruiser *San
Juan*, and seven destroyers. This brought Fletcher's TF-61 to three carrier groups.
Compared with *Saratoga*, which had been modernized and fitted with new 5-inch
paired AA guns, and with *Enterprise*, the 14,700-ton *Wasp* looked out of character.

She was smaller and narrower but had higher funnels. Nimitz had only four carriers in the Pacific, and he took a chance by sending three of them to Fletcher. He instructed Fletcher to support the landing of Rear Admiral Richmond K. Turner's South Pacific Amphibious Force on Guadalcanal.

Fletcher chose *Saratoga* as his flagship and put Captain DeWitt C. Ramsey, an aviator, in charge of running the ship. Rear Admiral Thomas C. Kinkaid, a tough cruiser division man, moved up to command the *Enterprise* group. Captain Arthur C. Davis, another aviator, skippered the "Big E." Rear Admiral Leigh Noyes commanded the *Wasp* group, as well as all the air groups. Captain Forrest P. Sherman, *Wasp*'s captain, probably knew as much about carrier air tactics as anyone in the task force.

For the South Pacific Force, Guadalcanal became a weeding-out process. Fletcher anticipated immense problems putting Vandegrift's 1st Marine Division ashore on Guadalcanal. Nimitz intended the landing to be a surprise, and he expected Fletcher to have at least as many carriers as the enemy. Fletcher, however, fretted about being too close to Rabaul. He worried that Japanese search planes would spot his carriers, resulting in massive air attacks. According to his instructions, the carriers would have to remain within Wildcat range until Vandegrift's marines established a firm beachhead. Fletcher's concerns were partly justified. *Wasp*'s pilots were a cohesive air group, having served together in the Mediterranean, but they had never been in combat. The air groups on *Saratoga* and *Enterprise* contained a mixture of veterans and recent flight school graduates. Such a multitude of worries took the fight out of Fletcher and made him ultra conservative.

At dawn on August 7, 1942, Fletcher's TF-61 stood off southwestern Guadalcanal, while Turner's four cruisers and six destroyers, supported by carrier planes, softened up landing beaches. When the first bombs landed, two Japanese Construction Battalions, composed mostly of Koreans, abandoned their equipment and fled into the jungle. Nineteen large transports and cargo ships rounded into Ironbottom Sound and disembarked Vandegrift's marines. In the first American amphibious landing since 1898, marines went ashore on Guadalcanal without having to fire a shot. Wildcats from *Wasp* destroyed all the flying boats and floatplanes at Tulagi, Gavuto, and Tanambogo, and though the Japanese fought stubbornly from caves and bunkers on the islands, resistance ended the following day.

The success of the 175-ship expedition could be attributed to two factors: good planning and coordination on the part of Ghromley's staff, and horrible aerial reconnaissance on the part of Rear Admiral Sadayoshi Yamada, commanding air groups at Rabaul. Yamada attempted hurried face-saving countermeasures. He had 27 twin-engine Betty bombers and 18 Zeros already armed and fueled to strike New Guinea. Guadalcanal was 560 miles away, slightly beyond the range of Vals and barely in range of Zeros. Knowing he would be criticized for not taking immediate action, Yamada cancelled the New Guinea strike and at 8:30 A.M. sent the Bettys, Vals, and Zeroes to Guadalcanal. For Val pilots, it would be a one-way trip.

Bridge scene on the USS *Wasp* during the August 7, 1942, landing of marines on Guadalcanal. Douglas Dauntlesses wait in readiness on deck. (U.S. Navy photo)

At 1:15 P.M., radar operators on the cruiser *Chicago* reported the bogies 43 miles away. Wildcat pilots, most of them inexperienced, would be up against Lieutenant Commander Tadashi Nakajima's superb Tainan Air Group. Nakajima's pilots had fought in China, destroyed American fighter squadrons on the Philippines, and decimated MacArthur's P-39 and P-40 groups at Port Moresby. Saburo Sakai, one of Nakajima's three aces, had 57 kills. Had it not been for the Thach weave and broken cloud cover, the dogfight with Nakajima's Zeros could have been disastrous.

Betty bombers with Zero escorts came in high. Six Wildcats from carriers dove through the approaching bombers and tore the formation apart. As more Wildcat squadrons tangled with the enemy, young pilots received a harsh lesson in the multiple capabilities of Zeros. Admiral Noyes lost control of the fight, and the battle in the sky developed into a melee over Ironbottom Sound. At the peak of the dogfight, a flight of Dauntlesses from Bombing 6 flew over Tulagi looking for targets and were jumped by Sakai's Zeros. The Japanese ace got too close to the tail of one SBD. The rear seat gunner wounded Sakai in the head and eye and knocked him out of the war.

Late in the action, nine Vals made their appearance and dove on the destroyer *Mugford*, striking the ship's aftermount. Wildcats from *Enterprise* and *Saratoga* pounced on the Vals and shot down six. The other three ran out of fuel and ditched in the Solomon Sea.

Despite their inexperience, American pilots did well. They saved the transports, but paid for it with 11 Wildcats and one Dauntless. Nakajima lost two Zeros, nine Vals, five Bettys, and the services of his ace, Saburo Sakai. The attack disappointed Admiral Yamada. None of his planes had located Fletcher's carriers. Fletcher should have been pleased. It was the first American amphibious operation covered by carrier-based planes, and his young flyers admirably stood their ground against enemy fighters flown by veteran pilots. Fletcher, however, could not quiet his nerves.

On August 8, Admiral Yamada launched the last of his flyable planes—23 Bettys armed with torpedoes, 9 Vals, and an escort of Zeros. A coastwatcher on Bougainville spotted the flight heading for Guadalcanal and tipped off Admiral Turner about 80 minutes before the planes arrived. Wildcats high in the sky over Ironbottom Sound did not see the first low-flying Bettys as they crossed the eastern cape of Florida Island and dropped to 20 feet over the water. Three Wildcats from *Enterprise*, patrolling low over Nggela Channel, shot four of them down.

Admiral Turner's transports were already maneuvering when the first formation of Bettys angled in with their deadly aerial torpedoes. By the time the Bettys reached the launching point, they were so chewed up by Turner's AA fire that only nine survived. Only one torpedo connected, striking the destroyer *Jarvis*.

A second Betty formation followed, but Turner's AA cut it to pieces. Two Bettys with engines smoking attempted suicide tactics, and one struck the transport *George F. Elliott* with deadly effect.

Turner's arrangement of AA fire on August 8 won the battle, not carrier planes. During August 7, Fletcher had removed his flattops from Guadalcanal, leaving Turner with a thin air patrol of Wildcats but nothing else. After midnight on August 9, a Japanese force under Vice Admiral Gunichi Mikawa came down the Slot from Rabaul and clobbered Turner's cruisers in a night attack off Savo Island. Had Fletcher remained in the area, his search planes would surely have spotted the Japanese squadron. Instead, Turner lost his covering force and sustained 1,732 battle casualties. Without Fletcher's air cover, Turner was forced to withdraw. Tons of ammunition and supplies never got ashore to marines on Guadalcanal. Once again, Fletcher appeared to be more concerned about the loss of 21 planes and topping off his fuel tanks than protecting Turner's covering force. Turner, who became the navy's outstanding authority on amphibious landings, never forgave Fletcher. As one historian noted, "Fletcher had entered battle determined to accept no risks; he left it with the same determination."[1] In the coming days, marines on Guadalcanal paid heavily for Fletcher's hasty withdrawal.

The setback in the Solomons did not go unnoticed in Tokyo. Admiral Nagano conferred with IGH and agreed that Guadalcanal's unfinished airfield at Lunga Point must be recaptured. Marines were already putting the airfield, renamed Henderson Field, into condition to receive Wildcats.[2]

Yamamoto, still disturbed by his losses at Midway, agreed to the plan. Operation KA consisted of two large carriers (*Shokaku* and *Zuikaku*), four battleships, and a powerful force of cruisers and destroyers. Yamamoto wanted nothing left to chance and took personal command of the operation from the battleship *Yamato*.

Once again, Yamamoto designed a complicated plan, this time to trap and destroy the South Pacific Fleet. He split his force into four groups. The advance group under Vice Admiral Kondo consisted of heavy cruisers, a seaplane carrier, and destroyer escorts. Many miles behind came Rear Admiral Abe's fast battleships *Hiei* and *Kirishima* with more cruisers and destroyers. Following Abe came Admiral Nagumo, who had somehow survived the Midway disaster and remained Japan's leading carrier commander. Yamamoto's plan involved a clever gambit. By using Rear Admiral Hara's light carrier *Ryujo* and a small escort of one cruiser and two destroyers as bait, Yamamoto hoped to lure Fletcher into launching a full strike, thereby leaving the American carriers with insufficient protection. Yamamoto understood that whoever struck first had the advantage. If Fletcher attacked *Ryujo*, Yamamoto planned to launch full deckloads of Vals and Kates from *Shokaku* and *Zuikaku*.

Yamamoto also embarked an invasion force under Admiral Tanaka at Rabaul. As soon as Fletcher's carriers were destroyed, Tanaka was to bring a landing force down the Slot, land on Guadalcanal, and recapture Henderson Field, where, because of Fletcher's hasty withdrawal, marines were running out of supplies, ammunition, and medicine.

For two weeks, while Yamamoto assiduously plotted the destruction of the South Pacific Fleet, Fletcher cruised aimlessly outside the danger zone, wasting time and effort. He provided his command with a marvelous demonstration of how not to use aircraft carriers. Nimitz probably did not know about Fletcher's missed opportunities or his carrier commander's reluctance to use the most powerful weapon afloat when on August 17 he sent *Hornet*, with a cruiser and destroyer escort, to join the South Pacific Fleet. Fletcher gave no help to the marines on Guadalcanal, who were being attacked several times a day by aircraft and shelled at night by submarines and surface vessels. Even Admiral Ghormley, not known for aggressiveness, ordered Fletcher to counterattack, but he refused, claiming that the concealment of his carriers would eventually produce dividends. Finally on August 20, and with no thanks to Fletcher, Henderson Field received 19 Wildcats and 12 Dauntlesses from the recently arrived escort carrier *Long Island*. The planes formed the nucleus of what became Guadalcanal's Cactus Air Force.

Fletcher's argument for concealment translated into avoiding a fight. Yamamoto wanted a fight. On August 20, a Japanese flying boat spotted Fletcher's

An F2A-3 fighter gets tangled up in the catwalk after a landing accident on the USS *Long Island*, the first escort carrier to reach the South Pacific. (U.S. Navy photo)

carriers 500 miles east of Bougainville. Yamamoto lost no time detaching Kondo's force from escorting transports to Guadalcanal and ordered him to refuel and be ready to launch Operation KA.

Also on August 20, Admiral McCain's land-based search planes spotted Admiral Kondo's invasion force steaming down the Slot toward Guadalcanal. Admiral Ghormley told Fletcher to use his carriers to cover the island's sea approaches. Fletcher sent 31 Dauntlesses and 6 Avengers to look for the enemy. The pilots sighted no ships because Yamamoto had ordered Kondo back to Rabaul to refuel. Instead of returning to *Saratoga*, Fletcher's pilots spent the night at Henderson Field.

McCain's shore-based PBYs again reported the approach of a Japanese force. *Saratoga*'s SBDs searched for hours but sighted nothing. For the next two days, although the weather remained too thick for good observation, Fletcher consoled himself in the belief that no Japanese force had penetrated the range of his search planes.

On 9:00 A.M. on August 23, with *Enterprise*, *Saratoga*, and *Wasp* about 150 miles east of Guadalcanal, a search plane reported a Japanese carrier 280 miles to the north. Fletcher's flyers could not find the lone flattop, which happened to be

Yamamoto's "bait," the light carrier *Ryujo*. Reasoning that a major clash would not come for several days, Fletcher made the mistake of sending *Wasp,* which contained Admiral Noyes's air control group, away to refuel.

Fletcher enjoyed a distinct advantage in air power. His three flattops carried 215 aircraft, whereas Nagumo had only 177 planes on *Shokaku, Zuikaku,* and *Ryujo.* By detaching Noyes instead of bringing an oiler to *Wasp,* Fletcher deprived himself of 39 planes. He also reduced his strength by allowing *Saratoga*'s planes to spend the night on Guadalcanal because his pilots were not proficient at night deck-landings. On the morning of August 24, Fletcher still had 87 planes on *Enterprise,* but he sent 23 on a dawn search, leaving only 28 Dauntlesses for a strike.

At this critical hour, a PBY patrol bomber again reported the position of *Ryujo* and three escorts off Santa Isabel Island. Because *Enterprise*'s search planes had found nothing but empty sea, Fletcher ignored the report. The PBY continued to shadow *Ryujo* and an hour later reported her position again. Fletcher disregarded the second message. He overlooked the fact that his planes had not spotted *Ryujo* or Nagumo's carriers because they were beyond the range of his search planes.

At 11:00 A.M., Fletcher's Dauntlesses and Avengers, after spending the night at Henderson Field, began returning to *Saratoga.* Planes were still orbiting when at 11:28 another PBY reported *Ryujo*'s location. Two minutes later, *Saratoga*'s radar picked up a Kawanishi Emily flying boat at 20 miles. Wildcats shot it down, but not before the pilot reported Fletcher's position. This was exactly the information Nagumo needed for personal vindication, but he paused two hours before ordering a strike. At 3:37 P.M., the first strike force, composed of 18 Vals, 9 Kates, and 18 Zeros headed for Fletcher's carriers. As they disappeared out of sight, Nagumo prepared a second strike.

Fletcher lost time ruminating but finally radioed *Enterprise* to launch a search-strike mission. At 1:15, Kinkaid put 23 Dauntlesses and Avengers armed with 500-pound bombs into the air to search for *Ryujo.* After the planes launched, Kinkaid's radar operators reported blips from 15 Zeros and 8 Kates headed toward Henderson Field. Fletcher now knew that a Japanese carrier was somewhere nearby.

Fletcher worried constantly about being drawn into a trap, but he could not overlook the enemy's presence and ordered a strike. *Saratoga*'s most available planes were those on deck recently arrived from Guadalcanal. The pilots, after receiving little rest at Henderson Field, had already flown five hours. Fletcher then realized that by sending *Wasp* away, he had deprived himself of planes. For protection, he kept 53 Wildcats for CAP and held 13 Dauntlesses and 12 Avengers on deck for emergencies.

Hara knew *Ryujo* had been reported by a PBY, but the only American planes to annoy him had been B-17s from Australia, which, as usual, hit nothing. Hara also knew American carriers were nearby and launched more fighters for protection.

At 4:06, Commander H. D. "Don" Felt, leading *Saratoga*'s Air Group at 14,000 feet, sighted *Ryujo* and her escorts. His new Avenger with its powerful R-2600

Wright engine could fly faster than a Dauntless, range as far, and carry a heavy load of ordnance. He set up the strike by sending Dauntlesses first followed by Avengers. Looking below, he could see *Ryujo* turn into the wind to launch Kates, which meant that Zeros were already airborne.

As the first 20 Dauntlesses tipped over, Captain Tadao Kato, *Ryujo*'s skipper, masterfully maneuvered the light carrier, making turns so sharp that every bomb missed. Felt called to the other bombers and told them to time their drops to the turns of the carrier, then he plunged into a dive himself. Zeros climbed quickly to do battle, but the Avengers went right through them. Felt's 1,000-pound armor-piercing bomb plunged into *Ryujo*'s deck and exploded below, setting the carrier on fire. Three more bombs connected after Felt pulled up. Lieutenant B. L. Harwood's five torpedo-armed Avengers peeled off and came in at 200 feet. Using the anvil tactic learned from the Japanese during the Coral Sea fight, three Avengers targeted on *Ryujo*'s starboard bow and two on the carrier's port bow. At 800 yards, the Avengers dropped. One torpedo struck home. Having not lost a plane, Felt led the group back to *Saratoga*.

Flames swept through *Ryujo*. She listed to starboard, dead in the water. Her planes, returning from the Henderson Field strike, ditched. As darkness approached, two more B-17s flew over the wreck and missed. Then *Ryujo* sank.

At 3:55, 18 minutes after Nagumo launched the first air strike, search planes from *Enterprise* spotted *Shokaku* and *Zuikaku*. Pilots dropped their bombs, missed, and radioed Fletcher that the Japanese carriers were preparing an air strike. They did not know the first wave was already airborne.

Fletcher confronted a quandary because at that moment *Saratoga*'s planes were attacking *Ryujo*, *Enterprise* had scouting missions in the air, and he had recklessly detached *Wasp*. Between the two carriers, he still had 12 Avengers, 13 Dauntlesses, and plenty of Wildcats, but he could not decide how to use them.

At 4:32, *Enterprise*'s radar located Nagumo's strike force at 12,000 feet 88 miles to the north. *Enterprise*'s returning search planes were leading Nagumo's pilots straight to the carriers. Fletcher finally launched all of his Wildcats and reserve aircraft to meet the attack. The last Wildcat flew off just as Japanese planes arrived overhead. Fletcher hastily dispatched the last of his Dauntlesses and Avengers to make a counterstrike without briefing them. None of the planes had good navigation equipment on board. An airman would not have made this mistake, but Fletcher was a battleship man.

Fletcher launched his reserve Wildcats too late for the pilots to climb and get organized. There were now so many blips on the radarscope that *Enterprise* controllers could not distinguish friend from foe. Moments later, *Enterprise*'s single radio channel jammed, making it impossible for fighter-direction control officers to communicate with CAP.

Wildcat pilots, struggling to 18,000 feet to intercept Vals, found Zeros in their front and on their tail. At such altitudes, the F4F-4's supercharged Wasp R-1830 engine could match the Zero, but too many enemy planes came in low

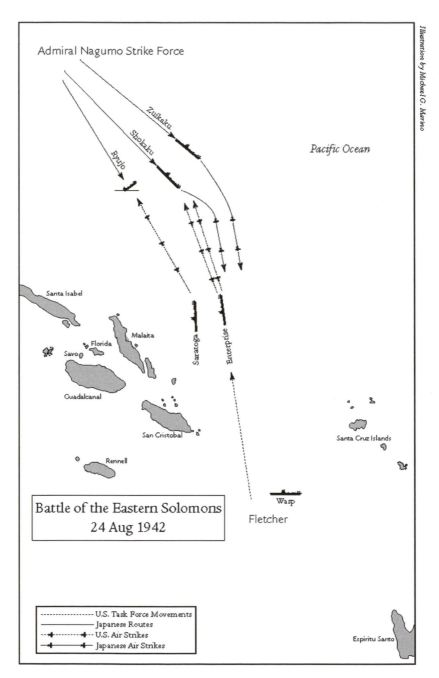

Battle of the Eastern Solomons, August 24, 1942. (Michael G. Marino)

and passed under the fighter screen. Despite a large number of airborne Wildcats, pilots intercepted few Vals before they tipped and dove.

The Val formation split. One bore on *Enterprise* and the other attacked the battleship *North Carolina*. In an action lasting less than four minutes, Vals leveled off at 1,200 feet, released their bombs, and did not miss. One 550-pounder buckled *Enterprise*'s flight deck. The next one plunged through No. 3 elevator, penetrated three decks before exploding, and partially knocked out the carrier's power. Two more bombs struck and started fires. Several near misses ruptured the hull and caused a three-degree list. *North Carolina* came out of the attack unscathed, thanks to her tremendous volume of AA fire. None of the Vals went after *Saratoga*, but they spotted her about six miles astern of *North Carolina* and informed Nagumo. The Kates never showed up. Wildcats intercepted them 60 miles from *Enterprise* and shot them down.

Fletcher's last-minute launch of Dauntlesses and Avengers from *Saratoga* flew in the general direction of *Ryujo*. Because the pilots had not been briefed, they may not have known of *Shokaku* and *Zuikaku*. They could have followed Nagumo's strike force back to the carriers but failed to do so. Commander Leslie was to have led the planes, but AA fire from *North Carolina* damaged his Avenger. Leslie fell behind and lost his command, which stumbled about without him.

At 5:40 P.M., *Saratoga*'s pilots accidentally located Admiral Kondo's Advance Force about 40 miles west of Nagumo's position. Five Avengers attacked the cruiser column and missed. Two wandering SBDs found the seaplane carrier *Chitose*, which they mistook for a battleship. The pilots dropped a pair of 1,000-pounders that missed but exploded on contact beside her hull. The concussion set the ship on fire, tore into the engine room, and flooded it. Captain Seigo Sasaki corrected a list that almost capsized *Chitose* and limped back to Truk.

Leslie used his ZB homing equipment to return to *Saratoga*, and at 11:33 P.M. made a night landing. He was the last. All the others flew to Henderson Field. Their arrival proved providential. For the next few days the Japanese made a full-scale effort to reinforce the island, but the Cactus Air Force, augmented by *Enterprise*'s Dauntlesses and supplemented by McCain's land-based aircraft, repulsed the effort.

Mechanics patched the deck of *Enterprise* and at 7:00 P.M. Kinkaid resumed flight operations. Radar operators reported Nagumo's second strike approaching when *Enterprise*'s rudder suddenly jammed, forcing her to travel in circles. Japanese planes inexplicably veered to the south, then to the west, and flew off without attacking. Mechanics corrected the problems with *Enterprise*'s rudder, and Kinkaid ordered her to Pearl Harbor for repairs.

Although Fletcher took Yamamoto's bait, Nagumo failed to deliver. No American plane attacked Nagumo's two heavy carriers, but the delays cost Yamamoto what could have been a well-executed Japanese victory.

Through good luck rather than good tactics, Fletcher earned a victory, having sunk the light carrier *Ryujo*. He failed to take advantage of reconnaissance, but most of all his indecisiveness and the untimely detachment of *Wasp* wasted an opportunity to destroy Nagumo's flattops. On the night of August 24, Fletcher pulled away from the area and headed into the Coral Sea to refuel. *Wasp* returned from refueling and cruised east of Guadalcanal. On August 25, after her last plane returned from a 200-mile search and reported an empty sea, Fletcher knew that the Battle of the Eastern Solomons had ended.

In the aftermath, Yamamoto still had more carriers in the Pacific, but six of his flattops had been sunk against two. His aircraft losses also were severe, and Yamamoto was beginning to feel the pinch of attrition. At first he believed two American carriers had been damaged and ordered Nagumo to finish them off. He soon learned the truth. Disillusioned, Yamamoto withdrew his flattops to Truk.

The Battle of the Eastern Solomons marked the third carrier battle of World War II, but unlike Midway, it ended indecisively. Carrier commanders and pilots provided the reasons. They deplored Fletcher's tactics and asked for more AA protection and better aircraft identification systems. They also wanted fighters capable of operating at longer range, better radio communications, better combat training for carrier pilots, and the greater use of long-range PBYs and floatplanes for reconnaissance instead of wasting carrier planes. Some suggestions received immediate attention. Wildcats were fitted with newly designed underwing drop tanks, and carriers began adding more AA guns, but torpedo quality and communication systems continued to be a problem.

The same group of after-action analysts soon discovered another deficiency: inadequate protection against submarines. On August 29, *Hornet* arrived, bringing Fletcher's command back to three carriers. Two days later, Japanese submarine *I-26* slipped through the destroyer screen and torpedoed *Saratoga*. She flew off her planes before limping back to Pearl Harbor, and the Cactus Air Force received another 20 Wildcats and 9 Dauntlesses. By the time Admiral King learned of the loss, he had already digested the after-action reports from the Eastern Solomons. Even Nimitz had exhausted his patience with Fletcher's alibis. What carriers needed were fighting admirals. King recalled Fletcher to Washington and eased him into retirement.

The Battle of the Eastern Solomons was over, but the fight for control of the Solomons had just begun. Nimitz needed ships, but more than anything else, he needed carriers, carrier commanders, aircraft, and men.

CHAPTER 9

The Battle for Guadalcanal

After the engagement in the Eastern Solomons, coupled with setbacks in New Guinea and Guadalcanal, IGH felt an urgent need to concentrate efforts on retaining its grip on the Solomons or risk losing all its gains in the South Pacific. During September, Prime Minister Tojo agreed to an all-out campaign to recapture Guadalcanal, which Rabaul had been bombing during the day and shelling every night.

Attrition, malaria, and the lack of supplies had worn down the marines defending the island. General Vandegrift's growing impatience with Admiral Ghormley's failure to reinforce Guadalcanal caught the attention of Nimitz. Admiral Turner had been holding a trained marine regiment in reserve waiting for instructions from Ghormley. When direct orders arrived from Nimitz to reinforce Guadalcanal, Ghormley committed *Wasp* and *Hornet* to the expedition.

On September 15, Admiral Noyes led the carriers into position south of the island and began spotting planes to cover Admiral Turner's landings. Two Japanese submarines, *I-15* and *I-19,* were there and waiting. At 2:20 P.M., *Wasp* turned into the wind to launch 18 Dauntlesses and 8 Wildcats. The captain of *I-19* knew *Wasp* would rudder right to resume course, and, as she began to turn, he launched six torpedoes. Three struck *Wasp* on the starboard side and set her afire. Captain Forrest Sherman did what he could to keep the carrier afloat, but the flaming wreck could not be saved. Sherman abandoned the ship, and a destroyer finished her off.

Five miles north-northeast of the burning *Wasp*, the commander of *I-15* fired on *North Carolina*. One torpedo struck the battleship on the port side 20 feet below the waterline but never slowed her down. Another torpedo caught the bow of the destroyer *O'Brien* and opened a gaping hole, but she made it to Pearl Harbor. Noyes believed the attack had been made by one submarine, not two, and both got away. Admiral Turner deposited the 7th Marine Regiment safely on Guadalcanal, but Nimitz lost *Wasp*. The sinking of the carrier emphasized another deficiency in carrier operations. Two Japanese submarines penetrated the

The USS *Wasp*, while turning into the wind to launch airplanes, is hit by Japanese torpedoes and is abandoned. (National Archives)

escort screen because of inadequate sonar detection and accomplished, in part, what Nagumo's carriers failed to do in the Eastern Solomons.

Carrier losses ended the career of Admiral Ghormley, who like Fletcher preferred to conserve his ships rather than fight them. Nimitz named Vice Admiral Halsey commander of the South Pacific Fleet, and the news resonated with jubilation throughout the theater. Two days later Halsey sent *Hornet* to Guadalcanal to help repulse an effort by the Japanese Seventeenth Army to recapture Henderson Field. Had Fletcher been in command, *Hornet* would probably have been elsewhere refueling.

Yamamoto acted swiftly. If he could eliminate *Hornet*, the IJN would have complete control of the South Pacific. He added three more carriers—*Hiyo*, *Junyo*, and *Zuiho*—to the Combined Fleet. The additions, coupled with *Shokaku* and *Zuikaku*, gave the Japanese a carrier ratio of five to one.

Yamamoto wanted to use his carrier advantage to recapture Guadalcanal and regain dominance in the South Pacific. *Enterprise* was still undergoing crash repairs at Pearl Harbor, and the wounded *Saratoga* was still limping north at 13 knots. Never had there been a better opportunity to assault Henderson Field. Yamamoto developed plans for transporting the entire Japanese 2nd Army Division by destroyer using Nagumo's five carriers with five fresh air groups as a strike force.

Once again, Pearl Harbor cryptanalysts intercepted Yamamoto's battle plans. On October 16, the hastily repaired *Enterprise* sailed from Pearl Harbor with the battleship *South Dakota* and the usual cruiser-destroyer escort. Having been fitted with new 40 mm quad-mounted AA guns with Bofors mounts and eight more 22 mm guns, *Enterprise* returned to the South Pacific with twice the firepower. Admiral Kinkaid, commanding TF-16, brought Air Group 10, which had been specially trained by combat veterans.

On October 23, during the second day of the battle for Henderson Field, *Enterprise* joined Rear Admiral George D. Murray's *Hornet* group (TF-17), and Willis A. Lee's battle line (TF-64.) Halsey ordered Kinkaid to push north around Santa Cruz Island and engage the enemy. Neither Halsey, at Nouméa, New Caledonia, nor Kinkaid knew exactly how Yamamoto had organized his fleet.

Having enough antiaircraft protection for aircraft carriers was partly solved by the installation of the new 40-mm quad-mounted AA guns on Bofors mounts. (National Archives)

Yamamoto still believed that Halsey's force contained one carrier. To destroy it, he sent Nagumo's Carrier Group (*Shokaku, Ziukaku,* and *Zuiho*), Kondo's Advance Force (with the carrier *Junyo*), and Admiral Abe's Vanguard Group of battleships, cruisers, and destroyers. The fifth carrier, *Hiyo,* developed engine problems and turned back. *Hiyo*'s absence deprived Nagumo of 55 aircraft, but he still had 87 Zeros, 68 Vals, and 57 Kates. Nagumo and Kondo operated about 100 miles apart because Commander Minoru Genda, in charge of air operations, believed that if the Americans spotted one carrier group, they would not think to look for another.

Ordered into battle by Halsey, Kinkaid had neither the carriers, surface vessels, nor aircraft to contend on an equal basis with Yamamoto's fleet. For aircraft, *Hornet* and *Enterprise* carried 70 Wildcats, 72 Dauntlesses, and 27 Avengers—43 fewer planes than Nagumo. Kinkaid enjoyed a small advantage in dive-bombers, but Dauntless pilots were notoriously inaccurate.

Nagumo also had the advantage of a head wind and could launch directly into it. Kinkaid had to come about to launch. Nagumo's group also was covered by an overcast sky with pockets of rainsqualls. If Kinkaid's radar or CAP failed to pick up an incoming flight, Vals and Kates might not be detected until they dropped from the clouds.

At dawn on October 26, Kinkaid began to worry. He liked neither the wind nor the overcast. A scouting PBY spotted Nagumo's carriers, but the report went to land-based communications and not to Kinkaid. The PBY remained overhead long enough to drop a payload of bombs that nearly hit *Zuikaku.* The incident unnerved Nagumo. He reversed course and moved away.

At 5:00 A.M., Kinkaid launched a 200-mile search with 16 SBDs armed with 500-pound bombs "just in case." He then ordered Admiral Lee's battle line to tighten formation.

Eighty-five miles north, two SBD pilots, flying together, spotted 8 Kates and 16 Japanese seaplanes heading south on reconnaissance. Lieutenant Vivian W. Welch and his wingman ignored the flight and continued flying north. At 7:17 A.M., they sighted Kondo's Advance Force and the carrier *Junyo.* Thirteen minutes later, Welch was still transmitting when Japanese scouts spotted *Hornet.*

At 7:50, Lieutenant Commander James R. Lee sighted Nagumo's three carriers and snapped on the transmitter. Before he could dive on the carriers, eight Zeros fell on his tail. Using the Thach weave, Lee and his wingman whipped around 180 degrees, knocked down three Zeros, and flew back to *Enterprise.* Had Lee and his wingman been able to bomb any of the three carriers, they would have caught the Japanese spotting planes for Nagumo's first strike.

At 8:18 A.M., Nagumo launched 27 Zeros, 22 Vals, and 18 Kates. As soon as the first wave cleared the decks, he began spotting planes for a second strike.

At 8:40, Kinkaid launched a smaller strike, with 8 Wildcats, 15 Dauntlesses, and 6 Avengers from *Hornet* but only 8 Wildcats, 9 Avengers, and 3 Dauntlesses from *Enterprise.* The other SBDs had not returned from search missions.

Japanese fighters prepare to launch from a Japanese carrier thought to be either the *Zuikaku* or the *Shokaku*. (U.S. Navy photo)

After overhearing Jim Lee's transmission, Lieutenant Stockton B. Strong and Ensign Charles B. Irvine changed course, located Nagumo's force, and at 8:40 dove on *Zuiho*. A 500-pound bomb struck the light carrier's flight deck, set her on fire, and made it impossible for her to recover aircraft. Nagumo ordered her back to Truk. The Japanese now had radar, but Nagumo's operators never spotted the SBD.

At 9:15, *Hornet* launched a second strike with the last of her planes, nine Wildcats, nine Dauntlesses, and seven Avengers armed with bombs. To conserve fuel, Avenger pilots flew in loose formation. Sixty miles from *Enterprise,* Japanese and American strike forces began passing each other. Zeros from *Zuiho* attacked *Enterprise*'s Avengers and shot four down. Radar operators on *Enterprise* and *Hornet* picked up blips but were unable to distinguish friend from foe.

At 9:55, Lieutenant Commander Mamoru Seki's air group spotted *Hornet*. *Enterprise*, located 10 miles east, was smothered in a rainsquall and remained concealed for about 25 minutes. Seki lost planes during the approach, but 15 Vals and 12 Kates penetrated the fighter screen. At 10:12, the first two Vals came screaming down through streams of flak and AA fire. Steaming at 28 knots, *Hornet* twisted and turned, and the first bombs landed in the sea. Seki led the second pair. During the dive, his Val started to smoke. Seki made a quick decision to sacrifice himself. His plane nipped *Hornet*'s smokestack, started a fire

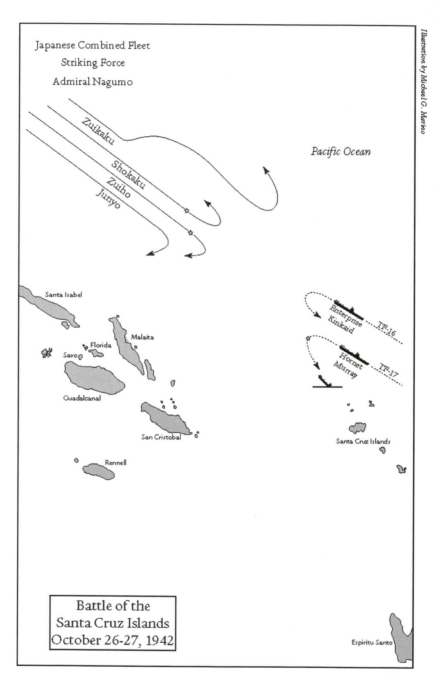

Japanese Combined Fleet
Striking Force
Admiral Nagumo

Zuikaku

Shokaku

Zuiho

Junyo

Pacific Ocean

Santa Isabel

Malaita

Florida

Savo

Guadalcanal

San Cristobal

Rennell

Enterprise
Kinkaid
TF-16

Hornet
Murray
TF-17

Santa Cruz Islands

Espiritu Santo

Battle of the
Santa Cruz Islands
October 26-27, 1942

Battle of the Santa Cruz Islands, October 26, 1942. (Michael G. Marino)

on the signal bridge, and caromed across the flight deck. One of his 100-pounders exploded, but the 550-pounder failed to arm.

While Vals streamed down from above, Kates came in low, launching torpedoes. Two fish detonated against *Hornet*'s hull and damaged the engine room. Several 550-pound bombs hit the carrier in succession, some penetrating to the fourth deck before exploding. At 10:17, as the attack ended, the pilot of a burning Kate who had missed with his torpedo followed Seki's example and flew his fiery plane into the port forward gun gallery of the drifting carrier and started more fires.

During the eight-minute attack, the Japanese lost 25 planes but rendered *Hornet* dead in the water. She was finished as a fighting ship, although Captain Mason and his crew tried valiantly to save her. *Enterprise* would have to service *Hornet*'s planes. If all returned, there would be more than she could handle.

At 10:30 A.M., *Hornet*'s 15 first-strike Dauntlesses, led by Lieutenant Commander William J. Widhelm, passed high over Admiral Abe's Vanguard Group of battleships and cruisers and continued north, searching for Nagumo's carriers. Attacked by Zeros, Widhelm's squadron lost four SBDs, among them his own, before sighting *Skokaku* and the smoking *Zuiho. Zuikaku* remained out of sight to the east.

In the absence of Widhelm, who had been forced to ditch, Lieutenant James E. Vose took command of the squadron, tipped, and dove with the remaining Dauntlesses on *Shokaku*, Nagumo's flagship. Four to six short-fused 1,000-pound bombs ripped *Shokaku*'s flight deck to shreds, started fires below, shut down communications, stopped flight operations, and put her out of the war for nine months. Like *Hornet, Shokaku* could no longer recover planes, leaving *Zuikaku* and Kondo's *Junyo* to recover the returning strike force.

Lieutenant Vose later learned that *Hornet*'s Avengers and the entire *Enterprise* air group had flown too far to the west. Widhelm, who was later rescued by a PBY, never stopped transmitting Nagumo's position, but the Japanese jamming system that had fouled communications during the Battle of the Eastern Solomons prevented his messages from getting through.

Hornet's six Avengers, unable to locate Nagumo's carriers, launched their faulty Mark 13 torpedoes on the cruiser *Suzuya* in Admiral Abe's group. One jammed on the hanger, two ran erratically, and one exploded prematurely and detonated the three that were about to hit the cruiser. Five Avengers from *Enterprise* went through the same convolutions with the same results. A few minutes later, three Dauntlesses dropped their bombs on the battleship *Kirishima* and missed.

Hornet's second strike went no better. At 10:40 A.M., after failing to find Nagumo's carriers, nine Dauntlesses led by Lieutenant J. J. Lynch dove on the heavy cruiser *Chikuma*. Four 1,000-pounders struck and partially disabled the ship, but the instantaneously fused bombs were meant to tear up carrier flight decks and not designed to penetrate armored decks. Had they been delayed-fuse bombs, *Chikuma* would not have made it back to Truk.

On October 26, 1942, Japanese dive-bombers strike the USS *Hornet*. Kates followed a few minutes later and struck *Hornet* with torpedoes, rendering her dead in the water. (U.S. Navy photo)

Hornet's nine Avengers flew over the burning *Chikuma* searching for carriers. They found nothing, turned around, and dropped four 500-pounders on the heavy cruiser *Tone*. Of 36 bombs, only one came within 50 meters of the ship. Had it not been for Lieutenant Vose's Dauntlesses, Kinkaid's air strike would have been an unparalleled embarrassment. Had the wandering American air groups teamed up and located *Zuikaku*, all of Nagumo's carriers might have been rendered useless.

At 10:30 A.M., *Enterprise* emerged from the rainsquall and began recovering planes and those of *Hornet*. Admiral Kinkaid had been spotting nine Dauntlesses to fly off at 11:00 when the returnees began to land. During the confusion, radar operators reported the approach of more planes. Some were Commander Lee's SBDs from Scouting 10, but the others were 20 Vals from *Zuikaku*, 12 Kates from *Shokaku*, and 16 Zeros. Another flight of 18 Vals and 12 Zeros, 30 minutes behind, had not yet registered on the radarscope.

The radar report came almost too late for Kinkaid to react. Patrolling Wildcats were too low to intercept the Vals, and lookouts on *Enterprise* were too distracted by flight deck mayhem to spot the leading planes. At 11:15, the Vals tipped and came screaming down from the sky. Only two bombs struck *Enterprise*, mainly because the carrier's new arsenal of AA weapons ripped the Vals to pieces before they dropped their payloads.

Both bombs, however, damaged the flight deck, set two SBDs armed and gassed for takeoff on fire, jammed the forward elevator, and made a mess of the second, third, and fourth hanger decks. The attack lasted four minutes, but 30 miles to the north *Zuikaku*'s 12 Kates began putting fresh blips on *Enterprise*'s radarscope.

Lieutenant Stanley W. Vejtasa had the good fortune to be patrolling 10 miles out with four wildcats. He climbed to 13,000 feet using the same vector as the Vals and located the incoming Kates. Vejtasa's pilots shot down five Kates and chased some away, but others passed through and closed on *Enterprise*. One Kate, flying too fast to drop its torpedo, crashed into the bow of the destroyer *Smith*.

Captain Osborne B. Hardison twisted *Enterprise* through a spread of torpedoes and almost collided with the burning *Smith*. When the Kates reformed for the kill, Hardison reduced the target area by showing them the ship's stern. If the Kates circled for an anvil attack, AA shot them down. The last Kate dropped from astern, but Hardison conned *Enterprise* to starboard and the torpedo slithered harmlessly by.

Hardison believed the worst was over and began recovering planes when radar operators reported more blips on the scope—18 Vals from *Junyo* commanded by Lieutenant Maseo Yamaguchi. Until the last attack, Nagumo believed the Americans had only one carrier in the area. Now he knew there were two, and so did Yamaguchi. The lieutenant passed up the burning *Hornet* to search for *Enterprise*. He led the Vals into Big E's murderous AA fire and in the process lost his life and the lives of eight others. One bomb nipped *Enterprise*, caromed off the side, and exploded under water. The concussion caved in the ship's side but otherwise did no damage.

The Japanese lost 45 planes, and many others returning to *Zuikaku* and *Junyo* would never fly again. American losses could have been worse. Some flyers had exhausted their ammunition and were compelled to keep out of the way. *Enterprise* lost 17 aircraft but only 9 pilots. She was about to lose more. Dozens of Dauntlesses, Avengers, and Wildcats orbited the carrier waiting for crews to remove wreckage and make repairs so they could land. At 12:35 P.M., Lieutenant Robin M. Lindsey, the landing signal officer, began waving them in. Against the advice of the deck officer, Lindsey brought in 95 planes without an accident before he ran out of room. Destroyers rescued many of the pilots who were then forced to ditch.

Sonar operators reported submarines in the area, and as no flights could be launched from *Enterprise*'s crowded deck, Kinkaid took her out of the battle zone and steamed south. According to reports, Nagumo still had one heavy and one light carrier.

Kinkaid gave up notions of rescuing *Hornet* and left Admiral Murray, commander of the carrier's task force, behind with four cruisers and six destroyers. Murray requested air cover, but Kinkaid could not provide it because of congestion on *Enterprise*'s flight deck. Kinkaid could not have provided air cover for either carrier, but he felt compelled to save *Enterprise* even if it meant losing *Hornet*.

With help from escort vessels, Captain Mason contained *Hornet*'s fires. The cruiser *Northampton* took her in tow but could only make four knots, too little to exit the battle zone before nightfall. Using lanterns, engineers worked frantically to raise steam in salvaged boilers. At 3:45, one boiler registered 300 pounds. Fifteen minutes later, engineers turned on the ship's generator, hoping to produce enough power to switch on the pumps and get the engine working. A new surge of optimism took hold of the men. It lasted exactly 20 minutes.

At 4:20 P.M., lookouts reported nine Kates approaching: *Junyo*'s second strike, ordered by Rear Admiral Kakuji Kakuta, a man far more aggressive than Nagumo. There were no Wildcats in the air to drive them off. *Northumberland* cast off the towline and concentrated on dodging torpedoes. AA put a few Kates out of business, but not enough. One torpedo struck *Hornet*'s damaged starboard beam, exploded, and flooded the previously dry after engine room. Minutes later, five Vals dove on the drifting carrier and missed. With enginerooms flooded and the carrier listing 18 degrees, Captain Mason lost all hope of saving *Hornet* and ordered her abandoned. At 4:55 P.M., while sailors were still being removed from the carrier, six twin-engine Bettys from Rabaul dropped a pattern of bombs, but only one struck *Hornet* in the corner of the starboard flight deck.

An hour later, four Vals from *Zuikaku*—the only planes Nagumo could put into the air—dove on the abandoned carrier and scored a single ineffectual hit. Two American destroyers, *Mustin* and *Anderson*, tried but failed to sink her with a pattern of faulty torpedoes. Late that night, a Japanese surface force arrived to mop up any cripples and spotted *Hornet*'s fires. They tried to take her in tow, but when that failed they fired four Long Lance torpedoes into her hull and she sank. *Hornet* testified to the durability of American carriers, and had Kinkaid been able to give her air cover, Captain Mason's engineers may have started her engines, pumped her out, and saved her for another fight.

Nagumo exaggerated the action off Santa Cruz by claiming to have sunk two carriers, but he paid a huge toll, losing 92 planes and many of his finest pilots. Despite the usual rash of mistakes by American pilots, *Shokaku* and *Zuiho* were knocked out of the war for several months. The Battle of Santa Cruz also knocked Nagumo out of the war. When Yamamoto later discovered that his timid admiral had failed to follow up his advantage and pursue *Enterprise*, he recalled Nagumo to Japan and transferred him to the Sasebo Naval Station where he could do no harm.

Enterprise, although badly damaged, was now the only American carrier in the South Pacific. Halsey wanted after-action recommendations and went directly to Hardison, *Enterprise*'s captain. Hardison pointed to the ship's radar fighter direction control, citing it as working well in practice but useless in battle. Halsey said that new VHF (Very High Frequency) radios were already on the way and would correct the problem. Hardison also offered new ideas on carrier tactics. He recommended that whenever search planes within a sector located the enemy, that all bomb-equipped search planes rendezvous and form the first attack wave. He also suggested a night tactic that Halsey immediately adopted. Henceforth, Wildcats were to strafe enemy carriers at night to cripple air groups spotted on the flight deck and set the ship on fire.

One issue remained unresolved. Hardison believed that two carriers should operate together for mutual support and in battle should never be more than five miles apart. Captain Mason, although bitter over losing *Hornet*, vociferously disagreed. He argued that carriers should be well separated and capable of operating their own fighter direction control. The issue remained temporarily moot. There was only one carrier in the South Pacific, and most of the battles for Guadalcanal would have to be fought between battleships, cruisers, and destroyers.

Kinkaid identified one of the problems that had distressed carrier commanders since the beginning of the war. Scouting PBY pilots, searching at long range, had often located and shadowed the movements of Japanese squadrons but sent their reports back to land bases. As a consequence, carrier commanders never received the intelligence or received it too late to be useful.

Halsey passed all the comments to Nimitz, who could not afford to lose carriers because of oversight.

Yamamoto believed that Nagumo had destroyed every American carrier in the South Pacific, so he turned his attention to eliminating the Cactus Air Force on Guadalcanal. Thirty thousand Japanese infantry had been put on the island, but they were running out of supplies, dropping from disease, and dying in battle because the Cactus Air Force prevented supplies and reinforcements from getting to the island.

IGH agreed that the defense of the Solomon Islands justified an all-out effort to recapture Guadalcanal and authorized 60,000 infantry for the campaign. Authorizing the task and accomplishing it created a conundrum. To land the IJA's 38th Army Division with all its artillery and mechanized equipment required 150 transports or 800 destroyers, neither of which was available. So on November 8, Yamamoto began planning for multiple landings staggered over several days using eleven transports and Vice Admiral Kondo's surface fleet, which now contained the CVLs *Junyo* and *Hiyo*. This time there would be no tricky traps set for American carriers because Yamamoto believed there were none in the area.

On November 9, Nimitz's code-breakers intercepted Yamamoto's orders and developed a fairly accurate analysis of his intentions. Nimitz forwarded the intelligence to Halsey, who had just returned to Nouméa from Guadalcanal. Halsey asked how long it would take to repair the injured *Enterprise*, and the officer in charge said three or four weeks. Halsey stopped the work and ordered Kinkaid to get TF-16 to sea and rendezvous with Admiral Lee's battle line. Captain Hardison warned that Big E's forward elevator might not work, even though the repair crew said they had fixed it. If the elevator stuck, *Enterprise* would be unable to launch planes.

On the night of November 12–13, Admiral Hiroaki Abe's battleship group steamed down the Slot before *Enterprise* arrived. At 1:50 A.M., Rear Admiral Daniel J. Callaghan's task group, composed of two heavy cruisers, three light cruisers, and eight destroyers collided with Abe's force of two battleships, one cruiser, and fourteen destroyers off Lunga Point. Callaghan led his group straight through the wedge-shaped Japanese formation and lost his life in the opening minutes of the engagement. The light cruiser *Atlanta* and three destroyers were so badly damaged that at daybreak the navy scuttled those not sunk. Other American ships also suffered damage, and the crippled light cruiser *Juneau* went down during the afternoon when the submarine *I-22* ventured into Ironbottom Sound and sank her. During the 15-minute night fight, the Japanese lost only two destroyers, but the battleship *Hiei* sustained 85 hits. With damaged steering, she staggered north off Savo Island.

At dawn on November 13, *Enterprise* stood about 280 miles south of Henderson Field. Kinkaid had not learned of the battle off Lunga Point and was more interested in finding *Junyo* and *Hiyo*. At daylight he launched SBD search planes, but he also sent eight torpedo-armed Avengers to Henderson Field. When approaching Guadalcanal, Flight Leader Lieutenant Al Coffin swept north of the island and when east of Savo Island sighted the crippled *Hiei*. In the distance, Coffin also observed Zeros escorting Vals and Kates and concluded that *Junyo* and *Hiyo* must be somewhere in the area.

While climbing to gain altitude, Coffin split his Avengers into two four-plane sections to anvil the battleship. They broke off and dove at 250 knots, one section on *Hiei*'s starboard, the other on her port. At 150 feet, all eight pilots throttled back, aligned *Hiei* in their hooded sights, and at a thousand yards dropped their load of unpredictable Mark 13 torpedoes. Once again, three torpedoes appeared to hit the target but may have detonated before contact. One torpedo so disarranged *Hiei*'s steerage that she could only circle. For the rest of the day planes from *Enterprise* and Henderson Field pummeled the injured battleship with bombs and torpedoes. Years later, the Japanese reported that only three torpedoes exploded on contact; the others were either duds or exploded prematurely. At nightfall, the crew scuttled *Hiei*. Faulty American ordnance and poor targeting could not sink her.

Admiral Abe withdrew without having shelled Henderson Field, and the loss of *Hiei* infuriated Yamamoto. He wasted no time relieving Abe from sea command.

By now, Yamamoto should have suspected that Nimitz had broken his code. Every move he made had been miraculously parried. Whatever his concerns may have been after failing to soften up Henderson Field, he continued to pursue his plans to reinforce Guadalcanal.

While Abe's bloodied force withdrew up the Slot, Admiral Kondo's Attack Group came down the Slot, borrowing Abe's ships along the way. Vice Admiral Gunichi Mikawa's Support Group took an easterly route around the Solomons, while Rear Admiral Raizo Tanaka's 11 troop-bearing transports and 11 destroyers came directly down the Slot. The Japanese came in force, and why should they not? Yamamoto believed that after damaging Callaghan's force there would not be many enemy vessels around to challenge the assault. Kondo's group consisted of the battleship *Kirishima*, three heavy cruisers, one light cruiser, and eleven destroyers. Mikawa brought two heavy cruisers, a light cruiser, and four destroyers to bombard Henderson Field after midnight. Tanaka did not want to expose his transports until Mikawa neutralized the airfield.

Early on the morning of November 14, Mikawa's cruisers and destroyers opened on Henderson Field and after firing 1,000 shells withdrew. The bombardment missed the bomber strip and barely touched the fighter runway. At dawn, six Avengers and seven SBDs flown by *Enterprise* and Marine pilots attacked the heavy cruiser *Kinugasa*, blew open her hull, and set her on fire.

An hour later, two search planes sighted Mikawa's force just as 17 SBDs lifted off *Enterprise*'s deck. At 9:15 A.M., the two search planes dove on the wounded *Kinugasa*, scored two hits, and set her on fire again. Thirty minutes later, *Enterprise*'s SBDs arrived and bombed the cruisers *Isuzu* and *Chokai*. While returning to Henderson Field, Dauntless pilots looked down just as *Kinugasa*'s bow tilted upward and slipped beneath the waves.

While *Enterprise*'s SBDs were striking Mikawa's force, search planes from Henderson Field sighted Tanaka's transports in the Slot. An hour later, two planes from *Enterprise* spotted the same ships, dove on a big transport, and damaged it. During the melee, American pilots engaged aircraft from *Hiyo*, which they suspected was somewhere to the north.

Planes from *Enterprise* joined marine flyers from Henderson Field and struck the transports. Kinkaid decided to "shoot the works" and sent every plane he could put into the air but 18 Wildcats for CAP. Only four Japanese transports survived the air attack. Despite the disaster, Tanaka continued south with the remnants of his convoy and lost the remaining four transports the following day.

Because Tanaka did not retire, Admiral Kondo pushed his group down the Slot to support the landing of the Hiroshima Division at Cape Esperance. Mikawa believed he had destroyed most of Henderson's planes, but the air action during the day over Ironbottom Sound changed Kondo's mind. Angry and misinformed, Kondo felt duty-bound to destroy the airfield and started down the Slot. Had he reached Guadalcanal, he would have caught *Enterprise*'s planes on the ground because Kinkaid had taken the carrier south and left his aircraft at Henderson Field.

Around nightfall, Admiral Lee's TF-64, composed of the battleships *South Dakota* and *Washington* and four destroyers, slipped into Ironbottom Sound and began searching for Japanese transports. At 11:00 P.M., radar operators reported ships coming down the Slot. Fifteen minutes later, firing began off Savo Island and continued to intensify. Lee soon realized that the ships were not transports but Kondo's attack group. In another wild midnight battle, Lee's TF-64 sank the battleship *Kirishima* and the destroyer *Ayanami* at the cost of three destroyers and considerable damage to *South Dakota*. Kondo, completely shocked by the unexpected reception, withdrew up the Slot, leaving Tanaka to fend for himself.

The naval battle for Guadalcanal gave the IJN its second worst day of the war, eclipsed only by the Battle of Midway. Yamamoto lost two battleships, *Hiei* and *Kirishima*, one heavy cruiser, three destroyers, and eleven transports. The transports alone put another 77,608 tons of shipping into Ironbottom Sound. Only 2,000 of the 10,000-man Hiroshima Division embarked for Guadalcanal landed. When Halsey received the news, he bluntly quipped, "We've got the bastards licked!"[1] Halsey was right. On January 4, 1943, IGH issued orders to abandon Guadalcanal.

With help from *Enterprise*, the Marine Corps held Guadalcanal and permanently checked Japan's plans of conquest and expansion. Yamamoto dolefully admitted to a friend, "I do not know what to do next."[2] The turning point had come.

CHAPTER 10

Refining Carrier Tactics

The navy learned from its battles, but changes took time. For four weeks, Admiral Halsey held onto Guadalcanal and the South Pacific with a scratch team of cruisers and destroyers. He kept *Enterprise* in reserve at Nouméa for repairs but would use her if needed. He agreed with other air admirals that carriers should work in pairs, not individually, so he waited for the return of *Saratoga,* soon to be on her way.

On November 26, 1942, Halsey received his fourth star. He removed non-aviator Kinkaid from command of *Enterprise,* put him back in charge of a cruiser division, and turned TF-16 over to aviator Rear Admiral "Ted" Sherman, who commanded *Lexington* during the Battle of the Coral Sea. Admiral King recalled Kinkaid from the South Pacific and replaced him with Rear Admiral Carleton H. Wright. Halsey did not like the change. It came at a time when Kinkaid, an expert in cruiser tactics, was to execute a battle plan that four days later developed into the Battle of Tassafaronga, from which Wright limped away with one cruiser sunk and other ships damaged.

In mid-December, Rear Admiral DeWitt C. Ramsey sailed into Nouméa with a second carrier group organized around *Saratoga.* "Duke" Ramsey, another airman, and Halsey were old friends, having flown together since 1927. By the beginning of 1943, Halsey's force was as strong as ever, and more ships were on the way.

Admiral Nimitz had been the unlucky victim of peacetime politics. In 1936, the navy had given construction of battleships higher priority than carriers. Finally, on the last day of 1942, *Essex* (CV-9) went into commission at Newport News. Five months would pass before she reached the Pacific, and nine more of her class would follow. *Essex* scaled out at 27,100 tons, length 872 feet, beam 147 feet, and draft 28 feet 7 inches. Four propeller shafts generated 150,000 horsepower and pushed the flattop at 33 knots. Her AA consisted of 5"/38 guns, 40-mm Bofors, and 20-mm Oerlikon light machine guns. She carried 103 planes and a complement of 360 officers and 3,088 enlisted men. Between the commissioning of

Hornet on October 20, 1941, and the commissioning of *Essex* in December 1942, not a single fleet carrier had been commissioned.

On January 14, 1943, *Independence* (CVL-22), the first of the navy's nine light aircraft carriers, went into service at New York. CVLs were conversions from light cruisers. It came as quite a shock to the New York Shipbuilding Company when on January 10, 1942, the firm received orders from the Navy Department to finish the cruiser *Amsterdam* as a light carrier, and *Amsterdam* became *Independence*. The precedent harkened back to the 1920s when two 45,000-ton battle-cruisers became the 33,000-ton *Lexington* and *Enterprise*.

Issuing the order was easier than complying with it. Cruisers had to be ripped apart and rebuilt to support a flight deck, which made the ship top-heavy. Builders added beam-broadening blisters to improve the ship's stability. To compensate for the weight of the island built on the starboard side, blisters on the port side were filled with concrete. Four funnels, looking oddly out of place, dispersed stack gases off both sides of the stern. The new 11,000-ton *Independence*-class carriers shaped out at 622 feet 6 inches long, 109 feet 2 inches wide, with a draft of 26 feet. The engines fed 100,000 shaft horsepower into four propellers that despite the added weight drove the flattops at 32 knots. Because they were originally built as cruisers with knife-edged bows, *Independence*-class carriers sacrificed 50 feet of flight deck. Jammed for space, they carried only two 5-inch guns, standard AA, 35–40 planes (less than half the number of *Essex*), and 1,569 men. *Independence* reached Pearl Harbor in July 1943, six months after commissioning.

Then the carrier dam began to break. In August, the new *Lexington* (CV-16) and the light carriers *Princeton* (CVL-23) and *Belleau Wood* (CVL-24) arrived, followed in September by *Cowpens* (CVL-25) and *Monterey* (CVL-26). Manning them became a problem. Hundreds of enlisted men reported for duty directly from boot camp the morning the ships went into commission. Most men had never been on an oceangoing vessel, and most CVLs sailed with only 70 percent of their complement. Nimitz dipped into his veterans at Pearl Harbor to fill the crews. Manpower problems were aggravated by demands in the Atlantic, where a dozen *Bogue*- and *Sangamon*-class escort carriers became available at the same time.

Japan could not match America's carrier-building capacity but they tried. During the last six months of 1942, the IJN commissioned the CVL *Ryuho* and the CVE *Chuyo*. During the first six months of 1943, they commissioned none. Japan started the war with eleven carriers and by January 1943 had lost six of them. During the next 32 months, they attempted to build 12 more.

In January 1943, Halsey received two *Sangamon*-class escort carriers, *Suwannee* (CVE-27) and *Chenango* (CVE-28). Converted from merchant tankers and commissioned in September, the 11,400-ton escorts were shorter (553 feet), wider (114 feet 3 inches), and heavier than light aircraft carriers. Their 18-knot speed prevented them from working with fast combat carriers. They were lightly armed, carried 30 planes (a mixture of Wildcats, Avengers, and Dauntlesses), and a complement of 1,080 men. When they arrived in the South Pacific, Halsey moved them into TF-18, Rear Admiral Robert C. "Ike" Giffen's cruiser command. Giffen had just arrived from Casablanca, where he had seen no air action, and Halsey wanted him to "get his feet wet in the Pacific."[1] He ordered Giffen to join forces with the four-destroyer "Cactus Striking Force" for a daylight sweep up the Slot. Instead of sending the slower escort carriers ahead for CAP, Giffen left them behind. On January 29, off Rennell Island, Japanese land-based Bettys intercepted TF-18 and torpedoed the heavy cruiser *Chicago*.

Chenango and *Suwannee*, joined by *Enterprise*, came up to protect the disabled *Chicago*, which Giffen was attempting to tow to safety. A Japanese snooper reported the position of *Enterprise*. Soon a dozen land-based Bettys began looking for *Enterprise* but ran into planes from *Chenango* and *Suwannee*, so the Bettys turned back on the crippled *Chicago*. Wildcats knocked down 10 Bettys, but not quickly enough. Four torpedoes smacked into the hull of *Chicago* and sank her. Three days later, the Japanese began evacuating Guadalcanal.

Halsey blamed Giffen for the loss of *Chicago*, citing his mishandling of *Chenango* and *Suwanee* as the cause. After all, Giffen was a cruiser man. Nimitz took him off Halsey's hands and put him back in a battle fleet where he belonged.

Knowing of Nimitz's carrier shortage, Admiral Sir Dudley Pound, Britain's First Sea Lord, approached Admiral King and proposed sending the HMS *Victorious* to Halsey. King was not enthusiastic about the offer, but because of the condition of *Enterprise* and the scarcity of flattops he agreed to find a place for her.

Victorious carried 45 planes, half the number of *Enterprise*. The Fulmar fighters and Albacore torpedo planes had to be disembarked and replaced with American-made Wildcats and Avengers. Avionics, aircraft parts, and communications equipment all had to be changed, and every British pilot had to be retrained. On May 17, 1943, *Victorious* arrived at Nouméa. On that day, *Enterprise* went into drydock at Pearl Harbor. For the next four months, the reconditioned *Saratoga* and HMS *Victorious* kept close company but saw limited action as marines worked through the Solomons.

Nimitz understood that the first new fleet carriers for the Pacific would not be ready until mid-1943, and any major campaign in the Central Pacific required carrier parity with Japan. The JCS in Washington used the time to plot a four-pronged offensive, the objectives being the Aleutians, the Solomons, the Central Pacific, and the Southwest Pacific (New Guinea). Quite by accident, Admiral Yamamoto also became a target. During the planning phase, navy code-breakers discovered Yamamoto's itinerary for an inspection tour. Discussions ensued over the possibility of eliminating him. "It's down in Halsey's bailiwick," Nimitz said. "If there's a way, he'll find it."[2] Admiral Mitscher, Commander Air Solomons, arranged a reception. On April 18, 16 Lockheed P-38 Lightnings from Henderson Field intercepted two bombers transporting Yamamoto and his staff to

Kahili, Buin, and shot them down, killing everyone on board. More than six months passed before the Japanese decided on a successor, Admiral Mineichi Koga, and despite warnings from Rabaul that America had broken the Japanese code, IGH declared the code unbreakable.

To deal with the Aleutians problem, Nimitz put Admiral Kinkaid in charge of the North Pacific Force. The targets were Japanese-occupied Attu and Kiska, and Admiral Hosagawa's battle group. Given only one escort carrier, the *Bogue*-class *Nassau* (CVE-16) for CAP, Kinkaid used her for reconnaissance and close air support. He wiped out the enemy on Attu in May and successfully ended the campaign in July.

At the opposite end of the Pacific, Admiral Halsey and General MacArthur met with Nimitz in March and worked out a plan. As marines, supported by Halsey's Third Fleet, moved up the Solomons, airfields would be captured to neutralize Rabaul. Meanwhile, MacArthur's Sixth Army would leapfrog along the north coast of New Guinea toward the Celebes Sea.

For Halsey, the logical place for airfields was on Bougainville—200 miles from Rabaul—but to get there required the capture of New Georgia's airfield at Munda Point and Kolombangara's airfield at Vila. Halsey organized TF-36 under himself, which consisted of 2 battleship divisions, 9 light cruisers, escort carriers, 13 destroyers, 4 minelayers, and 11 submarines. Rear Admiral Richmond Kelly Turner commanded the amphibious force, and Admiral Mitscher provided CAP from Henderson Field for simultaneous assaults on New Georgia and Rendova.

CAP had dramatically changed since the early days of Guadalcanal. Grumman F4F-3 Wildcats gave way to new F6F-3 Hellcats, which had almost twice the horsepower and gave the navy a heavier, faster, and tougher fighter. In combat, a green pilot could handle a Hellcat much easier than a Wildcat. F6Fs came with a belly tank for greater range, six improved .50-caliber machineguns, and a greater supply of ammunition. They also could carry a 1,000-pound bomb and double as a fighter-bomber.

Even more remarkable were the new Chance-Vought F4U Corsairs, a gull-winged fighter that could climb faster than a Zero, cruise at 341 mph, and fly twice as far as a Wildcat. The navy, however, preferred Hellcats because Corsairs caused deck-landing accidents. The Marine Corps took the F4Us off the hands of the navy, added them to Henderson Field, and turned them into the most versatile fighters in the Pacific.

The navy also tried Curtiss SB2C Helldivers, which could carry twice the bomb load of a Dauntless. Pilots did not like them, and for good reason. The "Big-Tailed Beast" tended to shed its wings during a dive, tail-hooks failed on landing, and tail-wheels collapsed. Carrier commanders demanded that Helldivers be removed until Curtiss solved the problems. Until mid-1944, the Dauntless SBD-5 continued to be the navy's bomber, despite its slower speed and inability to fold its wings.

Without Yamamoto at the helm and nobody to fill the void, the IJN missed a marvelous opportunity to bring down carriers and knock Admiral Turner's

transports to pieces. Instead, Japan based their carrier planes at Rabaul and resumed a war of attrition they could not win.

On June 30, MacArthur launched his offensive on New Guinea, and Admiral
Turner and Major General John H. Hester put the first of 15,000 men ashore on
Rendova and New Georgia. *Saratoga* and *Victorious* remained well south of the
Solomons, available if needed. At first, all the trouble came from air attacks
delivered from Rabaul, but the new Hellcats and Corsairs exacted a heavy toll on
enemy planes.

On July 6, the Japanese decided to hold Kolombangara and dispatched reinforcements by destroyer. In a confused midnight naval battle in the Kula Gulf
that lasted until dawn, Rear Admiral Teruo Akiyama's "Tokyo Express" lost two
of its ten destroyers while disembarking the troops.

A week later another midnight action occurred off Kolombangara with the
same result, and more enemy troops filed ashore. American skippers were getting
a good taste of night fighting. When the Tokyo Express came down the Slot the
night of August 6, Commander Frederick Moosbrugger intercepted four destroyers in the Vella Gulf and sank three of them.

Admiral Halsey ran out of patience with the slow progress on New Georgia
and bolstered Hester's three army divisions with the 1st Marine Raider Regiment.
On August 5, after fierce jungle fighting, the Japanese abandoned Munda airfield,
but organized resistance continued for another three weeks. Halsey later declared,
"Our original plan called for 15,000 men to wipe out 9,000 Japs on New Georgia;
by the time the island was secured, we had sent in more than 50,000. When I look
back on [New Georgia] the smoke of charred reputations still makes me cough."[3]
Noting that many of the enemy had skipped across Kula Gulf to join Japanese
forces on Kolombangara, Halsey bypassed the island, leaving the garrison to rot.
On August 15, he leapfrogged to Vella Lavella Island, halfway between Bougainville and New Georgia—and took it with little cost.

Faced with unacceptable losses, especially in aircraft and destroyers, IGH
decided to reinforce the Solomons no longer. Halsey still had battles to fight for
the island chain, and some especially dirty jungle action ahead on Bougainville.
He conducted the Solomons operation without risking his carriers. Nor had the
Japanese risked theirs. Most of the surface action occurred between cruisers and
destroyers.

Admiral Koga, the new commander of the Japanese Combined Fleet, expected Bougainville to be attacked. He considered sending the carriers *Shokaku*,
Zuikaku, and *Zuiho* to Rabaul, but they were all at sea training fresh pilots. In late
October, he began to worry that if Bougainville fell, his massive air and sea base
at Rabaul would be neutralized—exactly what Halsey intended. Instead of sending
carriers, Koga detached seven heavy cruisers, one light cruiser, four destroyers,
and a train of support vessels—nineteen ships in all—under Vice Admiral Takeo
Kurita to reinforce Vice Admiral Tomoshige Samejima's Eighth Fleet at Rabaul.
After Koga dispatched the force, he developed second thoughts and decided to
include his carriers, but they were off Japan.

On November 4, four days after the 3rd Marine Division went ashore on Bougainville, an American search plane flying over Rabaul's harbor reported a buildup of Japanese warships. When Halsey received the message, his first inclination was to form a powerful naval force and deal the enemy a fatal blow, but Nimitz was preparing for the invasion of the Gilbert Islands, scheduled to begin in three weeks, and had committed Halsey's carriers to the operation. Halsey managed to retain Ted Sherman's TF-38, built around *Saratoga* and *Princeton*, which had been left with him for the Bougainville invasion. Nimitz now wanted them, but after Halsey explained the importance of attacking Rabaul, Nimitz agreed. Besides, Sherman was near Rabaul and could be in position to launch a strike the following morning.

Every American pilot balked at the thought of flying over Rabaul, one of the most heavily defended bases in the Pacific. Antiaircraft guns ringed the harbor. From six airfields Zeros protected the harbor's airspace. The Japanese believed Rabaul's defensive shield could not be penetrated, and American pilots worried those claims might be true. Any air strike would be dangerous. Sherman's two flattops were under strength, having only 22 Dauntlesses, 23 Avengers, and 52 Hellcats to protect the strike force and provide CAP. Major General George C. Kenney promised to send AAF bombers from the Southwest Pacific Air command in Australia, but Sherman knew they could not get there until after the carrier strike.

At 9:00 A.M. on November 5, 230 miles southeast of Rabaul, Sherman launched his strike. The sky was perfectly clear, and from 20 miles pilots could see 28 cruisers and destroyers lined up neatly in the harbor. Commander Henry H. Caldwell, leading the strike in an Avenger, kept the Hellcats high above the bombers. At 11:10, the Dauntlesses swung over St. George's Channel in tight formation, picked their targets, and screamed down through bursting flak. The Japanese fighters, ranging above, waited too long, and when they attacked found themselves riddled by their own AA. The attack came as a complete surprise to the Japanese, who were caught flat-footed fueling Kurita's vessels.

Caldwell knew his air group had to strike hard, fast, and hurry away. Bombs struck the heavy cruisers *Atago*, *Chikuma*, *Maya*, *Mogami*, and *Takao*, and the light cruiser *Agano*. Avengers torpedoed the light cruiser *Noshiro* and the destroyer *Fujinami*. Near misses added to the toll. Minutes later the Americans were gone. Shortly after noon, 27 B-24s flew over the smoke-filled harbor. The pilots found no planes on the ground because they were all searching for Sherman's carriers, so they dropped their payloads on shore installations.

Every carrier plane had been hit, but only five Hellcats and five Dauntlesses failed to return. Some planes were beyond repair, so Sherman ordered them jettisoned. Lieutenant H. M. Crockett's Hellcat had 200 holes. Many flyers returned with wounds, including the two men of Caldwell's crew.

Halsey's gamble paid off. The strike temporarily crippled operations at Rabaul. Admiral Koga, however, enjoyed a short celebration when Admiral Samejima falsely reported, "One large [American] carrier blown up and sunk,

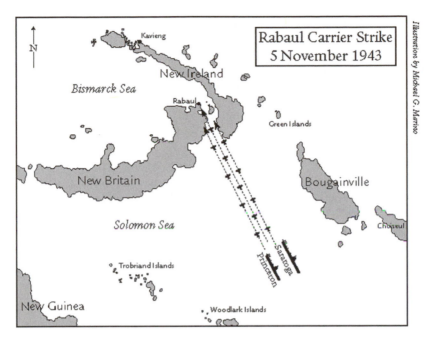

Rabaul Carrier Strike, November 5, 1943. (Michael G. Marino)

one medium carrier set ablaze and later sunk, and two heavy cruisers and one [light] cruiser and destroyer sunk."[4] When the smoke finally settled over Rabaul, Koga eventually learned the truth when six cruisers and a half dozen destroyers steamed to Truk for repairs, and the heavy cruiser *Mogami* went into drydock at Japan. Sherman's small carrier force had stopped a major Japanese offensive and made it possible for Halsey to turn his full attention to mopping up the Solomons.

Leapfrogging tactics worked so well in the Solomons that Nimitz decided to apply them to the Pacific. The strategy was not new. Marine Colonel "Pete" Ellis originated the idea back in 1921 under the code-name Plan Orange, but in 1921 neither Ellis nor anyone else in the navy envisioned the importance of carriers.

In August 1943, Nimitz knew the time had come to revamp the entire carrier command system. He gave Vice Admiral John H. Towers, his number one man on matters concerning naval air, the task of determining how best to operate the Pacific Fleet's carrier divisions. Towers assembled a committee of three admirals, captains of all the fleet carriers, and several staff officers to discuss flattop tactics. They all agreed that to launch far-flung strikes in the Pacific required changes in command and control.

The Pacific Fleet now contained six fleet carriers, five light carriers, and eight escort carriers. Each group had different capabilities, and Towers sought ways to effectively use them. No one could fully agree on how to integrate light carriers with fleet carriers. Captain Donald B. Duncan made the point that large flattops carried too many planes and suggested the number be reduced from 90 planes to 78 Dauntlesses and Hellcats, and that CVLs carry only Avengers and Hellcats. His suggestion received support, but Towers questioned whether aircraft could be reduced during Central Pacific operations because lost planes could not be readily replaced. Japanese aircraft from mutually supporting atolls would outnumber carrier planes. He also expected Koga's flattops to contest Pacific operations.

Nimitz did not have unlimited time to make several very important decisions. In Washington, the JCS had already directed him to seize Tarawa, Makin, and Betio in the Gilbert Islands by mid-November 1943, and to assault the principal islands of the Marshalls in early 1944. Nimitz needed an air base in the Gilberts for photographing the heavier defenses of the Marshalls, and he wanted land-based planes to neutralize enemy airfields before amphibious landings began.

With time short, Nimitz decided on an experiment. With the scale of operations planned for the Central Pacific, he abandoned the system of organizing every flattop as an independent task force and began coupling carriers into a single task force. He chose Japanese-controlled Marcus Atoll as the test site and in August 1943 sent TF-15, composed of *Essex, Yorktown* (CV-10), and *Independence*, to shake up the island.

Naval aviator Rear Admiral Charles A. Pownall commanded the group, and Rear Admiral Alfred E. Montgomery collaborated as an observer. Pownall launched the attack at night, timing the first of four strikes to occur at dawn. Not one Japanese plane got off the ground. The strikes silenced the island's AA batteries, clobbered ships in the harbor, and blew up shore installations. Pownall and Montgomery found that operating three carriers in circular fashion improved the group's AA defenses. Of equal importance, communications officers reported that the new four-channel VHF voice radio sets were remarkably interference free, which had been a chronic problem for flyers since the beginning of the war. The planes also were equipped with new airborne radar that enabled flyers to target Marcus Atoll in the dark. *Yorktown* lost three Hellcats and an Avenger to AA fire, but Pownall believed the lessons learned from the action outweighed the cost.

When Pownall returned to Pearl Harbor, he learned that Admiral Spruance had been given command of the Fifth Fleet and Operation Galvanic, the assault of Tarawa Atoll. Spruance explained that for the first island-hopping campaign, Pownall would command TF-50's 11 carriers. Pownall went to Vice Admiral Towers to share the good news. Towers had not been informed of Nimitz's reorganization plan and merely replied that such an arrangement made no sense because there was no need for an overall carrier commander. Towers also believed if Nimitz went ahead with consolidating carrier command, Admiral Ted Sherman (class of 1910), Montgomery (1912), and especially Radford (1916) were better qualified. Pownall's (1910) seniority still carried weight in the navy, but for the present neither Nimitz nor Spruance made any announcements.

Nimitz's code-breakers learned that strategists at IGH, using the same logic as the JCS, expected trouble and were reinforcing Tarawa and Betio with fighters, Mavis flying boats for reconnaissance, and long-range Bettys flown by pilots trained in night aerial torpedo tactics. Nimitz could no longer spend time deliberating. Tarawa and Makin had to be assaulted as soon as possible. In mid-September, Nimitz directed Pownall, who was already at sea with three new carriers—*Yorktown* (CV-10), *Lexington* (CV-16), and *Cowpens* (CVL-25)—to pummel Tarawa and Makin's airfields. Pownall launched seven strikes, wiped out the Bettys and Mavis flying boats, and obtained low-level oblique photographs of the atoll's beaches, which were rushed to Marine Corps amphibious planners. He described the strike as a good training exercise but recommended that the number of planes on large carriers be reduced to 36 Hellcats, 30 Dauntlesses, and 19 Avengers. Pownall's pilots could not see the enemy's well-hidden defenses buried in the ground, layered with logs and sand.

Nimitz ordered another experiment, this time with three CVs and three CVLS under the command of Admiral Montgomery. Nimitz chose Wake Island. Because Pownall had struck the southern flank of the Marshalls and Wake lay on the northern flank, Nimitz hoped the Japanese would interpret the Wake strike as a precursor to an amphibious landing and turn their attention away from Tarawa and the Marshalls. Wake had only one airfield with three runways but enough AA to give attacking American pilots a boisterous welcome.

Montgomery divided his six carriers into three task groups of two each, using the flagship *Essex* to coordinate tactics. Each group had its own flag officer. The experiment was important because it contained the largest group of carriers ever assembled by the U.S. Navy, but three were CVLs with mostly green pilots.

Montgomery sailed from Pearl on September 29, and early on the morning of October 5 came within striking range of Wake. Before launching, the column divided into three task groups. Hellcats from *Independence* and *Belleau Wood* provided CAP. Avengers patrolled far and wide in a precautionary search for Japanese surface vessels. All went well until Montgomery tried a tactic suggested by Admiral Towers—launching a four-ship strike from *Essex*, *Yorktown*, *Lexington*, and *Cowpens* in two air groups. Montgomery planned to hit Wake's airfield a half-hour before sunrise, but radar picked up Japanese planes already in the air. This forced Montgomery to rearrange his deck to put more Hellcats in the air. During the dogfight, inexperienced American pilots developed respect for the fast Zeros, and Japanese pilots soon discovered that the navy's new Hellcat was a far more dangerous fighter than the Wildcat. Rookie pilots paid the highest price in planes and personnel. Nimitz had the foresight to have the submarine *Shark* in the area to pick up downed pilots, but subs had not been equipped with VHF voice radio equipment to find the flyers.

The two-day battering of Wake Island cost Montgomery 13 combat and 14 operational losses. Considering that 738 sorties were flown, the losses were light. Wake Island took a pasting, and Montgomery returned to Pearl Harbor with another list of recommended changes. He praised *Shark*'s lifeguarding efforts but recommended that subs be fitted with VHF radios. He also commended the circular aircraft screen, which happened to be a prewar tactic developed by Nimitz. Montgomery also used new deck catapults with good success, and his only complaint concerned an old problem: inadequate night training caused operational losses.

Nimitz turned the recommendations of Pownall and Montgomery over to his staff and said there would be no more training missions. The time had come for action.

While Admiral Spruance put the final touches on Operation Galvanic with Admiral Turner in charge of the assault force, and Major General Holland M. Smith commander of the newly established V Amphibious Corps, Admiral Koga was trying to divine the movements of the Pacific Fleet from his headquarters at Truk. Montgomery's Wake Island strike puzzled him, so on October 17 he sent *Shokaku*, *Zuikaku*, and *Zuiho* to Eniwetok Atoll to await developments. When none occurred, he recalled them. Koga then turned his attention to the Solomons and considered sending the carriers to Rabaul. When Pearl Harbor code-breakers deciphered Koga's communications, Nimitz informed Halsey. This led to Admiral Sherman's November 5 strike on Rabaul, which tore up Kurita's cruisers and destroyers and left Admiral Samejima without a fleet. Koga still had his flattops but not Kurita's cruisers. Sherman's carrier strike occurred fifteen days before D day on Tarawa.

On November 13, while Marines mopped up the Solomons and MacArthur's forces advanced along the northern coast of New Guinea, planes from American aircraft carriers began pounding Japanese installations in the Gilbert and Marshall islands. Shortly before air strikes began, Spruance put Pownall officially in charge of TF-50, the Fast Carrier Task Force, and divided it into four groups, each with a special mission. Cruising at 30 knots, the only ships that could keep up with the carriers were the newer battleships and cruisers. Older ships and escort carriers were relegated to bombarding enemy shore positions, tactical targets, and supporting amphibious landings. Nimitz intended fast carrier groups to range far at sea, strike island airfields, and seek battle with enemy surface groups. Spruance, however, differed with Nimitz's tactical concepts, preferring to keep the fast carriers nearby until his assault force was ashore and supply ships unloaded.

Pownall personally commanded Carrier Interceptor Group (TG 50.1), which included the new carriers *Yorktown* (CV-10) and *Lexington* (CV-16), the CVL *Cowpens*, and supporting battleship groups. Beginning on November 19, Pownall's orders were to bomb airfields in the Marshalls and maintain air supremacy against enemy flights attempting to aid Tarawa.

Rear Admiral Arthur W. Radford commanded Northern Carrier Group (TG 50.2), composed of *Enterprise*, the CVLs *Belleau Wood* and *Monterey*, and another gunship group. On November 19–20, TG 50.2 bombed and shelled Makin, opening the way for marines to go ashore against light resistance. Radford spent the next several days fighting off enemy air attacks.

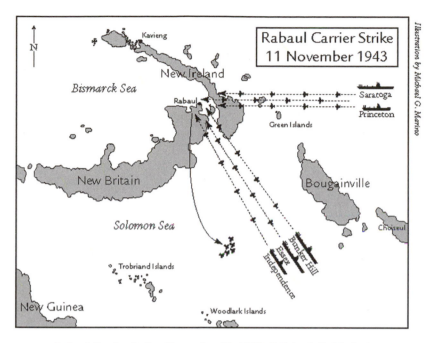

Rabaul Carrier Strike, November 11, 1943. (Michael G. Marino)

Rear Admiral Montgomery commanded the Southern Carrier Group (TG 50.3), composed of *Essex* (CV-9), *Bunker Hill* (CV-17), and *Independence*. On November 11, he rendezvoused with Sherman's Southern Attack Force (TF-38) to strike Rabaul. Koga had sent most of his carrier planes to Rabaul for an all-out attack on American shipping off Bougainville. When Japanese radar picked up the incoming American strike, Admiral Samejima got most of the carrier planes, numbering about 120, and many of his own aircraft into the air.

Samejima's search planes located Montgomery's Task Group and soon the first enemy bombers, some 40 miles out, registered on *Bunker Hill*'s radarscope. Hellcats performing CAP went to work on the incoming Kates but could not down all of them. Halsey had taken Montgomery's cruisers to support the Bougainville beachhead, leaving only destroyers and the carriers to provide AA coverage. Montgomery bellowed over the loudspeaker on *Bunker Hill*, "Man your guns and shoot those bastards out of the sky!"[5] Fighters and AA shot down 115 Japanese planes and killed 86 of Koga's best pilots. The Japanese admiral now had too few planes for his carriers at Truk. Had Montgomery and Sherman known this, they may have steamed over to Truk and destroyed Koga's flattops, which were sitting ducks, but Spruance wanted Montgomery available on November 19 to bomb preselected targets on Betio and Tarawa.

Rear Admiral Ted Sherman commanded the Relief Carrier Group (TG 50.4), *Saratoga* and the CVL *Princeton*, better known as Halsey's Southern Attack

Force (TF-38). After striking Rabaul on November 5 and again with Montgomery on November 11, Halsey declared that "Five air groups ... ought to change the name of Rabaul to Rubble," and it very nearly did.[6] Sherman then separated from Montgomery and on November 19 struck enemy airfields on Nauru, after which he returned to Nouméa to pick up garrison troops for Makin and Tarawa.

Admiral Koga had a rare opportunity to take his three-carrier battle force to sea and strike each of Pownall's widely scattered task groups separately, but Sherman and Montgomery's raid on Rabaul neutered Koga by depriving him of planes and forced him to stay at Truk.

Nimitz and Spruance now believed they had the necessary resources in place to launch the island-hopping campaign. The war with Japan now shifted to three fronts: MacArthur's Southwest Pacific Force in New Guinea, Halsey's South Pacific Force in the Solomons, and Spruance's Central Pacific Force operating out of Pearl Harbor.

For the Japanese, there would soon be little left but honorable death.

CHAPTER 11

Island-Hopping in the Pacific

Nimitz wanted airfields, and the best way to get them was to take them from the enemy. He especially wanted the Marianas, from which long-range bombers could reach Japan. Going directly to the Marianas created problems because of enemy bases in the Marshalls, and going directly to the Marshalls created problems because of enemy bases in the Gilberts. So the JCS decided to clean the Japanese out of the Gilberts and make use of the airfields on Tarawa and Makin before attacking the Marshalls.

The Marshalls lay about 500 miles northwest of the Gilberts. The two island groups were mutually supportive so long as their airfields remained operational. Capturing the Gilberts would provide airfields for strikes against the Marshalls, which in turn would provide airfields for strikes against the Marianas, and capturing the Marianas would isolate Truk and provide airfields for strikes against the Carolines, Iwo Jima, Okinawa, the Philippines, and Japan. Every leap toward the Marianas represented a leap toward Japan.

Montgomery's October 5–6, 1943, air strike against Wake Island baffled the Japanese high command and reduced the flow of reinforcements to the Gilberts. Aircraft usually based on Mili Atoll were flown off to replace losses at Rabaul. Koga could not decide where take his carriers because Sherman's strike at Nauru and Pownall's strike in the Marshalls kept him confused. Pownall wanted to continue through the Marshalls and bomb the airfields on Wotje, Maloelap, and Kwajalein, which were in range of Tarawa, but Admiral Spruance wanted the fleet carriers back to cover the landings. This later proved to be a strategic error with consequences.

On November 20, 1943, Spruance launched the assault on the Gilberts, and a detachment from the 27th Army Division went ashore on Makin. What should have taken one day took four. There were only 284 Japanese naval infantry on the atoll, but they all fought to the last man.

On Tarawa's Betio Island, the 2nd Marine Division waded into stiff resistance because a strongly entrenched enemy force of 4,500 naval infantry had weathered the softening-up strikes in bombproofs. Carrier support provided little help, and it took marines six days to blast the enemy out of their dugouts. Americans paid dearly with 990 dead and 2,391 wounded. Only 17 Japanese defenders surrendered.

There were lessons to be learned, both on land and at sea. Spruance decided that keeping the big flattops so close to the action was not a good idea. Islands under attack attracted enemy aircraft and submarines. *Liscome Bay* (CVE-16) operated near the center of conflict and was launching planes when torpedoed by *I-175*. A single torpedo, or perhaps two, blew the insides out of the little carrier and took 614 lives, including the life of Rear Admiral Henry Mullinix, commanding the air group.

On November 12, Koga had only 46 planes in the Marshalls, having sent the others to Rabaul. During the next eight days, the planes returned, including 16 Bettys with night-trained pilots. At dusk on November 20, snoopers sighted Montgomery's TG 50.3 about 15 miles southwest of Betio. In the fading light, Hellcats from *Bunker Hill* pounced on the Bettys, but the enemy had flown in low and at close range dropped their torpedoes. One struck *Independence* aft and knocked the propeller shafts out of alignment. In all, 17 men died and 43 suffered injuries. *Independence* departed under escort to the nearest navy base, 700 miles away.

Admiral Radford's *Enterprise* from TG 50.2 also got into trouble from night-flying Bettys. Although Spruance declared Tarawa and Makin secure on November 23, the area still attracted snoopers. On the night of November 26, *Enterprise*'s radarscope registered bogies. Lieutenant Commander Edward H. "Butch" O'Hare, commanding Air Group 6 and flying a Hellcat, volunteered to go airborne and intercept the incoming Bettys. Lieutenant Commander John L. Phillips, flying a TBF-1C Avenger equipped with a new model of intercept radar, and Ensign Warren Skon, flying wing on Phillips with a Hellcat, agreed to make it a threesome. O'Hare had already inked a remarkable record, having become the navy's first ace. With directional guidance from Phillips's airborne radar and shipboard controllers, O'Hare vectored on the Bettys. For a short while, the three-pronged attack worked precisely as planned. After shooting down two Bettys, Phillips, Skon, and O'Hare regrouped and began searching for more. A plane suddenly passed between Skon and O'Hare. Phillips's turret gunner fired 30 rounds. O'Hare disappeared, never to be found, leaving Admiral Radford to wonder who shot down America's first navy ace: Phillips's turret gunner or a Japanese Betty.

The bizarre outcome, tragic as it was, broke up a night attack of three Bettys targeting *Enterprise*. It also validated the importance of night interceptor squads, but those of the future would all be equipped with airborne radar.

With the Gilberts in American hands, Nimitz turned his attention to the Marshalls. For planning the next amphibious landing, he needed low-level oblique aerial photos of Kwajalein, Wotje, Maloelap, and Roi and told Pownall to strike the islands and get the pictures.

During carrier air operations in November 1942, Rear Admiral (later Admiral) Arthur W. Radford commanded Task Group 50.2 from the USS *Enterprise*. (U.S. Navy photo)

On December 1, Pownall headed for Kwajalein with his own task group (*Yorktown*, *Lexington*, and *Cowpens*) and with Montgomery's TG 50.3 (*Essex*, *Enterprise*, and *Belleau Wood*). Together, the flattops carried 193 Hellcats, 104 Dauntlesses, and 89 Avengers. Pownall decided to first neutralize the enemy airfield at Roi, but he cautiously withheld half of his planes. He then put Commander Ernest M. Snowden of *Yorktown* in charge of tactical air command. This made Snowden responsible for assigning specific targets to 249 planes over a lagoon 66 miles long by voice radio as the attack progressed, a virtual impossibility.

At 6:30 A.M. on December 4, Pownall launched the first strike. Radar on Roi picked up the incoming planes, sounded the alarm, and Zeros from Rear Admiral

An F6F Hellcat fighter prepares to take off from the new USS *Yorktown* (CV-10).
(U.S. Navy photo)

Monzo Akiyama's 6th Base Force took to the air. Snowden tried but failed to
contact the Hellcat leader from *Essex*, whose VHF set had failed. The confused
strike fell far short of its goal, and most of the bombs fell harmlessly into the
lagoon. The light cruiser *Isuzu* sustained damage and four freighters sank. The
Japanese lost about 50 planes, but there were plenty more untouched in camouflaged revetments. When Pownall received the action reports and discovered that
none of Akiyama's three airstrips had been damaged, he worried about repri-
sals. *Yorktown*'s captain, "Jocko" Clark, lobbied for another strike, arguing that
leaving the airfields untouched would invite air attacks. Pownall overruled Clark
and departed from Kwajalein without completing his mission. Clark responded
by pounding his chart desk and grumbling to his staff, "Goddammit, you can't
run away from airplanes with ships!"[1]

   With the task groups underway, Pownall decided on a passing attack on
Wotje's small airfield. At noon on December 4, as *Yorktown*'s Dauntlesses and
Hellcats took off, Kates from Roi and Maloelap began appearing on *Yorktown*'s
radar, just as Clark predicted. Concentrated AA fire shot down many and drove
others away, but several torpedoes came dangerously close to *Lexington* and
Yorktown. The air attack on Wotje netted only five enemy planes, and when the
flyers returned, Pownall attempted to exit the area before nightfall.

Forty minutes after sunset, 37 planes from Roi spotted Pownall's retiring carriers under a full moon and began dropping streams of flares to mark the task groups' course. Some Bettys carried airborne radar, which enabled enemy pilots to select targets in the dark. With the heavy stream of AA fire coming from escort vessels, Montgomery opted not to reveal his carriers' positions by opening fire. Pownall did the opposite, opening with every gun in the group. At 11:30, a Betty came in low and dropped a torpedo that jammed *Lexington*'s rudder, causing her to travel in circles. Mechanics straightened out the rudder but had to steer by manipulating her propellers. When the moon set at 1:27 A.M., Bettys faded from the radarscopes, and Pownall set a course for Pearl Harbor.

On December 23, after Nimitz reviewed photographs and read action reports from Pownall's strikes, including the comments of "Jocko" Clark, he went directly to his senior staff to discuss changes in fast carrier command. Admiral Towers, an ambitious man himself, recommended relieving Pownall and replacing him with Marc Mitscher, whose years of naval aviation experience traced back to *Langley*. The change involved the approval of Admiral King and triggered a massive reorganization. Mitscher had never commanded more than a single carrier (*Hornet*), which created questions in King's mind. Nimitz, however, wanted someone who would aggressively use the carriers, so he made Mitscher temporary commander, Fast Carrier Task Forces, Pacific Fleet, to see how he performed.

While TF-50 took a breather at Pearl, King and Nimitz also "adopted the principle that all major commanders in the Pacific Fleet who were non-aviators must have aviators as their chiefs of staff or seconds in command, and all major commanders who were aviators must have surface officers in the second position. By this principle, Mitscher would have to have a gunship officer as his chief of staff."[2]

The policy also created one of the best duos in the Pacific when Nimitz teamed Rear Admiral Willis A. Lee with Mitscher. "Putting 'Ching' Lee and 'Pete' Mitscher together was one of the smartest things the Navy ever did," Halsey recalled. "You had the best surface tactics and the best air tactics the world has ever known."[3]

Another meeting between Nimitz, King, Halsey, and planning chiefs at San Francisco concerned three topics: the Marianas and Japan's two massive air and naval bases in the Central Pacific, Rabaul and Truk. Forrest Sherman suggested bypassing Truk and concentrating on the Marianas. Halsey agreed with Sherman, and during a later conversation with King said that he saw "no need to storm Rabaul."[4] The idea took root at once. The Marianas became the primary target, and Truk and Rabaul were left to decay in the rear.

As more carriers arrived at Pearl, Nimitz wanted them deployed aggressively. He told Mitscher to finish the mission Pownall left undone in the Marshalls. No damage could be inflicted on the enemy by avoiding combat. Henceforth, American carriers were to be used as a strike force in every sense of the word.

Under Mitscher, TF-50 became TF-58 with four task groups: TG 58.1 with *Yorktown*, *Enterprise*, and *Belleau Wood*; TG 58.2 with *Essex* and the new carriers *Intrepid* (CV-11) and *Cabot* (CVL-27); TG 58.3 with *Bunker Hill*, *Cowpens*, and *Monterey*; and TG 58.4 with *Saratoga*, *Princeton*, and the new *Langley* (CVL-28). The temporary loss of *Lexington* and *Independence* created no reductions in carrier strength. Nimitz augmented the task groups with eight new fast battleships and dozens of cruisers, destroyers, service ships, and oilers.

On January 13, with everything in order, Mitscher transferred his gear to *Yorktown* and settled into the quarters previously occupied by Pownall. On the night of January 22, the last ships cleared the harbor. Admiral Turner's amphibious force of 84,000 marines and army infantry was on the way with Operation Flintlock set for the last day of the month. Mitscher had only a few days to soften up the Marshalls. On the morning of January 23, Nimitz looked down on Pearl Harbor from his headquarters on Makalapa Hill and observed that it was nearly empty. He would not see the carriers of TF-58 again until the end of the war.

The decision to assault Kwajalein and Roi before neutralizing Wotje and Maloelap could not have been made without carrier strength. Leaving nearby enemy air bases operational was always risky, but Operation Flintlock's planners believed that by going directly to Kwajalein and bypassing the outer Marshalls it would shorten the war and save American lives. What influenced the decision was a photograph taken during Pownall's November strike that showed an airstrip on Kwajalein that could be lengthened into a runway capable of accommodating heavy long-range bombers. If the airstrip could be secured quickly and expanded, then aircraft could be flown in to neutralize Wotje and Maloelap's airfields and relieve TF-58.

Mitscher did not want to use his carriers as a defensive weapon to shield Admiral Turner's amphibious forces during the Kwajalein assault. He believed in air supremacy. His carriers were offensive weapons, and he intended to use them to destroy enemy planes before they got off the ground. He also believed carriers should remain at sea, fueling and rearming as necessary, thereby avoiding the long respites and time-wasting inactivity by making the 2,000-mile trip to Pearl Harbor.

Unlike Pownall, Mitscher put together a plan to strike four Marshall Island airstrips simultaneously at daybreak on January 29, D day minus 2. He assigned Rear Admiral John W. Reeves's TG 58.1 to strike Maleolap, Montgomery's TG 58.2 to strike Roi, Ted Sherman's TG 58.3 to strike Kwajalein, and Rear Admiral Samuel P. Ginder's TG 58.4 to attack Wotje. Mitscher wanted no time wasted neutralizing Maleolap because he had to give Montgomery help at Roi.

Admiral Spruance, Fifth Fleet commander, followed in the heavy cruiser *Indianapolis*, partly to watch and partly to screen Montgomery's task group. Spruance intended to use Mitscher's carriers as protective cover for the assault. In this respect, he and the more aggressive Mitscher disagreed on carrier tactics.

Montgomery launched two hours before dawn, and at first light six Avengers illuminated Roi's airfield with incendiary bombs. Hellcats flew in low, firing arcs of tracers into revetments. The Japanese had picked up the incoming attack on

Rear Admiral (later Vice Admiral) Alfred E. Montgomery, commanding
Task Group 50.3, continued to serve throughout the war as one of
Admiral Mitscher's top carrier commanders. (U.S. Navy photo)

radar and got 27 Zeros off the ground. Japan's young pilots quickly learned that
the once nimble Zero could no longer compete with the swift and rugged Hellcat.
By 9:30 A.M., the only resistance on Roi's airfield came from AA guns.

The other three strikes went like clockwork. At Maleolap, Reeve's air group
delivered eight strikes and demolished Taroa airfield, destroying 37 planes on the
ground and 13 Zeros in the air. Ginder's pilots intercepted only one plane over
Wotje, shot it down, and smashed the facilities on the ground. Sherman's TG 58.3
found only eight planes on Kwajalein Island, shot them up, and bombed the supply base and ammunition dumps.

On February 1, Admiral Turner's V Amphibious Corps went ashore on the twin islands of Roi-Namur and 24 hours later declared them secure. By February 5, all resistance ended. Because of air supremacy, losses were so light that Admiral Turner never put his reserves ashore.

Eniwetok, 360 miles northwest of Kwajalein, remained the last Japanese stronghold in the Marshalls. Mitscher sent Sherman and Ginder's task groups to give the atoll a pasting. After clobbering the airfields, Ginder remained behind to support the February 18 amphibious assault, while Sherman rendezvoused with TF-58.

Vice Admiral (later Admiral) Frederick C. "Ted" Sherman served under Halsey, Mitscher, and Spruance, and probably saw more action in the Pacific than any of them. (U.S. Navy photo)

Mitscher collected three task groups to strike Truk Atoll, 669 miles west of Eniwetok. Discussions were still underway with the JCS regarding the necessity of capturing Truk. It had become Admiral Koga's advanced headquarters for the Combined Fleet and the homeport in the Central Pacific for his carriers and the superbattleships *Yamato* and *Musashi*. The JCS wanted aerial photos of the atoll: Mitscher wanted to smash its defenses. A few days after the capture of Roi, TF-58 fueled, turned westward, and picked up Sherman's TG 58.3 off Eniwetok.

At daybreak on February 11, Truk's commander, Rear Admiral Chuichi Hara, awoke to the news that radar had picked up an incoming swarm of aircraft. Hara scrambled about 45 Zeros to meet 72 Hellcats launched from five different carriers. In the opening dogfight, 30 Zeros went down in flames against a loss of 4 Hellcats. Avengers lit up the airfields with incendiary bombs, and Hellcats strafed the enemy's four airfields, but Koga was not there.

On February 10, Koga had moved the fleet to the Palaus because IGH had pulled the Japanese defensive perimeter back to the Marianas and the Philippines. At Truk, Koga left behind only two old light cruisers and a few destroyers and supply ships under Vice Admiral Kobayashi Jin, commander of the Fourth fleet. Truk and Rabaul had both been written off by IGH, which meant that the two bases would be defended by those there but not reinforced.

Disappointed by the absence of Japanese capital ships, Mitscher's pilots concentrated on other Truk targets. They flew 1,250 sorties and dropped 500 tons of bombs, sank 200,000 tons of Japanese shipping, pulverized runways, and strafed plane storage revetments. Hara reported more than 250 planes destroyed, including 110 transient aircraft on the way to Rabaul. Admiral Jin especially lamented the loss of six tankers because of Japan's growing shortage of fuel oil and aviation gas.

At 7:00 P.M., Hara mustered six radar-equipped Jill carrier-type torpedo planes for his one and only counterattack. For a while, AA fire held them off. Mitscher made his only mistake by launching a night fighter from *Yorktown* to bring down the Jills. He temporarily shut down AA fire, but the night-fighter failed to find the enemy planes. One Jill slipped through and launched a torpedo. It struck *Intrepid* on the starboard quarter near the sternpost and jammed the rudder. *Intrepid* returned to Eniwetok, steered by her propellers.

On February 18, 8,000 marines went ashore on Eniwetok and five days later secured the atoll. In 24 days, the combination of Mitscher's carriers and Turner's V Amphibious Corps captured the Marshall Islands and decimated Truk. The campaign cost Mitscher's task groups 85 planes and 56 flyers from combat.

The JCS removed Truk from the planning table as a strategic target, and Nimitz had found his carrier man. On March 21, Marc Mitscher officially became Vice Admiral, Commander Fast Carrier Forces, Pacific Fleet.

After losing the Marshall Islands, IGH retracted its southern defensive perimeter and formed a new line through the Marianas (Saipan, Tinian, and Guam) and the western Carolines (Ulithi, Yap, Ngulu, and Palau). To protect the perimeter, Admiral Koga dissolved the Combined Fleet, which had been inactive, and formed the First Mobile Fleet, composed of the Second Fleet and the Third Fleet. The Second Fleet contained the battleships *Yamato, Musashi, Nagato, Kongo*, and *Harawa*, 11 cruisers, and 14 destroyers. The Third Fleet operated three carrier divisions, which on paper looked deceptively impressive. Carrier Division 1 consisted of *Shokaku, Zuikaku*, and *Taiho;* Carrier Division 2 the CVLs *Junyo, Hiyo*, and *Ryuho*, and Carrier Division 3 the CVLs and CVEs *Chitose, Chiyoda*, and *Zuiho. Chitose* and *Zuiho* had been converted from tankers, and *Chiyoda* from a naval auxiliary ship.

After crafting the new organization, Koga discovered problems. Between November 1943 and April 1944 he had lost an enormous number of planes and pilots. Carrier Division 1 lost flyers at Rabaul; Carrier Division 2 lost flyers in the Marshalls; and Carrier Division 3, organized in February 1944, had no pilots with combat experience.

Koga expected the next strike would come against the Marianas, and to counter the threat he developed Z Plan, which called for an attack on the American fleet at any time it entered the Philippine Sea. Koga hoped to avoid carrier exposure by shuttling planes to island airbases, from which he hoped to increase their combat effectiveness by providing them with multiple landing fields.

On March 22, while Koga put the final touches on Z Plan from his new fleet base in the Palau Island group, Mitscher departed with 11 carriers from the Marshalls to pay him a visit. Mitscher brought three task groups, Reeves's TG 58.1, Montgomery's TG 58.2, and Ginder's TG 58.3, which now contained the repaired *Lexington*.

On March 29, Japanese radar picked up the approach of TF-58. Koga immediately launched two groups of Bettys armed with torpedoes. Hellcats and AA fire wiped out both flights. Koga also obtained considerable help from planes based on Yap and Peleliu, but after most of them were shot down he discarded Z Plan as unworkable.

At dawn on March 30, Mitscher launched the first strike against the Marianas. With the Hellcat sweep came a new innovation—Mark 10 moored magnetic mines and long, cylindrical Mark 25 ground magnetic mines that were designed to rest on a shallow bottom. The Japanese observed the mine drop and decided to keep their ships in the harbor, but Koga's carrier divisions were not there. Dauntless dive-bombing had never been accurate, but bomb-carrying Hellcats got into the action and tried skip-bombing: approaching low and bouncing a bomb with a delayed fuse across the water and into the side of a ship. The Japanese lost 36 vessels; the toll would have been greater had there been more delayed-fuse bombs available.

Avenger crews used a new weapon against airfield revetments, a 5-inch HVAR (high-velocity aircraft rocket). First tried at Kwajalein, it hit with the impact of a 6-inch shell and could blow whatever it penetrated to pieces.

During the strike, Mitscher's air groups flew 2,645 sorties, dropped 600 tons of bombs, launched 35 torpedoes, and lost only 17 Helldivers, 5 Avengers, and 3 Dauntlesses. Deck crashes accounted for another 18 planes.

On April 6, Mitscher returned to Eniwetok to begin a period of replenishment that would last a week. New plans were afoot for the New Guinea campaign. General MacArthur intended to leapfrog to Hollandia and strand the Japanese Eighteenth Army in the jungle at Wewak, but he wanted carrier support for the amphibious phase of the operation.

Nimitz expected trouble from Koga's newly formed First Mobile Fleet, and he told Mitscher that given the opportunity, to put the Japanese permanently out of business. Neither Nimitz nor Mitscher knew that, toward the end of March, Koga had decided to move his base of operations to Davao in the southern Philippines, and while en route in two flying boats, he and his staff encountered a tropical storm and crashed. Koga did not survive, and the IJN lost its second commander of the Japanese fleet.

Mitscher sailed for Hollandia with 5 task groups, 12 carriers, and Admiral Lee's battle line. He assigned the softening up to carrier aircraft. If the Japanese fleet showed up during MacArthur's landing, Lee's battlewagons had the responsibility for blowing it to pieces.

Mitscher arrived on April 20 to empty skies. General Kenney's Fifth Air Force had already pulverized the area, wiping out 340 Japanese planes in five heavy raids between March 31 and April 16. Mitscher found no reason to remain there. The leaderless Japanese fleet never showed, and bombing possible enemy positions in the jungle only wasted tons of valuable ordnance.

Admiral Reeves, commanding TG 50.3, used the opportunity to test the new F4U-2N Corsair night fighters equipped with airborne radar. On April 23, *Enterprise*'s air controller reported bogies at 30 miles. Lieutenant Commander R. E. Harmer took Lieutenant (jg) R. F. Holden as wingman and at 6:11 P.M. lifted off the deck. Using his own airborne radar and vectoring from *Enterprise*, Harmer came up behind a twin-engine Yokosuka P1Y "Frances," dropped flaps to slow his speed, and in an erratic dogfight in the dark, sent the enemy plane into the sea. Had his guns not jammed, he may have wiped out a following formation of six more bombers.

Before departing from Hollandia, Mitscher received orders from Nimitz authorizing another Truk strike. Unknown to Nimitz or Mitscher, Koga had previously flown in planes from other locations, bringing Truk's total to 104. On the morning of April 29, Hellcats from TF-58 strafed Truk's airfields. Bombers followed in overlapping flights. At the end of the day Truk had about a dozen planes left in impregnable revetments. Having dropped most of his bombs and shot up a fair amount of ammunition, Mitscher set a course for Eniwetok, making intermediate stops at Ponape Island and Satawan Atoll to give Admiral Lee's battle group an opportunity to shell enemy installations.

For Mitscher and his hard-working task force, the next objective would be across 700 miles of open water and into the Marianas and the Philippine Sea. Koga had pledged to check American advances in the Philippine Sea, but he would never keep that pledge because the admiral was dead.

CHAPTER 12

The Marianas Turkey Shoot

By the spring of 1944, Japanese factories were producing 1,700 planes a month. The new models were faster, better armed, more versatile, but still without safety features. Carriers received the latest version of the Mitsubishi Zero fighter, the A6M5 "Zeke 52," which could fly 351 mph at 20,000 feet, but, like Nakajima B6N Jills and Aichi D4Y Judys, they were without armor or self-sealing tanks. CVLs carried Zero 52b fighter-bombers; planes with strengthened wings that could dive at 460 mph and carry a 550-pound bomb. They had bulletproof windscreens and automatic fuel tank fire extinguishers, but when carrying bombs they required an escort.

Despite improvements in Japanese fighters, the 375-mph Grumman Hellcat still held a small advantage in speed and an enormous advantage in armoring and pilot protection. The new Judy dive-bombers could make 343 mph at 16,000 feet, but they could not outrun a Hellcat. The heavier Nakajima-built Jill 12, with its 1,850-hp Kasei 25 engine, was far superior to Kates and Vals and better protected, but at 300 mph fell easy prey to Hellcats.

Admiral Shigetare Shimada, the IJN's chief-of-staff, tried to fill gaps created by the death of Koga by sending 1,644 planes to the Marianas, but he could not rush enough pilots through flight training. By mid-May, Shimada had been able to send only 175 aircraft to the Marianas' seven airfields—Zeros and Jills, and a few Betty and Frances twin-engine bombers. Most planes went to carriers to support "A-Go" (Operation Victory), a plan developed by Admiral Koga before his death. In Koga's view, victory depended on the skill of Japanese flyers and the ability of Zero escorts to keep Hellcats off the Jills and Judys.

Koga and Shimada designed a plan to draw Mitscher's task force into battle. They expected the next assault to come in the Marianas, specifically Saipan, Tinian, and Guam, where airfields were located. When the strike came, they expected to find Mitscher committed to landing-support operations and busy receiving and launching planes for strikes against beach installations. They understood Spruance's tactics and believed the American admiral would not allow

Mitscher's carriers to stray from the beachheads. If so, Mitscher would be too involved in the assault to notice the approach of Japan's First Mobile Fleet.

During Mitscher's air operations in the Marshalls and the Carolines, there had been no contact with the Japanese fleet because Koga had withdrawn his carriers from the area to prepare for A-Go. He filled their decks with new aircraft and trained the pilots in tactical operations. His untimely death disrupted the schedule.

On May 3, IGH named Admiral Soemu Toyoda commander of the Combined Fleet. Toyoda adopted Koga's plan to seek a decisive battle during the next major American assault, but he wanted every battleship and heavy cruiser in the navy to accompany the carriers. The navy did not have enough oilers to support the operation, nor did they have enough refined oil for the fleet to reach the Marianas and return.

While studying alternatives, the IJN named 57-year-old Vice Admiral Jisaburo Ozawa commander of the First Mobile Fleet. Ozawa had relieved Admiral Nagumo of the Third Fleet in November 1943 after the Battle of Santa Cruz Islands. Since then, Nagumo had received command of the Fourth Fleet based at Saipan, but he had no fighting ships, only harbor craft distributed among the islands. Ozawa inherited the problem of how best to utilize the First Mobile Fleet with little time left to decide.

Toyoda attempted to solve Ozawa's fueling problems by sending all ships to Borneo to be filled with unrefined oil. Crude oil could be fed directly into firerooms, but it was volatile and highly explosive. Nevertheless, Toyoda believed the urgency justified the risk.

On May 5, two days after Toyoda authorized A-Go, IJN intelligence picked up sudden increases in American radio transmissions, much like the pattern observed prior to other assaults. Toyoda expected the next amphibious assault to occur in the Marianas, but he changed his mind when on May 27 eight carriers aided U.S. Army landings at Biak Island off the coast of New Guinea. Toyoda then wondered whether American efforts were shifting to MacArthur's theater. He did not know the eight flattops at Biak were escort carriers.

To gather more intelligence, Toyoda sent long-range suicide reconnaissance missions from Truk to overfly the Marshall Islands. On June 5, a flying boat spotted Mitscher's carriers and dozens of transports at Eniwetok. Four days later, another flight reported them gone. Toyoda remained circumspect, but on June 13, IGH finally decided that the next big battle would be fought near Saipan. On that day, Ozawa's fleet steamed from Borneo and set a course for the Philippine Sea.

The radio chatter detected by Japanese radio intelligence emanated from the planning of Operation Forager. On March 12, 1944, the JCS decided on Nimitz's next plunge: a giant stride across the Pacific to assault Saipan. They set June 15 as D day for the landing, which happened to be nine days after D day in Normandy, France. The setup called for Admiral Spruance to carry 531 combat ships of the Fifth Fleet, including Mitscher's TF-58 at full strength, and 127,571 marines and GIs to the Marianas.

Vice Admiral Jisaburo Ozawa, IJN, commanded the Japanese First
Mobile Fleet and lost most of his aircraft and three of his carriers during
the Marianas campaign. (National Archives)

The JCS wanted the Marianas' air bases, from which B-29 Superfortresses
could bomb Japan and the Philippines. An invasion of the Philippines, high on the
list of General MacArthur's priorities, could then become possible. Nimitz and
MacArthur had been recapturing territory taken by the Japanese during the war,
but the Marianas, ceded to Japan by the Treaty of Versailles, were different and
had a large Japanese population. Saipan, Tinian, and Guam's airfields represented
the key to controlling the Marianas. Invasion of Japan's inner defensive perimeter
could bring on a major naval engagement, which was exactly what Mitscher
wanted.

On June 11, Mitscher's TF-58 paid a visit to the Marianas and destroyed
80 planes on Saipan and Tinian and 25 more on Guam. The strike wiped out most

of Rear Admiral Kakuji Kakuta's air groups and left him with scattered aircraft sheltered in revetments. During the next four days, carrier strikes destroyed the rest of them. According to the A-Go plan, Kakuta was to destroy a third of Mitscher's carriers, but to accomplish this he needed replacement planes from Truk and Yap.

On the morning of June 15, two marine divisions went ashore on Saipan under close air support from carriers. Japanese army and navy troops, numbering 29,662, put up a stiff and bloody resistance for four weeks. Most fought to their deaths. Only 1,780 eventually surrendered.

On the night after marines went ashore, 10 Frances twin-engine bombers, 3 Judys, and 11 fighters from Truk registered on *Enterprise*'s radarscope. Once again, Commander Harmer with wingman Holden lifted off the deck in F4U-2N night-fighters to hunt for kills. A 20-mm bullet from one of the Zeros shorted Harmer's formation lights to the "on" position and forced him to retire. The bombers roared over the fleet without scoring a hit. Radar-directed AA fire knocked down 11 planes. The others returned to Yap. Four days passed before the carriers indulged another attack.

Early on June 15, word of the Saipan assault reached Ozawa by an order from Admiral Toyoda to initiate Operation A-Go. "The destiny of our Empire lies in the outcome of this battle. Each member will fight to the end."[1] After navy cryptanalysts decoded the message, Nimitz said, "I hope they stick to that idea. I don't know anything more we can do to provoke these people into a fleet action."[2]

The failure of Japanese intelligence to discover the date of Operation Forager drastically altered the strategy built into A-Go. Instead of having his fleet near the Marianas on the day of the assault, Ozawa had it in the western Philippines. He could not come within striking distance of Saipan before the morning of June 19. Toyoda realized that Ozawa would be delayed and began shuttling planes from Japan to Iwo Jima and thence to the Marianas with specific instructions to ignore all other targets and sink the American carriers. Spruance miscalculated. "He assumed the Japanese [would go] after Turner's transports."[3] The miscalculation led to one of the navy's greatest missed opportunities.

Two days before the Saipan assault, Mitscher detached "Jocko" Clark's TG 58.1 and Rear Admiral William K. Harrill's TG 58.4 with orders to clobber Chichi Jima and Iwo Jima's airfields. On June 14, both task groups made a hurried 600-mile run north. Spruance wanted the carriers back in three days because he expected trouble from the Japanese fleet. With 20 hours required to reach the Jimas and another 20 hours required to return, Clark and Harrill had no time to waste. The weather worsened as they steamed north, storms piling up 15-foot waves.

Off Iwo Jima at 1:34 P.M., Harrill catapulted 44 Hellcats into thick, squally weather. As soon as the fighters cleared the deck, Helldivers and Avengers formed for a full-scale strike, waiting for Hellcats to down any Zeros in the air.

Iwo Jima, shaped like a pork-chop, had two airstrips, a few medium bombers, and 120 Zeros manned by green pilots. When Iwo radar picked up incoming

Hellcats, Captain Kanzo Miura rushed 37 Zero interceptors into the air. Offshore, a severe dogfight developed beneath a 7,000-foot overcast. In a matter of minutes Miura lost 28 fighters. Hellcat pilots swung over the island and in successive strafing runs chopped up 86 enemy planes neatly aligned on Iwo's two airfields. Minutes later Helldivers and Avengers arrived, dropped their payloads, and pockmarked the airfields.

Clark, having found only one small airstrip on Chichi Jima, concentrated on the island's installations, seaplane base, and ships in the harbor. He rejoined Harrill during a night of worsening weather to discuss the feasibility of launching another strike in the morning. They decided to wait until noon, July 16, and almost on schedule the weather moderated. At 1:00 P.M., *Yorktown*, *Hornet*, and *Princeton* put planes into the air. Because of storms, Captain Miura had not bothered to send up a fighter patrol. He still had 60 aircraft lined up on his airstrips, although many had been damaged during the previous day's attack. The July 16 strike wiped the rest of them out. Mitscher's two task groups lost 12 planes, but Admiral Ozawa would find no reinforcements from Iwo Jima when he came within striking distance of Saipan.

While crossing the Philippine Sea, Ozawa designed tactics for making A-Go an operational success. His Jills and Judys had a range of 400 miles, a hundred miles more than Hellcats. While American carriers were still recovering from his first strike, he would steam swiftly forward and launch a second strike. Planes from both strikes would land on Saipan, Tinian, and Guam to refuel, rearm, and deliver another strike as they returned to the carriers, which would then be 250 miles west of Guam.

At 3:30 P.M. on June 18, Ozawa's reconnaissance planes reported the position of part of Spruance's fleet west of Saipan. Rear Admiral Suemo Obayashi, commanding Carrier Division 3, began launching planes. Many were already in the air when Ozawa ordered them back. A strike so late in the afternoon required night landings, and Ozawa feared unnecessary losses from inexperienced pilots. He decided to wait until morning. Then, after maintaining radio silence for three days, he sent a message to Admiral Kakuta on Saipan announcing a morning strike and requesting support from land-based aircraft.

Before dawn on June 19, Ozawa launched 16 seaplanes and 14 scout bombers to locate the enemy. Eleven attack bombers followed to carry out a mini-strike. At 7:00 A.M., he began receiving reports of the enemy organized into three groups, each with carriers, 300 miles due east. Ozawa ordered an immediate attack. A delay occurred when air group commanders on each carrier made ceremonial promises to their admirals pledging to avenge Midway losses.

Emotions ran high at 7:30 when the first strike of 48 fighters, 54 bombers, and 27 torpedo planes lifted into the air, young pilots shouting "victory" over the roar of their engines. Nobody effused more optimism than Ozawa, who believed his strike would come as a surprise to the Americans. A false report claiming that planes from Yap had damaged eight flattops on the 17th boosted his optimism.

Yap pilots believed they had injured TF-58, but the ships were escort carriers. One had been slightly injured.

Admiral Mitscher welcomed a carrier battle and knew it was coming. American submarines had been tracking Ozawa's force since June 13 when *Redfin* and *Bowfin* reported it moving through the Philippines. On June 15, *Flying Fish* observed two groups heading east through San Bernardino Strait and into the Philippine Sea. Mitscher plotted Ozawa's course, estimated the speed, and doubted whether the force could be within range sooner than June 18. He expected Ozawa to launch beyond the range of his Hellcats and use Marianas' airfields to refuel. If so, enemy strikes could continue for days. As a countermeasure Mitscher had the airfields strafed and bombed every day. The Japanese repaired them at night, and carrier pilots hammered them again in the morning, always observing a few more planes from Truk and Yap on the ground.

On June 17, the submarine *Cavalla* reported the course and speed of Ozawa's two groups and counted nine carriers populated with 450 planes. The intelligence gave Mitscher a full day's advantage in locating the enemy fleet. Although still 770 nautical miles apart, Mitscher wanted to begin moving toward the Japanese force. With both fleets steaming at about 25 knots, he expected to come within striking

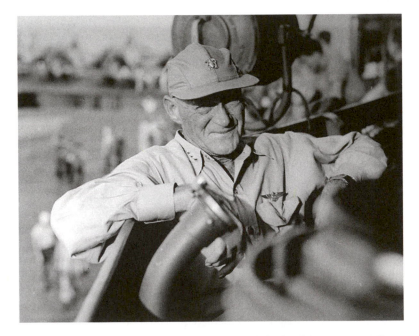

In 1943, Vice Admiral (later Admiral) Marc A. Mitscher began commanding all the fast carrier forces in the Pacific and developed into the navy's best tactical commander of the war. (U.S. Navy photo)

distance in eight hours. His air groups were ready and eager. They could make air contact with Ozawa's fleet by late afternoon, July 18, and attack that night.

Spruance's patent conservatism intervened. Against the advice of his own staff, and he told Mitscher that, "Task Force 58 must cover Saipan and our forces engaged in that operation."[4] He vetoed a night attack and turned Mitscher's task force southeast. Spruance still had illusions of the Japanese being better night fighters. As a consequence, Mitscher lost contact with the Japanese fleet until late that night when Ozawa broke radio silence to confer with Admiral Kakuta. Pearl Harbor intercepted the transmission, triangulated it with receiving stations in the South Pacific and the Aleutians, and relayed Ozawa's position to Mitscher.

Mitscher lost his opportunity for a night attack, but if he turned quickly west, he could launch a dawn strike. Mitscher took his plan to Spruance, who shuddered at the thought of detaching carriers and sending them into a possible trap. Mitscher bristled over another lost opportunity, certain that Spruance's decision handed Ozawa the initiative. "That course did not surprise the Japanese," wrote the historian Edwin P. Hoyt. "Their assessment of Admiral Spruance was shrewd. They knew that he was a man of extremely limited imagination who would never take a chance."[5] The assessment was partly true. Spruance "wanted to sink the Japanese fleet if he could, but only if the opportunity arose without risk to Turner's ships."[6]

When Spruance rendezvoused with TF-58 on June 17, by his presence he took over the supervisory command of the carrier force and prevented Mitscher from taking the two actions that could have put the Japanese fleet out of business. After Clark and Harrill's task groups returned from Iwo Jima on the 18th, Mitscher had more than enough planes to cover Marianas operations and still strike Ozawa. Spruance balked, even though Admiral Turner declared that his escort carriers were enough to protect the beachhead and advised Spruance to turn Mitscher loose. Despite radar and advanced technology, coupled with Ozawa's fleet being 400 miles away, Spruance still worried that Ozawa would slip by Mitscher during the night and have his carriers off Saipan at daylight. His concerns were not without merit. A recently captured Japanese naval document suggested a new battle doctrine, calling for "a feint at the center to draw the enemy's attention, followed by a flanking attack."[7] Spruance's concerns, however, did not take into account Ozawa's capabilities, which were greatly outmatched by TF-58.

After two and a half years of war and his experience at Midway, Spruance had not learned how to use fast carrier strike forces, and Nimitz let Spruance have his way. Nor since Pearl Harbor had the Japanese advanced much farther in their tactical thinking. Midway had thrown the IJN on the defensive. Now they had to act.

Spruance persisted in the notion that his primary task was to protect troops and supply vessels before, during, and after amphibious landings. Mitscher and Halsey had a clearer conception of what carriers could do, and they were bringing air admirals like Radford, Clark, Ginder, McCain, Montgomery, and Sherman along in their wake. As long as Spruance remained in overall command, carriers would be relegated to a support force instead of a strike force. During the meeting the night of June 18, when Mitscher pleaded for permission to attack Ozawa, Spruance ordered him to attack Japanese airfields. "This we did not like," Admiral Burke recalled. "It meant that the enemy could attack us at will . . . the next morning. We could not attack the enemy."[8] Montgomery fumed to the point of insubordination. Mitscher interceded and said he would strike the airfields. Mitscher then ignored Spruance's wishes and saved most of his planes for the battle he expected in the morning. To Spruance's credit, he gave Mitscher and Lee's battle group considerable latitude, saying, "I shall issue general directives [only] when necessary and leave details to you and Admiral Lee."[9]

At 2:00 A.M. on July 19, *Enterprise* launched 14 night-flying Avengers armed with torpedoes and sent them on a combined search-strike mission to the westward. Because Ozawa kept his ships 40 to 50 miles beyond the range of American search planes, the scouts reported no sightings. Had any of Ozawa's planes registered on the Avenger's airborne radar, Mitscher would have turned some of his carriers around and headed for the Japanese fleet.

Ozawa's scouts, however, located Mitscher's carriers at dawn, and at 8:25 A.M. Admiral Obayashi launched 69 planes—16 fighters, 45 fighter-bombers, and 8 Jills—from the 653rd Air Group on Carrier Division 3 (*Zuiho*, *Chitose*, and *Chiyoda*). A half hour later, Ozawa launched 48 fighters, 53 bombers, and

The USS *Enterprise* (CV-6) probably saw more action in World War II than any other carrier. She lands aircraft during operations in the Marianas. (U.S. Navy photo)

27 torpedo planes from Carrier Division 1 (*Shokaku, Zuikaku,* and *Taiho*). Ozawa now had two air groups and 197 planes headed for Mitscher's carriers. They would arrive about 30 minutes apart.

Spruance had put Mitscher at an enormous tactical disadvantage. His carriers were too far away to strike Ozawa's fleet, but Ozawa's planes were in range to strike Mitscher's fleet. Mitscher was also in range of Japanese land-based aircraft, but he had more planes (956) than Ozawa (475), better planes, and twice as many fighters.

As Obayashi's strike group headed for TF-58, Admiral Kakuta, in response to Ozawa's radio instructions the previous night, had brought in planes from Yap, Palau, and Truk. Before dawn, he put fighters and bombers in the air to strike Mitscher's carriers. Instead of the first attack coming from carrier planes, as Mitscher expected, it came from a lone land-based Zero search plane that attempted to drop a bomb on the destroyer *Stockham* but missed. Kakuta's air group now knew, as did Ozawa's, the new position of Mitscher's task force. Thirty minutes later, blips began appearing on carrier radarscopes.

Six fighters from *Belleau Wood* went to investigate and at 6:30 A.M. orbited at 16,000 feet above Guam's Orote Field. They observed planes taking off toward the carriers. Four Zeros, 4,000 feet higher, dove on the Hellcats but did no damage. As they passed, Hellcat pilots shot two down. Moments later, the first great air battle of the day erupted over Guam when a second Hellcat squadron from *Belleau Wood* entered the dogfight.

Hellcats from *Hornet, Yorktown,* and *Cabot* joined the fight. They dominated the action, surviving tail attacks and then blowing Zeros to pieces as they passed. Hellcats could out-turn and out-dive Zeros, and when engaged in head-to-head contests, outshoot them. The Zero's small advantage in maneuverability was no longer enough to compensate for the rugged durability of the Hellcat.

Japanese pilots, however, employed a new tactic that sometimes worked. With a Hellcat on their tail, they would dive toward the sea and quickly pull up. The heavier Hellcat, not quite as nimble, either splashed into the water or became vulnerable at lower altitudes. The enemy trick lasted about a day.

As the dogfight over Guam escalated, Montgomery added fighters from *Bunker Hill*. One air group noticed large numbers of enemy planes, apparently coming from distant islands, heading straight for Guam. Surmising that they were reinforcements in need of fuel, Hellcat pilots waited until they formed for landing. Once the planes committed to a runway, Hellcats swooped down and tore them apart. Soon planes were piled up and burning all over Orote Field. Without a place to land and short of fuel, Japanese aircraft began nosing into the ground and flipping over. Conditions on Saipan's Aslito Field were no better, and arriving reinforcements ran out of places to land.

Carrier planes fighting above Guam were still fully engaged as the stage set for the second great air battle of the day. Having launched strikes at 8:30 and 9:00 A.M., Ozawa waited for news from the first strike before sending another. Ten o'clock

On June 19, 1944, at the height of the Marianas Turkey Shoot, a pilot from *Yorktown*'s
VF-1 prepares to takeoff in a Hellcat fitted with a belly tank. (National Archives)

came and went. Still he heard nothing. He could not curb his restlessness. To
maintain his plan he needed to get a third strike ready for launch, so he cut loose a
second strike of 130 planes from Carrier Divisions 1 and 2.

At 10:00 A.M., radar operators on the battleship *Alabama*, using the latest
equipment, picked up blips from Obayashi's planes 150 miles to the west.
Minutes later, the flagship *Lexington* picked up the same contacts. This gave
Mitscher 30 minutes to get fighters in the air. He called back all planes short of
fuel and all search planes not engaged over Guam or Saipan. At 10:20, all 15
carriers began launching fighters and fighter-bombers to meet the incoming attack, but some flattops were slow in getting planes into the air. Had the Japanese
planes struck immediately, they would have caught several carriers with decks
crammed with planes coming and going, but the Japanese hesitated, wasting
about 10 minutes to organize their attack.

Mitscher's carrier commanders used the time to launch more fighters. Flight
Director Lieutenant Joseph R. Eggert's air controllers, noting the enemy at
18,000 feet, began screaming at Hellcat pilots to get up to 25,000 feet. Eggert
then put 23 Hellcats returning from Guam into orbit west of the carriers while
Admiral Lee's battle group formed an anti-torpedo screen. By 10:35, Mitscher
had 222 fighters in the air on the western flank and another 192 Avengers, 174
Helldivers, and 59 Dauntlesses airborne to defend the eastern flank. He now had
his decks free for continuous recovery and launching.

As Ozawa's strike force approached, language specialist Lieutenant Charles A. Sims picked up the Japanese 653rd Air Group commander's instructions to pilots and relayed the information to carrier flight controllers. With the new technology, Hellcat pilots knew exactly how to respond to Ozawa's attack.

Hellcats plunged through the incoming wave of Japanese aircraft and shredded it. One pilot from *Lexington*'s VF-16 shouted over the radio, "Hell, this is like an old-time turkey shoot."[10] The comment became legendary, and the air battle for the Marianas on June 19, 1944, passed into history as the Marianas Turkey Shoot. Flyers going into the dogfight with one or two kills came out aces. Before the day ended, Lieutenant (jg) Alex Vraciu knocked down six planes.

Obayashi's first strike never reached the carriers. Any planes penetrating the Hellcat screen got blown apart by Admiral Lee's battle line. Only 20 Japanese planes survived, scattering in different directions. Some flew to Saipan and found the airfield under attack by American ground forces. Others tried Guam, only to be strafed as they landed.

By the time Ozawa's second wave arrived, Mitscher had so many Hellcats in the air that the enemy had no chance of getting near a carrier. Commander David McCampbell, leading nine Hellcats from *Essex*'s VF-15, got into the fight too late to intercept the first wave. Earlier, the pickings had been good, but when McCambell arrived on the scene there were no bogies in the sky. He felt better when air controllers vectored in the approach of Ozawa's second wave. McCampbell knocked down four Japanese planes before his guns jammed. His air group then finished off one whole formation of Jill dive-bombers. As surviving Japanese planes scattered toward land bases, McCambell grumbled into his radio set, "The sky is getting short of enemy planes." Before the Marianas campaign ended, McCambell added seven kills to his record.[11]

Of 373 carrier planes and more than a hundred land-based planes sent against Mitscher's task force, Japan lost 315 aircraft during the daylong fight. Ozawa started the day with 473 planes. Now he had fewer than 200. TF-58 lost 18 fighters and 12 bombers but rescued most of the pilots.

Other American losses were negligible. One bomb struck the battleship *South Dakota*, causing 50 casualties, and another scored a near miss on the cruiser *Minneapolis*. A few enemy planes, possibly from Marianas airfields, flew about undetected. In a sky full of Hellcats, lone enemy planes were difficult to track on ship's radar. One wounded Jill pilot crashed into the side of the battleship *Indiana*. *Wasp* took a single 550-pound bomb through her deck. Two near misses punched a hole in the side of *Bunker Hill*, killing 76 men. Some of the planes could have come from *Taiho*, Ozawa's flagship, which because of a deck accident never got off until noon.

Ozawa could not understand why the Pacific Fleet did not attack him. He did not know that Spruance had ordered TF-58 eastward, taking Mitscher's flattops further out of range. While Mitscher and his air admirals fumed over the order, American submarines began looking for Ozawa's fleet.

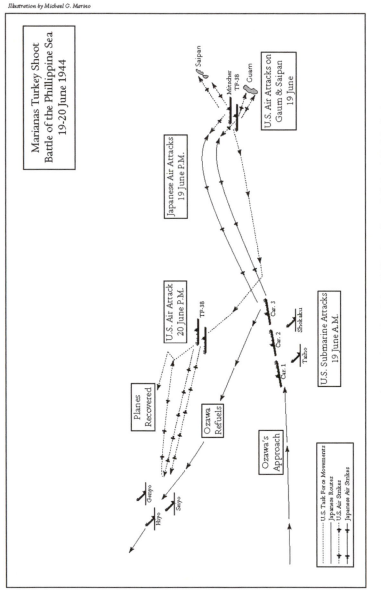

Marianas Turkey Shoot and Battle of the Philippine Sea. (Michael G. Marino)

Vice Admiral Charles A. Lockwood, Nimitz's commander of submarines, had correctly anticipated Ozawa's course and sent the submarines *Albacore, Finback, Bang,* and *Stingray* to patrol an area 60 miles in diameter about 350 miles west of Guam. At 8:16 A.M., Commander James W. Blanchard of *Albacore* observed Japanese planes flying eastward and knew the enemy ships must be over the western horizon. Thirty minutes later, Carrier Division 1 came in sight. Blanchard let one carrier pass, waiting for Ozawa's 29,300-ton flagship *Taiho* to come in range. As Blanchard prepared to fire, *Albacore*'s torpedo data targeting computer failed to respond. With time running out, Blanchard upped periscope and fired a six-torpedo spread by eye. One struck the carrier on the starboard side near her forward gasoline tanks and jammed the forward elevator to the "up" position. A second torpedo might also have struck had it not been exploded by a suicide pilot who dove into it.

At first, Ozawa did not consider the damage serious. The carrier had been ingeniously compartmentalized for maximum safety and built sturdier than her predecessors. Mechanics went to work repairing the damage and corrected the list by flooding compartments on the port side. The ship leveled and her speed barely dropped a knot. Except for the damage to the jammed forward elevator, Ozawa anticipated no problems sending off another strike.

Ozawa was too preoccupied to notice gasoline and volatile unrefined oil seeping into the forward elevator pit. The mixture of gases created a time bomb. An inexperienced damage-control officer ordered ventilating ducts opened full blast to release the fumes, but the carrier was going 26 knots into the wind. Instead of blowing out the well, the fumes filled the ship's lower decks. Now aware that a spark could turn his flagship into a blazing inferno, Ozawa shuttled *Taiho's* aircraft over to *Zuikaku,* although this did not decrease the danger.

Two hours later and 60 miles east of where *Taiho* had been torpedoed, Ozawa crossed the path of Commander Herman J. Kossler's submarine *Cavalla.* Kossler had been stern-chasing the Japanese carriers ever since reporting them on June 17. At first, Kossler could not ascertain whether they were Japanese carriers or part of Mitscher's group. "There was the Rising Sun, big as hell," Kossler recalled.[12] "The picture was too good to be true! A large carrier with two cruisers ahead on the port bow and a destroyer about 1000 yards on the port beam!"[13]

Kossler's torpedo data computer worked fine and told him that at least four of the six torpedoes ready for launch would hit. He fired all six and at 12:20 P.M. heard three explode. *Shokaku* lurched out of position, burst into flames, and began what became a progressive list. Kossler, who sustained a three-hour battering from depth charges, stayed near enough to hear *Shokaku* explode, break apart, upend, and sink at 3:00 P.M.

Thirty minutes later, *Taiho,* now a gigantic supercharged canister waiting for ignition, picked up the inevitable spark. The explosion lifted up the flight deck, blew out the sides of the hangar, blasted holes in the bottom, and killed everyone in the engine rooms. The first explosion set off a chain reaction that engulfed *Taiho* in a mass of flames. She began to settle. By 5:00 P.M., no ship could approach because of the heat. Ozawa and his staff transferred to the cruiser *Haguro,* bringing with them a portrait of the emperor and the admiral's flag. At 9:50 P.M., *Taiho* sank. Only 500 of her crew of 2,150 survived.

Two American submarine commanders accomplished what Mitscher had hoped to do since the very beginning of the campaign. Spruance had gotten in the way, but that was about to change.

After losing *Taiho* and transferring to *Haguro*, Ozawa no longer had the communications equipment required to manage three carrier divisions. Not until the morning of June 20 did he learn that of 473 planes, only 102 of them were left— 44 fighters, 17 fighter-bombers, 11 dive-bombers, and 30 torpedo planes. He hoped his other aircraft were safe on land bases in the Marianas. He did not know how much damage his planes had inflicted on the enemy, but according to the reports coming from the previous day's actions, his flyers had won a stunning victory, destroying four or five American carriers, a battleship or heavy cruiser, and more than 160 planes. Ozawa believed the reports; otherwise Mitscher would surely have attacked him. Now he had to decide whether to use his last planes and finish off the enemy. Because he needed to refuel he bought time, slowly backtracking to rendezvous with his oilers.

Meanwhile, the results of the Turkey Shoot made Spruance aggressive. After pulling TF-58 farther to the east, he now decided to let Mitscher go after the Japanese fleet. The decision came a day late.

At 3:00 P.M. on June 19, Mitscher turned his carriers west but was forced to remain in the area for several hours to recover planes. At 10:00 P.M., he finally got underway but had to cut cruising speed to 23 knots to conserve fuel. He was not sure where to look for Ozawa's carriers because none of his search planes had sighted them, and he did not want to put night-flyers in the air, although he had several Hellcats, Corsairs, and radar-equipped Avengers available. Instead, he relied on long-range PBY flying boats operating out of Saipan to find the enemy during the night.

Before dawn on June 20, Mitscher launched search planes, but his carriers were no closer to Ozawa than the night before. Uncertain of conditions in the Marianas, Ozawa had moved west during the night to stay beyond the range of carrier search planes. Spruance told Mitscher he had until nightfall to find Ozawa's fleet, and if unsuccessful, to turn back. He also suggested looking for Ozawa's damaged carriers, not knowing that both had sunk. When the last search plane returned at noon, Mitscher began to suspect that Ozawa had withdrawn. He had heard nothing from scouting PBYs and nothing from Pearl Harbor because Ozawa maintained radio silence.

Early in the afternoon, Mitscher authorized another search, this time with Hellcats armed with bombs and fitted with auxiliary tanks. It would be the longest search (475 miles) ever flown by carrier planes, but the Hellcats flew too far north and found an empty sea.

Without knowing it, Mitscher began closing rapidly on the Japanese fleet, which was moving slowly west and refueling.

Ozawa knew that Jake seaplanes had spotted American search planes to the east early in the morning, but these did not concern him. At 1:00 P.M., he transferred his flag to *Zuikaku*, and there received a fuller report of his plane losses. Admiral Kakuta, radioing from Tinian, reported that carrier planes had landed safely on the islands, but he neglected to say that most of them were shot up and useless. Although somewhat troubled by his losses, Ozawa shrugged off the bad news and began planning another strike. As a precaution, he sent six Kates on a search mission. Three hours passed without a sighting, but at 4:05 the cruiser *Atago* intercepted a radio message from Avenger pilot Lieutenant R. S. Nelson reporting the position of the Japanese fleet and adding that the ships appeared to be fueling. Nelson stayed long enough to correct the coordinates given on his first report, which would have sent Mitscher's planes 60 miles off course. Ozawa realized that his fleet was being stalked and hurried the fueling effort.

Nelson's final report placed the Japanese fleet 275 miles northwest of TF-58. Mitscher faced a tough decision. If planes launched quickly, they would arrive over the enemy 30 minutes before nightfall. With Ozawa's forces at maximum range of carrier aircraft, returning pilots would be faced with night recovery, which took many times longer than daylight recovery. Few wartime-trained pilots had ever landed at night. Mitscher knew this might be his last chance to strike the enemy a decisive blow, and he expected unavoidable losses once he gave the order.

Mitscher turned to Fleet Air Officer Lieutenant Commander William J. Widhelm and asked, "Well, can we make it?" Widhelm replied, "We can make it, but it's going to be tight." Mitscher nodded and said softly, "Launch 'em."[14]

At 4:10, Mitscher radioed Spruance: "The carriers are firing their bolt."[15] Then he turned to his pilots and said, "Give 'em hell, boys: wish I were with you."[16]

Every minute counted. Pilots scrambled from the ready room to their planes. At 4:21, *Lexington, Enterprise, Yorktown, Hornet, Bunker Hill, Wasp,* and five CVLs turned east and into the wind. Ten minutes later, 216 planes—85 Hellcats, 54 Helldivers, 51 Avengers, and 26 Dauntlesses—winged westward, led by Lieutenant Commander B. M. Strean of *Yorktown*'s VF-1. Hellcats carried 400 gallons of 100-octane fuel, Helldivers 310 gallons, Avengers 330 gallons, and Dauntlesses 254 gallons. Hellcats had plenty of fuel, but the others, especially the Dauntlesses, would be cutting it close. To conserve fuel pilots climbed slowly, forming as they gained altitude. Lieutenant Commander R. A. Winston, fighter-director for TG 58.4, watched *Cabot*'s Air Group 31 launch. He did not expect her planes to return.

Lieutenant Commander J. D. Arnold, leading *Hornet*'s Air Group 2, knew flyers might have to ditch at sea. He told them to "retire as far as possible before darkness set in, notify the ship . . . then have all planes in the group land in the same vicinity so that rafts could be lashed together and mutual rescues could be affected."[17] Arnold did not know that, five minutes after being airborne, Lieutenant

Colonel Ralph Weymouth, leading *Lexington*'s Bombing 6, received a corrected position report placing the enemy 60 miles farther to the west. Mitscher, who planned to launch a second strike, immediately cancelled it.

In Tokyo, Admiral Toyoda received Kakuta's unnerving report on aircraft losses. Then he received word of the loss of *Shokaku* and *Taiho*. Toyoda knew the battle was lost and ordered Ozawa to break off the fight and steam for Okinawa. Late that afternoon, the ships got underway.

At 6:40 P.M., with the sun beginning to set, Commander Strean sighted six oilers and six destroyers moving slowly west. Ahead and fanned out over 30 miles he could see the dark shapes of Ozawa's carrier divisions. Strean had no time to organize an attack. In 20 minutes, it would be dark.

Air Group 14 from *Wasp*, hoping to prevent Ozawa from refueling, targeted the oilers and disabled two, which Ozawa later scuttled. The other air groups flew on, looking for larger game.

Flak lit up the sky, followed by streams of bright AA fire. The attack caught Ozawa unprepared. His carriers were recovering search planes when radar picked up the incoming strike, but he still managed to launch 75 planes. Hellcats jumped the Zeroes and shot 65 down, opening the way for the bombers.

The rapid approach of nightfall gave American pilots only minutes to pick targets, dive, and drop their payloads. The young flyers, already stressed and fatigued from a long flight into the sun, now faced the dark. Conscious that their gas gauges had already bumped the half-full mark, they wanted to get it over quickly. Air groups picked targets but attacked wildly. What they needed were torpedoes, but most planes carried bombs. For several months Avenger pilots had been bombing and firing rockets at island installations. They had neglected torpedo tactics because Spruance wanted Marianas airfields bombed. Most of Mitscher's planes were already armed with bombs when orders came to attack Ozawa's fleet, and there was no time to change to torpedoes.

What might have been a splendid victory fell far short of expectations. Nightfall, poor targeting, fuel depletion, and the lack of torpedoes all contributed to a lackluster performance. One or more bombs from *Enterprise*'s Avengers struck the carrier *Ryuho* but did little damage. Dive-bombers from *Yorktown, Hornet, Bataan,* and *Belleau Wood* set Ozawa's flagship *Zuikaku* on fire, which was partially abandoned but recovered after fires were quenched. A combined attack from *Bunker Hill, Cabot,* and *Monterey* planes struck the light carrier *Chiyoda,* started fires, and tore up the flight deck. Bombers put *Junyo* temporarily out of commission, but she survived.

One squadron carrying torpedoes was Lieutenant (jg) George P. Brown's four Avengers (Torpedo 24) from *Belleau Wood*. Antiaircraft from *Hiyo* wounded Brown in the leg and knocked off a section of his Avenger's wing, setting the plane on fire and filling the rear of the cockpit with smoke. He told his two-man crew to bail out, but he stayed with the plane, dove, and doused the fire in the slipstream. Instead of breaking off after dropping his torpedo, Brown flew directly down the length of *Hiyo*. The tactic completely distracted the ship's AA batteries, enabling Lieutenant (jg) Warren R. Omark, who had been on Brown's starboard, to come in low at 240 knots and at 400 feet drop his torpedo close to the ship. As Omark banked sharply away, his radioman and gunner saw the fish explode against *Hiyo*'s forward quarter. Brown's two crewmen watched from the water as *Hiyo* burst into flames. Two hours later *Hiyo* slipped beneath the waves. Wounded and with his plane crippled, Brown rode it into the sea and was never found.

What could have been the greatest carrier battle of the war ended inconclusively when, at 7:00 P.M., a curtain of darkness draped the Philippine Sea. Stars twinkled overhead, lightning flashed in the north, a few fires dotted the sea below, but there was no moon and a slight overcast for pilots to contend with on the long trip back to the carriers. Another battle began for the flyers of 190 planes winging eastward. Some planes had been damaged, and after three hours in the air after a stressful battle, pilot fatigue began creeping into the cockpits. Outside there was only darkness, water, and the monotonous drone of engines, but inside there was a small panel light illuminating a gauge approaching empty. For some, the inevitable became clear. They would not make it back.

A few cripples ditched along the way, but the mass ditchings did not begin until most planes were a few miles from the carriers. Helldivers got about two miles to the gallon. Five of them went down together, ditching 50 miles west of the fleet. Three carriers and a cruiser passed by before a destroyer picked the flyers out of their rafts and brought them on board.

Mitscher had been steaming west at full speed, hoping to reduce the distance for returning planes. He ordered the lights switched on and, in a unique trick never attempted before, beamed searchlights into the thin overcast above the carriers. He launched night-fighters with airborne radar to intercept planes and lead them back home. At 8:30, an air controller reported visual contact with the first returning planes. Mitscher stopped the carriers in their tracks, swung them east into the wind, and ordered cruisers and destroyers to illuminate the area with starshells.

At 8:50, two-hours of chaos began when a plane from *Hornet* landed on *Lexington*. Fearing that pilots would deplete their fuel looking for their home carrier, Mitscher issued instructions for planes to land wherever they could. With fuel tanks empty, pilots headed for the nearest flattop, causing numerous deck crashes. Deck handlers shoved the planes overboard. Some pilots—dazed, confused, and panicky—tried to land on battleships and cruisers. Others, unable to find a clear deck, crashed in the water beside the carrier. Destroyers searched through the waves, looking for little jabs of light coming from waterproof flashlights carried by pilots afloat in the water. Admiral Montgomery praised the work of the destroyers, writing, "had it not been for their persistent and effective efforts, our loss in pilots would have been staggeringly large."[18]

In the morning, Spruance ordered a wide search to find the Japanese fleet, which he knew had already retired, and to finish off cripples. Although Ozawa escaped, the search proved productive in other ways. Pilots located dozens of flyers in yellow rafts.

A morning-after tally showed a loss of 100 planes: 20 by combat and 80 by ditching or deck-crash. Picked up near the carriers or by floatplanes and destroyers were 163 pilots and airmen. Only 43 flyers were lost at sea. Another six died in deck crashes.

When the carrier phase of the Marianas campaign ended, the Japanese lost more than 500 planes and three flattops—*Shokaku*, *Taiho*, and *Hiyo*. Among Mitscher's admirals the rejoicing was restrained. They knew the opportunity to destroy the Japanese fleet had been lost, not because of a lack of willingness on their part, but because of Spruance. Mitscher tried to suppress his bitter feelings over what he perceived as Spruance's mismanagement of the naval phase of the Marianas campaign, but he only went halfway, writing, "The enemy had escaped. He had been badly hurt by one aggressive air strike. His fleet was not sunk."[19]

Nimitz recognized that Spruance had muffed an opportunity, but Spruance had become his most trusted fleet commander. Nimitz also recognized that while his objective had been to use TF-58 to find and engage the enemy in a conclusive battle, he had never specifically ordered Spruance to do it. Captain Emmet P. Forrestel, who was then Spruance's operations officer and later his biographer, wrote, "[Admiral Spruance's] primary mission was to take Saipan, Tinian, and Guam, and the amphibious landing on Saipan was at that time in a critical stage with troops ashore with partial supplies and a vast fleet of loaded ships in the vicinity."[20] Forrestel must have forgotten Admiral Turner's advice, who, soon after the landing on Saipan, urged Spruance to cut Mitscher loose because the escort carriers of his own command could maintain air supremacy.

The naval phase of the battle for the Marianas had ended, but the battle of the air admirals had just begun.

PART IV

Ascent of the Air Admirals

"Ninety-one years ago, a Naval officer [Matthew C. Perry] opened up the ports of Japan and now another officer is doing his damndest to close them."[1]

CHAPTER 13

The New Air Navy

Operations on Tinian and Guam continued into early August, but on July 12 the fighting ended on Saipan. By then, Nimitz and his staff had digested the flood of carrier commander action reports pouring into Pearl Harbor since the beginning of the Marianas campaign. Some of those reports were not what he expected.

Admiral Montgomery, speaking for TG 58.2, said it was unfortunate "our entire strength was deployed for this purpose [covering Saipan] and therefore not permitted an opportunity to take the offensive until too late to prevent the enemy's retirement."[2] Rear Admiral Ted Sherman wrote, "Spruance was still thinking of a surface action. He did not grasp the tremendous power of our air weapons or their ability to strike in any direction to the limit of their fuel supply."[3] Sherman's point was that a carrier group could have steamed 250 miles west of Saipan, fought a battle with Ozawa's fleet, and still covered the Marianas.

Spruance seemed unable to understand this simple concept because he was fundamentally a battleship and cruiser man, not an airman. His staff was also composed of gunship men without an airman among them. When Admiral King came to Saipan on July 17, he told Spruance that "he had done exactly the right thing . . . no matter what anyone else might say," but two weeks later, after reading dozens of action reports, he removed nonaviator Captain Carl Moore as Spruance's chief of staff and replaced him with veteran aviator Rear Admiral Arthur C. Davis of his own staff.[4]

The tactical training of Mitscher and his air admirals dated back to May 1937 and Fleet Problem XVIII, during which carrier and battleship commanders disagreed on tactics. Carrier commanders argued, "Once an enemy carrier is within striking distance of our fleet no security remains until it, its [air] squadrons, or both, are destroyed."[5] The fleet commander, a battleship man, disagreed and wanted carriers confined to supporting beach assaults. In the mock battle that followed, the landing succeeded but *Langley* was theoretically sunk and *Saratoga* and *Lexington* damaged.

Navy airmen learned a lesson from the exercise: if enemy carriers were in the area, the greatest gamble was to wait until they struck you. Airmen classed carriers as offensive weapons of enormous power. Battleship men thought of them mainly as mobile air bases. The greatest mistake was to restrict the mobility of carriers, which was precisely what Spruance did during the Saipan campaign. On June 19, 1944, had Spruance turned the carriers loose as Mitscher wanted, the most decisive battle in naval history would have been fought. Instead, Mitscher's airmen enjoyed a turkey shoot but were not released from the defensive mode soon enough to destroy the Japanese fleet.

During the summer of 1944, while marines mopped up the Marianas, air admirals of the navy became more assertive. Their goal was to redefine the character of the fleet and control it. They won support from James Forrestal, who in April 1944 succeeded Frank Knox as Secretary of the Navy. Forrestal, an early navy pilot, sided with the strongest advocates of naval air—Mitscher, Towers, Halsey, and the Shermans—but the internal scuffle in mid-1944 had more to do with postwar budget planning than wartime carrier operations. Gunship admirals still outnumbered air admirals, but the outstanding performance of fast carrier groups in the Pacific had diminished the importance of battleships. The Marianas Turkey Shoot and the Battle of the Philippine Sea, during which carriers delivered crushing blows to the enemy and gained air supremacy of the Central Pacific, convinced Nimitz that the fast carrier program should be given top priority. Admiral King did not completely agree, but Forrestal did, so on July 31 Nimitz got what he wanted: more planes, more pilots, and more carriers. There were already 35 carriers on active duty or under construction, and the new authorization provided for three more fast carriers, a battle carrier, and two light carriers. In mid-1944, nobody expected the war to end before 1946, but postwar requirements were already being discussed in Washington and air admirals were having their say.

During the summer of 1944, the IJN began losing face in Japan. General Tojo and his military cabinet collapsed, and the emperor's advisers admitted that the loss of Saipan marked the turning point in the war. The U.S. Navy had breached Japan's inner defensive shield, causing Fleet Admiral Osami Nagano to lament, "Hell is on us."[6]

Admiral Ozawa assessed his losses after the Battle of the Philippine Sea and tried to resign, but Nagano rejected the request. Despite Ozawa's disappointing performance, Nagano could not afford to waste time looking for a replacement. The Japanese fleet had been worn down and the carrier air force severely depleted, but the IJN still had plenty of airbases and planes in the Pacific. The problem was deciding where to deploy the remaining aircraft.

Unless the Japanese could strike a decisive blow against the Pacific Fleet, there could be no hope of winning the war. Their carrier forces had been whittled down by the loss of *Shokaku*, *Hiyo*, and *Taiho*. Japan had lost the battle of carrier and plane production to the supercharged American shipbuilding and aircraft industry. After Midway, the Japanese government had authorized 20 fast carriers but only *Taiho* and six *Unryu*-class carriers were laid down. Two conversions were also underway—the huge 64,800-ton *Shinano* and the 12,500-ton CVL *Ibuki*, both due for commissioning in early 1945—but progress was slow.

IGH predicted MacArthur's intentions to mount a campaign against the Philippines during the autumn of 1944. Since securing New Guinea in late July, there had been little else on MacArthur's mind. Any attack on the Philippines or Formosa threatened to shut off Japan's supply routes to crucial East Indies oil fields, which were already in jeopardy because of American submarine activity. The IJN concluded that the defining naval battle of the war would be fought in the Philippines, and to succeed, more carriers were needed. To this end, said Nagano, the three carriers lost in the Marianas must be immediately replaced.

In August, Japanese shipyards hurriedly commissioned two fast carriers, the 17,150-ton *Unryu* and a sister ship, the 17,460-ton *Amagi*. Each flattop carried 54 aircraft and could steam at a respectable 34 knots. Admiral Ozawa shifted his flag to the new *Amagi*, which with *Unryu* and the battle-scarred *Zuikaku* brought Carrier Division 1 back to strength. On October 15, the 17,260-ton *Katsuragi* (another *Unryu*-class carrier) went into commission. Instead of adding it to Carrier Division 2, which had lost *Hiyo*, Ozawa placed it in his own carrier division. He dissolved Carrier Division 2 and transferred *Junyo* and *Ryuho* to Carrier Division 4, commanded by Rear Admiral Chiaki Matsuda, whose other carriers were actually the half-battleships *Ise* and *Hyuga*. Carrier Division 3 remained as before with *Chitose*, *Chiyoda*, and *Zuiho*.

For carrier use, the Japanese developed the new 400-mph Shiden-kai fighter. They had also been working on the 390-mph Reppu fighter as a Zero replacement. It never got beyond the prototype stage, but the Shiden-kais did.

If the new carriers completed their accelerated shakedown cruises and new aircraft plans stayed on track, Admiral Toyoda anticipated having a respectable navy and new air groups by mid-November. Ozawa's Mobile Fleet would have five fast carriers, four light carriers, and two half-battleship carriers. The most serious obstacle was a shortage of pilots and insufficient time to train them. Another troubling problem was a shortage of aviation fuel. All things considered, only masterful Japanese tactics combined with great bungling on the part of American carrier commanders could prevent the IJN from suffering irreparable damage.

Captain Eiichiro Jyo of the CVL *Chiyoda* thought he had answers to the tactical questions. "[We cannot] hope to sink the numerically superior enemy aircraft carriers through ordinary attack methods," Jyo told Ozawa. "[We must organize] special attack units to carry-out crash-dive tactics."[7] At first, Ozawa did not like the idea, but his senior air admirals did. Vice Admiral Takajiro Onishi knew that most of the new pilots had a better chance of hitting a ship with their plane than with a bomb. Onishi did not to wait for Ozawa to decide and began organizing a kamikaze corps of suicide planes.

After the Battle of the Philippine Sea, the U.S. Navy roamed at will in the Central Pacific while Ozawa's Mobile Fleet seemed to have evaporated in the hot tropical winds. For several weeks, war in the Pacific took a respite.

During the summer, three *Essex*-class carriers joined the Pacific Fleet: *Franklin* (CV-13), *Hancock* (CV-19), and *Ticonderoga* (CV-14). New *Essex*-class carriers continued to be commissioned at the rate of one a month: *Bennington* (CV-20) in August, *Shangri-La* (CV-38) in September, *Randolph* (CV-15) in October, and *Bon Homme Richard* (CV-31) in November. Some of the carriers were of the new *Essex* Long-Hull group with slightly longer flight decks. The popular 20-mm Oerlikon AA guns had been replaced by heavier, longer-range 40 mm Bofors, and a new proximity-fused shell with improved accuracy replaced standard ordnance on 5″/38 guns.

Mitscher never brought his carriers back to Pearl Harbor. The improvements in technology came to him in the form of retrofits wherever his task force went. A vastly improved Mark 22 radar system, which could be adapted to older shipboard fire control systems, gave air controllers a better fix on incoming enemy aircraft, and together with improvements made in AA weapons, provided better fire-direction control.

For the navy, one of the stumbling blocks concerned aircraft, and especially fighters. The Grumman F6F-3 Hellcat, flying at 376 mph at 17,000 feet, had defeated Japan's best planes in every combat. So did land-based F4U Corsairs. Many authorities believed that to spend large sums of money to produce better aircraft was unnecessary, but others worried that the Japanese might be developing fighters to match Hellcats and Corsairs. Indeed they were with Shiden-kais. There was also the question of postwar requirements because Germany and Great Britain were experimenting with jet-propelled aircraft. The debate would continue into the future, but in 1944 the navy settled for going ahead with the Grumman F6F-5, a better armored and slightly faster plane than the F6F-3 Hellcat.

The changeover to F6F-5 fighters had an immediate impact on heavy carriers. The new Hellcats carried a 500-pound general-purpose bomb and in late August began replacing SB2C Helldivers, which in turn began replacing Dauntlesses. During the summer of 1944, fast carrier air groups began the changeover to new Hellcats. A new F4U-4 Corsair fighter, which could fly at 446 mph and was qualified for use on carriers, became the standard Marine Corps land-based "Jap-killer" and was not assigned to flattops. Avengers, Helldivers, and F6F-5 Hellcats remained the aircraft of preference for fleet carriers, but better and faster planes with improved radar, instrumentation, and firepower were being rapidly developed by America's aircraft industry.

Admiral King wanted a night carrier division built around *Enterprise*, *Independence*, and *Bataan*. Grumman F6F-5Ns became the night fighter and Avengers the standard torpedo-bomber. Hellcats carried new APS-6 airborne radar, which could detect an enemy ship 22 miles away. Avengers carried ASD-1 radar, which could identify a flattop 40 miles away. Planes had to be retrofitted with night-flying equipment, pilots had to be trained, and the flattops converted from day carriers to night carriers, all of which took time.

The summer interlude of 1944 also ushered in organization changes that had been brewing ever since the war began. In May 1944, Admirals King and Nimitz met with Halsey and adopted a two-platoon system that made sense to them but confused others. The two-platoon system involved the rotation at sea of commanders and their staffs without a change in ships. Halsey was no longer needed in the Solomons and his Third Fleet had been downgraded to the equivalent of a task group. Halsey came to Pearl Harbor with his staff as one of two planning platoons, Spruance and his staff became the other. If Halsey went to sea, his command became the Third Fleet (TF-38). If Spruance went to sea, his command became the Fifth Fleet (TF-58). There was only one big fleet, and its numerical designation depended on who commanded it. Halsey would use the task force for operations he planned, Spruance for operations he planned. On June 17, while Spruance was overseeing operations in the Marianas, Halsey began planning the next operation at Commander in Chief Pacific (Cincpac) headquarters.

Admirals King and Nimitz had finally and permanently reached the conclusion that fast carriers were the future of the navy. This caused radical changes throughout the fleet, and especially in Spruance's command, where he was forced to shed trusted battleship men for aviators. Nor did the rule settle well with most officers of the "Gun Club," because in 1944 they began losing control of the navy. The aviators had not yet taken complete charge because men like Spruance still carried weight, but it was only a matter of time. Battleships and cruisers had been reduced to protecting carriers, and this created squabbles between aviators and nonaviators. Admiral Lee, a superb battle group commander, became distraught because he would never be able to fight an action as a tactical commander.

Admiral King observed dissention mounting between the Gun Club and aviators. During the summer of 1944, he visited Cincpac to resolve the issue. He sent grumbling Gun Club men stateside to make room for air admirals. Rear Admiral George Murray, who had not distinguished himself as a carrier commander in the Solomons, was nonetheless an airman and part of the team. King gave him another chance, and named him Commander Air Force Pacific Fleet on August 16. Because of increased emphasis on air power, Murray became a vice admiral. During the summer months, King made dozens of changes, taking air captains from fast carriers and promoting them to admirals in charge of escort carrier groups. King was looking down the road. By the summer of 1945 the Pacific Fleet would have 17 heavy carriers and nine light carriers, enough to break the flattops into two separate task forces, Mitscher with one and McCain with the other, and eliminate the practice of rotation.

After taking the steps necessary to transfer the future of the U.S. Navy into the hands of air admirals, King departed for Washington and left the details of fighting the war in the Pacific with Nimitz, Halsey, and Spruance.

Admiral John Towers, Nimitz's deputy, viewed the changes as a major victory for airmen. He wrote, "Thank Heaven that Halsey and Mick Carney [Halsey's chief of staff] have stepped into the driver's seat."[8]

Admiral Mitscher never participated in the discussions. He was too busy knocking out enemy airfields and running errands for Nimitz's planners. They wanted photographs of the Palau group, and in particular the islands of Peleliu, Yap, and Ulithi. Nimitz's timetable called for a strike on the Palaus in September, thereby eliminating the last Japanese salient in the western Carolines.

Home base for TF-58 became Eniwetok, and for the next four months Mitscher, when not at sea, directed operations from there. On July 22, he sent Jocko Clark's TG 58.1, Davison's TG 58.2, and Montgomery's TG 58.3 to the six main islands of the Palaus to gather photographs and bomb airfields. The carriers stayed in the area for four days. When returning home on July 29, there was not a flyable enemy plane to bid them goodbye.

Mitscher learned the Japanese intended to bring planes through the Bonin Islands and Iwo Jima, so he ordered Clark and Montgomery to pay the area a visit. On August 4, TG 58.1 and 58.3 launched planes against Chichi Jima, Haha Jima, and Iwo Jima. Hellcats strafed 25 planes on Iwo's airfields but found no more. Clark's pilots spotted eight freighters and three escorts departing from the area and sank all but two. Had Clark and Montgomery sent a landing team ashore on Iwo they may have taken it, but Nimitz's planners had no knowledge the island was so vulnerable. Over the next six months, the desolate volcanic island became a Japanese stronghold.

On August 10, Nimitz arrived at Eniwetok and learned the carrier task groups had just returned from bombing the Jimas. Remembering some old navy history, he took Mitscher aside and said, "Ninety-one years ago, a Naval officer [Matthew C. Perry] opened up the ports of Japan and now another officer is doing his damndest to close them."[9] Until the mid-1800s, Japan had not penetrated the world beyond its shores.

While TF-58 enjoyed a two-week rest, Nimitz brought Mitscher up to date on the Pacific Fleet's organization changes. On August 12, Rear Admiral Ted Sherman relieved Montgomery in command of TG 58.3, and six days later Vice Admiral John S. McCain relieved Clark in command of TG 58.1. Montgomery and Clark were long overdue for a furlough. Rear Admiral Gerald F. Bogan remained in command of TG 38.2, and Rear Admiral Ralph E. Davison continued to command TG 38.4. Every admiral in charge of a task group, and every captain in charge of the 16 carriers comprising the task force were aviators. On August 26, Halsey relieved Spruance. The Fifth Fleet became the Third Fleet and Mitscher's TF-58 became TF-38. The only nonaviators were Halsey's chief of staff, Rear Admiral Robert B. Carney, and Mitscher's chief of staff, Commodore

Arleigh A. Burke, because early in 1944 Nimitz had decreed that every fleet command and every task group must have one airman and one nonaviator in the top echelon.

When Halsey took command of the Third Fleet, he looked upon himself as being the *real* carrier commander. He made little allowance for the tactical expertise of Mitscher and his men, all of whom were superb carrier men. Halsey lacked the hands-on experience of Mitscher, and carrier tactics had significantly changed since the Solomons campaign. When Halsey stepped on board Mitscher's flagship, he recalled, "I hadn't been with the fleet for more than two years: I wanted to see what the new carriers and planes looked like."[10] Halsey had more homework to do than he first realized. He could not do it without help from Mitscher, but he brought on board his staff from the South Pacific and many of them, his chief of staff and his operations officer in particular, were fiery nonaviators as stubborn as Halsey.

Meanwhile, Mitscher needed to be briefed on plans hatched at Cincpac headquarters while his task force was rampaging through the Central Pacific. Nimitz now had a new timetable: to strike the Palaus, and Peleliu in particular, on September 15, while MacArthur landed on Morotai in the Celebes Sea. Nimitz and MacArthur believed that both islands were essential steppingstones to the Philippines, now on the planning table. During one of the sessions, Halsey suggested that both islands be leapfrogged in favor of a direct landing on Kyushu in southern Japan. Nimitz did not agree, stating that American forces must first establish intermediate fleet and air bases. Halsey wanted to say, "We have air bases. They are called aircraft carriers," but held his tongue.[11] For the JCS and Nimitz, future plans beyond the assault of Peleliu and Morotai remained unresolved.

On August 31, while discussions continued between the JCS and Nimitz's staff over how best to defeat Japan while warring in Europe, Halsey cut loose his 16 carriers. For three days, Admiral Davison's TG 38.4 pounded Iwo and Chichi Jima, following it with strikes against Wake Island and Yap. On September 6, the main event began when McCain, Bogan, and Sherman's task groups spent three days hammering air bases and military installations in the Palaus.

On September 9, Halsey left Davison among the Palaus, took the other three groups west, and on September 12 struck Mindanao's Lumbia and Cagayan airfields. The attack came as a complete surprise. Halsey found light opposition, broke off Mindanao raids, and ranged through the southern Philippines, destroying enemy aircraft, ships, and ground targets with impunity. The moment Zeros appeared in the air, Hellcats shot them down. A few new Shidens flown by green pilots showed up and met the same fate.

Halsey's raid ranked among the best ever planned by a carrier group. On the first day, navy pilots knocked out all enemy radar stations in the southern Philippines. Because of the loss of intelligence, Japanese long-range search planes waited on the ground for directional information that never came. They were still there when the first wave of Hellcats flew over the field and cut them to pieces. On Cebu's Lahug airfield fighter squadrons, gassed up and fully armed, waited in line for reports from the same search planes. Hellcats swooped over the airfield and decimated the fighters. A few Zeros got into the air and experienced short and disastrous careers.

More strikes followed, and the 11 primary and secondary Japanese airfields on Mindanao, Leyte, and Cebu received heavy doses of carrier air power. Later, a few planes from Lahug flew into the night looking for Halsey's carriers and never returned. They may have been kamikazes. The records did not say.

On September 13, Halsey's planes swarmed over the islands of the Visayan Sea and found more planes on Negros Island's airfields. Some were parked on runways, others hidden in revetments or covered with camouflage. Commander David McCampbell of *Essex* had learned to recognize camouflage markings. After strafing enemy planes attempting to get airborne, McCampbell turned his group on camouflaged aircraft. He found it impossible to count the number of planes destroyed on the ground, but he could see 12 twin-engine bombers and 7 fighters on fire. Before the day ended, McCampbell's group encountered a swarm of 40 enemy fighters and shot 21 of them down, losing 1 Hellcat in the process.

During September 12–13, 2,400 sorties struck 21 Japanese primary and secondary airfields on Mindanao, Leyte, Cebu, Negros, and Panay. Carrier planes also strafed and bombed airfields in the central Philippines, hammering airstrips on Luzon.

Halsey began to wonder where the Japanese had hidden their aircraft and whether they were holding back. To some extent, his concerns were valid. Photographs showed planes where the previous day there had been none and some interesting examples of clever camouflage at the Damagusto airfield on Negros Island. Two days later, Ensign Thomas C. Tillar, who had been shot down over Leyte, was recovered by a PBY "Dumbo" and returned to *Hornet*. Tillar reported that the natives who sheltered him said that Japanese air defenses on the Philippines were nothing "but a hollow shell."[12]

Halsey suspected there were still enemy aircraft hidden somewhere among the islands, but he decided to end the four-day raid after photographs failed to reveal more targets. He informed Nimitz that TG-38 had complete command of the air and that MacArthur's Sixth Army should go directly to Leyte as soon as possible instead of waiting until late December. Halsey also stated that the Peleliu-Morotai operations scheduled for September 15 were no longer necessary and should be canceled. Nimitz and MacArthur ignored Halsey's suggestion. This proved most unfortunate. Major General William H. Rupertus, commanding the 1st Marine Division, had predicted that Peleliu could be taken in a few days. Instead, the fighting lasted two months and resulted in 9,170 American casualties. Peleliu was not worth the cost. As Halsey said, the island could have been bypassed. Other landings among the Palaus were postponed and the troops shifted to the Leyte campaign.

The decision to invade the Philippines had been decided by President Roosevelt and General MacArthur during a meeting with Nimitz at Pearl Harbor. MacArthur held the highest regard for Halsey. The general also had a keen sense of politics. In June, the invasion of France by the Allies had succeeded and it was only a matter of months before Germany surrendered. The time now seemed ripe for another major invasion, this one in the Pacific. Everyone in America knew that when MacArthur withdrew from the Philippines he had promised to return. His "return" would make good publicity for Roosevelt, so D day on Leyte was moved up to October 20—17 days before the national election. If the invasion succeeded, Roosevelt expected it to propel him into an unprecedented fourth term as president. MacArthur did not want Spruance to spoil the show. He wanted Halsey at the helm.

After deciding on the Leyte campaign, the JCS began looking beyond the Philippines. Nimitz vetoed an assault on Formosa and Amoy. He preferred going from Leyte to Luzon, from Luzon to Iwo Jima in January 1945, to Okinawa in March, and then Japan. King did not want Halsey's carriers tied up for months off Luzon, but MacArthur said he would not need them for more than a few days. Once ashore on Leyte, he believed his own land-based aircraft coupled with support from Admiral Kinkaid's Seventh Fleet escort carriers could command the air. Discussions continued regarding how best to assault Japan, but the JCS, along with Nimitz and MacArthur, finally agreed to the Leyte-Luzon-Iwo-Okinawa approach about two weeks after Halsey reported Leyte vulnerable to immediate attack.

After MacArthur moved D day for Leyte from December 20 to October 20, Mitscher resumed strikes on Manila and the Visayas. By the end of September, TF-38 air groups had destroyed 893 Japanese planes and had sent 224,000 tons of shipping to the bottom.[13]

On September 23, Halsey detached himself from TF-38 and returned to the Palaus. He issued orders for Rear Admiral W.H.P. Blandy to pass up the scheduled assault of Angaur and put TG-32.2's floating reserve ashore on undefended Ulithi Atoll. Ulithi had a fine natural harbor and a good coral shelf for airfields, and a week later Halsey made it the new advanced base for the Pacific Fleet. On October 1–2, Bogan and Sherman brought their carriers into Ulithi Lagoon and rode out a violent three-day typhoon. By the middle of October, Ulithi's harbor became a 400,000 barrel fuel center with repair facilities, hospital ships, oilers, salvage ships, and airfields for CAP and replacement planes for carrier losses. No longer dependent on Eniwetok, Halsey transferred everything for the Leyte campaign to Ulithi.

The survival of Japan depended on the ability of the IJN to control the South China Sea. By securing the Philippines, the United States could "cork" it up, and, once corked, Japan would no longer be able to draw oil from the East Indies. Such penetration of Japan's inner defense line would create great consternation in IGH. Japan would be compelled to throw every ship and soldier the empire could spare to prevent the recapture of the Philippines. The survival of the Japanese government depended on it.

Halsey's carrier commanders prepared for what they expected to be the greatest sea battle of the war. Spruance had allowed Admiral Ozawa to slip away during the Battle of the Philippine Sea. Halsey had no intention of allowing Ozawa to do it again.

CHAPTER 14

Prelude to the Philippines

Defending the Philippines put an enormous strain on the rapidly dwindling resources of the Japanese Empire. The islands acted as the western flank of Japan's inner defense circle and the eastern flank of Japan's vital lines of communication and raw materials from the East Indies. Controlling the Philippines kept Japan in the war. Under no circumstances could IGH allow the Philippines to fall into the hands of the Allies. MacArthur intended to cork those supply lines. Recapturing the Philippines would enable his command to link up with British forces in India and Chiang Kai-shek's army in China.

As a preventive measure, IGH authorized the transfer of ships and aircraft from other areas to defend the Philippines. Admiral Toyoda had no choice but to commit Ozawa's Third Fleet at Japan and Admiral Kurita's Second Fleet at Singapore. Toyoda admitted, "There would be no sense in saving the fleet at the expense of the loss of the Philippines."[1]

Toyoda expected MacArthur to assault the Philippines in December, and he worked toward having all his defenses in place by November. The battle fleet included Ozawa's Northern Force of three carrier divisions, Kurita's Center Force of two battleship divisions and three cruiser divisions, and a combined Southern Force of one battleship division and two cruiser divisions under Vice Admirals Kiyohide Shima and Shoji Nishimura. Toyoda also planned to assemble more than 1,000 land-based and carrier-based aircraft for defense, along with scattered squadrons of suicide planes.

Although Toyoda erred in predicting the date of the assault, MacArthur and Nimitz's planners erred in anticipating Toyoda's countermeasures. After MacArthur advanced the Leyte landing to October 20, he also moved up Mindoro landings to December 5, and Luzon landings to December 20. Navy planners expected the assault on Mindoro or Luzon would draw the Japanese fleet into a major action. They did not except it to come at Leyte.

Accelerating the Leyte assault by two months created loose ends. Operations against the Philippines fell under General MacArthur's Southwest Pacific

A partial view of the U.S. fast carrier fleet, which acted as the Third Fleet under Admiral Spruance or the Fifth Fleet when under the Command of Admiral Halsey. The USS *Essex* is in the foreground with other *Essex*-class and *Independence*-class carriers in the background. (National Archives)

command. He had his own land-based air force under Lieutenant General Kenney and his own surface ships, the Seventh Fleet ("MacArthur's Navy"), under Admiral Kinkaid. Kinkaid had been the last nonaviator to command a carrier division, and in 1942 King had removed him from carrier command. Kinkaid's Seventh Fleet consisted of battleships, cruisers, and destroyers. Because Mac-Arthur had chosen to bypass Mindanao, Kenney's land-based planes were too distant to provide adequate air cover for Leyte landings, so Nimitz detached Rear Admiral Thomas L. Sprague's Escort Carrier Group (TG 77.4) and sent 18 of the baby carriers with light cruiser and destroyer supports to MacArthur. Kenney balked because he knew nothing about operating aircraft from escort carriers. Kinkaid could not help much, so Nimitz pulled Captain Richard Whitehead from leave and sent him to Kinkaid as Commander Air Support, Seventh Fleet.

Halsey planned, if necessary, to support the Leyte landing with the Third Fleet, but he was a free agent from the Southwest Pacific Command and responsible to Nimitz. Halsey viewed his principal task as destroying the enemy fleet, and in this Nimitz fully agreed. The arrangement left nobody in overall command. Halsey and MacArthur were each in charge of his own activities. Neither man established a common communications link with the other. All messages between the Third Fleet and MacArthur or Kinkaid had to be routed and rerouted through a slow, cumbersome system. Nimitz would never have trusted MacArthur with Halsey's fast carriers, and MacArthur did not want the all-army Leyte operation shared with the navy, even though the Seventh Fleet and Nimitz's escort carriers were already part of the general's amphibious force.

Earlier, MacArthur had declared that escort carriers could cover the Leyte operation and that Halsey would not be tied down during the landings. Nimitz used MacArthur's statement to inform Halsey, "In case opportunity for destruction of major portion of the enemy fleet is offered or can be created, *such destruction becomes the primary task.*"[2] Regardless of MacArthur's needs, Halsey clearly understood Nimitz's priorities, which coincided fully with his own.

Halsey, however, had a sloppy way of communicating with his task force. He used abrupt dispatches instead of meticulously crafted orders. The system worked when he commanded a single carrier, but with four divisions of 17 carriers and Admiral Lee's battle group thrown into the mix, Halsey's loosely worded dispatches often caused confusion. This worrisome trait annoyed Mitscher and his carrier commanders, and in the weeks to come would annoy them even more.

Halsey set out to bring on a battle with Ozawa's carriers before they could disrupt MacArthur's plans. On October 7, the Third Fleet rendezvoused 375 miles west of the Marianas and with more than 1,000 aircraft steamed toward Formosa and Okinawa to neutralize Vice Admiral Shigero Fukudome's Second Air Fleet. Halsey next planned to move south and strike Admiral Onishi's First Air Fleet on Luzon and Visayan. Somewhere during the two operations, he expected to clash with Ozawa's carrier divisions.

Halsey's operation began on October 10 when TF-38, operating closer to Japan than ever before, struck Okinawa's airbases with Hellcats and caught most of Fukudome's planes on the ground. Dive-bombers followed, dropping high explosives on runways, control towers, hangars, and fuel dumps. Two hours later, the second wave struck. This time Fukudome had all his aircraft aloft, including a number of trainer planes. Hellcat pilots shot down or chased off everything Fukudome put in the air.

One strike followed another, sweeping across the full length of the island. After destroying Yontan's airbases, pilots began looking for other airfields and found them scattered about, including a new one on Ie Shima. By day's end, TF-38 had flown 1,400 missions, damaged all the airfields on Okinawa, and destroyed more than 100 aircraft. Planes also struck Okinawa's harbor and sank 18 ships, 2 midget submarines, and 22 sampans. Halsey lost 21 planes, but American submarines recovered most of the flyers.

Halsey found too few planes on Okinawa and suspected they were being rapidly shuttled to Luzon and Formosa. On October 11, he sent part of his carrier force to strike Aparri airfield on northern Luzon, hoping the raid would deflect the enemy's attention from Formosa. By evening, there were not enough enemy planes left in northern Luzon to interfere with operations against Formosa.

The sudden strikes by TF-38 in October wrecked Admiral Toyoda's plans for a major carrier battle in November. He ordered Admiral Fukudome to commit all land-based planes to the destruction of Halsey's carriers. He then flew to Formosa to personally direct the air attacks, for it was there that he had based his veteran pilots. Fukudome had about 750 planes on Formosa, and Onishi had about 450 planes in northern Luzon. So on the morning of October 12, as Mitscher launched the first strike against Formosa, Fukudome could muster about 1,300 planes for operations against the Third Fleet.

Before dawn, Fukudome sent scout planes to find TF-38. Pilots located the carriers and reported the entire force steaming for Formosa. Fukudome had 100 fighters in the air when the first Hellcat sweep preceding the bombers appeared over Formosa.

Commander David McCambell of *Essex*, leading the first strike group of 32 Hellcats, had been looking for Kobi airfield. Old maps from American intelligence showed three airfields. From 19,000 feet McCambell counted about as many as 15. He also discovered that the enemy had developed a system for jamming his fighter control frequency, which added to the difficulty of choosing the right target. Then to his surprise he sighted Shidens at 23,000 feet and had to climb to engage them. This put McCampbell's flyers at a disadvantage, but the Shidens broke formation and sacrificed their altitude advantage. Operating as single planes made them easy targets. McCampbell's pilots stayed in four-plane divisions until the moment of contact, breaking then into two-plane sections so each pilot had a wingman to cover his tail. Hellcats fought the first big air battle of the day at 15,000 to 25,000 feet, and at this altitude Hellcats matched the swift Shidens.

McCampbell encountered the first new Japanese Radens, called "Jacks," and observed that they could outclimb a Hellcat at high altitudes. He spotted only four of them and his pilots shot one down.

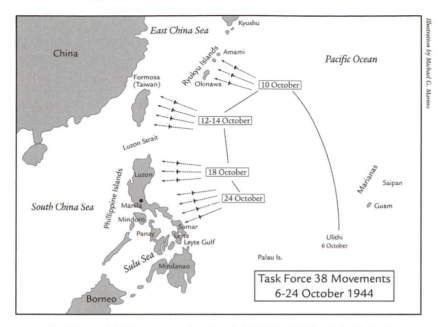

Task Force 38 Movements, October 6–24, 1944. (Michael G. Marino)

Japanese pilots fought with desperation but failed to stop Hellcats from sweeping over airfields and strafing and firing rockets into rows of fighters taxiing for takeoff. Other waves followed, striking airfields at Kobi, Keishu, Rokko, Toyohara, and Nikosho. Dozens of fully gassed single- and twin-engine planes on the ground burst into flames. Helldivers and Avengers, following behind the fighters, blew up buildings, hangars, and ammunition dumps.

At every airfield Mitscher's pilots met fierce AA fire that caused more damage than the dogfights. TF-38 lost 48 planes, but the enemy suffered enormous losses in the air and on the ground.

Admiral Toyoda arrived at Formosa during the latter part of the day. IGH had prepared three separate plans for countering an American attack: SHO-1 for the invasion of the Philippines; SHO-2 for the invasion of Formosa; and SHO-3 for the invasion of Okinawa. On reaching Formosa, Toyoda executed SHO-2. Exaggerated reports by returning pilots led him to change his air defense plans from making his stand on the Philippines to making it on Formosa. He ordered Ozawa to detach all planes from Carrier Divisions 3 (3rd Naval Air Squadron) and 4 (4th Naval Air Squadron) and send them to Formosa to join in an all-out attack on Halsey's task force.

While the transfers were being made, IGH met with senior officers in Tokyo to determine exactly what the Americans intended to do and to decide what measures to take. The meeting ended indecisively, so IGH left matters in the hands of Admirals Fukudome and Toyoda. Fukudome brought the elite Thunderbolt Torpedo Squadron—100 of the improved Tenzan Jill torpedo-bombers—from Kyushu to Formosa to destroy Halsey's carriers.

During the afternoon of October 12, Japanese search planes located three of Halsey's task groups off eastern Formosa. At 2:00 P.M., 55 Tenzans went airborne and began searching for the carriers. The day was dark and cloudy and the torpedo-bombers never sighted a ship. Only 29 returned to base; the others either became lost or were shot down by American fighters.

On the morning of October 13 Mitscher resumed operations against Formosa, but pilots found few Japanese planes in the air. Fukudome had received reinforcements overnight, but he kept them all under cover for a major battle the following day. Hellcats and Helldivers concentrated on shipping, but without notable results. The bad weather of the previous day had settled over Formosa. The absence of enemy resistance deluded Halsey into believing that his pilots had neutralized the island and the moment had come to move on the Philippines.

Late that afternoon, Fukudome launched a massive air attack against the American fleet, which had moved about 60 miles southwest of Ishigaki Island off Formosa. Fukudome scheduled the strike to arrive just after dark, when carriers were the most vulnerable. If the planes arrived early, Fukudome instructed his pilots to hide in clouds until sunset. Some pilots followed his instructions; others could not wait and attacked during daylight.

At 5:00 P.M., *Essex* radar picked up an incoming flight of a dozen torpedo planes. AA warded off the first attack and shot down four planes. *Essex* avoided a number of torpedoes, but this was only the beginning.

The attack became general and lasted all night. Planes attacked furiously, the pilots never able to see whether damage had been done. Those who survived returned to Formosa with glowing reports. The first group informed Fukudome that three carriers had been sunk. Japanese planes were being shot down at a staggering rate, but in Fukudome's mind his young pilots were winning the battle. As night wore on, returning pilots reported more sinkings. They pleaded to be rearmed and refueled, so off they went again, many never to return. Fukudome took no time to count losses because in his mind a great battle was being won.

Toyoda reported the stunning victory to Tokyo, and IGH released the good news to the press. Accounts flooding Tokyo's streets on October 14 read, Sunk: three aircraft carriers, three warships of unidentified category, and one destroyer, plus another aircraft carrier and warship damaged, along with 160 American planes shot down. By October 16 claims ballooned to 35 American ships sunk or damaged, including five more carriers, a battleship, and a dozen lesser ships. Two days later, the Japanese press reported that the American task force had lost 1,000 planes and 25,000 men. On October 19, IGH upped the claims to 42 ships destroyed, including 11 carriers, 2 battleships, and 7 more carriers damaged. These last figures resulted from search planes spotting a small detachment of ships escorting two crippled cruisers back to Ulithi and thinking they were the only survivors from Halsey's fleet.

For three days, the Japanese believed they had won the war, and IGH seemed obliged to let the public enjoy their misbegotten euphoria.

One small item in the Japanese account was partly true. On October 13, Halsey had detached Admiral Davison's TG 38.4 with instructions to strike airfields in northern Luzon. Four Japanese Jills attempted to torpedo the carrier *Franklin* (CV-13), but she outmaneuvered the "fish" and shot down all four planes. Rear Admiral Masafumi Arima, commanding the 26th Air Flotilla of the First Air Fleet, decided to show his group how the coming contest for the Philippines could be won. Against orders, he took off from Luzon in a bomber and deliberately crashed it into *Franklin*. The plane exploded in flames and did a small amount of damage to the carrier, but not enough to knock her out of action. The attack marked the beginning of what was to become a new carrier war. Arima became the first suicide pilot to actually plan his attack in advance.

On October 15, Admiral Toyoda began tallying his losses and discovered that more than 500 planes had been lost. He had sacrificed a third of his air strength and diluted his ability to defend the Philippines. He would eventually learn that none of the American carriers but *Franklin* had been damaged, though a few Japanese torpedo planes did get through the protective AA screen and struck the heavy cruiser *Canberra* and the light cruiser *Houston*, which Halsey sent under escort to Ulithi for repair. Halsey also detached the light carriers *Cabot* and *Cowpens* and sent them along with the escorts, hoping that Japanese search planes would locate the slow-moving cripples and lure Vice Admiral Kiyohide Shima's three cruisers from Japan. Despite heavy clouds, planes from Clark Field did locate the cripples and reported them as the last remnants of Halsey's fleet. It was this report that misled IGH into believing that Halsey's task force had been destroyed. Shima took the bait but soon learned that TF-38 was far from defeated and prudently turned back.

After reviewing aerial photographs taken over Formosa, Halsey decided that little could be accomplished by further attacks. His planes were low on ammunition, and MacArthur wanted him nearby for the Leyte assault.

On October 17, the Third Fleet steamed for the Leyte Gulf to support MacArthur's amphibious landing. On the way, planes from McCain, Bogan, and Davison's groups pummeled Luzon, in particular the vast facilities at Manila's Clark Field where most of the enemy's air opposition originated. Halsey believed the Japanese fleet would not interfere until the Mindoro or Luzon assaults, which were scheduled later. By keeping three carrier groups in the area, he felt capable of responding to any emergency. All four of his hard-working groups needed to rotate to Ulithi for rest and replenishment, but he could only detach one at a time, beginning with Ted Sherman's TG 37.3. In his opinion, General Kenney's long-range AAF planes could aid MacArthur's landing if help was needed.

On the same day, a Japanese garrison on tiny Suluan Island spotted American ships putting troops ashore near their observation post and reported the landings to Tokyo. The situation quickly became clear to Toyoda. MacArthur intended to invade the Philippines, not Formosa. Toyoda now regretted activating SHO-2 because it sapped his air strength. Having depleted his inventory of planes, Toyoda had no other alternative but to launch SHO-1 and call into action Japan's battle fleet.

When Admiral Onishi arrived at Manila to take command of the First Air Fleet, Admiral Teraoka informed him that he had fewer than 100 planes. New aircraft were coming through the pipeline from Kyushu, but, for every plane landing on Clark Field, one had been shot down along the way.

Admiral Fukudome rounded up about 200 serviceable planes from Formosa's Second Air Fleet and flew them across Luzon Strait to Clark Field. Then he relayed Onishi's call for hundreds more from China and Japan. Onishi became annoyed when he discovered that inexperienced pilots flew the planes. He adopted the tactics employed by Admiral Arima and began organizing his navy pilots into a special attack force and on October 19 officially launched the Kamikaze Corps. He instructed each pilot to prepare himself to die for the emperor. The plane became the bomb, directed solely by the pilot.

The sudden activation of SHO-1 came as a shock to Admiral Ozawa, who at Admiral Toyoda's directive had sent most of his planes into Halsey's mincing machine. He now had three carrier divisions, two of them without aircraft. Ozawa had to hurriedly develop a new plan for the defense of the Philippines. When Admiral Toyoda returned from Formosa to Tokyo, Ozawa suggested that Admiral Kurita's battleship-cruiser group be brought from Singapore to destroy MacArthur's amphibious landings while he employed his planeless carriers to lure Halsey's fleet away from Leyte Gulf. He believed if Halsey took the bait, Kurita could creep in from the South China Sea undetected, but Ozawa underestimated the strength and composition of Kinkaid's Seventh Fleet. After the war Ozawa admitted that he "expected complete destruction of [his] fleet, but if Kurita's mission was carried out that was all [he] wished."[3]

Toyoda agreed to the plan, and on the morning of October 18 Ozawa prepared his Northern Force to act as decoys. He still had 116 planes, just enough to attract Halsey's attention, but few experienced pilots. Before sailing, he dissolved Carrier Division 1 and left behind three new but unready *Unryus*-class flattops. He also detached the CVLs *Ryuho* and *Junyo*, originally part of Carrier Division 4, and assigned them to duty as aircraft ferries. He then switched his flag from *Amagi* to the old veteran *Zuikaku* and took direct command of Carrier Division 3, which also included the CVLs *Chitose*, *Chiyoda*, and *Zuiho*. Rear Admiral Chiaki Matsuda commanded Carrier Division 4, which was not a true carrier division but two half-battleships, *Ise* and *Hyuga*, whose planes had been previously sent to Formosa. Ozawa wanted the ships for their 14-inch guns. On October 20,

10 hours after MacArthur's troops began landing on Leyte, Ozawa's decoys steamed from the Inland Sea.

On October 22, Admiral Kurita departed from Brunei Bay with two battleship-cruiser groups. The Center Force consisted of the superbattleships *Yamato* and *Musashi*, 3 old battleships, 10 heavy cruisers, 2 light cruisers, and 15 destroyers. Kurita planned to bring the group into the Sibuyan Sea, through San Bernardino Strait, down the east coast of Samar, into Leyte Gulf, and trap MacArthur's landing force inside the gulf.

Kurita's Southern Force, commanded by Vice Admiral Shoji Nishimura, consisted of two old battleships, one heavy cruiser, and four destroyers. Nishimura sailed on October 21. He planned to cross the Sulu and Mindanao seas, pass through the Surigao Strait, and strike MacArthur's forces from the south. Nishimura expected support from Vice Admiral Kiyohide Shima's command, which sailed from Japan on October 22 with two heavy cruisers, one light cruiser, and seven destroyers. Shima planned to come through Suriago Strait behind Nishimura's force.

The plan made perfect sense. All three of Kurita's gun groups would come together the morning of October 25, crush MacArthur's landings, and win a great battle.

Although supported wholeheartedly by Toyoda, Ozawa's strategy contained all the features of a suicide mission. His carriers would be sacrificed, and Kurita's battleship-cruiser force would be up against Kinkaid's Seventh Fleet and Halsey's Third Fleet. Ozawa's one hope was to draw Halsey's carriers away from Leyte, thereby paving the way for Kurita, supported by Admiral Ohnishi's kamikazes, to pull off a surprise victory and by the greatest of good luck destroy MacArthur's assault and preserve Japan's lifeline to the East Indies. If Halsey did not take the bait and waited for developments off Leyte, Kurita's battleship-cruiser force would be doomed as soon as it passed through San Bernardino Strait.

Ozawa's planning depended on outwitting Halsey, but Toyoda and his advisors seemed to be unconcerned, if not oblivious, to the presence of "MacArthur's Navy." Kinkaid's Seventh Fleet was quite capable of dealing with Kurita's three-prong attack. In addition to 18 escort carriers, Kinkaid had 6 battleships, 4 heavy cruisers, 4 light cruisers, and 28 destroyers.

On October 20, MacArthur's Sixth Army began landing on Leyte. Captain Whitehead, commanding support aircraft for the Seventh Fleet, provided air cover from Rear Admiral Thomas L. Sprague's escort carriers. Hellcats, Wildcats, and Avengers from Sprague's three "Taffy" groups and Halsey's fast carriers quickly destroyed 100 Japanese planes and established air supremacy over the landing beaches. The Sixth Army moved inland, captured two airfields on Leyte, and began preparing for a Japanese counterattack by land, air, and sea.

With the army ashore, Kinkaid and Halsey began to relax. During the interlude, Halsey decided to take a closer look at San Bernardino and Surigao straits, the two most likely routes for a counterattack by sea. Because Kurita's Center and Southern forces did not sail from Borneo until October 22, search planes found no warships in the straits. On this day, Admiral Sherman returned from Ulithi with TG 38.3, and as part of the rotation program, Halsey detached McCain's TG 38.1.

McCain was on his 600-mile trip to Ulithi when Halsey learned that two U.S. submarines, *Darter* and *Dace*, had spotted Kurita's force in Palawan Passage west of the Philippines. The subs sank two heavy cruisers, one being Kurita's flagship *Atago*, and damaged a third. Halsey now knew that a Japanese battle fleet was headed for the Sibuyan Sea, but he did not know its size or whether it contained carriers.

On the morning of October 23, another submarine spotted Admiral Shima's cruisers and destroyers of the Southern Force in the Sulu Sea and steaming south. The only force not reported were Admiral Ozawa's carrier decoys, which on the morning of October 23 were still east of Formosa. Halsey immediately regretted detaching McCain's five carriers. *Bunker Hill* had also departed for Ulithi to pick up more fighters, leaving Halsey with 11 carriers to possibly face the full might of the Japanese navy.

At daylight on October 24, Mitscher's search planes reported two enemy battle groups approaching the Philippines from the west. According to the pilots, neither group contained carriers. This puzzled Halsey. Hence, the carriers must be somewhere else.

Halsey believed in going straight at the enemy, and when he made a decision, no one on the Pacific Ocean acted with more alacrity, regardless of where the move might take him.

And Halsey was on the move.

CHAPTER 15

Leyte Gulf

On the morning of October 24, while Kurita's center force and Nishimura's southern force approached the Philippines from the west, Halsey dispersed his three carrier groups to search for the enemy. Sherman's TG 38.3 (*Essex, Lexington, Langley*, and *Princeton*) steamed north scouting the skies off central Luzon. Sherman halted 60 miles east of Polillo Islands and launched air strikes against Clark Field. Bogan's weakened TG 38.2 (*Cabot, Independence*, and *Intrepid*) took position off San Bernardino Strait and scouted the Sibuyan Sea. Davison's TG 38.4 (*Belleau Wood, Enterprise, Franklin*, and *San Jacinto*) roamed off lower Leyte, watching Surigao Strait. After making his deployments, Halsey recalled TG 38.1 from Ulithi, thereby forcing McCain to backtrack and refuel at sea. Halsey should not have detached McCain until the question of Japanese countermeasures had been clarified by intelligence, but Halsey was prone to rash acts that often resulted in positive outcomes. In Admiral Robert B. Carney's assessment, "Halsey's constant purpose was to keep the enemy off balance and in the dark, and by avoiding fixed patterns and objectives, tactics, communications, etc., he achieved tactical surprise on many occasions."[1] Those same traits also got Halsey into trouble.

At 8:00 A.M., search planes from *Intrepid* reported five enemy battleships, eight cruisers, and thirteen destroyers off the southern tip of Mindoro Island. Halsey suspected the Japanese force would come through San Bernardino Strait, where he had posted his weakest (Bogan's) carrier group. He ordered air strikes and radioed Sherman to hurry back from central Luzon to support Bogan.

When Halsey's orders arrived, Sherman's Hellcats were engaged in a furious dogfight. While he waited to recover planes, McCampbell's veterans from *Essex*'s Air Group 15 downed or chased off 50 enemy planes. McCambell added nine more kills to his total and his wingman, Lieutenant Roy W. Rushing, shot down six more. Despite another turkey shoot, one Japanese dive-bomber came screaming out of a cloud and dropped a 550-pound bomb on the busy flight deck of *Princeton* when she was recovering planes. The 14-inch hole in the deck did not look menacing, but the bomb penetrated to the interior and started fires in the

Admiral William F. Halsey, Jr., as he appeared during operations off
the Philippines. (U.S. Navy photo)

torpedo storage room. Torpedoes began exploding and eventually blew the guts
out of the ship. Sherman ordered her scuttled. The first score of the day went to
the Japanese, and Halsey lost his first carrier.

Because of the weakness of Bogan's group, Halsey radioed Davison to move
up to San Bernardino Strait. Davison had search-strike planes aloft looking for
Nishimura's force in the Sulu Sea. Halsey made a snap decision. He decided to
leave Nishimura to Kinkaid and Rear Admiral Jesse B. Oldendorf's battleships
and ordered Davison to recall his planes. Davison still had aircraft to recover
before responding to Halsey's call, but, like Sherman, he was close enough to
send planes against Kurita's force in the Sibuyan Sea.

Halsey's decision to leave Nishimura's force to Oldendorf's battleships and
escort carriers made good tactical sense, but he neglected to tell Kinkaid. The
Japanese army and navy were notorious for failing to communicate with each
other, and they lost battles because of it. There was no excuse for Halsey to make
the same mistake, but because Kinkaid reported to MacArthur, it happened.
Halsey also knew the speed of Nishimura's battle fleet, knew it would be arriving
in Surigao Strait after dark, and failed to warn Kinkaid to expect a night battle.

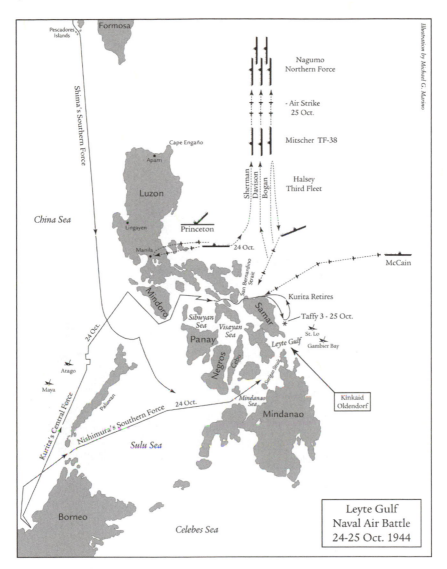

Leyte Gulf Naval Air Battle, October 24–25, 1944. (Michael G. Marino)

Spruance would never have allowed the fast carriers to stray from an important landing operation, and Kinkaid expected the same from Halsey. But Halsey was not Spruance. He itched for a fight and expected to find it off San Bernardino Strait. During the summer King-Nimitz strategy conference in San Francisco, the pros and cons of Spruance and Halsey's tactics had been a subject of

Vice Admiral Takeo Kurita, IJN, brought his naval force through San Bernardino Strait and eventually retired after losing about half of his force. (U.S. Navy photo)

discussion. While laying plans for the future, King suggested that Spruance "be put in charge of landings when they came to Japan so that Halsey could go out and fight."[2]

At 10:00 A.M., Hellcats, Helldivers, and Avengers from *Cabot* spotted Kurita's battleships and cruisers moving through the Sibuyan Sea. Pilots waited in the overcast for other air units to arrive before launching a coordinated attack. They encountered noy air opposition because Onishi and Fukudome had decided it was more important to engage Sherman's carriers than provide air cover for Kurita. Five waves from Bogan and Davison's flattops—259 planes in all—pounded the center force for more than three hours. At 2:00 P.M., Kurita ordered a withdrawal. The 72,000-ton battleship *Musashi*, repeatedly struck by bombs and torpedoes, rolled over after dark and sank. The heavy cruiser *Myoko* took a torpedo and fell behind. Other Japanese vessels suffered hits, but Kurita still had four battleships (three with damage), six heavy cruisers, and his destroyer escort.

Pilot reports of immense damage to the enemy fleet persuaded Halsey that Kurita had withdrawn for good. Mitscher had grown accustomed to exaggerated claims by pilots and spent time personally interviewing *Lexington*'s air group. He concluded that Kurita's force had been damaged but not disabled. He also noted duplication in the reporting of ships damaged and ships sunk. Halsey, on the battleship *New Jersey*, had no direct contact with pilots, nor did he bother to confer with Mitscher.

When Admiral Toyoda learned that Kurita had turned back, he became furious. The whole Sho plan depended on Kurita disrupting MacArthur's landings. That evening, while carrier search planes reported Kurita's force retiring, Toyoda radioed Kurita and ordered him to go back and stop the Leyte landings.

At 4:40 P.M., while the Toyoda-Kurita messages were being exchanged, Admiral Sherman's search planes reported a Japanese carrier force off the northeastern tip (Cape Engaño) of Luzon and moving south. The sighting came as great news to Halsey, for here was the *real* Japanese navy. He still envisioned it as the once-powerful Combined Fleet, merged together with battleships and cruisers into a mighty strike force. He did not know that Ozawa's decoys could barely strike anything, but here was his chance to deliver war's fatal blow. Having thumped Kurita's battle force, he could now thump Ozawa's.

Before turning north Halsey arranged to form TF-34 under Admiral Lee by detaching four battleships, two heavy and three light cruisers, and fourteen destroyers to keep an eye on San Bernardino Strait. Admiral Kinkaid accidentally intercepted the message. He was relieved to learn that Kurita had withdrawn, and should the enemy return again, that Lee's battle line would be there to meet him. Kinkaid, however, did not intercept Halsey's second message, which clarified the first message by stating that TF-34 would not be formed unless "the enemy sorties" and until "directed by me."[3] Kinkaid acted on the only message he received from Halsey and ordered his Seventh Fleet to "Prepare for night engagement" with Nishimura and Shima's forces, which were then crossing into the Mindanao Sea, but he said nothing to Admiral Oldendorf about San Bernardino Strait because he expected Lee to be there.[4]

Meanwhile, Admiral Ozawa raced south, doing everything in his power to be detected so he could reverse course and lure Halsey into a stern chase. The opportunity unfolded when Sherman's search planes located the Japanese carriers off Cape Engaño. Despite losing *Princeton* earlier in the day, Sherman was all for going after the carriers on his own, believing that "they were close enough so that they could not get away if we headed to the northward."[5]

Halsey still had Kurita and San Bernardino Strait on his mind, but he had to make another snap decision. Although his staff on *New Jersey* disagreed, Halsey decided not to form TF-34 or to hold any ships back to guard the strait. To Halsey, destroying Ozawa's carriers took precedence. He kept the Third Fleet together and ordered Lee to follow with his battle line. Under no circumstances did he want Ozawa to join forces with Kurita, even though he doubted Kurita would double back. He expected heavy attacks from land-based planes on Luzon and wanted Lee's AA batteries for protection. Halsey relied on old fleet doctrine emanating from his days at the Naval Academy. He believed the doctrine still applied, even though many on his staff disagreed.

Halsey doubted whether Kurita could reach San Bernardino Strait before noon the following day. He also believed that if Kurita tried, Sprague's escort carrier planes and Oldendorf's battleships would cut the Japanese force to pieces. Halsey also expected to strike Ozawa at dawn and be in position to send supports back to Kinkaid by midday. Having assessed the situation from his own perspective, Halsey declared, "We will run north at top speed and put those carriers out for keeps."[6] Having made his decision, Halsey radioed Kinkaid, "[Kurita's] central force heavily damaged according to strike reports. Am proceeding north with *three groups* to attack carrier forces at dawn."[7] Kinkaid interpreted the message as meaning *three carrier groups* exclusive of Lee's battle line.

Halsey saw no reason to mention that he was taking Lee because he did not know Kinkaid had intercepted his earlier message. Kinkaid, however, expected Lee to be off San Bernardino Strait. Lee had prepared to guard the strait and was troubled when Halsey ordered him to follow the fleet. Lee had been monitoring reports transmitted from search planes watching Ozawa's carriers and sensed a trick. So did Captain Arleigh Burke, Mitscher's chief of staff. Just before dark, Lee flashed his concerns to Halsey by light. Halsey had already rejected similar warnings voiced by his staff. Burke took the problem to Mitscher, who under Halsey felt like a man without a command. Mitscher said, "Well, I think you're right, but I don't know you're right," and refused to "butt in."[8]

Halsey learned that Kurita's force had indeed turned around and was again headed at 12 knots for San Bernardino Strait. He sent the contact report to Kinkaid, ordered Bogan and Davison's task groups to close up on Sherman, and after two days without sleep went to bed. More reports on the movements of Kurita arrived from night-flying search planes, but no one woke Halsey and Kinkaid received no more intelligence.

Halsey did not know that Kurita had communicated with Nishimura and Shima, instructing them to rendezvous with the center force at 10:00 A.M. off the southern tip of Samar for the purpose of launching a coordinated attack on MacArthur's Leyte beachhead. As the hours passed, and the Third Fleet sped north through the night, it began to look as if Toyoda's SHO-1 plan might work after all.

Kurita's instructions to Nishimura and Shima arrived too late. At 11:00 P.M., Seventh Fleet PT boats operating south of Bohol spotted Nishimura's force crossing Mindanao Sea and headed toward Surigao Strait. On the far side of the strait, Oldendorf waited with battleships and cruisers arranged in a neat "T" to greet the enemy. The Japanese were old hands at dealing with PT boats and soon drove them off. When Nishimura's force reached Limasawa Island, 15 miles from the strait, more PT boats attacked but were again repulsed.

At 1:00 A.M., the Japanese force began rounding into Surigao Strait. All Nishimura had seen were a few torpedo boats. He had no idea what was waiting for him in the mouth of the strait.

At 2:40 A.M., Captain J. G. Coward's Destroyer Squadron 54 picked up the approach of Japanese ships 15 miles away and alerted Oldendorf. Soon two battleships, *Yamashiro* and *Fuso*, became visible on radarscopes, followed by smaller blips as the minutes passed. At 3:00 A.M., Coward's destroyers launched torpedoes at Nishimura's ships. Oldendorf's battleships opened, and the destroyermen soon became lost in the smoke of battle. At 3:15, Admiral Shima's smaller force steamed in behind Nishimura, passing by the wreckage of the battleship *Fuso*. Moments later the battleship *Yamashiro* blew up, taking the life of Nishimura. At 4:20 A.M., the fight ended. One division of the southern force no longer existed; only the destroyer *Shigure* survived. Admiral Shima beat a hasty retreat and fled, losing two light cruisers and three destroyers. Neither Nishimura nor Shima would meet Kurita off Samar in the morning.

During the night of October 24–25, Kinkaid expected to engage the enemy in Surigao Strait, but he also expected Admiral Lee's battle line to have pickets in San Bernardino Strait. Kinkaid enjoyed a false sense of security. Neither Halsey nor Lee were anywhere near the area.

At 11:30 P.M. on October 24, Kurita's center force came through the San Bernardino Strait without firing a shot. Leyte Gulf lay ahead, but Kurita waited off Samar for Nishimura and Shima to arrive, with whom he expected to gain a great victory. Four hours later, Kurita received a message from Nishimura that three enemy ships had been sighted. Two hours passed before he learned from Shima that Nishimura's force had been destroyed. Kurita's communications on the battleship *Nagato* had been knocked out during the previous day's air attack, causing long delays in receiving messages.

Kurita still had 22 ships and expected heavy air support from Luzon at daylight. He did not know that American carrier planes had decimated Japanese air strength, leaving scattered squadrons of kamikazes, but after passing through the strait he was pleasantly surprised to find Halsey's Third Fleet nowhere in sight.

After abandoning his watch on San Bernardino Strait, Halsey went to bed at 8:30 P.M. and left matters in the hands of Mitscher, who was shocked to find Lee's battle line with the fleet. Commander James H. Flatley, Mitscher's operations officer, pressed the admiral to radio Halsey and urge that Lee's battleships be returned to the strait. Having lost tactical command weeks earlier to Halsey, Mitscher growled: "If he wants my advice he'll ask for it."[9] Admiral Bogan sent

Rear Admiral Gerald F. Bogan (later Vice Admiral) was one of the fine air admirals who commanded fast carrier groups throughout the war. (U.S. Navy photo)

the same recommendation to the snoozing admiral, but Halsey's staff would not wake him.

Mitscher, now back in temporary tactical command, steamed north at 25 knots looking for Sherman. Mitscher had one purpose in mind: to overtake Ozawa, put him out of business, and get back to San Bernardino Strait as quickly as possible. At 11:00 P.M., Sherman's carriers fell in with the Third Fleet, and Mitscher picked up the pace. An hour later, one of Halsey's staff officers ordered the carriers to reduce speed to 16 knots. Burke received the message and asked Mitscher who was in charge of tactical command. Mitscher replied, "We are the tactical commander. Why do you ask?" "Well," Burke replied, "Admiral Halsey is giving tactical orders."[10]

Mitscher told Burke that Halsey was asleep, to ignore the order, and to inform carrier commanders to stay on course at 25 knots. Fifteen minutes later, Burke received another order from the flagship to slow down. Mitscher said the officer was acting on his own and told Burke to slow to 20 knots and then return to 25. Halsey woke at 1:00 A.M. and found the fleet moving at 25 knots. He ordered it slowed to 16 knots because he worried about overrunning Ozawa's carriers. Mitscher followed Halsey's order, although he thought it absurd.

The next dispute occurred when Halsey ordered night search planes launched from *Independence*. Mitscher argued that the Japanese would spot the planes on radar and run for home. Halsey did not believe Mitscher's theory that Ozawa's carriers were acting as decoys. Mitscher then argued that instead of sending a few night search planes, a search-strike force should be sent. Halsey rejected the suggestion and instead sent a small section of radar-equipped Hellcats on a 350-mile search. Thirty minutes later, night pilots from *Independence* sighted several destroyers, the van of Ozawa's force, 80 miles north. Halsey made a quick calculation and concluded that by 4:30 A.M. his fleet would be engaged in a night surface action.

Halsey did not like night fighting, even though radar and fire direction control had vastly improved since his days in the Solomons. At 2:55 A.M., he ordered Admiral Lee to bring his surface ships through the fleet and post them 10 miles ahead of the carriers. Lee did not like close maneuvering at night any more than Mitscher. This meant slowing the fleet, pulling six battleships out of three task formations, and rearranging them in the dark to form a new battle line of 6 battleships, 12 carriers, 8 cruisers, and 41 destroyers. Lee eased back to 15 knots, pulled the battle line to the side to reform, and then steamed ahead of the carriers to a position in the van.

During Lee's maneuvers, Halsey learned that Nishimura had attacked Oldendorf in the Surigao Strait but nothing more. Minutes later, the pilot shadowing Ozawa's carriers lost contact when his radar malfunctioned. Halsey suffered a few troubled moments of indecision and issued orders to slow down and await further developments. When at 4:30 A.M. no surface contact with the enemy had been made, Mitscher knew that Halsey's search planes had triggered Ozawa's turnabout for home. He could do nothing but keep his planes ready for search-strike sorties at dawn.

At 4:00 A.M. on October 25, as Oldendorf's battle with Nishimura's southern force sputtered to a victorious conclusion, Kinkaid called a staff meeting to ask whether anything may have been overlooked. Whitehead recommended that flights be readied from escort carriers to mop up cripples at dawn. He also suggested a search to the north, particularly around southern Samar and the San Bernardino Strait. When Kinkaid asked him why he wanted to search there,

Whitehead said he merely wanted to finish off any enemy ships that may have slipped by Lee's battle line. Kinkaid paused to consider the proposal without making a decision.

After the meeting ended Captain Richard H. Cruzen returned and said, "Admiral, I can think only of one other thing. We have never directly asked Halsey if TF-34 is guarding San Bernardino."[11] Kinkaid agreed there would be no harm in asking and at 4:12 sent a message in cipher to Halsey requesting confirmation. Twenty minutes passed, and when no answer came Kinkaid told Whitehead to go ahead and launch 10 planes at dawn.

At the same hour and 300 miles north of San Bernardino Strait, Halsey dallied in the Philippine Sea waiting for a night action that never materialized. Two and a half hours passed before Halsey received Kinkaid's message. It came as a complete surprise. At 7:05, Halsey replied, "Negative. Task Force 34 is with carrier groups now engaging enemy carrier force."[12] The reply came too late to help Kinkaid. Oldendorf's surface fleet had gone through the Surigao Strait to mop up Japanese cripples, and the only force protecting Leyte's beachhead were 16 escort carriers with destroyers. Oldendorf, however, had taken Hellcats and Avengers off some of the carriers to cover his pursuit.

Kinkaid had not received any reports of trouble off San Bernardino Strait, and he believed that Halsey would have posted pickets to keep him informed. A PBY night patrol flying over the area reported no activity. Besides, in 1941 the Naval War College had opined that San Bernardino Strait was too narrow and shallow for capital ships to navigate. Captain Cruzen, who opened Kinkaid's eyes to the possibility that Lee may not be there, had been a party to the college's conclusions. Suddenly at 6:45, just as the 10 search planes requested by Whitehead were launching, escort carriers off southern Samar sighted Kurita's force bearing down on Leyte Gulf. Minutes later, 18.1-inch shells from the super-battleship *Yamato* began dropping around Rear Admiral Clifton A. F. Sprague's "Taffy 3" escort carriers.

What Kurita saw was the northernmost element of Kinkaid's Seventh Fleet: the escort carriers *Gambier Bay*, *Kitkun Bay*, and *White Plains*, along with three destroyers and four destroyer escorts. Further to the south and not visible to the Japanese were three more escort carriers with destroyers. Inside Leyte Gulf were another 10 escort carriers interspersed among the transports. Each mini-flattop carried 30 planes, but Oldendorf had borrowed a number of them for his pursuit through Surigao Strait.

At 7:07 A.M., Kinkaid radioed a plain-language message to Halsey that his ships were under heavy attack off Leyte. An hour later, Halsey received the communiqué. Minutes later, he received another plain-language message, this one from Admiral Sprague, reporting that Taffy 3 was under attack from battleships and cruisers. Halsey figured that Kinkaid, with 16 escort carriers and more than 450 planes, could take care of himself. He did not know that all of Sprague's planes were armed for CAP, antisubmarine action, and close air support. Without torpedoes and bombs, Sprague's Hellcats and Avengers could do nothing but make dummy runs. Halsey doubted that Kinkaid and Sprague, with all their planes, could have been caught unprepared, and because Kinkaid did not specifically request help, Halsey continued searching for Ozawa.

Meanwhile, Mitscher launched his search-strike force at dawn. When Japanese radar picked up the incoming flight, Ozawa knew that Halsey was indeed taking the bait and put another 40 more miles between his force and Halsey's. Mitscher had 10 strike groups orbiting above his carriers waiting for word from the search planes. By 7:30, they were all on the way with Commander McCambell acting as target coordinator. When Japanese radar operators reported a swarm of American planes approaching, Ozawa launched his last 29 planes.

While Halsey listened to radio chatter from *New Jersey*'s bridge, he received another message from Kinkaid: "Fast battleships are needed immediately at Leyte Gulf!"[13] Mitscher had planes in the air, and Halsey was not inclined to stop the attack and rush back to Leyte. He did not believe Kinkaid needed help. He knew McCain was fueling TG 38.1 at sea 300 miles east of San Bernardino Strait and radioed him to make the best possible speed to Leyte Gulf. Halsey radioed Kinkaid that McCain was on the way and resumed following the progress of Mitscher's strike on Ozawa. He was determined to finish off the Japanese fleet.

Halsey did not know that Kinkaid had scattered the escort carriers, leaving only six small flattops near the gate to Leyte Gulf. In Halsey's mind, doing so had not been the battle plan, but Halsey never discussed a battle plan with Kinkaid. Nimitz at Pearl Harbor and King in Washington also received Kinkaid's pleas for help. King turned blue with rage. He paced the floor, cursing Halsey in the presence of "Jocko" Clark.[14] Nimitz, taken completely by surprise, fired off a curt message to Halsey in cipher: "From Cincpac ... where is, repeat, where is Task Force 34. The world wonders."[15] Nimitz simply wanted Halsey, wherever he was, to send Lee's battle line to the aid of Kinkaid, but the yeoman preparing the message caught the emphasis in Nimitz's voice and padded the message, adding the words "repeat" and "The world wonders."

Halsey interpreted those four words as undeserved censure from Nimitz. "I was stunned as if I had been struck in the face," Halsey recalled. "The paper rattled in my hands. I snatched off my cap, threw it on the deck, and shouted something that I am ashamed to remember. Mick Carney rushed over and grabbed my arm: 'Stop it! What the hell's the matter with you? Pull yourself together!'"[16]

Pilot reports were coming in from Mitscher's air strikes when Nimitz's coded message arrived. Helldivers had sunk the light carrier *Chitose*. A torpedo had struck the heavy carrier *Zuikaku*, forcing Ozawa to transfer his flag to a cruiser. Subsequent air strikes finished her off and she sank at 2:14 P.M. The second air strike set *Chiyoda* afire and forced her abandonment. The light carrier *Zuiho* sank an hour later. The two carrier-battleships, *Ise* and *Hyuga*, and a number of destroyers had not been in the battle area, but Halsey knew of their presence and sent Lee after them with orders to mop up any cripples.

Lee's battleships were already in pursuit when at 10:00 A.M. Halsey received Nimitz's message. Fifty-five minutes later, Halsey angrily ordered Lee to reverse course and hurry down to Leyte with Bogan's carriers for air support. Lee's battle line was about 400 hundred miles from Leyte Gulf when Halsey turned it around. Then he radioed Kinkaid, "I am proceeding toward Leyte with Task Group 38.2 and 6 fast battleships . . . but do not expect arrival before 0800 tomorrow."[17]

Halsey left Mitscher with Sherman and Davison's task groups to finish off the Japanese carriers and steamed south with Lee. Kinkaid continued his barrage of messages, first advising Halsey that Kurita's force had turned back and later that it was still threatening Leyte. Kurita was actually retiring, but Halsey knew that Nimitz would be listening to Kinkaid's reports and wanted no more rebuffs. He detached his two fastest battleships, two cruisers, and eight destroyers with orders to get down to San Bernardino Strait at full speed and take whatever action necessary. The advance force reached the strait around midnight and found only one enemy destroyer, left behind by Kurita to pick up survivors, and destroyed it. During the previous 24 hours, Lee's battle line had steamed 700 miles without making contact with an enemy fleet.

At dawn on October 25, while Halsey was chasing Ozawa, Admiral Clifton Sprague, commanding Taffy 3, launched eight Hellcats to search the sea north of Leyte Gulf. The pilots sighted no enemy ships because of rain and poor visibility.

At 6:44 A.M., lookouts from Kurita's force spotted Sprague's three escort carriers—*Gambier Bay*, *Kitkun Bay*, and *White Plains*—and seven support vessels off southeastern Samar. Farther to the south and out of sight were the rest of Taffy 3, escort carriers *Fanshaw Bay*, *Kalinin Bay*, and *St. Lo*.

At 6:58, shells fired from a range of 20 miles by the battleships *Yamato*, *Haruna*, *Kongo*, and *Nagato*, began falling among the escort carriers. The attack came as a complete surprise to Sprague and jarred the nerves of Kinkaid. Minutes later, three planes from *Gambier Bay* spotted the enemy fast approaching. *Gambier Bay* absorbed the first shots, followed by *Kalinin Bay*, *Fanshaw Bay*, and *White Plains*, and several near misses damaged *Kitkun Bay*.

Rear Admiral Thomas L. Sprague, positioned in Leyte Gulf and commanding the Escort Carrier Group, had 10 more flattops spread out among the transports and ordered all of them to launch strikes against the enemy. *Gambier Bay* got 15 planes in the air, but none of them were armed with bombs or torpedoes. They ineffectually strafed Kurita's ships but put on a good show. Meanwhile, destroyers and cruisers from Kurita's force bracketed *Gambier Bay* and pummeled her with shells. *Kongo's* guns got the range, and *Gambier Bay* broke in two and sank.

Between rainsqualls and smokescreens laid across the water by Taffy 3, the Japanese lost the ability to bracket targets. They had the added problem of carrier planes diving out of clouds and strafing their decks, and American destroyers creeping out of the smoke and firing torpedoes. At one point, lookouts on *Yamato* observed six torpedoes bearing toward the battleship. Rear Admiral Nobuei Morishita turned in an effort to outrun the torpedoes and ended up 25 miles away.

This maneuver may have given Kinkaid the impression that Kurita was retiring because Morishita took *Yamato* completely out of the fight.

Kurita put a scout plane in the air to determine what forces lay beyond the smoke. The pilot reported carriers guarded by destroyers withdrawing to the south. This emboldened Kurita, so he pressed forward. Destroyers and destroyer escorts did yeoman's work protecting the flattops but paid a huge price. Enemy battleships and cruisers spotted the destroyer *Hoel* advancing to fire torpedoes and sank her. The destroyer *Samuel B. Roberts* went down while doing the same. *Heermann* sustained several hits but survived. The destroyer *Johnston* sank after valiantly holding back one of Kurita's destroyer divisions. Taffy 3 put up a magnificent fight against overwhelming odds and kept Kurita's battleships from concentrating their fire on the carriers. Kinkaid, however, believed that the Japanese were again attacking and once more radioed Halsey that he needed immediate help.

Tom Sprague now had planes in the air from 15 serviceable carriers but no one to coordinate an attack. A few planes carried bombs or torpedoes, and when the pilots got into the air they teamed up with planes from other flattops. One group damaged the heavy cruiser *Chikuma* and another group disabled *Chokai*. Kurita peeled off two destroyers to tow the cruisers to safety. Before the day ended, all four went to the bottom.

Sprague's planes from Leyte began landing on Taffy 3 flattops to rearm. It soon became clear to Kurita that the Americans had shifted to the offense. More planes appeared in the sky. For two hours, Japanese ships had been maneuvering at high speed, consuming fuel at a voracious rate. Kurita never realized that he was fighting Kinkaid's escort carriers and not Halsey's fleet. He knew fast carriers could steam at 30 knots, which meant he would have to apply maximum speed to get his battleships out of harm's way. Had he known the force in his front were escort carriers incapable of more than 18 knots, he might have changed his tactics. Sixteen escort carriers, however, could deliver the same air power as six fleet carriers, and Kurita had no intelligence to warn him of the other ten baby carriers lying inside Leyte Gulf.

Late in the morning, while Kurita's ships were still dueling carrier aircraft, Admiral Onishi's first organized flight of kamikazes arrived. Hellcats shot them down, but a few planes slipped through the fire. One crashed into *St. Lo* and sank her. Other kamikazes appeared over Taffy 1 and registered on *Petrof Bay* (CVE-80). "I saw three Zekes begin to dive toward our ship," Captain John D. Ahlstrom recalled. "Planes were parked aft. One of the Zekes made a well-aimed, almost vertical dive . . . but no crewmember left a gun. The Zeke's tail was shot off when it was about 500 feet from the ship's deck. The plane crashed into the sea about 50 feet astern."[18]

Kamikaze attacks pulled Sprague's aircraft away from harassing Kurita's force and gave him time to reconsider his options. His mission was not to fight Halsey's Third Fleet but to wreck MacArthur's beachhead. So, at 11:20, now minus 7 of his 22 ships, Kurita ordered his force into Leyte Gulf. While approaching, he developed grave misgivings. At 11:40, ships in the van reported an American battleship and four destroyers ahead. Attacks from carrier planes intensified, and Kurita began to wonder what had happened to the promised air support from Admiral Onishsi's land-based planes.

At noon, Kurita received a message warning him that more enemy carriers (McCain's) were approaching from the east. He could see American carrier planes landing on Leyte to refuel, which meant that MacArthur's forces were already ashore and could no longer be kept from landing. He also knew that the Seventh Fleet had battleships in the Surigao Strait, so he decided to go back to his position off Samar and destroy what he still believed were Halsey's fast carriers. He then learned that Halsey was not in his front but off Cape Engaño chasing Ozawa. "The destruction of enemy aircraft carriers was a kind of obsession with me," Kurita admitted after the war, "and I fell victim to it."[19] So Kurita decided to steam north and go to a glorious death fighting Halsey. The superbattleship *Yamato* still had a full supply of 18.1-inch shells, and one well-directed shot could sink a 33,000-ton carrier.[20]

At 12:30 P.M., Kurita again changed his mind and without consulting his staff ordered a withdrawal through San Bernardino Strait. His ships were low on fuel, and American planes were everywhere. Had he pressed into Leyte Gulf, Old-endorf's battleships would have returned to engage him. Had he delayed any longer, McCain's TG 38.1, coming from the east, and Halsey's battleships, coming from the north, would have caught him off Samar.

McCain launched one strike while his five carriers were still far to the east. The pilots found Kurita's force off Samar. With gas gauges registering near empty, pilots made a quick pass, scored few hits, and began looking for a place to land.

At 9:45 P.M., as Halsey approached, six night Avengers from *Independence* spotted Kurita's ships passing through the strait. Flyers from *Independence* urged Halsey to authorize a night attack. The admiral waited too long. Finally, at 3:00 A.M. on October 26, he authorized a strike of five Hellcats and four Avengers. A thunderstorm intervened, the shadowing torpecker lost contact with Kurita's force, and the planes returned.

At daylight, Bogan's pilots located Kurita's force deep in the Sibuyan Sea. The first wave disabled the cruiser *Noshiro*, which later sank, and dropped two bombs on the superbattleship *Yamato*. Ninety minutes later, a second wave torpedoed and bombed the big battleship. Kurita begged for air support, but Fukudome and Onishi had too few planes. A third wave dropped three more bombs on *Yamato* and damaged the battleship *Nagato*. An hour later, 30 B-24s from southern air bases plastered *Yamato*, and although she had taken more than 3,000 tons of water and was down several feet in the water, the remarkable ship still floated. Late that night, 14 of Kurita's 22 ships limped into Manila. Few of them were fully operational. Kurita fueled and departed the following day for Brunei Bay.

Yamato survived to become the only effective surface vessel in the Japanese navy. Embellished news reports touted the performance of the great battleship and gave Japanese morale a boost. With the carrier *Katsuragi* under construction and *Unryu* and *Amagi* being prepared for duty, the Japanese still held hope. The public never learned of the devastating losses sustained by the IJN during the Leyte campaign.

During the three-day battle, the U.S. Navy lost the light carrier *Princeton*, two escort carriers, *Gambier Bay* and *St. Lo*, two destroyers, and one destroyer escort, all together totaling 36,000 tons. The IJN lost almost half the ships engaged: one heavy carrier (*Zuikaku*), three light carriers, three battleships, six heavy cruisers, four light cruisers, and nine destroyers, totaling 305,710 tons.[21] With better coordination, no Japanese ships would have survived.

At Leyte, mistakes in command piled up against both sides but most decisively against Japan's admirals. The root cause of the problem came from a near-complete breakdown of communications. Admirals Nishimura, Shima, and Kurita had been assured of having maximum air support when there was none to give. They were completely unaware of the immense power vested in Kinkaid's battleships and escort carriers. Kurita could not tell the difference between an escort carrier and a fleet carrier, and this affected his judgment. None of the four Japanese naval groups, the two naval air groups, or the army knew what was happening in the area. SHO-1 utterly failed because of poor communications. Had Admiral Toyoda known that Nishimura had been decisively whipped in the Surigao Strait on the night of October 23–24, he may have changed his orders to Kurita and Ozawa and saved his ships.

One Japanese tactic worked almost to perfection, that of decoying TF-38 from Leyte, but, as Halsey had predicted, Kinkaid had enough firepower to take care of himself. Halsey's mistake, however, can be blamed on the absence of an overall commander. Kinkaid's Seventh Fleet reported to MacArthur. Halsey reported to Nimitz. For policy reasons, neither wanted to report to the other. The arrangement made Halsey a free agent, but he still had an obligation to communicate with Kinkaid. This he did sparingly and inadequately. Plain-language communications took an hour to transmit and receive. Coded messages took up to five hours. Halsey blamed Kinkaid for not having planes in the air on October 25 to watch San Bernardino Strait. Kinkaid blamed Halsey for leaving the strait uncovered without telling him. Both were correct in their criticism of the other, and both were wrong by neglecting the strait. Admiral King eventually came to the same conclusion.[22] For many years, military historians and armchair quarterbacks would study the Leyte operation *ad nauseum*. MacArthur explained the problem in one sentence: "Of all the faulty decisions of war, perhaps the most unexplainable one was the failure to unify the command of the Pacific."[23]

Halsey never admitted error, but he ever after lamented having run south with Lee the afternoon of October 25 instead of staying with the carriers and finishing off Ozawa's group. Kinkaid stayed clear of the verbal skirmish. The Seventh Fleet had defeated three Japanese surface groups and successfully protected MacArthur's beachhead. That was his job.

Halsey suffered from an obsession. Illness had kept him from command during the Battle of Midway, and he wanted to capstone his career by finishing off the Japanese fleet. He admitted, "Missing the Battle of Midway was the greatest disappointment of my life—but I'll sink those damned Jap carriers yet!" Knowing Halsey's impulsive nature, nothing could have prevented him from pursuing that pledge.[24]

When Halsey took command of the Third Fleet, he would not listen to Mitscher, who undoubtedly was the most skillful carrier air commander of the war. Mitscher did not like the way Halsey ran the fleet, but he kept his opinions to himself. After several years passed and naval tacticians had picked to pieces the Leyte operation, Halsey finally admitted: "I wish that Spruance had been with Mitscher at Leyte Gulf and I had been with Mitscher in the Battle of the Philippine Sea."[25] Halsey finally got it right. He was not a meticulous and efficient planner like Mitscher or a cautious and thorough planner like Spruance. He came out of the environment of the Solomons where every carrier was priceless and before improvements in concentrated AA fire, fire direction control, radar, and better aircraft became a reality. He did not have Mitscher's experience in the Central Pacific, and he had never completely made the transition from being a carrier commander to a fleet admiral. Despite the many times he made mistakes that drove King to the point of removing him from the Pacific, King would then turnabout and say, "[Halsey] is the greatest leader of men that we have. The men are crazy about him, and they will follow him anywhere."[26]

In addition to Mitscher, any one of the Third Fleet's task group admirals—Sherman, Bogan, McCain, and Davison—probably understood carrier tactics better than Halsey. Even Admiral Lee developed a taste for carrier tactics and believed that going after Ozawa was a sucker move. Mitscher, Bogan, and Lee would have split the Third Fleet, sending half after Ozawa and half after Kurita, and probably decisively defeated both. This would have defied the outdated Nelsonian doctrine of concentration, but it would have worked, especially if the night *Independence* had been left with Lee. The most serious error was the lack of communication between Halsey and Kinkaid, and for that omission, Halsey received the blame. In April 1945, Kinkaid received his fourth star, and Halsey had to wait until December to receive his fifth star.

Organization changes also occurred in the Japanese navy. Vice Admiral Ozawa became the designated hero of the battle because he carried out his orders and sacrificed four carriers. Admiral Toyoda received the blame because he used up his aircraft before the Leyte battle began. In May 1945, Ozawa relieved Toyoda as Commander-in-Chief, Combined Fleet, but he never received promotion to full admiral because he had no fleet to command. But in the autumn of 1944, the Japanese still believed in miracles.

CHAPTER 16

The Setting Sun

On October 29, 1944, Admiral Ozawa returned to the Inland Sea and recommended that the Mobile Force be disbanded because all that remained were two battleship-carriers. Admiral Toyoda agreed, declaring that carriers were no longer needed. The battle area had become so constricted that land-based aircraft could cover defensive requirements. IGH did not agree. Japan still had five carriers: *Unryu, Amagi, Katsuragi, Junyo,* and *Ryujo.* Toyoda lumped them into Carrier Division I under Rear Admiral Keizo Komura, but American submarines and the lack of planes and fuel kept the group confined to the harbor.

On November 11, the huge 68,059-ton *Shinano,* originally laid down as a sister ship to the superbattleship *Yamato,* slid into Tokyo Bay and one week later went into commission. With 17,700 tons of armor, Toyoda called her impregnable and loaded her decks with 50 Yokosuka MXY7 Oka piloted bombs. Oka, a rocket-powered kamikaze, carried 4,700 pounds of explosives in the nose and was to be launched from the belly of a Mitsubishi G4M2e attack plane. Oka's suicide pilots were trained to guide the missile to the target at 576 mph, but the weight "deprived a bomber of all maneuverability and made it a sitting duck for [American] fighter planes."[1]

On November 29, the giant carrier steamed out of Tokyo Bay for training exercises in the Inland Sea. The submarine USS *Archerfish* fired a spread of torpedoes into her hull and she sank. During December, *Unryu* suffered the same fate in the East China Sea, and torpedoes crippled *Junyo* off Nagasaki. After that, Japanese ships remained in port, and in March 1945 all war materials shifted to the defense of the Home Islands. The IJN decommissioned the remaining carriers—*Amagi, Hyuga, Ise, Katsuragi,* and *Ryuho*—and mothballed them to the Kure Naval District. No longer was there a fleet, but Japan still had suicide planes. Thousands of young half-trained carrier pilots, willing to sacrifice their lives, shifted to the Kamikaze Corps, and American flattops became the primary targets.

On October 27, 1944, General MacArthur turned air operations over to General Kenney and told Halsey to stop attacking Philippine land targets unless requested. This suited Halsey. His pilots were exhausted. He detached McCain and Sherman's task groups and sent them to Ulithi for replacements and supplies. Halsey planned to remain off Leyte until Kenney brought up enough P-38 Lightnings to provide close air support. Because of rain-soaked airfields, Kenney moved only one air group to Leyte. Weeks passed, leaving Bogan's TG 38.2 and Davison's TG 38.4 with the AAF's workload.

The IJN rushed air groups to Luzon from all over Southeast Asia. As the units arrived, Admiral Fukudome turned them over to Onishi's Kamikaze Corps. Onishi declared that two or three suicide planes could sink an enemy carrier. Conventional methods required at least 8 bombers escorted by 16 fighters to accomplish the same task.[2]

On October 28, the day that Halsey detached McCain and Sherman, kamikazes pounced on Bogan's and Davison's task groups and during the next eight days damaged *Franklin, Belleau Wood, Intrepid, Lexington,* and the escort carrier *Suwanee.* Kamikazes also struck four destroyers, the light cruiser *Denver,* and sank the destroyer *Abner Read.* Halsey then sent Davison's task group to Ulithi for repairs, and Kinkaid released Sprague's escort carriers, leaving MacArthur with Bogan's three carriers and a few AAF P-38s and P-61 Black Widow night fighters. The carriers should not have been released. Kenney's Fifth Air Force did not reach Leyte for two months because of construction delays caused by wet weather. Having detached three of his four carrier groups, Halsey now needed them.

On the way to Ulithi, Mitscher suffered a mild heart attack, and Nimitz sent him home to recover. McCain took command of the fast carriers, but not for long. Mitscher wanted to be there when the war ended. Nimitz also wanted Mitscher back to work with Spruance, who needed an aggressive carrier commander. Mitscher and Halsey were too much alike to get along well because neither needed the other to command a task force.

In Washington, Admiral King reacted to the kamikaze menace by creating a special study team to develop methods for eliminating the problem. The group moved carriers and support vessels into Casco Bay, Maine, and simulated suicide tactics in an effort to design new defensive methods. They decided that as long as pilots were willing to sacrifice their lives to destroy ships, some would always stand a chance of succeeding. The study team suggested adding more AA guns and fighter planes. Other than greater vigilance, they offered no solution.

Halsey developed his own strategy, which also happened to be the one preferred by Mitscher. On November 5–6, after reunifying his carrier divisions, he struck Japanese airfields on Luzon and destroyed 450 planes on the ground. The strike put a huge but temporary dent in kamikaze operations.

Halsey grew impatient waiting for MacArthur to build airfields. He wanted to strike Brunei Bay, Borneo, and wipe out Kurita's surviving elements, but neither MacArthur nor Nimitz would let him go. Carrier planes continued to take a toll on Japanese shipping, but on November 25 kamikazes jumped on Halsey's flattops and damaged *Intrepid* and *Cabot.*

On December 17–18, the IJN received a boost when Halsey wandered into a strong typhoon east of Luzon. Three destroyers, top heavy with added guns and other equipment, capsized. Three light carriers, the cruiser *Miami*, and 22 other ships suffered damage. Wind and waves swept 200 planes overboard and killed 790 men. Halsey called the disaster "the Navy's greatest uncompensated loss since the Battle of Savo Island."[3] Halsey paid a price for the failure of his meteorological staff. A court of inquiry found him principally responsible for not avoiding the path of the typhoon.

On January 27, 1945, as arranged by King and Nimitz, Halsey rotated command of the Third Fleet to Admiral Spruance and went home for a rest. The Japanese navy was no longer a threat, but suicide planes would harass the Pacific Fleet until the end of the war.

When Spruance took command of the Fifth Fleet, Mitscher, fully recovered and full of fight, resumed command of his former task force, now designated TF-58. The U.S. Navy had grown to 88 aircraft carriers, 23 battleships, 62 cruisers, 371 destroyers, 378 destroyer escorts, and 238 submarines.[4] All 15 fleet carriers and the 8 CVLs were in Mitscher's command.

The JCS was hard at work putting finishing touches on two more operations: Iwo Jima as a forward air fighter base for escorting B-29s over Tokyo, and Okinawa as an assault-launching platform against mainland Japan. Because MacArthur fell behind schedule at Luzon, the JCS delayed landings until February 19 on Iwo Jima and until April 1 on Okinawa. A third operation, summer assaults on the coast of China, drew opposition from the AAF and the navy, so the JCS began advancing the invasion of Japan.

Six days before Mitscher returned, McCain's carrier planes struck Formosa and Okinawa. A kamikaze damaged *Ticonderoga* and a torpedo plane crashed into *Hancock*. *Ticonderoga* retired for repairs, but *Hancock* stayed with the fleet. Four new *Essex*-class carriers joined the fleet, *Bennington, Bon Homme Richard, Randolph,* and *Shangri-La*. *Ticonderoga* would not be missed.

To counter kamikaze attacks, carrier commanders wanted more fighters. Grumman proposed replacing F6F-5 Hellcats with F8F-1 Bearcats. Mitscher did not want Hellcat production stopped and got his way. The navy went ahead and ordered 2,000 Bearcats, but Hellcats remained the navy's number one fighter.

When Mitscher went stateside in November 1944, Admiral Clark took him aside at San Diego and suggested putting marine pilots on fast carriers. Mitscher took the proposal to Washington, and later, during a meeting with Nimitz and King in San Francisco, obtained approval. On December 2, King authorized 10 Marine Corps fighter squadrons (18 planes each) be assigned to fast carriers. This took time. Landing Corsairs on carrier decks required training, but by year's end two marine units joined Mitscher's carriers.

At 446 mph, the F4U-4 Corsair was already faster than the F8F-1 Bearcat (421 mph) and the F6F-5 Hellcat (386 mph). Some Corsairs came equipped with 20 mm cannon, others with .50-caliber machine guns. The navy wanted speed and

Corsairs provided it. In early 1945, the navy demanded more speed. The first FR-1 Fireball turbojets and McDonnell's full jet XFD-1 Phantom went into production, but they were still months away.

Fast navy fighters could not carry heavy bomb loads, but this deficiency was offset by the development of 5-inch Holy Moses and 11.75-inch Tiny Tim rockets. Holy Moses became the rocket of choice because of its accuracy. Tiny Tim delivered a powerful punch but tended to wander from the target.

The navy also asked for a faster and more powerfully armed bomber and during the spring of 1945 looked at five prototypes, among them the Grumman TB3F Guardian with a turbo-jet booster. None would be ready until after the war. The navy continued to depend on Hellcats, Helldivers, Avengers, and a small number of F4U-4 Corsairs.

In the setup for the final months of the war, Mitscher's TF-58 contained task group veterans who had fought in many battles:

TG 58.1—Rear Admiral J. J. "Jocko" Clark, with *Hornet, Bennington, Wasp,* and *Belleau Wood.*

TG 58.2—Rear Admiral R. E. Davison, with *Lexington, Hancock,* and *San Jacinto.*

TG 58.3—Rear Admiral Ted Sherman, with *Essex, Bunker Hill,* and *Cabot.*

TG 58.4—Rear Admiral A. W. Radford with *Yorktown, Randolph,* and *Langley.*

TG 58.5 (night)—Rear Admiral Matthew B. Gardner with *Enterprise* and *Saratoga.*

In the mix of admirals and captains making up TF-58, only Spruance and Arleigh Burke, Mitscher's chief of staff, were nonaviators.

The organization of the task groups on February 10 never remained static. Mitscher exchanged carriers between groups as he saw fit. Sherman suggested a tactical change. He believed that carrier divisions made up of eight flattops would improve air strike efficiency. Mitscher set the limit at four and, with few exceptions, kept it there.

Mitscher confronted an entirely different kind war, not a war against battleships and carriers, but a war against suicide planes. King and Nimitz wanted Halsey out of the way when they put Spruance in charge of the assault on Iwo Jima and Okinawa. Spruance would never deviate from protecting the invasion force, and Mitscher could be trusted to do exactly what Spruance wanted. After spending six months under the thumb of Halsey, Mitscher was ready to work with Spruance again.

Nimitz made another tactical change. He pulled Captain Whitehead out of Kinkaid's Seventh Fleet and put him in charge of air support *during* the assault. After the beachhead was secured, he planned to transfer the reigns from Whitehead to Colonel Vernon E. Megee, USMC. The Marines had perfected close air support at Leyte and Luzon, and the plan at Iwo and Okinawa was for Megee to take command of all tactical air, including Mitscher's air groups. No one evaluated how this arrangement would work during unrelenting kamikaze attacks.

Three days before D day on Iwo, Mitscher moved into position 60 miles off Honshu and sent the first carrier air strike against Tokyo since launching Jimmy Doolittle's desperate raid in 1942. Foul weather and Japanese fighter planes prevented the destruction of Mitsubishi's aircraft engine and production facilities at Nagoya, but American pilots destroyed 350 planes in the air and 200 more on the ground. Because of a number of rash young navy pilots who broke formation to chase enemy aircraft, Mitscher lost 90 flyers, mostly rookies but among them some of his best pilots. When TF-58 turned south to support Iwo Jima operations on February 19, the Japanese still had the capability of producing 500 to 600 planes a month.

Admirals Clark and Radford pinned the blame for failing to destroy Japan's aircraft plants on imperfect carrier tactics, claiming that the task force carried too many fighters for CAP and not enough bombers for air strikes. They argued that CVLs should carry CAP fighters and that Avengers on CVLs should be transferred to fast carriers. Mitscher sent the recommendation to Spruance and waited for an answer.

On February 18, after bombing Chichi Jima, Mitscher returned to Iwo on D day. For three days eleven escort carriers, five old battleships, four cruisers, and ten destroyers had been softening up the eight-square-mile island. Mitscher's carriers shifted to air support and remained in that mode for four days. Hellcats carried a 500-pound bomb and six 5-inch Holy Moses rockets. Helldivers and Avengers carried only bombs and napalm.

As marines waded ashore on February 19, carrier day fighters and *Enterprise* night fighters broke up feeble enemy air attacks. Two days later, Mitscher sent *Saratoga* to Rear Admiral Calvin T. Durgin's escort carrier command to provide night defensive cover. Fifty kamikazes dove on her at twilight. Three bombs and two suicide planes struck the old flattop, but she pulled away, only to be struck again after dark. The sudden kamikaze attack killed 123 men and destroyed 36 planes, but *Saratoga* limped away. One suicide plane sank the escort carrier *Bismarck Sea,* killed 218 of her 943 officers and men, and another kamikaze struck and damaged *Lunga Point.* Mitscher wanted no more surprises. He sent *Enterprise* to Durgin with instructions to keep fighters in the air night and day. No more enemy air attacks occurred, but for the next seven days nobody on *Enterprise* obtained any rest.

On February 25, Mitscher took 11 fleet carriers, 4 escort carriers, 8 battleships, 18 cruisers, and 75 destroyers for strikes on military installations on Honshu and Okinawa. The attacks destroyed hundreds of Japanese planes and 300,000 tons of shipping. Despite fierce fighting on Iwo Jima and Luzon, Spruance no longer needed fast carrier support and sent TF-58 to Ulithi to prepare for the Okinawa assault.

While rotating air groups at Ulithi, a suicide plane from a distant airfield crashed into *Randolph* after dark and put the big carrier out of action for a month.

During operations off Okinawa, a TBM Avenger is catapulted from the USS *Makin Island*. (U.S. Navy photo)

Days later, *Franklin*, *Intrepid*, and *Bataan* arrived after overhauls and made up the loss. Mitscher retained the same five task groups, but he wanted two more fleet admirals available on standby. He recalled Bogan from leave and put him on *Franklin* in Davison's task group, which did not make the aggressive Bogan happy. He also brought Thomas Sprague, who commanded Kinkaid's escort carriers at Leyte, and put him on *Wasp* in Jocko Clark's division.

On March 14, TF-58 steamed from Ulithi and headed for Japan. Kamikazes worried Mitscher. Okinawa, being so close to the home islands, would invite suicide attacks. He even considered the possibility of enemy planes dropping poison gas on his fleet. With this on his mind, he set out to eliminate as many enemy planes as possible on Okinawa, Kyushu, and Kure.

After the fall of Manila on February 3 and the Iwo Jima assault 16 days later, IGH expected the home islands to be struck next. Vice Admiral Matome Ugaki, who had been Yamamoto's chief of staff, now commanded the Fifth Air Fleet with headquarters at Kanoya airbase in southern Kyushu. He controlled more than 1,000 planes, most of which were kamikazes, and more were on the way.

Ugaki began tracking Mitcher's movements on March 14, the day TF-58 sortied from Ulithi. Three days later, search planes reported the task force 175 miles south of Kyushu. Ugaki ordered up the first of two strikes—27 kamikazes and 25 torpedo-bombers. Next morning, while Mitscher's planes were strafing and bombing Kyushu airfields, Ugaki's planes damaged *Enterprise*, *Intrepid*, and *Yorktown*. Ugaki tried to mount another strike but his airfields were in shambles.

On March 19, Mitscher changed tactics and sent strikes against the Japanese fleet at Kure. Swift new Shiden-kai fighters, flown by veteran instructors, aggressively attacked the Hellcats but without success. So few planes could not stop Mitscher's air groups, which scored hits on the carriers *Amagi* and *Ryuho* and the battleship *Yamato*.

While Mitscher's planes hammered Kure, Ugaki's bombers and kamikazes approached through a low layer of haze and struck *Franklin* and *Wasp*, killing and wounding 990 officers and men on *Franklin* and 370 on *Wasp*. The second wave hit *Franklin* and *Wasp* again, setting off explosions on *Franklin* that could be heard from 50 miles away. *Franklin* went dead in the water, but changes in compartmentalization and damage control kept the ship from sinking.

Ugaki believed that if his flyers damaged enough carriers, he could keep Americans from invading Japan. His kamikaze attacks produced encouraging results, forcing Mitscher to withdraw periodically to assess damage. Admiral Davison had to transfer his flag from *Franklin* to *Hancock*. *Enterprise* caught fire from friendly AA fire. The situation could have become worse on March 20 had Jocko Clark's Hellcats not intercepted and shot down 18 enemy bombers carrying Oka piloted rocket bombs. TF-58 escaped another attack when several squadrons of IJA pilots assigned to Ugaki's Fifth Air Fleet scattered and ran at the first sight of Hellcats.

On March 22, Mitscher reformed TG 58.2 into a task squadron of three cripples—*Franklin*, *Enterprise*, and *Wasp*—and sent them under escort to Ulithi. Jocko Clark's TG 58.1 received *San Jacinto* in place of *Wasp*, and Radford, having lost *Enterprise*, picked up *Independence*. Ted Sherman's TG 58.3 received *Hancock* and *Bataan*, which with *Essex*, *Bunker Hill*, and *Cabot* brought his group to five carriers. Sherman would have preferred eight carriers, but five gave him an opportunity to test his tactical theory that "the larger the task group the better."[5]

On March 23, Mitscher returned to Okinawa to carry out a week of preinvasion strikes. Attacks on Kyushu had destroyed 500 enemy planes, but the supply of kamikazes seemed limitless. Japanese pilots discovered that American radar was less efficient if they flew low, singly, or in pairs. This forced Hellcat pilots to rely on visual contact. Because of improved carrier combat air control, kamikazes shifted their efforts from flattops to destroyers and cruisers. On the eve of the Okinawa invasion, suicide planes damaged the heavy cruiser *Indianapolis* and forced Spruance to transfer his flag.

On March 25, during the softening up of Okinawa, the British Pacific Fleet arrived. For several months, the Royal Navy had been assembling a carrier strike force for deployment in the Pacific. With the Normandy invasion ten months old, the invasion of Southern France seven months old, and German U-boats no longer a threat, capital ships of the Royal Navy found little employment in the Atlantic. Admiral King had never been enthusiastic about Royal Navy help and saw no need for British carriers in the Pacific. With the Japanese navy obliterated, he believed he had more than enough sea power to finish the war. King also believed that the presence of a British squadron would create confusion because everything the Royal Navy did, from guns and ammunition to communications, differed from the Pacific Fleet. But King had no say in the matter because President Roosevelt approved the plan.

The idea of sending the Royal Navy to the Pacific took root during the spring of 1944 when HMS *Illustrious* began joint operations with *Saratoga*. The plan called for making each ship familiar with the other's procedures. For several months, the two carriers worked together striking Japanese installations in the Dutch East Indies. During the summer of 1944, the fast carriers *Victorious* and *Indomitable* arrived and joined in operations.

In November, the Royal Navy changed the name of the squadron from the East Indies Fleet to the British Pacific Fleet, although headquarters remained in

The HMS *Illustrious* has a group of U.S.-built Corsairs (wings tipped upward) interspersed with British Barracudas (wings flat) during operations with the U.S. fleet. (Imperial War Museum)

Ceylon. Soon the fleet carrier *Indefatigable* arrived with the escort carriers *Amere, Atheling, Battler, Begum*, and *Shah*. On December 20, 1944, Rear Admiral Philip Vian led relentless attacks on East Indies oil refineries and was instrumental in shutting down Japanese naval and air operations during the winter of 1945. During the strikes on Sumatra and Palembang, British pilots proved to be as adept at shooting down Japanese aircraft as American pilots. The British Pacific Fleet moved its base to the Admiralty Islands in the Bismarck Sea and assimilated six more escort carriers.

On March 15, the British Pacific Fleet, now under the tactical command of Vice Admiral Sir H. Bernard Rawlings, reported for duty with the U.S. Pacific Fleet. With three American carriers crippled and removed from operations at Okinawa, Nimitz welcomed the additions and sent Rawling's TF-57 with Vian's TG 57.2 of four fleet carriers (*Illustrious, Indefatigable, Indomitable*, and *Victorious*) to Spruance. The British also had discovered the importance of choosing air admirals to command carriers, the only battleship man being Vian's chief of staff.

On March 26–27, Vian's short-range Seafires provided CAP while Hellcats, Corsairs, Helldivers, and Avengers strafed and bombed Japanese aircraft-shuttling bases on Sakishima Gunto, which lay between Okinawa and Formosa. Vian's commanders had never seen a kamikaze until four days later when one crashed into the deck of *Indefatigable*. The British discovered that 20 mm and two-pounder AA guns could not stop a diving kamikaze, but the armored decks of their carriers could. A kamikaze killed and wounded several men but did no damage. Another struck *Illustrious*, bounced off the armored deck, and toppled into the sea. Kamikaze attacks on British flattops set the stage for more to come.

On April 1, more than 500 planes from Mitscher's fast carriers and Admiral Durgin's escort carriers covered the landings on Okinawa. The Japanese had dug into the hills and offered weak resistance as Lieutenant General Simon Bolivar Buckner, Jr., USA, began putting the first of more than 183,000 men ashore. Close air support over the landing beaches went smoothly, but pilots found few targets. Captain Whitehead anticipated enemy air attacks and as an early warning system posted specially trained radar picket destroyers around Okinawa, but for five days only spotty flights of kamikazes bothered the invasion fleet. Most of them targeted transports, destroyers, and escort carriers.

From Kyushu, Admiral Ukagi had hoped to concentrate 4,500 planes for Operation Ten-Go: the launching of a massive air attack against Spruance's amphibious force. He developed the tactics himself, planning to use immense waves of suicide planes and hundreds of fighters to keep Hellcats busy so kamikazes could get to the ships. By April 6 he had mustered only 699 aircraft, including 355 kamikazes. Instead of launching suicide planes for a mass attack, he sent them out in small groups. This gave Mitscher time to send up more fighters.

Kamikaze attacks lasted all day but scored only one near miss on *Belleau Wood*. Suicide pilots sought easier targets and sank three destroyers, two ammunition ships, and an LST. They also damaged 20 other ships, including

Vice Admiral Philip L. Vian, later (Sir) Admiral of the Fleet, Royal Navy, commanded the British carrier squadron during operations around Okinawa and the Japanese home islands. (National Archives)

The USS *Belleau Wood* (CVL-24) is struck by a kamikaze. The fire crew turns out in an effort to save planes positioned on the deck. (National Archives)

destroyers, destroyer escorts, and a minelayer. Thousands of Americans lost their lives, but Admiral Ugaki lost 350 planes.

Operation Ten-Go also employed the superbattleship *Yamato*. Followed by one light cruiser and eight destroyers, *Yamato* sortied from the Inland Sea on April 6 for a suicide run to Okinawa. Admiral Ryunosuke Kusaka, chief of staff for the nonexistent combined fleet, radioed Ugaki for air support. The admiral had no planes to spare and only a few hundred unskilled kamikaze pilots capable of making one-way flights into oblivion.

Despite being occupied by kamikaze attacks, Mitscher had the good sense to keep Hellcat and Helldiver search-strikes in the air. Jocko Clark also had a squadron of Avengers armed with torpedoes aloft, even though most TBFs now carried bombs because of the scarcity of enemy ships. At 8:30 A.M. on April 7, a search patrol from *Essex* spotted *Yamato* in the East China Sea. Mitscher radioed Jocko Clark and Ted Sherman to go after *Yamato* and directed Radford to sink the cruiser. It had been so long since Avenger pilots had dropped a fish that Torpedo Nine skipper Lieutenant Thomas H. Stetson remarked, "Take a good look at it, fellows. That's a torpedo, remember? We haven't seen one in six months. Do you suppose you still know how to drop 'em?"[6] At 12:30, Stetson's Avenger pilots struck *Yamato* with four torpedoes.

By 10:15, Clark and Sherman had 280 planes in the air with 106 more launching from Radford's group. At 12:41, flyers from *Bennington* struck *Yamato* with two bombs and four minutes later the first torpedo. More planes from Clark's and Sherman's groups found her on fire and hit her again. At 1:30, Avengers from Radford's *Yorktown*, *Intrepid*, and *Langley* arrived and came in low. "I suddenly saw all five torpedoes hit—bang! bang! bang! bang! bang!" said Lieutenant Stewart Bass. "For a moment, nothing seemed to happen. Then she began erupting. Flames belched through holes in her deck, and great holes were blown in her portside."[7] At 2:23 P.M. the giant 72,000-ton battleship rolled over and sank, taking 3,000 lives. As the historian Clark Reynolds observed, "For naval aviation, the sinking of *Yamato* was final proof of the obsolescence of the battleship."[8] The destroyers went down with her, marking the last sortie of the Imperial Japanese Navy.

During the attack on *Yamato*, Admiral Ugaki launched another suicide strike. Already on alert, American planes ripped the kamikazes apart, but four wiggled through. One suicide plane smashed into *Hancock's* hangar deck, killing 72 men, wounding 82, and destroying 20 aircraft. Others struck the battleship *Maryland*, the destroyer *Bennett*, and the destroyer escort *Wesson*.

To carrier pilots, it seemed that for every 100 kamikazes they shot from the skies, 100 more appeared in the days that followed. Every plane that could be spared from home defense went to Admiral Ugaki, and on every day that planes could fly, he sent wave after wave against the Allied fleet. Spruance never budged, keeping Mitscher's carriers off shore. While American troops fought desperate battles against suicide troops on the ground, American flyers battled suicide pilots in the skies. The attacks never ceased. On April 11, a kamikaze struck *Enterprise*. Five days later, another kamikaze struck *Intrepid*. When Admiral Davison returned with two repaired carriers, Mitscher sent him back to Ulithi with two more.

Nimitz decided to go to Okinawa and size up the situation for himself. Before leaving, he learned that on April 12 President Roosevelt died. Like most men in the service, Nimitz knew little about Vice President Harry S. Truman. In a letter to his wife, Nimitz wrote, "Whether or not we liked all the things [Roosevelt] did, and stood for—he was always for a strong Navy...."[9]

Army engineers were supposed to be building fighter airstrips on Okinawa so carriers could be freed to strike Japan, but construction crews were not getting the job done. Mitscher was still offshore providing close air support. Spruance heard a rumor that General Henry H. "Hap" Arnold, commanding the AAF, had been privately exhorting General Buckner's engineers to build bomber fields instead of fighter strips. Spruance doubted the rumor, but when Nimitz arrived from Hawaii, both men went ashore. They discovered that of 22 sites selected for airfields, the only ones under construction were for bombers. Nimitz took Buckner aside and said, "I'm losing a ship and a half a day. So if this line isn't moving within five days, we'll get someone here to move it so we can all get out from under these stupid air attacks."[10] Buckner did not like the navy meddling in army business, but five days later construction crews began excavating fighter strips.

In early May, after HMS *Formidable* relieved *Illustrious* for a scheduled overall, Admiral Vian took the carriers to the Sakishimas to bomb enemy airfields. On May 4, kamikazes crashed into *Formidable* and *Indomitable* but did not damage the armored decks. Five days later, suicide planes struck *Victorious* and *Formidable,* proving again that British armored decks were superior to American decks. As an example, on May 11 a kamikaze shattered the deck of *Bunker Hill*, Mitscher's flagship, and killed more than 350 men and most of the ship's air group. Forced to transfer his flag to *Enterprise*, Mitscher detached *Bunker Hill* for repair, and having lost 13 members of his staff in the explosion, he temporarily transferred tactical command to Ted Sherman.

The Okinawa campaign marked the first time Royal Navy carriers joined operations with the Fifth Fleet. Spruance remarked that during the campaign the British Pacific Fleet gained the experience necessary to share operations with Mitscher's carriers.

For four weeks, Mitscher's task force had been under continuous attack from kamikazes, all because Spruance would not let TF-58 stray more than 60 miles from Okinawa. During Nimitz's visit in late April, he said, "We are a high speed stationary target for the Japanese air force," but Spruance did not interpret the comment as an order to change carrier tactics.[11] Mitscher understood the meaning and patiently waited for new orders. Finally, on May 18, he asked for permission to strike Japan, but Spruance thought he still needed the carriers for close air support. So TF-58 remained off Okinawa performing the function of escort carriers.

Everyone in the upper echelon of the navy studied tactical methods for fighting kamikazes. None of them worked. Mitscher privately blamed Spruance for keeping his carriers in a defensive mode. He also blamed General Buckner for snail's pace operations on Okinawa and for delays in building fighter airstrips, both of which tied down his ships and exposed them to daily attacks.

Out of the turmoil came Halsey, who claimed he could stop kamikaze attacks. His theory was the same as Mitscher's: using carrier air to clobber enemy airstrips and production facilities. Nimitz had become frustrated because General Curtis LeMay of the 20th Bomber Command in the Marianas preferred burning Japanese cities with incendiaries to targeting enemy aircraft plants. Mitscher asked permission to do what LeMay refused to do, but Spruance kept him handcuffed to Okinawa.

In late April, Halsey flew to Guam, Nimitz's new forward base for the Pacific Fleet. He explained the importance of taking the offensive, and Nimitz agreed.

Halsey then flew to Okinawa to confer with Spruance about changing carrier tactics. Spruance refused to budge, insisting the only way to dispose of kamikazes was to shoot them down. Halsey reported the discussion to Nimitz, who decided to relieve Spruance under the pretense of needing him to plan future operations. Nimitz also decided to give Mitscher a rest and put McCain in command of the carriers. During discussions, the war in Europe ended, and everybody looked to the day it would end in the Pacific.

On May 27, Halsey relieved Spruance and took command of the Fifth Fleet, which then became the Third Fleet. He told Spruance that his orders were to discontinue the current static defense arrangement and take the task force wherever it had to go to stop kamikaze attacks, which meant striking the Japanese homeland. With Halsey back in command and the mission changed, officer and pilot morale, which had been backsliding for eight weeks, received an enormous boost, even though ships, men, and aircraft remained the same.

On June 2–3, carrier pilots caught the enemy off guard and destroyed scores of planes on the ground and dozens more in the air. As flyers returned, Halsey received word that another typhoon was approaching, and this time he tried to avoid it. Meteorologists at Pearl Harbor fed him erroneous information and sent TF-38 into the eye of the storm. Three destroyers capsized, 29 ships suffered damage (among them carriers), wind swept 150 planes into the sea, and more than 750 men died. Halsey had recommended weather-tracking methods after being caught in the first typhoon, which included constant monitoring by specially equipped planes, but no one listened. After the weather improved, Halsey returned to the coast of Japan and spent a week hammering airfields and factories. He doubled CAP, and no more kamikazes reached the ships. The tactics worked. On June 21, Japanese resistance on Okinawa ended. The 11-week struggle cost the Japanese 6,810 aircraft, including 1,900 suicide planes. American carriers lost 565 aircraft and British carriers 160, including 61 deck-landing accidents caused by Seafires.[12]

Spruance's insistence that TF-58 remain off Okinawa created an enormous toll in Allied shipping, which stopped after Halsey took command. The Fifth Fleet lost 36 ships with another 371 injured. Kamikazes and Okas did most of the damage. One out of 10 suicide planes struck a ship. Dawn or moonlight attacks were the most successful. By the time Halsey arrived on May 27, the Japanese had lost most of the night-trained suicide pilots and the half-trained day pilots.[13]

After Okinawa, Japan could no longer obtain supplies. Kamikazes, the Rising Sun's last desperate hope, had failed to drive Allied forces away from the home islands. The future looked hopeless, but the proud and battered nation would not surrender.

After a respite during the latter weeks of June, TF-38 returned in July and resumed operations against Kyushu and Honshu, bombing and strafing anything resembling a military target. On July 14, in the first major shore bombardment of the war, battleships, cruisers, and destroyers pounded the home islands, blasting steel factories on Honshu. On July 17, carrier planes soared over Tokyo, striking ships at the Yokosuke Naval Base and in Tokyo Bay. The British Fleet returned and struck airfields on Hokkaido and Honshu. Carrier pilots found no planes on airfields and met none in the sky. McCain concluded that Japan had dug in, sheltering their aircraft for the final defense of the homeland.

In late July, with thousands of American troops preparing for the assault on Japan, Admiral Ugaki resumed kamikaze raids. He hoped to destroy the amphibious fleet, and suicide planes sank enough transports to bring part of McCain's task force back to Okinawa.

On August 6, an AAF B-29, *Enola Gay,* dropped the first atomic bomb on Hiroshima, a city of 500,000, and killed 70,000 people. Still the Japanese held out. The generals refused to surrender, even though 2,409 kamikaze pilots had been killed and everyone else had known for weeks that the war was lost. On August 9, a second atomic bomb killed 20,000 people in Nagasaki. The emperor lobbied the Supreme War Council to surrender, but the generals still resisted.

Halsey added to the devastation. On August 10, planes from TF-38 flew at treetop level over northern Honshu and riddled 175 enemy planes hidden beneath camouflage. Three days later, they repeated the attack over the Tokyo plain, destroying 254 enemy aircraft and damaging more. Japanese AA shot down 15 American and 6 British planes. TF-38 commander Admiral McCain had no idea the war's end was only hours away. On August 14, IGH agreed to unconditional surrender providing no harm came to the emperor. McCain recalled the last strike of the war, launched at 4:15 A.M. on August 15, when he received word of Japan's capitulation.

At breakfast on the battleship *Missouri*, Halsey began pounding the backs of men at the table, and said, "God be thanked. I'll never have to order another man out to die." Then he went on deck and ordered a flag hoist run up with the message, "Well done."[14]

The war in the Pacific started as an air war with the bombing of Pearl Harbor. Until the atomic bomb, the most powerful weapon of the war had been the aircraft carrier. The Japanese, having a widely distributed island empire, understood the value of this weapon in the 1930s. On December 7, 1941, the United States came to understand it better.

At the beginning of the war with Japan, American military strategists believed that naval surface engagements between battleships and cruisers would decide the course of the war. They also believed that Japan would have to be invaded.[15] The concept emanated from old doctrine that harnessed carriers to battle lines for the purpose of providing reconnaissance and support for amphibious operations. Men like Halsey, Mitscher, and dozens of war-grown air admirals and captains proved the fallacy of this thinking, but it took most of the war to be understood by others. During 1941–43, such ignorance resulted in too much spending for battleships and not enough for carriers.

After the surrender of Japan, the United States Strategic Bombing Survey (USSBS) interviewed Japanese military and naval leaders. General Tojo attributed Japan's defeat to three factors: "the Navy's 'leapfrogging' strategy of bypassing important centers of Japanese military power . . .; the far-ranging activities of the Fast Carrier Forces Pacific Fleet . . .; and the destruction of merchant shipping by United States submarines."[16] Japanese officials agreed that "if the atomic bombs had not been dropped . . . Japan would have surrendered to the air attack even if no surface action invasion had been planned."[17]

The USSBS went a step further, reassessing the war in the Pacific from the beginning. They concluded that if U.S. strategy had been "oriented toward air power and air weapons," and if "air, sea, and land forces in the Pacific could have been directed along the most direct route to Japan: from the Solomons to the Admiralties, Truk, the Marianas, and Iwo Jima . . . MacArthur's entire Philippines campaign [would have been] unnecessary."[18] This would have eliminated all of Nimitz's costly campaigns in the Gilberts, Marshalls, and Okinawa, but the belief that Japan must be invaded induced the JCS to stick with a plan designed in the 1920s.

USSBS analysts had no further to look for corroboration of their postwar theories than to the Fast Carrier Task Force itself. Once new air weapons became available, Mitscher redefined carrier tactics. His task force was not needed for the battle line at the Marianas, and Spruance made a serious error by keeping it there. Spruance made the same mistake at Okinawa by hog-tying Mitscher's attack carriers to a defensive role. When Halsey resumed command of the Third Fleet, he did exactly what Mitscher wanted to do—he struck Japanese air bases and aircraft plants in whirlwind attacks that virtually drove the enemy from the skies and solved the kamikaze problem.

After the war, when discussing carrier commanders, Nimitz pointed to Vice Admiral Mitscher, not Halsey, and said, "He is the most experienced and most able officer in the handling of fast carrier task forces who has yet been developed. It is doubtful if any officer has made more important contributions than he toward extinction of the enemy fleet."[19]

Two major tactical problems remained unsettled at the end of the war. One concerned task group composition, the other close air support tactics. Admiral Ted Sherman still believed that fast carrier task force development had not reached its peak when Japan surrendered. He still believed that a task group should contain as many as eight fast carriers, whereas Mitscher held to a group consisting of three CVs and one CVL. In addition, marines believed that close air support should be controlled from shore, not from a ship, but their analysis did not provide for close air support of army forces, and the navy refused to change. As time, aircraft, and instrumentation changed, so would tactics, leaving discussions on the subject for the future.

After years of fighting in the Pacific, military and naval strategists finally understood the tactical value of aircraft carriers, and a few years of peace before the beginning of the Korean War provided the time necessary to understand it better.

For the Japanese and all mankind, the Rising Sun had set.

PART V

Command of the Seas

"Now that it [the war] is over, I pray that we shall not gamble away all we've gained by any hasty, ill-considered decision."

Admiral William F. Halsey, quoted from E. B. Potter, *Bull Halsey* (Annapolis, Md., 1985, 398)

CHAPTER 17

Korea: Carriers and Politics

On August 14, 1945, one day before the celebration of V-J Day, General of the Army Douglas MacArthur became Supreme Commander of the Allied Powers (SCAP). On September 2, after signing the surrender accord, he moved SCAP headquarters to Tokyo. The title gave him absolute authority over the emperor, the Japanese government, and all the military and naval forces in the Pacific. Like Nimitz, he had learned from firsthand experience the importance of fast carrier task forces. He also discovered the superiority of naval air support compared to his own AAF. He would not forget what he learned, but in the summer of 1945 no one expected war any time soon.

Admirals began going home. In December, Nimitz relieved Admiral King as CNO. After a short stint as Commander in Chief Pacific, Spruance became president of the Naval War College. Halsey went home, received promotion to fleet admiral in December, and retired in April 1947. Vice Admiral John H. Towers received the rank of full admiral. Barely known to the public, he did more to promote naval aviation and the formation of fast carrier task forces than any man in the Pacific. Vice Admiral Mitscher exited from the war as the acknowledged leader of carrier aviation. Secretary of the Navy James V. Forrestal urged him to become CNO, but Mitscher hated desk jobs. Promoted to full admiral in early 1946, he ended his career commanding the Atlantic Fleet. In February 1947, Mitscher's health failed and he died. In January 1946, Vice Admiral Ted Sherman, one of the finest carrier air admirals in battle, became commander of the Fifth Fleet and brought it home to Los Angeles. Soon everyone went home. In 1950, on the eve of the Korean War, there was only one fast carrier in the western Pacific, the 36,000-ton *Valley Forge* (CV-45), commissioned in November 1946.

During World War II, the Royal Navy also went through the radical transformation from battleships to carriers. All their fast carrier commanders went on to high flag rank. In 1946–47, Vice Admiral Vian became First Sea Lord (Air) and eventually admiral of the fleet. Although postwar conditions forced the British to reduce its fleet, they continued making technical improvements. When Vice Admiral Sir Denis Boyd took command of the British Pacific Fleet in 1946, he asked for no more battleships. Even though Britain's struggling economy forced a production halt on most of the navy's *Malta*-, *Majestic*-, and *Colossus*-class carriers, the 46,000-ton *Eagle* went into commission in 1951. A new problem faced every navy—designing carriers for operations with jet aircraft.

The atomic bomb created a new controversy, this time in Washington, D.C. AAF advocates claimed that all the United States needed for first-line defense were B-29s armed with A-bombs, and as there were no carriers large enough to carry B-29s, the navy and its flattops would not be needed. To prove the point, the government moved *Saratoga* and *Independence* to Bikini Atoll and, in July 1946, with an experimental nuclear blast, sank the former and scorched the latter. Contrary to the wishes of the navy, the AAF and the army used the blast to lobby for the consolidation of the services into a single defense department. In July 1947, President Truman agreed and on September 23, to placate the navy, named Secretary of the Navy Forrestal as the first Secretary of Defense. John Sullivan filled the downgraded position of naval secretary and continued the policy of demobilization.

On October 1, 1947, the 45,000-ton *Midway*-class *Coral Sea* (CVB-43) went into commission. If Truman and Congress had their way, she could be the last. Air admirals, after two more years of watching the fleet disappear, revolted when Congress cancelled the 60,000-ton supercarrier *United States* (CVB-58). Admiral Louis E. Denfield, CNO, led the revolt. He won his argument before the House Naval Affairs Committee but lost his job by irritating Secretary of Defense Louis A. Johnson. Johnson would never become a popular figure with navy personnel.

The supercarriers keel, laid-down in April, remained untouched until the outbreak of the Korean War. Congress suddenly realized that dropping an atomic bomb on South Korea was out of the question and that conventional ground warfare might actually be here to stay. They reversed their position and appropriated funds for 60,000-ton *Forrestal*-class carriers capable of launching nuclear air attacks. Much to the chagrin of the USAF, carriers recovered the strategic bombing initiative so recently won from them by the air force. More important to all the services, the Korean War demonstrated that although nuclear weapons might serve as political deterrents, they were too powerful for general use. Congress had been carrying the ball in the wrong direction.

On June 25, 1950, when war erupted in Korea, the U.S. Navy had only 270 combat ships in commission, including 15 carriers. North Korea's lightning strike on South Korea caught everyone napping. Vice Admiral Arthur D. Struble's TF-77 lay off Hong Kong with *Valley Forge*, Captain L. K. Rice, and the HMS *Triumph*, Captain A. D. Torliss. Neither carrier was war-ready. Struble sent TF-77 to Subic Bay in the Philippines for ammunition and supplies.

It would be *Essex*-class carriers that provided support for ground troops. Most of the 86 aircraft on the deck of *Valley Forge* resembled planes from World War II. There were two propeller-driven fighter squadrons equipped with

28 F4U-4B Corsairs and an attack squadron of 14 Douglas AD-4 Skyraiders—an upgrade of the Dauntless II divebomber. Two squadrons, each with 15 Grumman F9F-2 Panthers, added jet fighter support. Panthers were rugged aircraft armed with four 20 mm cannon. Over short ranges they could carry up to 3,000 pounds of bombs and rockets. A sixth group contained a mixed assortment of 14 planes specially configured for photographic, night, and radar missions. When it came to aircraft, the USAF short-changed the navy by overselling the importance of strategic bombing and used appropriated funds to advance their own programs.

On July 3, 1950, TF-77 steamed into the Yellow Sea and launched the first naval air strikes of the war. The HMS *Triumph* carried only 24 planes, MK1 Fireflies and MK47 Seafires, both propeller-driven leftovers from World War II. Some had actually fought in the war. British pilots enjoyed flying Seafires but hated to land them. If a Seafire hit the deck too hard it buckled and formed permanent creases in the fuselage. The problem traced back to the 1943 invasion of Salerno, Italy. During three days of operations from escort carriers, Seafires shot down two German planes without a loss, but 42 of them were damaged beyond repair from deck-landings.[1]

Seafires and Fireflies struck bridges and airfields at Haeju while 36 planes from *Valley Forge* bombed Pyongyang, North Korea's capital. Eight Panthers strafed Pyongyang's airfield, shot down two North Korean Yak-9 fighters, strafed nine on the ground, and created general mayhem. Sixteen Corsairs and 12 Skyraiders arrived minutes later, bombed the airfield, blew up fuel supplies, and clobbered the rail center. All planes returned, but one Skyraider hit by AA jumped the barrier, crashed into two Corsairs, and damaged six other planes.

On July 7, General MacArthur became Supreme Commander of UN forces in Korea. He could not strike North Korean supply lines without carriers, nor could he provide close air support for troops being shoveled ashore to bolster the crumbling Pusan perimeter. President Truman declared a blockade of North Korean waters, thereby increasing a need for more carriers. For four weeks, Admiral Struble's two carriers steamed back and forth protecting landings at Pohang one day and hitting targets in North Korea the next. On July 25, after helping Lieutenant General Walton H. Walker get the Eighth Army ashore at Pusan, Struble sent *Valley Forge* back to Okinawa for ammunition and supplies, leaving *Triumph* on blockade duty off North Korea.

From Okinawa, the fast carrier *Philippine Sea* (CV-46), sister ship of *Valley Forge*, joined TF-77. From across the Pacific came more flattops: *Boxer* and the escort carriers *Badoeng Strait* (CVE-116) and *Sicily* (CVE-118). The escorts brought two Marine Fighter Squadrons for desperately needed close air support along the Pusan perimeter. By mid-August, five U.S. carriers became active in the Korean War. Operating from the Sea of Japan, most of the planes flew close support missions, but *Philippine Sea* slipped away to hammer bridges, railroads, and supply routes feeding from the north into South Korea.

On September 4, while operating in Korea Bay, *Valley Forge* came within 100 miles of Red China and the Soviet airbase at Port Arthur on Liaotung

Peninsula. A little extracurricular action occurred when *Herbert J. Thomas*, a picket destroyer, reported an unidentified aircraft approaching from Port Arthur. *Valley Forge* radar picked up a blip 60 miles out. Two divisions of Corsair fighters performing CAP went to investigate and spotted a Soviet Tupolev bomber. When the Tupolev opened fire, the American squadron leader radioed *Valley Forge* for instructions and received permission to fire back. Cannon blasts from a single Corsair set the Tupolev on fire and it splashed into the sea.

On August 23, with the military situation improving along the Pusan perimeter, General MacArthur persuaded CNO Admiral Forrest Sherman and army chief of staff General J. Lawton Collins to support his plan for an amphibious assault at Inchon, South Korea's principal port on the west coast of Korea. After saying, "The Navy carriers were a vital factor in holding the Pusan perimeter," Mac-Arthur now commandeered all five flattops for the Inchon operation.[2]

Located 150 miles behind enemy lines, Inchon provided a gateway to Seoul and strategically located Kimpo Airfield, which lay beside a major highway that ran between the two cities. The North Korean People's Army (NKPA) ignored the port as a possible landing site because the narrow twisting channel ran through mud flats that could be easily blocked by sinking barges. A seawall enclosed Inchon, keeping out 30-foot tides, and the swift running tidal flow combined with paste-like mud made amphibious operations precarious. While finalizing plans for the Inchon invasion, MacArthur continued to feed troops into Pusan, ordering them to break out on the day of the Inchon assault.

At 6:33 A.M. on September 15, after a typhoon nearly wrecked MacArthur's timetable, Inchon operations began. Close air support from five carriers enabled components of the 1st Marine Division to secure a beachhead at Wolmi-do, which for two days had been plastered with bombs and napalm. As Marines moved onto the highway leading to Kimpo airfield, Corsairs from the escort carriers *Sicily* and *Badoeng Strait* blasted enemy tanks and infantry units attempting to block the road.

Squeezed between MacArthur's landings at Inchon and the Allied breakout at Pusan, NKPA divisions disintegrated and fled north through the Korean countryside. Carrier planes tore the retreating columns to pieces, and on September 17, USAF fighter squadrons moved onto Kimpo Airfield.

On September 25, the HMS *Triumph* departed from the area with only one flyable Seafire and a few Fireflies. HMS *Theseus* arrived with 24 planes to fill the slot, bringing improved Mark 4 Fireflies, and instead of Seafires, the new, faster Hawker Sea Furies, which could compete with Soviet MiG-15s.

By September 26, the NKPA had been destroyed below the 38th parallel but not above it. MacArthur obtained approval from the JCS to continue the pursuit into North Korea and mop up the remnants. The general needed a forward base and chose Wonsan on the east coast of North Korea. The plan sounded simple. While Republic of Korea (ROK) troops pressed north from the 38th parallel, Admiral Struble's task force would clear mines from Wonsan's harbor and put

An F4-U Corsair prepares to take off from the carrier *Boxer* stationed
off Korea. (U.S. Navy photo)

Major General Edward M. Almond's X Corps ashore. After two minesweepers
went down, Struble learned that Wonsan's harbor contained 3,000 contact and
magnetic mines. ROK troops entered the port city two weeks before the navy
could clear a narrow path through the minefield. Struble's carriers spent the next
12 days striking strategic targets and flying supplies into the city.

Detached from duty in the Mediterranean, the 21,100-ton *Leyte* (CV-32)
joined TF-77 on October 3 and became involved in action off Wonsan. She spent
the next 108 days flying 3,933 sorties during MacArthur's advance through North
Korea.

On October 19, Allied forces occupied the capital city of Pyongyang and
began pushing the last remnants of the NKPA toward the Yalu River on Manchuria's border. A few days later, the 1st Marine Division marched north from
Hungnam to the Chosin Reservoir while the 7th Infantry Division and two ROK

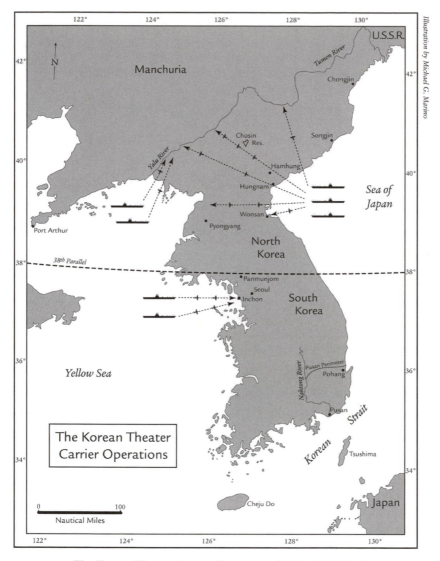

The Korean Theater: Carrier Operations. (Michael G. Marino)

divisions pressed up the east coast and into the interior. By late October, it appeared that the battle for Korea had entered the final days. MacArthur predicted that the men would be home for Christmas, and Admiral Struble detached his fast carriers for a breather in Japan, leaving only two escort carriers off Korea.

Reconnaissance aircraft keeping watch on the Yalu reported a buildup of Chinese Communist Forces (CCF) along the Manchurian shore. Intelligence operatives claimed that CCF units were already across the river and moving south. ROK units in eastern Korea soon reported heavy fighting. MacArthur became concerned and recalled Struble's carriers. On October 29, *Leyte* and *Valley Forge* departed from Honshu and crossed the Sea of Japan. Two days later, Soviet-built MiG-15s based in Manchuria flew across the Yalu and fired on UN reconnaissance aircraft.

From captured prisoners, army intelligence determined that elements from four CCF armies were already in North Korea. MacArthur ordered Vice Admiral C. Turner Joy to bomb 17 major Yalu and Tumen River bridges linking Manchuria to North Korea, hoping the action would prevent more Chinese from crossing. He also ordered armed air reconnaissance over northeast Korea, which meant attacking targets of opportunity.

Bombing Yalu bridges came with conditions. Joy advised Struble: "The Manchurian territory and air space under no circumstances must not, repeat *not*, be violated."[3] This meant that pilots could bomb the North Korean side of a bridge so long as they did not enter Manchurian airspace. Because of the snake-like meandering of the two rivers, B-29s could neither strike just one side of a bridge nor avoid Manchurian airspace. The only flyers capable of carrying out the order were carrier pilots, but they were trained in glide bombing, which invariably would carry them into Manchuria's airspace. This meant that flattop pilots would have to resort to perpendicular dive-bombing, with which they were unacquainted, and veer sharply away to avoid flying over Manchuria. They were also ordered "not to fire upon or bomb the antiaircraft guns on the Chinese side of the river...[or] pursue an attacking MiG back into Chinese territory."[4] Such tactical restrictions diminished the chances of hitting a bridge, and the condition of being under heavy anitaircraft artillery (AAA) fire without being able to fire back created a psychological barrier not conducive to good marksmanship. Although destroying bridges made tactical sense, it did not keep CCF out of Korea. The Yalu and Tumen Rivers would soon freeze, enabling troops and supplies to move across ice. Until then, the Chinese used pontoon bridges.

On November 9, carrier air strikes of 24 to 40 planes resumed. Launched from 100 miles offshore, Panthers provided top cover while a mix of Corsairs and Skyraiders struck bridges. Panthers, because of greater speed and lesser range, departed in staggered groups, the first flight 50 minutes behind prop-planes with the second and third flights leaving at 15-minute intervals. Long before the bridges came in sight, the first Panthers overtook the prop-planes and escorted them to the Yalu, the second flight provided air cover, and the third flight escorted the "props" back to the carrier. During November 9–21, carrier planes from *Valley Forge*, *Philippine Sea*, and *Leyte* flew 593 sorties and dropped 232 tons of 500-, 1,000-, and 2,000-ton bombs on Yalu bridges.

After the first attacks, the Chinese realized that AAA batteries on the south side of the river were the only ones being targeted. They sensibly moved all the batteries to the north shore and no longer bothered to camouflage them. After that, enemy flak became a serious impediment to effective bombing.

Panther pilots observed MiG-15s coming off airfields a few miles inside Manchuria. They noted the MiG's faster speed, shorter turning radius, and better maneuverability. American pilots countered with superior training, teamwork, and marksmanship. On November 9, Lieutenant Commander William T. Amen became the first navy pilot to register a jet-to-jet kill. Nine days later, Panther pilots from *Valley Forge* and *Leyte* shot down two more MiGs.

On November 24, MacArthur launched an offensive to hurl the CCF back across the Yalu and complete the occupation of North Korea. Approximately 300,000 CCF were already in North Korea largely undetected and poised for launching their own attack. The CCF struck MacArthur's Eighth Army in western North Korea with 180,000 troops and sent it reeling back in disorder. Another 120,000 CCF troops fell on the 1st Marine Division west of the Chosin Reservoir, the 7th Army Division at Hyesanjin, and two ROK divisions at Hapsu and Chongjin.

On December 10, Rear Admiral James H. Doyle's TF-90, which had been responsible for landings on the east coast of North Korea, now became responsible for evacuating 105,000 troops, including the 1st Marine Division, 91,000 civilian refugees, and 350,000 tons of supplies from the port of Hungnam.

Caught by surprise on every front, MacArthur recalled all of Admiral Struble's carriers. *Valley Forge, Sicily*, and *Badoeng Strait* moved back into

In 1950, the HMS *Triumph* joined the U.S. fleet at Subic Bay, the Philippines. (U.S. Navy photo)

combat, rejoining *Philippine Sea* and *Leyte*. *Princeton* (CV-37) arrived with a crew of reservists. The CVL *Bataan*, ferrying USAF fighters to Japan, flew them off, took on Corsairs, and on December 15 joined HMS *Theseus* off Korea's west coast. For the next two weeks, carrier planes provided air support for Mac-Arthur's massive withdrawal. By the beginning of the 1951, Struble had nine carriers in Korean waters with more coming. The mothballed fast carriers *Bon Homme Richard*, *Essex*, and *Antietam* were on their way, along with HMS *Triumph* and the escort carrier *Bairoko*. The CCF did not press the withdrawal at Hungnam, so Doyle's TF-77 concentrated on covering the retreat of the Eighth Army—the greatest defeat suffered by American troops since the fall of the Philippines in 1942.

By January 15, 1951, CCF forces in Korea numbered 500,000. They pushed UN forces below the 38th parallel and recaptured Seoul, but there they stopped. Against the advice of Struble, who believed his planes could better serve in close air support, MacArthur directed TF-77 to strike the railway and bridge network along North Korea's east coast.

Supplies continued to reach the CCF until, one day in March, flyers from *Princeton* discovered a partly concealed and untouched 600-foot bridge with tunnels at both ends. Rear Admiral Ralph A. Ofstie, who had taken command of TF-77, ordered a strike. Eight Skyraiders from *Princeton*, led by Lieutenant Commander Harold G. Carlson, "dropped one span ... damaged a second, and twisted two others" out of alignment.[5] *Princeton*'s crew called the area "Carlson's Canyon," and Hollywood moviemakers turned the event into "The Bridges of Toko-Ri."

Seventh Fleet commander Vice Admiral J. J. "Jocko" Clark took a personal interest in finding ways to plug tunnels and keep Carlson Canyon's bridge out of commission. For several months, two carrier air groups spent all their time blasting the span and the tracks leading to and from it. The Chinese finally shifted their supply lines to western Korea. Clark did not have enough carriers to cover both sides of Korea, so the USAF took the responsibility for interdiction in the west.

On April 11, President Truman relieved MacArthur and replaced him with Lieutenant General Matthew B. Ridgeway, who continued his predecessor's policies on using carriers. He expected the CCF to launch a spring offensive, and he planned to mount a counteroffensive with the Eighth Army.

The Chinese controlled the flow of water from the Hwachon reservoir, using sluice gates to flood advances made by UN troops but cut the flow of water when supporting CCF operations. Ridgeway wanted the Hwachon dam destroyed. After attacks by B-29s failed to do any damage, the Eighth Army called on the navy. Three hours later, Rear Admiral George Henderson, commanding *Princeton*, put a strike in the air. Skyraiders dropped 2,000-pound bombs but did not damage the sluice gates. Henderson then tried torpedoes. Six fish blew apart the sluice gates and emptied the dam, marking the only use of torpedoes in the Korean War.

On June 5, Ridgeway launched Operation Strangle, a plan designed to choke the enemy front lines by cutting their eight key supply lines or "strangle zones." The operation called for the Fifth Air Force to interdict three western routes while TF-77 took two central routes and the 1st Marine Air Wing took three eastern routes. TF-77 spent the entire summer, day and night, bombing truck routes, country roads, bridges, and railroads. The Chinese formed highly effective teams of manual labor to repair the damage or create new routes around bombed-cratered areas. The "strangle" raids had barely begun when on July 10, 1951, the first truce talks began.

During late October, however, the Eighth Army learned through guerrilla sources operating in North Korea that communist commissars and party officials planned to meet at Kapsan. Admiral John Perry, commanding TF-77, ordered aerial photographs taken of the area. On the morning of the meeting, eight Skyraiders flew off *Essex* to strike the compound. Each plane carried two 1,000-pound bombs, eight 250-pound bombs, and napalm. At 9:13 A.M., just as the gathering settled into chairs, Skyraiders swooped over a 6,000-foot range to the east, dropped into the valley, and destroyed the compound, killing 509 high-level Communist Party members.

Admiral Perry tinkered with several methods to save the lives of his pilots while meeting the demands of war. He obtained six World War II F6F-5 Hellcats fitted with remote guidance systems. During August–September 1952, he had the planes loaded with high explosives and catapulted into the air. Technicians guided the flying missiles into predetermined enemy targets. Photographic evidence collected the following day showed that the experiment actually worked.

Despite all efforts, Operation Strangle failed, and the Korean War settled into a stalemate near the 38th parallel. Carrier planes continued to pound supply lines, perform close air support for ground troops, and bomb strategic targets such as oil refineries, power plants, and the North Korean capital of Pyongyang. President Truman did not object to air strikes on strategic targets, but he wanted no more major assaults into North Korea. He also stopped the bombings of the CCF supply center at Rashin because of its proximity to Russian territory.

Admiral Perry's Action Report summarized the interdiction effort: "Operations resolved themselves into a day-to-day routine where stamina replaced glamour and persistence was pitted against oriental perseverance."[6]

During the autumn of 1952, aerial combat increased between Panthers and MiG-15s flown by Russian pilots at Vladivostok. After several skirmishes in the air, observers admitted that the Soviet MiG was a better plane than the Panther, but Americans were better pilots. After losing several MiGs, interference from Vladivostok stopped.

Until July 27, 1953, the day of the Korean Armistice, little change occurred in the tactics of fighting what the United Nations called a "police action," not a war. Carrier capabilities, however, continued to change. In addition to F4U-4s and Douglas ADs, new Grumman F9F-6 Panther models appeared with swept wings and were called Cougars. Flattops also began carrying HO3S-1 Sikorsky Helicopters for rescue and minesweeping operations. Helicopters could hover over mines and blow them up. Midway through the war the navy added the McDonnell F2H Banshee jet, which became an effective escort fighter. The Grumman F7F-3N Tigercat and the Corsair F4U-5N became the navy's night hecklers.

Night fighting, developed during World War II, never became an important factor in Korea. *Princeton*, designated for Operation "No Doze," developed the war's only night-fighting capability. Many of her Corsair pilots operated from land-based airfields after communist planes began flying night missions over American lines. Night jets were too fast to knock down enemy planes, so Corsairs did the work. Lieutenant Guy P. Bordelon shot down five planes in three night actions and became the first and only navy ace.

One night-fighting weapon made a difference, the 2.75-inch folding-fin aircraft rocket, nicknamed "Mickey Mouse." Designed initially as an air-to-air weapon, it became a popular night interdiction weapon late in the war. Mighty Mouse rockets came in pods of seven. Skyraiders carried six pods, flares, and 250- or 500-pound bombs. Pilots fired a pod in a ripple, with a split-second pause between each rocket. When deployed against ground targets, Commander

HRS helicopters fly off the USS *Sicily* (CVE-118) during operations in 1952 off Korea. (U.S. Navy photo)

F. G. Reynolds said, "Using them was like going after a bug with a flyswatter instead of trying to stab him with a pencil."[7]

Commander M. U. Beebe of *Essex*'s Air Group Five summed up his experience, writing, "Generally speaking, the war in Korea demanded more competence, courage, and skill from the naval aviator than did World War II. The hours were longer, the days on the firing line more, the antiaircraft hazards greater, the weather worse."[8]

Fifteen American carriers and five British carriers served in the Korean War. The U.S. Navy flew 167,552 sorties and marines flew 107,000 sorties, many from carriers. British Seafires, Sea Furies, and Fireflies flew 22,000 sorties. Carrier planes contributed a third of all air operations in Korea, dropping 120,000 tons of bombs. The aircraft-to-aircraft war was almost nonexistent. The navy claimed 16 kills in the air and the destruction of 36 aircraft on the ground. A few navy pilots flew North American F-86 Sabres, but Panthers and Banshees were the jets of choice for carrier pilots.[9]

The Korean War muffled the USAF's efforts to argue against keeping a strong navy. B-29s delivered some of the most ineffective bombing of the war.

In 1952, 27 months after canceling the carrier *United States*, work began on the 60,000-ton supercarrier *Forrestal* (CVA-59). Congress promised to build one every year for the next five years. With *Forrestal*, the navy began changing carrier designations. Attack Aircraft Carriers became CVAs; Aircraft Carriers, Large, became CVBs; light carriers remained CVLs and escort carriers CVEs.

With the introduction of jet aircraft and new weaponry, carrier technology changed so rapidly that no ship under construction ever went into commission as originally designed. In January 1953, landing tests began on *Antietam* (CV-36), retrofitted with the navy's first angled deck. Eight months later, the navy announced that every *Midway*-class carrier would be refitted with angled decks and steam catapults to accommodate jets. Had it not been for the Korean War, one might wonder whether the U.S. Navy would have been able to withstand attacks from Congress to diminish it.

The Korean conflict modified all the theorizing in Washington about nuclear arms dictating the tactics of future wars. The so-called Korean police action also defined the policies of Red China and the USSR in the postwar world. To exist, nations such as the United States and Great Britain had to remain in a perpetual state of readiness. Without new aircraft carriers to command the seas and better carrier planes to command the skies, there could be no national security.

A new arms race had begun.

CHAPTER 18

Vietnam: President Johnson's War

The Vietnam conflict began the day the war with Japan ended. In March 1945, after the IJA succeeded in driving the French out of Vietnam, Ho Chi Minh's fellow communists immediately seized all abandoned military stores. On August 11, the day of Japan's surrender, Vietminh forces struck Ha Tinh province and other key locations. On August 19, after ousting the emperor, Ho issued an imperial rescript to the country, asking that "all the different classes of people, as well as the Royal Family, to be all united, and to support the Democratic Republican Government wholeheartedly in order to consolidate our national independence."[1]

Despite Ho's allusions to democracy, U.S. operatives in Vietnam reported that the new government was dominated by "a 100% Communist party" that hoped "the United States would intercede with the United Nations for the exclusion of the French, as well as the Chinese, from the reoccupation of Indo-China."[2]

Because Ho Chi Minh had been an ally during World War II, he expected American support. President Roosevelt had once said, when referring to the "flagrantly downtrodden" Vietnamese, "Anything must be better, than to live under French colonial rule!"[3]

Meanwhile, Ho's Vietnamese Liberation Army, commanded by General Vo Nguyen Giap, entered Hanoi and seized a huge stock of Japanese weapons. On September 2, the same day Japan signed the surrender instrument on the battleship *Missouri*, Ho issued a "Declaration of Independence" modeled after the American document, and established himself as president over the "whole population of Vietnam."[4]

The new French government, however, decided to recapture Vietnam and retain it as a colony. Such a venture required ships. France still had the post–World War I carrier *Béarn*, but the antiquated ship could only be used for shuttling troops and supplies. In 1946, Great Britain shed two of its excess flattops and loaned France the escort carrier *Biter* (renamed *Dixmude*) and the 13,000-ton, 695-foot light carrier *Colossus* (renamed *Arromanches*). In 1951, France borrowed the well-traveled *Langley* (CVL-27) from the United States and renamed her *LaFayette*. Two years later, after the end of the Korean conflict, France borrowed another carrier, *Belleau Wood* (CVL-24), and renamed her *Bois Belleau*. France operated no other carriers until the 1960s, when the 32,000-ton *Foch* and *Clemenceau* were commissioned.

The first use of carriers in combat since World War II occurred on March 16–17, 1947, when *Dixmude* launched American surplus Douglas SBD dive-bombers from her 500-foot deck and provided air support for French troop landings on Vietnam's coast. The operation also marked the first combat in French history involving an aircraft carrier. Ten days later, *Dixmude* moved into the Tonkin Gulf. Two hundred SBDs dropped 65 tons of bombs on Minh bases northwest of Hanoi and started the Vietnam War.

On November 29, 1948, *Arromanches* arrived and *Dixmude* went home. *Arromanches* carried World War II Dauntlesses and British Seafires. The French asked for better planes and in 1950 *Dixmude* sailed to the United States, picked up F6F Hellcat fighters and SB2C Helldivers, and returned to Vietnam. France persisted in asking the United States for support. On April 26, 1953, the USS *Saipan* (CVL-48) arrived off Danang, and marine pilots flew 25 AU-1 Corsairs ashore.

Carriers could not overcome the difficulties France faced in recapturing Vietnam. As French forces increased, Vietminh resistance strengthened. Red China stood aside, studying opportunities for intervening in Vietnam or attacking Taiwan.

A crisis developed in November 1953, when General Henri Navarre, commanding French forces, dropped thousands of paratroopers into a remote northern post at Dienbienphu. Navarre also launched an offensive in the south. The reoccupation of Dienbienphu stirred up a hornet's nest. Vietminh, supplied with Chinese artillery, responded in force and surrounded the valley base. Pilots from *Arromanches*, attempting to strafe enemy positions and fly in supplies, found themselves under fire from Soviet 75 mm AAA guns. The flak, heavier than any during World War II, knocked down 47 planes and damaged 167. Instead of a forward base to interdict a Vietminh supply route, French paratroopers descended into a trap. Navarre asked the U.S. Navy for help, but Admiral Robert B. Carney, CNO, wanted no involvement in Vietnam.

Navarre's campaign, however, worried Carney. With the planned reduction of naval forces off Korea, he approached the JCS in 1954 and suggested that two carriers and six destroyers be retained at Subic Bay to "cover for possible operations to assist French in Indochina if such operations become necessary...."[5] Because of China's interest in Taiwan, Carney kept the Seventh Fleet at Tokyo and put First Fleet commander Vice Admiral William K. Phillips in charge of South China Sea operations. Phillips formed TG 70.2—*Wasp* (CVA-18), *Essex* (CVA-9), and a screen of eight destroyers—under Rear Admiral Robert E. Blick, Jr., and took the force, joined later by *Boxer* (CV-21) and four destroyers, into the South China Sea for readiness exercises.

On March 22, Blick, instructed by Phillips not to interfere unless Chinese aircraft attacked the French, moved TG 70.2 secretly into position south of

Tonkin Gulf. Admiral Carney, however, continued to lobby against any participation in the war. Despite urgent appeals from France for assistance, the JCS informed President Dwight D. Eisenhower that although an air strike might improve French morale, it would only lead to undesirable military and political complications. Eisenhower agreed. No air strike occurred, and on May 7 Dienbienphu fell to the Vietminh.

Delegates at Geneva, Switzerland, began immediate discussions to end the war. On July 20, 1954, France and the Vietminh concluded an accord involving Vietnam, Laos, and Cambodia. Ho's communists got half of what they wanted, North Vietnam. A demarcation line drawn at the Ben Hai River (17th parallel) provided a narrow DMZ (demilitarized zone) dividing Vietnam into two countries: the Democratic Republic of Vietnam (North Vietnam) and the Republic of Vietnam (South Vietnam). The agreement provided that Vietnamese citizens could live in whichever country they chose. U.S. Navy units transported 293,002 civilians and 17,846 military personnel from North to South Vietnam. An American-French mission remained behind to help President Ngo Dinh Diem build a nation and a military force for safeguarding South Vietnam. The war ended, but there was no peace. Viet Cong (VC) in South Vietnam did not migrate north. They had the full support of Ho Chi Minh, Red China, and the USSR, and they wasted no time creating civil strife. Laos and Cambodia fared no better, each threatened by communist-supported insurrection.

On July 31, 1958, Admiral Harry D. Felt became Commander in Chief of the Pacific and immediately faced three unstable situations—Laos, Taiwan, and Vietnam. On September 9, he moved a Seventh Fleet task group, commanded by Vice Admiral Frederick N. Kivette and formed around *Lexington* (CVA-16), into the South China Sea. He moved a second group, formed around *Shangri-La* (CVA-38), off Taiwan to discourage Chinese aggression. *Hancock* (CVA-19) and *Midway* (CVA-41) were both on the way. *Thetis Bay* (CVHA-1), also en route, contained helicopters to overfly South Vietnam and land marines in Laos. Admiral Kivette expressed concerns about putting Americans into Laos, to which Admiral Felt replied, "I am trying to keep us from having the same kind of experience as the French during their catastrophic Indo-China War when they won many [battles] but lost the campaign."[6] Concerns over instability in South Vietnam, however, led in March 1961 to the formation of TF-77, commanded by Rear Admiral Frank B. Miller, with the carriers *Lexington*, *Midway*, and *Bennington*.

Carriers of TF-77 first saw action in Vietnam on August 2, 1964, when the destroyer USS *Maddox* (DD-731), operating in international waters, reported an unprovoked attack in the Tonkin Gulf by North Vietnamese Soviet-made P-4 torpedo boats. From *Ticonderoga* (CVA-14), Captain D. W. Cooper launched four F-8E Crusaders, an all-weather fighter/interceptor that carried an arsenal of general-purpose rockets. Using UHF/ADF radar, the pilots flew to the scene of the attack and sank two enemy boats.

Two days later, on a perfect moonless night with low clouds, *Maddox*, joined by *Turner Joy* (DD-951), reported a second attack, but Crusaders found no

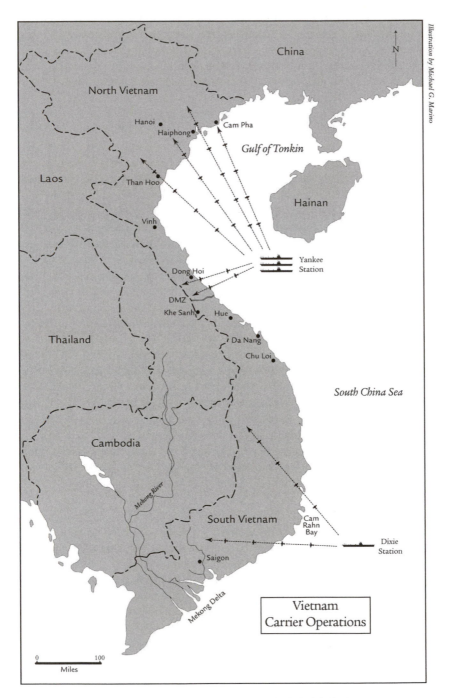

Vietnam: Carrier Operations. (Michael G. Marino)

vessels in the area. The search suggested that the reported radar blips were just blips and not torpedo boats, but Commander Herbert L. Ogier reported *Maddox*'s sonar had detected torpedo noises. Commander Robert C. Barnhart, *Turner Joy*'s skipper, reported sinking a torpedo boat, but from 6,000 yards no one could be certain. On August 4, there actually was no attack, just nervous sonar operators.

At 11:40 P.M. on August 4, President Lyndon B. Johnson announced that "renewed hostile actions against United States' ships in the . . . Gulf of Tonkin have today required me to order the military forces of the United States to take action and reply. . . ."[7] On August 5, he authorized Secretary of Defense Robert S. McNamara to order a retaliatory strike on enemy naval bases along North Vietnam's coast. Propeller-driven Douglas A-1 Skyraiders, A-4 subsonic jet Skyhawks, and F-4 Phantom Mach-2 fighters from *Constellation* (CVA-64) and *Ticonderoga* flew 64 sorties during the four-hour mission. The strike blew up 12 Mihn oil storage dumps and sank 8 and damaged 21 torpedo boats. Two planes from *Constellation* received a heavy dose of AAA. Lieutenant (jg) Richard A. Stather, flying a Skyraider, became the first navy pilot killed in Vietnam, and Lieutenant (jg) Everett Alvarez, flying a Skyhawk, became the first navy POW.

The slower, propeller-driven Douglas A-1H Skyraider on the USS *Intrepid* flew many sorties over Vietnam. In the background an A-4 Skyhawk is also preparing for takeoff. (U.S. Navy photo)

On August 10, Congress authorized President Johnson to "take all necessary measures to repel any armed attack," but six months of political indecision followed.[8] Johnson needed more than one incident to justify a restricted bombing campaign against North Vietnam, one heavy enough to persuade Hanoi to cease its aggression. For six months, Admiral Miller's TF-77 stood offshore with bomb loads and missiles fixed to planes waiting for orders. Not all the time was wasted. Photoreconnaissance missions and strikes against enemy truck convoys entering South Vietnam occurred whenever weather permitted.

On February 17, 1965, VC attacked a barracks at Pleiku Airbase in South Vietnam, killing 18 American servicemen and wounding 109. Johnson authorized Flaming Dart. *Hancock*, *Coral Sea*, and *Ranger* (CVA-61) launched 182 planes and struck North Vietnamese military installations. Nine hours later, carrier planes bombed Dong Hoi, north of the DMZ. Three days later, VC blew up an American billet at Qui Nhon.

Johnson could not have picked a worse time of the year to begin air strikes. Monsoon weather from the northeast kept planes out of the sky but did nothing to slow VC operations on land. Heavy torrential rains, low clouds, and poor visibility hid targets and screened enemy missile sites. Only Grumman A-6 Intruders, a subsonic low-level attack bomber, could operate with any success in such conditions. Better weather, except for occasional typhoons and tropical storms, occurred when the southwest monsoon blew from late April to mid-October. Meteorologists in Washington were of no help when scheduling Secretary McNamara's air strikes.

Carrier captains fumed because targets, routes, the number and types of mission aircraft, and the fuzing of weapons were commonly specified by remote control out of Washington without consideration given to weather or disposition of enemy antiaircraft. McNamara often specified the day and exact hour of attack but refused to permit pilots to perform prereconnaissance. Such micromanagement from Washington wasted the few clear days of winter and tons of ordnance. If bombs could not be dropped on a primary or secondary target because of weather, pilots released them over the South China Sea.

When flying in heavy, low scud clouds, pilots used "Snakeyes," a retarded bomb that could be dropped from 500 feet and not detonate until the plane passed the bomb-blast area. Washington added another complication. Pilots could not fire on enemy aircraft without first positively identifying them: a thorny problem when flying at Mach-2. Admiral Miller did what he could to protect his pilots, but Washington directives for political purposes led to preventable losses.

On March 2, Johnson authorized Rolling Thunder, a sustained bombing campaign organized around the strategic theory that a graduated and progressive bombing of North Vietnam would eventually touch the enemy's "ouch level," terminate Hanoi's support of the VC, and preserve the government of South Vietnam. To support his theory, Johnson authorized the landing of the 9th Marine Expeditionary Brigade at Danang near the DMZ, thereby committing the first American ground troops to South Vietnam. Johnson punctuated his resolve by informing the world: "We will not be defeated. We will not grow tired. We will not withdraw, either openly or under the cloak of a meaningless agreement . . . and we will remain ready . . . for unconditional discussion."[9] Over time, "meaningless" best described America's longest war.

Rolling Thunder may have been effective had Johnson not imposed barriers. He placed supply depots in Cambodia off limits, forbade pursuit of the enemy and the use of napalm, made Hanoi a sanctuary, and ordered that Haiphong, the key North Vietnamese port used by Soviet and Chinese supply ships, not be blockaded, mined, or crippled by air attacks. Carrier planes were permitted to destroy trucks carrying supplies offloaded at Haiphong, but only after the camouflaged vehicles left port and disappeared into the jungle. Washington added another restriction: only moving trucks could be attacked, and they must be military trucks. No one explained how a pilot flying 1,000 mph at 2,000 feet could distinguish a military truck from a nonmilitary truck. Nevertheless, General Giap began moving his military trucks only at night.

Admiral Ulysses S. G. Sharp, Commander U.S. Pacific Fleet, soon learned that planes from TF-77 and the USAF got misscheduled and occasionally appeared over the same target at the same time. Washington then divided North Vietnam into two sectors, established a geographic point in the Tonkin Gulf as the operational center for TF-77 and called it Yankee Station. In an effort to explain to carrier pilots Washington's strategy, Sharp said, "[Rolling Thunder] does not seek to inflict maximum damage on the enemy. Instead, it is a precise application of military pressure for the specific purpose of halting aggression in South Vietnam."[10] During March 1965, A-4 Skyhawk and F-8 Crusader pilots from *Hancock* and *Coral Sea* wandered about hitting Secretary McNamara's designated targets—mostly supply depots and radar installations far from Hanoi—and took their losses in aircraft and airmen grudgingly.

On March 17, Rear Admiral Edward C. Outlaw relieved Miller as commander of TF-77. Soon after his arrival, pictures from a *Coral Sea* RF-8 Crusader showed a surface-to-air missile (SAM) site under construction. Photographs showed more sites around Hanoi and Haiphong. Outlaw flew to Saigon to plan a joint strike with General J. H. Moore's Seventh Air Force. This required approval from Washington, and "after what seemed an inordinate delay," wrote Outlaw, "the proposal was returned disapproved. Such a refusal was beyond my comprehension." During the next five years, Soviet SA-2 SAM sites shot down 115 American planes, all of which, Outlaw added, "could have been destroyed at a minimum risk before they became operational. . . . We were restrained to carrying out a campaign which seemed designed *not* to win" because Russian technicians might be killed.[11] Secretary McNamara eventually authorized the USAF to take out two SAM sites but did not allow pilots to attack any installation where MiGs were based.

In April 1965, TF-77 received orders to fly close air support against VC positions in South Korea. Because of the absence of airfields, *Midway, Coral Sea*, and *Oriskany* (CVA-34) moved off Cam Ranh Bay and established Dixie Station. Three carriers could not effectively cover both Yankee Station and Dixie

Station, so Admiral Sharp and General William C. Westmoreland requested more flattops.

On the night of August 11–12, 1965, a new era of navy warfare began. SAMs struck two A-4E Skyhawks flying reconnaissance at 9,000 feet 60 miles south of Hanoi. Admiral Outlaw sent 76 planes to destroy the sites. They could not be found, but AAA downed five planes and damaged seven others. Photoreconnaissance showed that SAM sites could be packed up in three hours and moved elsewhere. SAMs changed the tactics of the war, forcing pilots to fly higher, which meant more misses, or fly lower, which meant more damage from visually controlled Soviet weapons.

On August 12, Outlaw launched Operation Iron Hand, an anti-SAM campaign using the new navy-developed Shrike missile. Shrikes homed on a SAM battery's guidance radar system. Because of initial problems with the guidance system, two months passed before Lieutenant Commander Cecil E. Garber, flying one of the new Grumman A-6A Intruders from *Independence* (CVA-62), knocked out the first SAM site.

During SAM site reconnaissance, TF-77 pilots reported 75 MiG-17 and Mig-21 Fishbed fighters and eight IL-28 Beagle light bombers in North Vietnam. Rear Admiral James R. Reedy, TF-77's new commander, applied for authorization to strike the planes on the ground. McNamara vetoed the request, leaving carrier pilots to fight it out in the sky.

During 1965, 10 different attack carriers participated in operations at Yankee and Dixie stations, including the new 85,830-ton, 35-knot, nuclear-powered *Enterprise* (CVAN-65), which arrived on December 2. She was 1,123 feet long, had a 4.5-acre deck, and carried a crew of 4,600. She cost $445,000,000, making her the most expensive ship ever built. Because of the cost, Congress voted to forego another nuclear carrier until *Enterprise* proved herself. With her came Admiral Miller, to resume command of TF-77 and put *Enterprise* through a battery of combat exercises.

Enterprise carried the first North American AJ-3/RA-5 Vigilante twinjet bombers and the first F4H Phantom II fighters. Vigilantes made a quantum leap in reconnaissance and electronic countermeasure support in an enemy air defense environment that became increasingly lethal because of Soviet- and Chinese-made weaponry. McDonnell Aircraft's new Phantom, capable of Mach-2+ speeds, became TF-77s all-purpose MiG-killer, performing escort, strike, and photoreconnaissance roles.

Despite Admiral Miller's efforts to inform Washington that half of the enemy's cargo moved on inland waterways in sampans and barges, two years passed before McNamara allowed the navy to mine rivers—but not the port of Haiphong. *Enterprise* and *Kitty Hawk* planes sowed the first minefields in the mouths of five principal rivers. So far, the Johnson-McNamara strategy of applying military pressure in gradual doses had not slowed the war or forced North Vietnam to the peace table.

The USS *Independence* cruises off Yankee Station. Four Douglas F-4 Phantom II fighters are at the catapults to be launched. (U.S Navy photo)

In 1965, the navy flew 30,993 sorties over North Vietnam and another 25,895 sorties over South Vietnam. More than 100 navy planes were lost, and 82 flyers were either killed, captured, or missing. Forty-six were rescued. Carrier planes struck trucks, rolling stock, military barracks, and roads and bridges, but the saddest reality was Washington's choice of targets—none had strategic importance.

During the early weeks of 1966, President Johnson called off all bombing and took a stab at opening discussions by offering North Vietnam $1 billion for economic reconstruction. Hanoi snubbed the offer, using the time to shove more supplies into South Vietnam, set up early warning and fire control monitors, build more SAM sites, and add 400 new AAA emplacements. Once again, Admiral Sharp beseeched Washington to use the navy to interdict Russian and Chinese shipments into North Vietnam. "It was evident to me," Sharp told the JCS, "that Ho Chi Minh intended to continue to support the Viet Cong until he was denied the capability to do so."[12] Once again, McNamara resumed Rolling Thunder during the monsoon season with the same restrictions as before.

Congress began scrutinizing McNamara's policies after Admiral Miller complained of shortages in aircraft, pilots, ammunition, rockets, and bombs. Some

Carriers such as the *Kitty Hawk* and *Enterprise* began flying the new Vought A-7E Corsairs over Vietnam. Five-hundred-pound bombs are mounted under the wings. (U.S. Navy photo)

pilots were flying 38 missions a month over North Vietnam. McNamara increased pilot training output, which took 18 months, and in the meantime ordered the navy to reduce the number of pilots in a 14-plane Skyhawk squadron from 24 to 20. This looked good on paper but did not solve the pilot problem. McNamara's staff tried to conceal bomb shortages by supplying leftover World War II ordnance not well suited to jet aircraft, and soon those supplies were depleted.

In February 1966, despite shortages, Johnson stepped up Rolling Thunder and let the navy strike a few previously protected targets. Admiral Reedy returned just in time to organize the strikes. *Kitty Hawk* and *Ticonderoga* provided the aircraft. Intruders, Phantoms, and Skyhawks hit power plants, railroads, supply depots, and communication centers. The strike on Cam Pha's harbor, however, rattled Washington, because a Polish freighter reported bomb damage. Navy flyers had carefully avoided the ship, even though it fired upon them. Reedy spent a week exchanging messages and statements of proof with Washington to show that the Polish ship had not been attacked.

Renewed bombing once again created air space problems between the USAF and the navy. The navy's new sector included Haiphong and coastal areas, whereas the USAF covered Hanoi and the area north of the DMZ. Bombing restrictions remained the same and excluded main supply depots located near the Chinese border.

Carriers came and went. In May 1966, *Kitty Hawk* and *Ticonderoga* received a rest while *Enterprise*, *Hancock*, and *Ranger* covered Yankee Station. *Intrepid* relieved *Hancock* at Dixie Station. Yankee Station never had fewer than three carriers; Dixie Station never fewer than one.

Hanoi and Haiphong became the most heavily defended cities in the world. SAM sites and MiG activity kept TF-77's EA-3Bs and EC-121M "Big Look" electronic warning aircraft constantly in the air. Dogfights with MiGs became more frequent, but North Vietnamese pilots could not cope with navy jets armed with GAR-83 (later AIM-9) Sidewinder infrared homing missiles and resorted to hit-and-run measures.

Successful night tactics began when Commander Harry Thomas developed a system involving two squadrons of A-4 Skyhawks, an E-2 Hawkeye for navigational assistance, and the new Mk-4 gun pod. One Skyhawk squadron carried flares and flew a thousand feet above the other. The lower squadron watched bridges, ferry crossings, and roads, calling for illumination when detecting movement. Magnesium flares lit up the entire area, sometimes revealing long lines of trucks, which were then strafed and blasted with bombs and rockets. Night flying at low levels remained risky, but Hawkeyes kept Skyhawk pilots out of trouble.

Intruder pilots used another trick when chased at night by a MiG. They flew over heavily defended areas to draw AAA fire, thereby forcing North Vietnamese pilots to veer away and terminate the chase. The tactic became known as

"Willard Egress," although the originators were Lieutenants R. S. Williams and J. E. Diselrod.

In April 1966, Secretary McNamara finally agreed to listen to proposals geared to disrupting North Vietnam's supplies of petroleum, oil, and lubricants (POL), all of which came from Red China. Because of President Johnson's bombing restrictions, major storage areas had all been moved to Hanoi and Haiphong.

After weeks of intensive debate, McNamara finally relented, but he restricted air strikes to only eleven targets because of concerns over collateral damage involving Chinese and Russian civilians. He also did not want any oil tankers bombed unless they clearly carried North Vietnam registry. Because of this restriction, Commander Frederick F. Palmer, leading *Ranger*'s Air Wing 14, put the slower A-4s in the van hoping that pilots might be able to see markings on ships before firing their payloads.

The 28-plane strike from *Ranger* included such specialties as anti-MiG, anti-SAM, and antiflak elements. Attack aircraft carried bombs and 2.75-inch Mighty Mouse rockets. *Ranger* pilots blasted North Vietnam's largest POL storage center at Haiphong, sending three huge fireballs 20,000 feet into the sky. Air groups from *Constellation* and *Hancock* bombed two POL facilities outside Haiphong and another near Hanoi.

The attacks continued until the end of the year, thoroughly disrupting the enemy's ability to escalate the war. China and Russia redoubled efforts to bring oil into North Vietnam, but carrier planes interrupted operations by destroying Hanoi's facilities and Haiphong's importation terminal. The POL campaign, however, came about 15 months too late: General Giap had already hidden thousands of barrels of fuel in the jungle.

Every carrier strike produced jitters in Washington for fear a bomb might hit a Soviet or Chinese vessel, or land in the city and destroy an embassy or hospital. Although the raids occurred years before the surgical strikes of the Iraqi war, navy pilots did their work well. No Soviet ships were struck, and the enemy began offloading cargo in China rather than Haiphong, thereby forcing North Vietnam to mobilize 300,000 civilians to transport supplies by foot.

In 1966, TF-77 flew 30,000 sorties against North Vietnam and 20,000 against VC. The carriers lost 120 planes in combat, and 89 flyers were either killed, captured, or missing. It had been a hell of a year.

In January 1967, Admiral Sharp, annoyed by the slow progress of the war, submitted a plan to force North Vietnam to the negotiating table, but his plan violated some of President Johnson's bombing restrictions. Sharp wanted strategic sites in Hanoi bombed and MiG airbases struck. After four months of debate, McNamara released a few new targets but still drew a 10-mile no-bombing circle around Hanoi.

In July, McNamara came to Saigon for a briefing, and once again Sharp explained the problems of interdiction and urged the secretary to remove all restrictions. McNamara relented and allowed supply lines coming through the buffer zone between China and North Vietnam to be bombed. Knowing President Johnson's sensitivity about being drawn into a broader war, the Soviets began complaining about being attacked. The charges rattled Johnson, and some of the choice North Vietnam targets went back on the no-bombing list. After that, little changed to end the war.

Vietnam provided a great testing ground for new weapons and new tactics. In March 1967, the navy introduced into combat the Walleye, the first TV-guided air-to-surface glide bomb. Pilots could lock the weapon onto a ground target, release it, and the TV eye would direct the bomb to the target with no further assistance from the pilot. Commander Homer Smith's Attack Squadron 212 from *Bon Homme Richard* made the first strike against a military barracks. Pilots watched the bomb go in through the window and explode. Thus began a new era in aerial warfare with "smart bombs."

Another tactical highlight of the Vietnam War was the development of combat search and rescue (SAR) by Admiral Reedy's staff. Submarines and floatplanes performed rescue efforts in World War II, but Vietnam was different. Some pilots landed in the sea, others in the jungle. Helicopters made it possible to recover flyers wherever they landed. No pilot wanted to be sent to a POW camp and be tortured or starved to death. Reedy believed that effective SAR operations not only saved lives but boosted flagging morale caused by having the capabilities for winning the war but being politically restrained from doing it. When pilots knew they had a good chance of being rescued, it made a positive impression on their outlook when stepping into the cockpit of their jet.

The fledgling SAR system developed in 1965 required an UH-1 or UH-2 Seasprite helicopter from *Ranger* working together with a destroyer. The unarmored helicopters carried one .30-caliber machine gun mounted in the cabin. The first recorded rescue occurred in North Vietnam when Lieutenant (jg) John R. Harris's Skyhawk from *Independence* went down east of Hanoi. An UH-1B flew in and transported him back to the task force.

In May 1966, the first armored and specially equipped SH-3 Sea Kings (Big Mothers) arrived armed with two M-60 machine guns. This marked the official beginning of SAR teams. Four Skyraiders and one or more helicopters followed behind air strikes to protect and recover downed pilots. Destroyers followed the action with in-flight refueling capabilities, enabling a helicopter to refuel while hovering above the ship. This enabled the helicopter to remain in the air and continue SAR efforts for 12 hours. Through October 1966, of 269 naval and Air Force pilots shot or forced down over North Vietnam, 103 were recovered. The others were killed, taken prisoner, or reported missing.

Every pilot in a damaged aircraft tried to reach water, where his chances of rescue increased to 90 percent. The North Vietnamese wanted prisoners and paid fisherman $200 per pilot (a virtual fortune) for every one they captured. Fortunately, helicopters were much faster than fishing boats, and as SAR techniques

Vought Crusaders, with a top speed of 1,100 miles per hour, fly in formation over the USS *Forrestal*. (U.S. Navy photo)

improved, dozens of carrier pilots remained forever grateful to the men in helicopters.

On October 1, 1965, the U.S. Navy commissioned *Forrestal* (CVA-59), the first of six supercarriers having a full load displacement of 76,000-tons. She was 1,039 feet in length with a 190-foot flight deck that could be extended to 236 feet using retractable extensions. Unlike *Midway-* and *Essex*-class carriers, she was specifically designed to carry jets and had an angled deck, larger elevators, steam catapults, a conventional safety barrier, and stronger arresting wires. She carried between 60 and 90 aircraft and as many as 428 officers and 4,155 enlisted men. She also carried the highly sophisticated Naval Tactical Data System (NTDS), which could launch and recover aircraft electronically as well as locate, identify, and track planes in the vicinity. The system also guided her planes to enemy aircraft more effectively than conventional radar systems, making her the most modern ship afloat.[13]

When on July 24, 1967, *Forrestal* arrived at Yankee Station, she had been an Atlantic carrier and never in combat. Five days later, while preparing to launch a strike, a Zuni rocket inadvertently discharged from a parked F-4B Phantom on the after starboard quarter of the flight deck. The warhead struck the fuel tank of a nearby Skyhawk and turned the deck into an inferno. The blaze set off bombs, killing firefighters and spreading flames below deck. Fourteen hours later, 134 men lay dead, 21 planes were incinerated, and another 41 damaged. *Forrestal*, the first of the great carriers, limped back to the United States for seven months of repairs. The accident marked the navy's largest single-day loss of the war.

Admiral Sharp, always disturbed by Johnson's handling of the war, went to Washington to ask permission to blockade Haiphong, through which 85 percent of the country's imports passed. If President John F. Kennedy could "quarantine" Cuba and risk war with the Soviets during the 1962 missile crisis, Sharp wanted to know why the same could not be done at Haiphong. He also asked permission to seed the harbor with mines. Despite inviting retaliation from the White House, he put the question before Congress. Secretary McNamara compromised, allowing TF-77 to bomb all the main bridges leading out of Haiphong and the harbor's dredges, which were used to prevent silt buildup from interfering with Soviet ship deliveries of some 200,000 tons of supplies a month. The effort to isolate Haiphong had an immediate though temporary effect. The city's defenses began running out of missiles and ammunition. A typhoon followed by heavy weather suspended air strikes for several days. When pilots resumed operations, they found the city as heavily defended as before.

Walleyes gave carrier pilots an opportunity to strike targets that McNamara had previously not released because of political concerns over collateral damage. The secretary began specifying Walleye-only targets, such as the thermal power plant and the Van Dien truck park on the outskirts of Hanoi. On May 17, 1967, two air wings of F-8 Crusaders and F-4 Skyhawks, one from *Bon Homme Richard* and the other from *Kitty Hawk*, blasted both sites. Pulling away with the F-4s, four Crusaders ran into ten MiG-17s. A major dogfight erupted southwest of Hanoi. After four MiGs went down, the others broke off, marking one of the biggest battles between navy and Soviet-built aircraft in the war.

Another air battle occurred on July 21 when eight MiG-17s attacked *Bon Homme Richard*'s Carrier Wing 21 over Ta Xa's petroleum works. F-8E Crusaders, flying fighter cover over Skyhawks, downed four MiGs, two with Sidewinders, one with a Zuni rocket, and the other with 20-mm fire. The navy lost no planes.

With the stepped-up use of Walleyes for surgical strikes, McNamara took PT-boats, ferry slips, shipyards, and railroads around Haiphong off the no-bombing list. AAA fire and SAMs became less distracting to pilots armed with Walleyes. Once sighted and released, the missile found its own way to the target, allowing the pilot to withdraw at supersonic speed. Despite the accuracy of Walleyes, Johnson still refused to bomb strategic sites inside Hanoi and Haiphong, and the North Vietnamese simply moved all their supplies, munitions, and military facilities into no-bombing zones.

On December 3, 1967, *Ranger* arrived at Yankee Station with two new aircraft, the A-7 Corsair II and the EKA-3B Tacos. The Corsair could carry a 15,000-pound bomb load and operated with advanced radar, navigation, and weapon systems. The EKA-3Bs were converted from the old A-3 Skywarrior and rebuilt specifically for the electronic warfare environment of North Vietnam. All the changes in aircraft, from radar and weaponry to targeting enhancements, meant little in terms of winning the war as long as Washington imposed restrictions. In August 1967, McNamara admitted to Congress that the bombing had not "in any significant way affected [North Vietnam's] war-making capability," yet it was he and the president that prevented the flyers from striking targets that could change the course of the war.[14] During 1967, 11 carriers had been on station, thousands of sorties had been flown over North Vietnam, 133 aircraft had been lost in combat, and those in the navy began to wonder whether it was all worth the trouble.

Bad weather during the first three months of 1968 kept carrier planes in shipboard hangers. The all-weather A-6 Intruders, although few in number, bore the brunt of winter monsoon missions. During the rains, North Vietnam rebuilt what carrier planes had destroyed in 1967. Johnson called for a standdown in January to give negotiations a chance, and North Vietnam used the interregnum to launch the Tet offensive. Air strikes resumed during spells of good weather and carrier pilots blasted more bridges and railroads with no permanent results.

In late January, the North Vietnam Army (NVA) surrounded Marines at Khe Sanh. Carrier planes flew 3,000 sorties, dropping ordnance on enemy trenches 100 meters from the marine perimeter. Johnson, now in a complete dilemma over North Vietnam, increased bombing pressure against Hanoi and Haiphong, but only on selected targets. On March 31, he called a partial bombing halt and followed it in October with a complete halt, and the slow and painful pullback from war in Southeast Asia began. Five years passed before the Paris Peace accord was signed. By then, Johnson was no longer president.

For 37 months, TF-77 had blasted North Vietnam's roads, bridges, railroads, petroleum installations, and military complexes without ever being given the opportunity to win the war. The carrier task force lost more than 300 planes in combat with 83 flyers killed and 200 captured or missing. Political differences between the United States, Soviet Russia, and Red China could have been settled in Vietnam or Korea, but no one wanted to risk a nuclear war. The embarrassment of all Americans came when President Johnson vowed to stand fast at Vietnam and created conditions through the Department of Defense making it impossible to do so.

Attack carriers operating in the Gulf of Tonkin were in a tactically good position to batter the enemy into submission. A carrier's tactical mission is to control the sea, not sit for 37 months 100 miles off the coast of North Vietnam and provide stationary airfields for land forces. As Admiral Halsey and dozens of World War II carrier commanders learned, supporting land battles was strictly a secondary task. Had Secretary McNamara understood this maxim, he may have found a different way to lose the president's war. One might hope that the United States never engages in another war where civilian control is so complete, pervasive, and detailed that it impairs the tactics and strategies necessary to win wars.

The Vietnam War produced one outcome that eventually drove the USSR to self-destruct: the development of electronic warfare and missile technology. Carrier aircraft could deliver precise strikes day or night in any kind of weather. Planes such as the A-7 Corsair II and the A-6 Intruder, covered by F-8 Crusader fighter/interceptors, made it possible to direct an array of bombs and missiles straight to the target. Behind Mach-2 attack planes came the AJ-3/RA-5C Vigilante multisensor reconnaissance plane, the E-1B Tracer and E-2A Hawkeye early warning aircraft, and the C-2 Greyhound cargo variant. Never in the history of naval aviation had so many planes armed with sophisticated instrumentation and weapons been developed specifically for carriers.

The array of aircraft ordnance included Walleyes (flying TV bombs), Sidewinders, Snakeyes, Sparrows, Focus, Rockeyes, Sparrows, Zunis, aerial seeded landmines, and cluster bomblets. Shrike and Standard antiradiation missiles (ARM) were developed to locate and destroy enemy missile and radar installations by electronically homing on the site's output of radiation. After SAMs appeared in North Vietnam, the navy developed electronic devices to detect missiles in flight and "spoof" them.

Toward the end of the war, *Enterprise* introduced the new Grumman F-14 Tomcats, an aircraft designed to overcome deficiencies in F-4 Phantoms. In addition to more maneuverability, the swing-wing Tomcat carried an M61 20-mm Vulcan multibarrel cannon for close-range support and an array of Sparrow and Sidewinder missiles. Tomcats also carried the AIM-54 Phoenix long-range homing missile, which was coupled to a radar and fire control system that enabled the pilot to engage multiple targets 100 miles away.

When the Vietnam War officially ended on January 27, 1973, the Cold War was 28 years old. The apogee came on April 29–30, 1975, when navy and Marine helicopters, supported by A-1, A-6, and A-7 fighter aircraft from *Coral Sea, Enterprise, Hancock*, and *Midway*, evacuated 9,000 people from Saigon, many from the rooftop of the American embassy.

President Johnson never realized that his attempts to control bombing strikes from Washington produced a side benefit reaped many years later, when Ronald Reagan became president. His restrictions aided the development of the most sophisticated aircraft and weaponry in the world. It also erased doubt in high places about the effectiveness of aircraft carriers. The USSR felt compelled to compete, and their attempts to do so eventually led in the 1980s to economic collapse. Had this been President Johnson's strategy, he may have departed from this world a great man. Instead, he lost a war that might have been won.

CHAPTER 19

Cold Wars and Brush Fires

The Cold War began in 1945 and lasted 43 years. In 1947, President Truman recognized the threat and on March 12 stated the policy of the United States "to support free peoples who are resisting attempted subjugation by armed minorities or outside pressure."[1] The validity of Truman's position became clear three months later when Secretary of State George C. Marshall announced that the United States would provide economic aid to war-torn nations, but the Soviet Union and its satellites refused to participate. A foreign service officer at the Moscow embassy, aware of Soviet expansionism, recommended "patient but firm . . . containment [by the] application of counterforce at a series of constantly shifting geographical and political points corresponding to the shifts . . . of Soviet policy."[2] The Truman Doctrine and containment by application of counterforce became the future of America's foreign policy, and the United States began flying reconnaissance missions in international waters off the Soviet coast.

The Soviet-supported overthrow of the democratic Czech government on February 24, 1948, authenticated the existence of a Cold War. Soviet efforts to impede the flow of supplies to West Berlin led to a six-week airlift. Cold War fighting spanned the Korean War, the Vietnam War, and numerous smaller confrontations until finally petering out in 1987–88 with the breakup of the Soviet Union. During the Cold War years, and because of the advent of nuclear power, nothing drove advancements in naval technology more vigorously than Soviet determination to dominate the world through communism. The British had always been more conscious of the Soviet threat. It took the Cold War to awaken Americans to the reality that the free world was under political attack by force of arms from the USSR and Red China.

In January 1954, Secretary of State John Foster Dulles reflected on the experience of the Korean War and admitted that although the United States held superiority in nuclear weaponry, "the overwhelming manpower superiority of the Communist powers could be countered . . . only through nuclear warfare."[3] When on August 20, 1953, the Soviet Union exploded its first hydrogen bomb, the nuclear arms race quickly accelerated. In 1958, the United States began forming a strategic doctrine "from emphasis on nuclear retaliation as a response to Communist aggression to adoption of a concept of flexible response," which meant adjusting the solution to the seriousness of the threat, and this became the policy of President Eisenhower's administration.[4]

One of the first brush fires occurred on July 26, 1956, when Soviet-supported President Gamal Abdel Nasser of Egypt attempted to take control of the Suez Canal. To block the effort, Great Britain and France mustered five carriers, the Royal Navy's *Eagle, Albion, Bulwark*, and the French navy's *Arromanches* and *LaFayette,* all commanded by British Vice Admiral M. L. Power. U.S. marines attached to the Sixth Fleet in the Mediterranean had studied the situation and suggested landing troops by helicopter, so Power added the helicopter carriers *Theseus* and *Ocean.*

On October 29, Israelis started the fight by dropping airborne troops on the Sinai Peninsula. Admiral Power used the action as an excuse to intervene. Two days later, British and French carrier planes bombed Egyptian airfields and shipping. On November 6, helicopter landings began. Before the war escalated beyond control, the United States and United Nations stepped into the conflict and settled it without further bloodshed. During the crisis, Admiral Power proved that when fast military response is required, only carriers could provide the support necessary to meet the requirements of flexible response.

In February 1958, Soviet-sponsored Egypt and Syria merged and formed the United Arab Republic, presenting a major threat to Jordan and Israel. On July 14, Arab nationalists seized the government of Iraq and killed the pro-Western king and prime minister. President Camille Chamoun of Lebanon felt threatened by invasion and asked for help from the United States. Three days later, Admiral James L. Holloway's Sixth Fleet carriers—*Essex* (CV-9), *Saratoga* (CVA-60), *Wasp* (CV-18), and the refitted antisubmarine carrier *Randolph* (CVS-15)— moved into position off Beirut, demonstrating an example of fast carrier response. Three marine battalions, covered by a mix of Skyraiders and North American FJ-3 Furies, went ashore, stabilized the situation by bringing an end to civil war, and arranged an election satisfactory to all parties.

The incident marked the first combat appearance of the new *Forrestal*-class supercarrier *Saratoga,* which together with the flattops of the Sixth Fleet flew more than 10,000 sorties during the three-month intervention.

During the Lebanese crisis, Red China tested American resolve by igniting another brush fire. With Taiwan as the objective, China began an intensive artillery bombardment of Matsu and Quemoy, two offshore islands held by Nationalist troops. President Eisenhower, bound by a congressional resolution to defend Taiwan, deployed six carriers from the Seventh Fleet. After a four-month standoff,

China disengaged, but her efforts to recover Taiwan continue as a permanent threat to world security.

The Cold War came closest to home when, on October 14, 1962, a U-2 reconnaissance plane flying over Cuba photographed a Soviet nuclear missile site under construction 100 miles west of Havana. Two days later, another group of photographs showed Soviet Il-28 bombers being assembled on Cuban airfields. President John F. Kennedy held marathon meetings to discuss an appropriate response. The JCS recommended a surgical strike. Other military advisors warned that such action could lead to war. Another option, a naval blockade, seemed less risky. Because a formal blockade could not be imposed without a declaration of war, the administration invented a naval "quarantine" to block the importation of Soviet-made offensive weapons.

Kennedy handed the details of arranging the quarantine to Vice Admiral Alfred G. Ward. Ward organized three task units from the Second Fleet: TF-136 with support carrier *Essex*, TF-135 with the nuclear carrier *Enterprise*, and Carrier Division Six with the attack carrier *Independence*. On October 24, when the quarantine commenced, 25 Soviet vessels approaching Ward's blockade stopped dead in the water. Hours later, 24 ships turned about for home. Ward allowed one ship to pass because it carried only oil.

Two days later, Kennedy received a phone call from Soviet Premier Nikita Khrushchev stating that Russia only intended to put missiles and planes in Cuba to discourage an American invasion. He agreed to remove them if Kennedy promised to lift the blockade and not attack Cuba. Kennedy agreed. Four weeks passed before the Soviets pulled their missiles and bombers out of Cuba, and the communist effort to move nuclear weapons into the Western Hemisphere ended.

After World War II, the United States enjoyed absolute command of the air at sea because of aircraft carriers. For more than 25 years, the only flattops at sea belonged to friendly nations. In February 1959, the U.S. Navy announced a plan to scrap 43 obsolete warships, including 5 battleships. There were still four fast *Iowa*-class battleships in the fleet, but they were becoming weapons of the past. In place of battleships, Secretary McNamara proposed building more supercarriers to prosecute the Vietnam War. He also proposed a new 15-carrier force with four nuclear-powered ships. Guided missiles had become the weapon of the future, and on May 13, 1964, the Sixth Fleet in the Mediterranean formed the first task group of nuclear-powered ships. It consisted of the attack carrier *Enterprise* (CVAN-65), the guided-missile cruiser *Long Beach* (CGN-9), and the guided-missile frigate *Bainbridge* (DLGN-25). In December 1965, *Enterprise* entered the South China Sea, launched strikes off Vietnam, and became the first nuclear-powered ship to go to war.

In the late 1960s, the Soviet navy's air arm began with two 16,300-ton antisubmarine cruisers carrying 18 helicopters. Not until the late 1970s were the Soviets able to commission the first of four 33,300-ton *Kiev*-class carriers.

The nuclear-powered USS *Enterprise* (CVAN-65) becomes the largest warship ever built. (U.S. Navy photo)

*Kiev*s operated with 18 helicopters and 12 Yak-36 Foragers, a vertical/short takeoff and landing (VSTOL) jet patterned after the British Sea Harrier. Fixed-wing aircraft were then withdrawn, and *Kiev*-class ships became helicopter carriers.

In 1990, during the disintegration of the USSR, the Soviets launched the 57,000-ton *Admiral Kuznetsov* with Su-27 and MiG-29 fighters. A sister ship launched in 1988 remained unfinished. The unraveling empire also planned a

70,000-ton nuclear-powered carrier, but the collapse of the USSR left the new Russian navy with an uncertain future.

Aircraft carriers made such an impact during World War II that seven other nations wanted at least one. The United States and Great Britain had enormous stockpiles. During World War II, Britain had lost only eight of its 79 carriers, the United States 11 of 110 carriers. Argentina, Australia, Brazil, Canada, India, and the Netherlands obtained theirs from the British, all light fleet carriers of the *Majestic* and *Colossus* classes. In 1967, Spain acquired an *Independence*-class CVL from the United States. Carriers that went to foreign nations were all with outdated technology. By then, the United States had launched *Kitty Hawk* (CVA-63), the first missile-armed carrier, and *Enterprise* (CVAN-65), the first nuclear-powered carrier.

During the 1970s, the world's navies began replacing fixed-wing aircraft with helicopters and Harriers. Some nations built their own carriers. Spain's 17,188-ton *Principe de Asturias* carried from 6 to 12 McDonnell Douglas AV-8B Harriers and a dozen helicopters. In 1987, Italy launched the 10,100-ton *Giuseppe Garibaldi*—a small flattop capable of carrying 16 Sea Harriers or 18 helicopters, or a mixture of both. With few exceptions, all the carriers in the world, outside of the few built by the USSR, France, Spain, and Italy, came from stocks of the United States or the United Kingdom.

The USSR, never able to match America's arsenal of flattops and aircraft, concentrated on producing submarines. The U.S. Navy answered the challenge by retrofitting a number of *Essex*-class attack carriers with sonar and new electronics for antisubmarine warfare. Instead of Hellcats and Helldivers, the venerable old veterans carried Grumman S2E Trackers and E2A Hawkeyes, Lockheed S-3 Vikings, and helicopters equipped with "dunking" sonar—an instrument that could be lowered into the sea while the helicopter hovered overhead.

The USSR also produced spy ships—seaworthy trawler-type vessels known as AGIs (auxiliary, general, intelligence). AGIs were crammed with electronic equipment and in international waters became a common nuisance during American carrier operations. AGI skippers developed a habit of playing chicken with carriers by passing in front at speeds designed to cause a collision. Rather than create an "incident," most carrier commanders changed course. In 1965, however, Admiral Holloway became exasperated with one bothersome AGI and ordered the 90,000-ton *Enterprise* to flank speed and headed straight for the spy ship. "And he got the hell out of the way," Holloway said. Holloway continued the tactic throughout the Vietnam War, and the bothersome AGIs kept their distance.[5]

In October 1973, one close encounter with the Soviet navy occurred in the Mediterranean during the Second Israeli-Arab War. The U.S. Sixth Fleet operated three carriers but deployed only *Independence* with escorts to keep watch on the war and provide Israel with additional aircraft if needed. By October 24, the Soviets had sent 80 ships into the area. All but 26 were submarines. To discourage the Soviets from launching a coordinated salvo of surface-to-surface

In 1990, Russia eventually commissioned the 57,000-ton *Admiral Kuznetsov* with a striking 12-degree ramp in the bow to assist the launching of Su-27 and MiG-29 fighters. (U.S. Navy photo)

missiles, Vice Admiral Daniel Murphy used cruisers, destroyers, and aircraft to circle and shadow the Soviet vessels. While Israelis fought on the ground, carrier aircraft gave Israelis the tactical advantage at sea should the Soviets attempt to land troops or launch a missile strike. A UN-brokered cease-fire cooled the war, but on October 25, American forces were thrown into a higher defensive posture (Defense Condition Three) when the Soviets sent 15 more ships into the area for a six-day anticarrier exercise. Murphy knew the exercises were just another bluff and moved his force west, but Admiral Elmo R. Zumwalt, CNO, later admitted that "major units of the U.S. Navy were [never] in a tenser situation since World War II ended than the Sixth Fleet in the Mediterranean was for the week the alert was declared."[6]

To some nations of the world, carriers became status symbols. Other than U.S. and U.K. carriers, few of them carried a punch. The major navies, however, envisioned their principal role as being participants in a major conflict between NATO (North Atlantic Treaty Organization) and Warsaw Pact nations. They also expected to be struck with nuclear weapons, which led to improving NATO air defenses with advanced warning systems at sea.

During the early 1970s, the first Harriers introduced a new era in jet aircraft. The planes could adjust the angle of engine thrust to vertically takeoff and land (VTOL) without impairing airborne maneuvers. Nine NATO nations conducted Harrier trials. All agreed that the aircraft's unique features no longer required 1,000-foot-long carrier decks. Vertical takeoffs, however, reduced the weight of payloads. The British partly solved the problem by modifying the Harrier for vertical and *short* takeoff and landing (VSTOL) by placing a ramp in the carrier's bow nicknamed the "ski-jump," thereby enabling Sea Harriers to carry an extra 2,000 pounds. For the Royal Navy, ski-jump retrofits came just in time for the Falkland Islands conflict with Argentina.

One of the rare wars in the 1980s occurred without encouragement from the USSR. As a former possession of Great Britain, Falkland Islanders enjoyed their sovereignty and wanted to keep it. Because the British no longer controlled the independent Falklands, Admiral Jorge Anaya of the Argentine navy convinced President General Leopoldo Galtieri that the conquest of the islands would not be challenged. Anaya predicted no trouble from the United States because Argentina, though fascist, served as a bulwark against communism in South America. Anaya also reasoned that the British, even though they maintained a Royal Marine Falkland garrison, would not bother to send an amphibious force half way around the world to defend islands of no importance.

When a group of scrap merchants landed on nearby South Georgia—another former British possession—and illegally raised the Argentine flag, the Royal Navy did nothing. Without South Georgia as a port, Anaya believed the British could not mount a sustainable operation. He also declared that if the Royal Navy came with planes, Argentina's French Mirage fighter jets would destroy them. So without further debate, on April 2, 1982, Argentine forces invaded and occupied the Falklands.

Three days later, while the Argentine junta celebrated the conquest, TF-40 and the antisubmarine carriers HMS *Hermes* and *Invincible* sailed from Plymouth. Instead of the usual antisubmarine aircraft, *Hermes* and *Invincible* mustered 20 Sea Harriers, 20 Sea King helicopters, and 9 Sea King HC-4 Marine transports. TF-40 went to South Georgia first and on April 26 recaptured the island. The ships then proceeded to the Falklands and established a total exclusion zone (TEZ) in which they would engage any intruders from Argentina.

Ships of the Argentine navy were far from modern, but their single carrier, *Vienticinco de Mayo*, represented a potentially formidable asset. Built as the *Colossus*-class HMS *Venerable*, the Dutch Royal Navy bought her in 1948 and 20 years later sold her to Argentina. Though antiquated, she carried an air group of eight A-4Q Skyhawks, five S-2A Trackers, and four Sea King helicopters. *De Mayo* could not operate the recently acquired Exocet-carrying Super Entendard fighter-bombers because inertial navigational reference system and enhanced landing aids had not been installed.[7] Aware of Argentina's Exocet missile capability, the Royal Navy refitted Sea Harriers with the U.S. Navy's advanced AIM-9L Sidewinder. All changes, including software, were made during the nine-day voyage to South Georgia.

To meet the crisis, the Royal Navy upgraded eight more Sea Harriers, flew them to Ascension Island, and embarked them on a transport for the Falklands. Having committed all but two of their stock of Sea Harriers, the Royal Navy borrowed GR-3 Harriers from the RAF, fitted them with Sidewinders and navy avionics systems for radar identification, and flew them to Ascension Island as reserve aircraft. By then, TF-40 Harriers operating in the TEZ had already seen action.

On May 1, a lone RAF Vulcan bomber with an inferior targeting system designed for dropping nuclear bombs flew over Port Stanley and cratered the airfield. Sea Harriers followed and cluster-bombed AA positions, the airfield, and an airstrip at Goose Green. Later, two British pilots received directions from fighter control that two Mirages were approaching. Flight Lieutenant Paul Barton locked on with a Sidewinder and blew the first Mirage to pieces. Lieutenant Steve Morris fired on the second plane, watched it and the Sidewinder disappear into a cloud, and never learned until later that the damaged plane, when attempting to land at Port Stanley, was mistaken for a Harrier and shot down by Argentine antiaircraft.

Admiral Anaya began worrying that the British might attack the mainland. He withdrew the Mirages, leaving the less proficient Skyhawks and IAI Dagger fighter-bombers to protect the Falklands. The Royal Navy lost a number of ships to Argentine air attacks, including the destroyer *Sheffield* to an Exocet missile, but lost only three Harriers, two of which collided in stormy weather. Twenty-eight Harriers flew 1,190 sorties, fired 26 Sidewinders, and destroyed 21 Argentine aircraft without a single loss in air combat.

The Falkland conflict established the tactical value of VSTOL aircraft but also highlighted their deficiencies. Harriers were lightly armed, carrying only two Sidewinders. The navy addressed the problem and added twin missile launchers, but what Harriers needed most were longer-range radar-guided missiles and better avionics.

Other than the U.S. Navy's attack carriers, most nations of the world still operated World War II–vintage light carriers with short flight decks. After the Falklands conflict, India, Spain, Italy, Australia, began replacing outmoded Douglas A-4 Skyhawks and Hawker Sea Hawks with McDonnell Douglas AV-8B VSTOLs and British Aerospace Sea Harriers. Russia and France launched their own programs. Harriers began changing carrier design, and the Falkland war provided the stimulus.

Before the Falklands, Great Britain had attempted to sell the World War II–era *Hermes* to Chile, India, or Australia. There were no takers. The 28-knot *Hermes* had low freeboard, no stabilizers, and still burned black oil. She rolled in the surf and took green water over the bow. Australia turned down *Invincible,* which had modern gas-turbine engines but was not designed with Harriers in mind. Great Britain was fortunate to have both carriers available for the Falklands conflict. They proved the value of short carriers in small wars while demonstrating operational deficiencies in a new technology-driven environment.

On May 3, 1975, the 81,600-ton nuclear-powered *Chester W. Nimitz* (CVAN-68) went into commission. Fully loaded and displacing 95,100 tons, the 1,092-foot-long ship carried 100 aircraft and helicopters. Her two pressurized water-cooled reactors could propel her at 30 knots for 13 years, covering more than a million miles before replacing the reactor's cores. Her armament included three Basic Defense Missile System launchers with Sparrow III missiles.

Two years later, *Dwight D. Eisenhower* (CVAN-69), the navy's third nuclear-powered carrier, went into commission, followed on March 13, 1982, by a third *Nimitz*-class carrier, *Carl Vinson* (CVAN-70). Three of the navy's 22 carriers were now nuclear-powered. They could do most anything: control the sea, hunt submarines, or project air power deep into enemy territory without refueling. Congress authorized a fourth *Nimitz*-class carrier, but President Jimmy Carter canceled it. Congress put it back into the budget, and Carter took it back out. Admiral Arleigh Burke, CNO, grumbled, "You cannot run a military campaign by changing your mind every morning. We must have national goals."[8]

During the summer of 1981, the first year of President Ronald Reagan's administration, John F. Lehman became secretary of the navy. He understood the president's goals and predicted that by the 1990s the United States would have "outright maritime superiority over any power or powers which might attempt to prevent our free use of the seas and the maintenance of our vital interests worldwide."[9] One year later, Colonel Muammar Qadaffi, who had seized power in 1967 and was now head of Libya's Soviet-supported government, decided to test Lehman's resolve. He repudiated the 12 nautical mile limitation on territorial waters and declared the entire Gulf of Sidra off limits. The incident created a chain reaction that began on August 19, 1982, when *Nimitz* appeared 60 miles off Libya's coast to conduct "freedom of navigation" exercises. Two F-14 Tomcat pilots shot down two Libyan-piloted Soviet SU-22 fighters when attacked over international waters in the gulf.

During the next four years, the center of gravity for terrorism shifted from the Middle East to Libya. Qadaffi took the lead in terrorism's spread and sent men to set off explosives at Rome and Vienna's airports. He underestimated President Reagan's resolve to stop it. On January 26, 1986, Vice Admiral Frank B. Kelso, commanding two battle groups of the Sixth Fleet, moved the carriers *Saratoga* and *Coral Sea* off the Gulf of Sidra for maneuvers. Qadaffi announced that any ship or airplane penetrating his so-called gulf-drawn "Line of Death" would be attacked and destroyed.

On the first day of maneuvers, Libyan MiG-25 Foxbats approached Kelso's CAP but were intercepted and chased off. The air minuet between MiGs and carrier planes continued for two months without a shot being fired. American aircraft flying CAP carried a full load of the latest Sparrow radar-guided and Sidewinder heat-seeking missiles. Aircraft flying surface CAP carried a variety of air-to-ground ordnance, including Rockeye cluster bombs, high-speed anti-radiation missiles (HARMS), and Harpoon antiship missiles. F/A-18s also carried a complete suite of air-to-air missiles, enabling pilots to respond wherever needed. Each CAP contained E-2c radar control aircraft with data link coordination and tankers for air fueling.[10]

Qadaffi's arsenal contained large quantities of Soviet and French hardware, including Soviet fighter aircraft (Mig-23s, MiG-25s, and Su-22 Fitters) and French Mirage aircraft, all armed with air-to-air, radar-guided, and heat-seeking missiles. He then surrounded himself with foreign technical advisors and his cities and military installations with overlapping SAM missile sites.[11] The constant intrusion of Libyan fighters made Admiral Kelso's tactical exercises a marvelous training ground for carrier pilots, and it also disclosed the vectoring and tracking limitations of Libyan surveillance.

In mid-March, the USS *America* (CVA-66) joined Kelso's Sixth Fleet, making it the most powerful force in the Mediterranean. On March 24, the three carriers groups stretched east to west 150 nautical miles north of Qadaffi's Line of Death. At 2:00 P.M., American cruisers and destroyers, covered by F/A-18s from *Coral Sea*, crossed the Line. Libya responded by firing dozens of SA-5 SAMs from Sitre. All missed. Planes from the carriers responded and, using Harpoons and Rockeyes, sank a Soviet-built missile corvette and severely damaged another. For the next five days, the Sixth Fleet operated inside the Line of Death without a challenge, so Kelso withdrew to the north gratified that Qadaffi chose no longer to challenge international law.

Qadaffi's terrorists, however, blew up a Berlin disco and a TWA airliner, killing Americans and others. *Saratoga* had already returned stateside, and on

April 9, *Coral Sea* was about to do the same when Admiral Kelso rearmed her for a resumption of operations against Libya. Pilots on *America* and *Coral Sea* already knew the location of key Libyan targets. Before dawn on April 15, 30 jets struck Benina airfield, Benghazi, and the Al Jamahiriyah barracks. F/A-18 Hornets armed with HARMs and EA-6B Prowlers with SAM radar jammers knocked out Libya's air defense system. From the night sky, Hornet pilots' last view of Benghazi showed a city in flames, backdropped by the distant glow of fires burning on Benina airfield. Not a plane had been lost.

Kelso waited for Qadaffi to counterattack, but none came. He sent *Coral Sea* home and replaced her with *Enterprise*. Never certain what the Soviets planned next, Secretary Lehman decided to keep two carriers in the Mediterranean—at least for a while.

During the Libyan disturbance, the Soviets had also been busy in the Western Hemisphere. Having been cast out of Cuba, they quietly began converting the island of Grenada into a missile base. On October 19, 1983, a Marxist coup overthrew Grenada's government after a communist general murdered the commonwealth's president. The former 133-square-mile British colony lay in the eastern Caribbean 1,600 miles from Florida. Soviet funds had already provided military installations and a naval base. One thousand Americans lived on the island, mostly students attending St. George's University Medical School.

President Reagan could not allow the USSR to create a "Russian Gibraltar" in the Americas. On October 25, at the invitation of the Organization of Eastern Caribbean States, he issued orders for Vice Admiral Joseph Metcalf, Jr., to occupy the island. Metcalf formed a task force around the carrier *Independence,* and with 11 other ships sailed to Grenada despite objections from Queen Elizabeth, still the former colony's head of state.

The Landing Platform Helicopter carrier *Guam* (LPH-9), specifically designed for amphibious operations, contained one reinforced marine battalion of 1,900 men and a helicopter squadron for inserting troops. The LPH program began in 1958 with the conversion of escort carriers and *Essex*-class carriers for special operations. Eventually, four new LPHs—*Iwo Jima, Okinawa, Guadalcanal*, and *Guam*—survived the 1960s budget-cutting process. At 5:30 A.M. on October 25, with SEALs already ashore, helicopters from *Guam* landed 400 men from the 22nd Marine Amphibious Unit on Pearls Airport, Grenada's only operational airfield. Thirty minutes later, C-5A and C-130 transport aircraft from Barbados dropped paratroops on a new unfinished 9,000-foot airstrip being built by Cubans on Point Salinas.

By 8:50 A.M., except for resistance at the Government House that ended the following morning, marines and airborne troops secured the island. At a cost of 18 killed and 116 wounded, they gathered up 49 Russians, 24 North Koreans, 13 Eastern Europeans, and 638 Cubans. They found warehouses crammed with Soviet weapons and documents containing plans for establishing a garrison for 6,800 Cuban troops. The sudden strike astounded both communists and American medical students and ended the USSR's efforts to put missile bases in the Western Hemisphere.

In 1987, on the heels of Grenada and the Libyan War, General Secretary Mikhail Gorbachev admitted the USSR had been driven into national bankruptcy by military competition with the United States. Reagan's bloodless war with the USSR cost an enormous amount of money, but a hot war would have cost immeasurably more. In 1990, the new Russian Navy eventually finished their only attack carrier, *Admiral Kuznetsov*, but scrapped plans for a nuclear-powered flattop authorized by the former Soviet regime.

At the end of 1987, Reagan and Gorbachev signed a treaty as the first step in reducing stockpiles of nuclear weapons, and the 43-year-old Cold War between the East and the West came to an end. The eight-year war between Iran and Iraq also came to an end, but the field of contention swiftly changed from communist expansion to aggression in the Middle East.

Incoming President George H. W. Bush, an old flattop pilot himself, would rediscover what he had already learned during his World War II experiences—the most powerful conventional weapon on earth was the aircraft carrier.[12] His administration would be compelled to call them into service again.

CHAPTER 20

The Desert Wars

The long Iran-Iraqi war during the 1980s marked the beginning of Saddam Hussein's campaign to dominate the Middle East. Both sides began targeting each other's oil tankers, forcing the U.S. Navy to step in during the summer of 1987 and provide convoy protection. *Enterprise* joined the effort, using Intruders, Corsairs, and helicopters to drive off Iranian naval vessels. Neither Iraq nor Iran wanted to involve the U.S. in their war, so they stopped attacking each other's tankers. The conflict ended in July 1988, leaving Iran and Iraq with huge debts and a staggering amount of rebuilding. Postwar problems for Saddam Hussein became the context for involving American carriers in the next round of Middle East disturbances.

By 1990, the Cold War had sputtered to a close with the breakup of the Soviet Union. Western nations began reaching for a "peace dividend" by reducing defense spending. This task fell on the year-old administration of President George H. W. Bush. Cuts in the military establishment were abruptly postponed when on August 2, 1990, Hussein's Iraqi army, reputed as being the fourth largest in the world, invaded Kuwait.

Hussein sought to liquidate Iraq's debts by acquiring Kuwaiti oil fields. He also believed that the United States, having supported his war against Iran, would not intervene. For a person acclaimed by some as a great strategist, Hussein made an enormous mistake. President Bush and Prime Minister Margaret Thatcher conferred on the invasion of Kuwait and agreed that Saudi Arabia could be next.

Admiral Carlisle A. H. Trost, CNO, had established three governing principles as the post–Cold War navy's future role. Henceforth, the navy would become "a deterrent force strong enough to discourage any enemy from considering an attack on the United States; an attack force capable of deploying rapidly in a crisis; and a Navy of alliances and with nations of the world that shared a common interest."[1] Trost already had forces in the Persian Gulf, and while the Bush administration formed a 33-nation military coalition, a battle group organized around the carrier *Independence* moved into the Gulf of Oman. A second battle group, formed around *Dwight D. Eisenhower* (CVAN-69), moved quickly from the eastern Mediterranean into the Red Sea. On arrival, both battle groups were in position for immediate, nonstop operations.

In 1990, Secretary of Defense Richard Cheney had kept military cutbacks to a minimum, retaining for the navy 546 combat ships, including 15 fast carriers. For Desert Shield—the deployment of troops to defend Saudi Arabia—240 ships responded to the call. Among them were six more carriers. *Saratoga, America, John F. Kennedy* (CV-62), and the fleet's newest nuclear carrier, *Theodore Roosevelt* (CVN-71), steamed into the Red Sea. *Ranger* and *Midway* took position in the Persian Gulf.

H hour, the campaign to liberate Kuwait, began on the night of January 16–17, 1991, with surgical air strikes against key Iraqi position. Two battleships, nine cruisers, five destroyers, and two nuclear-powered submarines fired the first 100 Tomahawk land attack missiles (TLAMs) against heavily defended targets in Baghdad. Six American carrier groups and two amphibious assault ships (LHAs) launched strikes against carefully designated Iraqi-held positions in and near Kuwait. A-7 Corsairs and A-6 Intruders introduced into combat the AGM-84E SLAM (stand-off land attack missile), whose TV-guidance system made broadcast news around the world. In the only air-to-air action of the war, two Hornet pilots demonstrated the new F/A-18Cs capabilities by shooting down two Iraqi MiG-21 fighters with Sidewinders while loaded with four 2,000-pound bombs and still carrying out their mission. After losing 90 planes, Hussein put his remaining MiGs underground and sent 122 aircraft into Iran. This came as some relief to the navy because Iraqi aircraft had used air-launched Exocet missiles during the war with Iran.

Intruders and Hornets using Skipper and Rockeye bombs and air-to-ground Harpoons sank or disabled most of Iraq's missile gunboats, minesweepers, patrol boats, and Silkworm antiship missile sites. Tactics had made quantum leaps since World War II when a pilot depended on his own eyes to locate and strike a target. While performing routine surface reconnaissance in the northern Persian Gulf on February 20, an S-3B Viking antisubmarine plane from the carrier *America*, guided by the Aegis cruiser USS *Valley Forge* (CG-50), searched the area with its forward-looking infrared system and inverse synthetic aperture radar, pin-pointed the position of a high-speed, heavily-armed gunboat, and sank it.

During the ground campaign, carrier based navy and Marine Corps Harriers and Intruders shifted from hitting stationary targets to strikes against tanks and truck convoys. The navy's new F/A-18D night Hornets, used for the first time in combat, prevented the enemy from moving masses of men and material after dark.

Although the USAF played a lead role from bases in Saudi Arabia, navy and marine pilots, using both rotary and fixed-wing aircraft, flew sorties off six carriers and several amphibious ships posted in the Red Sea and Persian Gulf. Some units operated from makeshift airstrips ashore. Carrier planes performed four missions simultaneously: in seven days they gained air superiority by destroying Iraq's strategic capabilities, knocked out the enemy's air defenses around

The USS *John F. Kennedy*, *Saratoga*, and *America* steam with their supports toward the Persian Gulf for Operation Desert Storm. (U.S. Navy photo)

Five A-7E Intruders and one A-6E Intruder line up in the air to receive fuel from a KC-135E Stratotanker. Under the wings are AGM-88 HARM missiles, Mark 83 1,000-pound bombs, and AIM-9 Sidewinders. (U.S. Navy photo)

Kuwait, attacked Iraqi positions in Kuwait, and provided air support for ground operations.

Missions from the Red Sea averaged 3.7 flying hours and required airborne refueling from KC-10 or KC-131 USAF tankers at both ends. Some targets were 700 miles away. Navy EA-6B Prowlers (defense suppression aircraft) aided air operations by first employing electronic jammers and then directing HARM attacks on radar sites, command centers, Scud missile launchers, electric power plants, and enemy nuclear, biological, and chemical weapons facilities. During the 100-day war, 1,000 navy and Marine pilots flew 30,000 sorties. Beginning with Desert Shield, having carriers on both flanks of the Arab coalition ensured the constant flow of logistics and enabled coalition Arab nations to participate without fear of retaliation.

Desert Storm provided the navy an opportunity to test in combat the reliability of an entirely new array of smart bombs. Carrier pilots using SLAM missiles, a variant of Harpoons, discovered they could accurately strike high-value targets from 50 miles away. F-14 Tomcats equipped with tactical air reconnaissance pod systems (TARPS) and armed with Phoenix missiles could pick out selective targets on the ground, even very small ones, and destroy them. British vessels used Sea Darts to intercept and destroy Silkworm missiles.

Desert Storm changed modern warfare and gave new meaning to the tactical strike strength of aircraft carriers. Although the Department of Defense spread new technologies across all the services, no entity at sea enjoyed a bigger bundle of the latest technology than carriers. Flattops had become the most powerful, responsive, and all-purpose weapon in the world. No insurgency within reach of carrier planes could any longer be safe from retaliation.

In 1993, incoming President William J. Clinton began looking for another "peace dividend," and a steady flow of defense spending cuts began neutering the armed forces. A-7 Corsairs were among the first to go. The production of F-14D Tomcats with new engines and better avionics was cut back to three squadrons, and one squadron had to settle for the older F-14Bs following another cut. Both models were equipped with the new low-altitude navigation and targeting infrared system for night (LANTIRN) targeting pods, which made them among the most effective strike aircraft in the world. The Clinton administration then cut the new A-12 Stealth aircraft and abandoned plans to upgrade the old reliable A-6 Intruder.

Cutbacks in aircraft directly affected supercarriers. Instead of carrying 82 to 90 planes, they were trimmed back to 56 planes—14 Tomcats and 42 F/A-18C Hornets. *Coral Sea*, retired in 1990 after the commissioning of *Abraham Lincoln* (CVN-72), was followed by *Midway*. Between 1993 and 1996 the Clinton administration withdrew from service *America, Forrestal, Ranger*, and *Saratoga*, all conventional-powered carriers, and finally in 1998, *Independence* went into retirement. Not all the voids remained unfilled. New carriers had been authorized during the Reagan administration. In 1989, *Abraham Lincoln* joined the fleet but was not ready for the Gulf War. *George Washington* (CVN-73) followed in 1992, *John C. Stennis* (CVN-74) in 1996, and *Harry Truman* (CVN-75) in 1999.

During the Reagan era, the U.S. Navy operated 15 fleet carriers. In 2001, when George W. Bush became president, there were only 11 attack carriers, 8 of which were nuclear powered. America's readiness for war had been squandered during the 1990s, but throughout the decade, wars of another kind percolated with little notice.

For 60 years, whenever a crisis occurred, there had been an *Enterprise* to respond. On December 7, 1941, the first *Enterprise* (CV-6), under the command of Admiral Halsey, lay 400 miles southwest of Hawaii when the Japanese struck Pearl Harbor. After the attack, Halsey began searching for the enemy fleet. During World War II, no carrier earned more battle stars. On December 2, 1965, the new *Enterprise* (CVAN-65) joined TF-77 at Yankee Station off North Vietnam. On September 11, 2001, after terrorists flew jetliners into the World Trade Center and the Pentagon, she raced at full speed for the North Arabian Sea and joined the *Nimitz*-class supercarrier *Carl Vinson* (CVN-70) to prepare for Operation Enduring Freedom, the war against Osama bin Laden's al-Qaida and his Taliban hosts in Afghanistan.

From out of Japan came the old *Kitty Hawk* (CV-63), a 1961 vintage flattop with the distinction of being the first missile-armed aircraft carrier. There were no air bases in Afghanistan, so *Kitty Hawk* became the staging base for U.S. Army Special Forces. As Vice Admiral John B. Nathman recalled, "Army special operations forces lived, trained, and lifted off for war from her deck."[2] After Special Forces teams dropped deep into Afghanistan, they developed a special relationship with F/A-18 and F-14 pilots who hung high in the air, flying eight- to nine-hour missions that required multiple trips to tankers while waiting for strike directions. No power on earth could respond so swiftly and with such force as an aircraft carrier. Lieutenant Commander Henry J. Hendrix wrote: "The success derived from mating the flexibility of special forces with the versatility of one of the Navy's floating airfields was astounding and led Special Operations Command ... to put the Navy on notice that it would be requesting its services in the future."[3]

The other weapons, born of the Cold War and Desert Storm, were Marine Expeditionary Units, Special Operations Capable [MEU(SOC)] teams, whose base was an amphibious assault ship such as *Wasp* (LHD-1) or *Peleliu* (LHA-5). MEUs operated from three to five assault ships. They moved rapidly and freely across the seas without the usual diplomatic restraints imposed by foreign nations guarding their territorial boundaries, and they were ready to perform any mission on six hours' notice. Amphibious assault ships carried 2,200 marines and sailors and contained four highly trained, specially integrated teams. The Ground Combat Element consisted of an infantry battalion supported by artillery, armor, engineers, amphibious assault vehicles, and reconnaissance. The Aviation Combat Element contained an amalgamated squadron of AV-8B Harriers, CH-53E Super Stallions and CH-46 Sea Knight helicopters, and scouting planes. The Combat Service Support Element provided a full range of logistical support from sea or shore with 15 days of supplies and equipment ready at all time for immediate deployment. The command element provided local command and control, communication with other command posts in the area, and linkage through the chain of command to the regional commander in chief and to authorities as far up as the Pentagon. The centerpiece of the MEU is the aircraft carrier.

The AV-8B Harrier saw its first sea-based combat action during Desert Storm. Flying from the amphibious assault ships *Tarawa* (LHA-1) and *Nassau* (LHA-4), the Harrier demonstrated the navy/marine team's versatility and effectiveness by flying both strike and close air support missions. Beginning on February 20, 1991, during an amphibious raid planned for Faylakah Island, *Nassau* launched her Harriers, flew 240 combat missions, dropped more than 900 bombs, and became the first LHA used as a Harrier carrier. The performance of LHAs and their carrier based Harriers during Desert Storm established new tactical standards for the future.

The combination of aircraft on MEU amphibious assault ships and fast supercarriers enabled the United States to "project its power over many thousands of miles from home bases and sustain that power for a long time [without] support from host nations and restrictions imposed on its forces on land."[4] Those tactical lessons learned in Desert Storm and Afghanistan would have telling impact in the wars to come.

The dust had not settled over Iraq when genocide and ethnic cleansing erupted in Somalia, Bosnia, and Kosovo. On December 9, 1992, after the 15th MEU(SOC) went ashore on Somalia, the carriers *Ranger* and *Abraham Lincoln* split time between the Somalian coast and the Arabian Gulf in support of operations. Fifteen months later, two Marine Amphibious Ready Groups organized around *Inchon* (LPH-12) and *Peleliu* (LHA-5) appeared offshore and removed troops from Mogadishu. During February/March 1995, *Essex* (LHD-2) returned with the helicopter carrier *Garibaldi* to cover the withdrawal of the UN humanitarian force.

In 1993, when ethnic cleansing began in Bosnia, President Clinton authorized an air umbrella that created a no-fly zone over Bosnia-Herzegovina to protect peacekeepers on the ground. Navy and Marine pilots from the NATO airbase at Aviano, Italy, and the carriers *Theodore Roosevelt, America,* and others flew 50,000 fighter, close air support, and strike sorties during a campaign that lasted until December 20, 1995. During operations over Bahja Luka, Bosnia, a Serb SAM shot down Captain Scott O'Grady's F-16C Fighting Falcon. For six days, Serb search parties combed the hills searching for O'Grady. The 24th MEU(SOC), embarked in *Kearsarge* (LHD-3), loaded two rescue teams on CH-53E Sea Stallions. Covered by AH-1 Cobra light-attack helicopters and AV-8 Harriers, marines located O'Grady in the wooded underbrush and pulled him to safety.

In March 1999, problems with Slobodan Milosevic's Serbian government migrated across the border and into Kosovo. For the first time in its 50-year history NATO engaged in hostilities. Until April 3, when the *Theodore Roosevelt* Battle Group arrived, the United States had no fast carriers on hand, only the amphibious assault ships *Kearsarge* and *Nassau.* In an engagement against Serbia lasting 12 weeks, planes from *Roosevelt* flew 4,270 sorties, and destroyed 400 tactical targets and scores of fixed targets without a single loss.

During the decade between the end of Desert Storm and the end of operations against the Serbian government, terrorism accelerated throughout the world. Nor were operations over Iraq's no-fly zone ever quiescent, keeping aircraft carriers on duty in the Persian Gulf to knock out radar and SAM sites.

Terrorism reached the shores of the United States in 1993 when militant Muslims bombed the World Trade Center in New York City. Unlike earlier incidents, terrorists were becoming better organized under the leadership of Osama bin Laden, the son of a Saudi billionaire. Bin Laden had gone to Afghanistan in the 1980s to fight the Soviets and later subsidized the warlords of Somalia. In 1995, his wealth supported the bombing of a building in Riyadh used by Americans. He also supported the 1996 Khobar Towers bombing in Dhahran that killed 19 U.S. flyers. A few days later, he called for a holy war against the United

States. In 1998 he told ABC News, "We do not differentiate between those dressed in military uniforms and civilians: they are all targets."[5] He kept his word, killing and injuring 5,036 people when he blew up U.S. embassies in Kenya and Tanzania. Although President Clinton authorized a mini-Tomahawk strike on four terrorist training camps in Afghanistan and a pharmaceutical plant in Sudan, he did not take bin Laden's threat seriously and refused to capture him when given an opportunity by the Sudanese government. New York City and the Pentagon paid the price when on September 11, 2001, bin Laden's trained assassins hijacked four fully fueled commercial aircraft and flew them into three of America's most prestigious buildings, taking more than 3,000 lives. Clinton avoided paying the price for his mistakes because he was no longer in office.

On September 12, 2001, President George W. Bush, who had taken office in January 2001, declared war on terrorism and authorized immediate retaliatory operations against bin Laden and the controlling Taliban government in Afghanistan. On October 7, 2001, Hornets and Tomcats from *Enterprise* and *Carl Vinson* launched the first surgical air strikes, hitting airfields, air defense sites, command-and control centers, al-Qaida training camps, and the Kandahar residential compound of Taliban leader Mullah Mohammad Omar. By mid-December, the two carrier groups had flown more than 6,000 missions without losing a plane.

On November 24, the 15th and the 26th MEU(SOC) amphibious ready teams on *Pelelieu* and *Bataan* landed by helicopter in southern Afghanistan and took over the Kandahar airfield, interdicted roads, collected prisoners, performed search and destroy missions, and carved safe pathways through a country infested with landmines. A day later, AH-1W Super Cobra helicopters spotted a Taliban column and provided fire direction control for F-14s from the carrier *Carl Vinson*.

As the weeks passed, General Tommy Franks called in AH-1W Harriers and CH-53E helicopters of the 13th MEU(SOC) from *Bon Homme Richard* (LHD-6) to fly combat sorties during Operation Anaconda, a mission designed to squeeze Taliban forces out of the rugged mountains around Torabora. Harrier pilots flew 400 sorties, dropping GBU-12 500-pound bombs and MK-82 bombs on specified targets.

For navy pilots, Afghanistan became an exercise for the coming war with Iraq. Each flight, from carrier to target to carrier, averaged 1,000 miles with in-flight fueling. EA-6Bs provided electronic suppression and jammed Taliban communications. F-14 Tomcats used tactical targeting capabilities to identify and transmit precision-targeting coordinates to navy and air force strikers. The USS *John C. Stennis* (CVN-74) arrived on December 16, relieved *Vinson*, and flew another 4,000 sorties. Of some 10,000 sorties, 84 percent hit a target. Compared with Desert Storm, 94 percent of the ordnance delivered was precision-guided. In Desert Storm, many aircraft were assigned to the same target. In Afghanistan, navy pilots on average struck more than two targets per aircraft. When pilots launched their ordnance, they did it against targets they could seldom see because remote fire-direction air controllers picked most of the targets and controlled the firing.

The Taliban regime and its 40,000-man army collapsed in a matter of weeks; the key to success in Afghanistan was once again Tomcats, Hornets, and Harriers—carrier air power. Dr. Milan Vego, who studied the lessons from Operation Enduring Freedom, said, "Without carriers in the area, it is difficult to see how success would have been achieved."[6]

At 9:34 EST on March 19, 2003 (5:34 A.M. local time in Baghdad on March 20), U.S. and U.K. forces began conducting military operations against Iraq to disarm Saddam Hussein of his weapons of mass destruction and to remove the Iraqi regime from power. During negotiation delays within the United Nations, Hussein transferred most of Iraq's chemical and biological weapons to Syria. President Bush clarified the attack on Iraq by addressing the American public, stating that coalition forces were in the "early stages of military operations to disarm Iraq, to free its people, and to defend the world from grave danger."[7]

Forty cruise missiles and carrier aircraft from *Abraham Lincoln, Constellation, Harry S. Truman,* and *Kitty Hawk*, struck targets of opportunity throughout Iraq. Those targets consisted of communications sites, SAM missile sites, early-warning radar defense systems, and elements of Iraqi leadership. F/A-18 Hornets from the USS *Constellation* and *Abraham Lincoln,* posted in the North Arabian Gulf, struck targets around Basra to pave the way for amphibious landings by the I Marine Expeditionary Force and the British Royal Marines. Two Amphibious Ready Groups in the USS *Tarawa* (LHA-1) and *Nassau* (LHA-4) waited offshore in readiness to land. Two Amphibious Task Forces also waited offshore, one organized around *Saipan* (LHA-2) and the other around *Boxer* (LHD-6). Both units carried helicopters and new AV-8B Harriers. As the day progressed, all four groups went ashore near the mouth of the Tigris River.[8]

On March 21, Baghdad time, F/A-18 Hornets, F-14 Tomcats, and Marine AV-8B Harriers from the navy's flattops, and RAF GR7/GR9 Harrier IIs and Royal Navy FA2 Sea Harriers from HMS *Ark Royal* went into high gear and launched hundreds of strikes on military targets using only precision-guided missiles to prevent collateral damage. On the following day, the USS *Theodore Roosevelt* arrived in the Persian Gulf and joined in the strikes. By then, coalition forces had flown 6,000 sorties.

On March 23, when Iraqi forces began luring Marines into ambushes by pretending to surrender, Hornets and Harriers responded quickly and provided close air support. For the next several days carrier planes concentrated on suppressing ballistic missile threats, degrading Republican Guard units, and neutralizing Iraq's control and intelligence centers. A two-day sandstorm that suspended ground operations on March 25–26 did not interrupt all air strikes. Working with S-3B Vikings, F/A-18Cs from *Constellation* knocked out three naval targets near Basra. One Viking, using an AGM-65E Maverick laser-guided missile, destroyed a fourth target, marking the first time in 30 years that a navy S-3B became involved in an overland strike. Vikings were normally relegated to tanking support, antisubmarine warfare, and electronic support missions.

On March 31, *Theodore Roosevelt*'s Carrier Air Wing 8 flew the longest night of sorties since the war began and struck enemy positions in northern Iraq, destroying SAM sites, artillery installations, and barracks. Carrier Air Wing 11 of *Nimitz* joined Carrier Air Wing 14 on *Abraham Lincoln* to provide a mix of F/A-18E/F Super Hornets with drop tanks and intermediate refueling from tankers for a 4,000-mile roundtrip strike in support of ground troops in northern Iraq.

The two-seat F/A-18F Super Hornet strike fighter made its first debut in combat during Operation Iraqi Freedom and came equipped with second-generation Advanced Targeting Forward-Looking InfraRed (FLIR) targeting pods and the new Shard Advanced Reconnaissance Pod (SHARP). Vice Admiral John Nathman praised the Super Hornet's performance, declaring, "It's really doing well. The multi-mission capability of the airplane is just gangbusters for us—it really is [a] great story."[9]

SAR helicopters remained in the air during every flight recovery. When a returning S-3B Viking veered off *Constellation*'s flight deck, slid to the port side, and fell into the water, an SAR swimmer dropped into the sea and rescued both pilots. Aside from a few bruises and lacerations, neither pilot was seriously injured. An F/A-18C pilot from *Kitty Hawk* was not so lucky when he came down in the desert. Although SAR operations continued for several days, the pilot was never found.

Twelve years after the LHA *Nassau* established the value of Harrier carriers during Desert Storm, *Bataan* (LHD-5) and *Bon Homme Richard* (LHD-6) repeated the performance during Operation Iraq Freedom. The only operating procedures available came from *Nassau*'s short stint as a Harrier carrier during Desert Storm. Each LHD carried 20 to 24 AV-8 Harriers. The most difficult problem to untangle was the division of air space between fast carriers, land-based aircraft, LHAs in the area, and LHDs. While waiting for air traffic problems to be resolved, *Bataan* transferred 1,900 Marines, 175 vehicles, 270 tons of cargo and equipment, and hundreds of pallets of ground ammunition on Iraqi's east coast. With the marines safely ashore and air control patterns resolved, Harrier squadrons from *Bataan* and *Bon Homme Richard* dropped 250 tons of ordnance, most of which was laser-guided, and destroyed, damaged, or removed 1,200 targets from the fight. Once again, Harrier carriers demonstrated the relevance of an Expeditionary Strike Group and have become the focus of new carrier doctrine.[10]

In early April, although carrier air strikes continued against strategic Iraqi communications and intelligence installations, most planes flew close air support against Republican Guard units defending Saddam International Airport, Najaf, and Basra. By April 7, conventional fighting ceased.

On April 12, marine forces moved out of Baghdad and headed toward Tikrit and Auja, the hometown of Saddam Hussein. Carrier planes covered the advance.

By then naval aviation had flown 7,000 sorties. The cities fell two days later after air and ground attacks destroyed the district's fortifications.

After freeing Iraq, carriers rotated but remained on duty to provide air support against attacks by militant insurgents who oppose democracy. The USS *George Washington*, after Persian Gulf deployment, returned home to Norfolk, Virginia, on July 26, 2004. Her six-month tour of duty covered 51,000 nautical miles. Carrier Air Wing 7 flew 7,592 sorties, dropped 82 tons of ordnance, and never lost a plane.

Three wars in the deserts and mountains of the Middle East reconfirmed the role of aircraft carriers as a platform of choice, especially when land-based air is not available. But to fight war effectively, both are needed because their capabilities are complementary. During the wars in Iraq and Afghanistan, it is difficult to see how rapid success could have been achieved without the flexible air power brought to the battlefield by carriers of the U.S. Navy.

From the USS *Langley* (CV-1) to the USS *Harry S. Truman* (CVN-75), aircraft carriers have become the most powerful weapon afloat.

Conclusion

Aircraft carriers leaped into eminence during World War II, mainly in the Pacific. During four years of intensive air combat at sea, no American carrier ever came within sight of a Japanese carrier. Carrier wars were fought between aircraft, and at such distances that the only encounter between a surface battle group and a carrier occurred at Leyte Gulf when Admiral Kurita's center force stumbled into Taffy 3's escort carriers off Samar in the Philippines. After World War II, with the possible exception of a foray in the Falklands, there has never been another air battle between aircraft carriers.

At the end of 2003, there were no fixed-wing aircraft carriers under construction outside of the United States, but a number of nations adopted the idea of building hybrid ships capable of carrying assault helicopters and vertical or short takeoff and landing fighters. The Indian Navy plans to build three "air-defense ships" patterned after American amphibious assault ships. Russia never completed the cruiser-carrier *Admiral Gorshkov*, but India has signed a contract to have it finished with a full-length flight deck and a ski-jump bow for carrying 16 fixed-wing fighters and 8 helicopters.

Russia plans no new carrier construction and continues to sporadically operate its sole survivor, the *Admiral Kuznetsov*. Her newer sister, *Varyag*, is rusting at a commercial pier at Dailan, China, with no apparent plan to mobilize her.

The Royal Navy wanted to build two 70,000-ton fixed-wing carriers but discovered the government could not afford them. They decided on a less-capable 50,000-ton design, the first of which will not be ready before 2012. Already named *Queen Elizabeth* and *Prince of Wales*, the two carriers are designed to carry around 25 Joint Strike Fighters (JSFs) and about 10 helicopters.

France is trying to justify the expense for building its own *Queen Elizabeth*-class carrier, but have not decided on whether to design it with conventional power or nuclear power. France has two helicopter-carrying assault ships in the works, the 21,500-ton *Mistral*, due for completion in June 2005, and a sister ship *Tonerre*, to follow in 2006.

Italy already has the 27,500-ton *Andrea Doria* under construction, but she will only be able to handle 8 AV-8B Harrier fighter-bombers or 12 helicopters.

Japan is planning four small carriers they officially refer to as "helicopter-destroying destroyers." They will displace 17,000 tons, have the classic appearance of a World War II full-length flight deck 640 feet in length, the standard starboard side island superstructure, and two aircraft elevators leading to hangars below. They are ostensibly designed to carry helicopters but have the capacity to carry Harriers. Japan is also planning another "helicopter-carrying destroyer" for 2008, which is also configured like a small conventional carrier but is designed to handle three SH-60K Sea Hawk and one MCH-101 Merlin helicopters or 11 CH-47 Chinook helicopters.

To keep pace with her European neighbors, Spain is buying a 28,100-ton, 664-foot, 21.5-knot amphibious assault carrier from the United States. It will have a ski-jump ramp for eight AV-8B Harrier VSTOL fighter-bombers, plus landing spots and hangar capacity for 12 helicopters.

South Korea is working on two small amphibious assault ships for carrying 10 helicopters and 600 troops, but no mention has been made of adding Harriers.

Aside from the Royal Navy's fixed-wing carrier program scheduled for the next decade, the only truly fast fixed-wing and named carrier under construction is the USS *George H. W. Bush* (CVN-77), scheduled to join the fleet in 2009. She will be the first new American carrier since the commissioning of the USS *Ronald Reagan* on July 12, 2003. The next generation of U.S. carriers, the CVN(X) class, has not been named. One might hope that the name USS *United States* might be resurrected from Secretary of Defense Louis A. Johnson's ill-conceived cancellation back on April 23, 1949.

Aircraft on U.S. carriers are being constantly modified while new types are in test. Although other nations of the world attempt to standardize on a single type of fighter aircraft, the U.S. government flirts with three: the F/A-18E/F Super Hornet, the F-35A/B Joint Strike Fighter (JSF) scheduled for 2010, and the F/A-22 Raptor. The Raptor is costly ($115 million) and has problems. It is not a bomber, has limited ground-attack capability, carries a light payload, and is less stealthy. F/A-18E/F Super Hornets cost half as much as Raptors, carry heavier payloads, and have a proven record of success striking ground targets. Weapons experts agree: "An F/A-18E fitted with the new shared reconnaissance pod can provide high-resolution wire-area coverage while maintaining its self-protection and offensive capabilities."[1] The best aircraft outside NATO are MiG-29s and Su-27s, but they have unimpressive avionics.

The F-35A/B is a short take-off and vertical landing aircraft employed on Amphibious Assault Ships and offers a superior ground-attack capability combined with excellent stealth characteristics and costs far less than Raptors. For some years to come, the standard fighter-bomber on fast carriers will be Super Hornets, and the standard VSTOL on Marine platforms will be the F-35s.

The Marine Corps is also trying to replace CH-46E helicopters with the MV-22 Osprey, a tilt-engine rotorcraft with vertical take-off and landing capabilities. The Osprey can travel twice as fast, carry three times the load, and go six times farther than the CH-46E. With improved avionics, and more time in test, the Osprey will "change everything about how maneuver warfare is conducted."[2]

Before the Iraq War, the average age of aircraft exceeded the average age of combat ships. Navy and Marine aircraft averaged 17.8 years. Strike fighters have an expected service life of 20 years and helicopters of 25 years. During the 1990s, both aircraft and the vessels to carry them were shortchanged during the Clinton administration. Super Hornets, Ospreys, and the aircraft of the future are now in the budget.

The world remains a tinderbox. China wants control of Taiwan, North Korea threatens nuclear war, Iran is developing missile and nuclear technology, and the world is filling over with 130 million Muslim radical fundamentalists espousing *jihad*. Wherever the next outbreak occurs, whether in the war against terrorism or elsewhere, aircraft carriers, both large and small, will be there to defend the free nations of the world, and on their decks will be the most advanced weapons technology in the world.

On November 14, 1910, Eugene B. Ely planted a small seed that germinated into an aircraft carrier when he became the first pilot to fly off a wooden platform built over the bow of the cruiser *Birmingham* at Hampton Roads, Virginia. The navies of the world took notice, and as better aircraft evolved to meet the requirements of modern warfare, ships also evolved to expand the range of aircraft. During World War I Great Britain put the first airfields to sea—*Hermes* and *Ark Royal*. During World War II the United States operated 25 fleet carriers, 9 light carriers, and 77 escort carriers. Another 30 escort carriers went to Great Britain. Today the U.S. Navy tries to keep about a dozen fleet carriers in service along with about two dozen amphibious assault ships.

In 1922, the USS *Langley* (CV-1) displaced 12,700 tons, carried 34 biplanes, and a complement of 350 men. *Lexington* (CV-2) and *Saratoga* (CV-3) displaced 38,500 tons and carried 80 aircraft (fighters, bombers, and torpedo planes) and a complement of 2,122 men. *Enterprise* (CVAN-65), the first nuclear powered carrier, displaced 89,600 tons, carried 99 aircraft (five attack squadrons, two fighter squadrons, and nine other aircraft), an array of missile systems, and a complement of 5,500 men and women. Today the USS *Ronald Reagan* (CVN-76), the ninth of the *Nimitz*-class, displaces 91,487 tons, carries up to 90 planes, including F/A-18 Hornets and Super Hornets, and a complement of 6,400 men and women.

One might ask this question: Where would the United States, NATO, and the free world be today without aircraft carriers? The former Third Reich, the former Soviet Union, the former Imperial Japanese Empire, North Korea, Red China, and Muslim radical fundamentalists have learned the answer the hard way. Some of them are still learning.

Notes

Chapter 1: From Dreadnoughts to Flight Decks

1. Quoted in William N. Still, *American Sea Power in the Old World 1865–1917* (Westport, CT, 1980) 157, 137.

2. O'Toole, *The Spanish War: An American Epic* (New York, 1984), 385.

3. Hagan, ed., *In Peace and War: Interpretations of American Naval History 1775–1984* (Westport, Conn., 1984), 192.

4. James D. Richardson, comp., *Messages and Papers of the Presidents 1789–1905*, vol. 10 (Washington, D.C., 1907), 831.

5. Frank L. Owsley, Jr., and Wesley Phillip Newton, "Eyes in the Sky," *Proceedings* Supplement, 1986, 18.

6. Ibid.

7. Thomas Ray, "Naval Aviation: The Beginning," *Proceedings*, 97, no. 1 (January 1971), 34.

8. Ibid., 35.

9. John Hammond Moore, "The Short, Eventful Life of Eugene B. Ely, *Proceedings*, 107, no. 1 (January 1981), 60.

10. Ibid., 61–62.

11. Ray, "Naval Aviation," 37.

12. Paolo E. Coletta, *American Secretaries of the Navy.* 2 vols. (Annapolis, 1980), 1:515.

13. Ray, "Naval Aviation," 38.

14. Ibid., 41.

15. Owsley and Newton, "Eyes in the Sky," 16.

16. Ibid., 8.

17. J. C. Hunsaker, *Forty Years of Aeronautical Research* (Washington, 1956), 241–45.

18. Layman and Boris V. Drashpil, "Early Russian Shipboard Aviation," *Proceedings*, 97, no. 4 (April 1971), 60.

19. Ibid., 61.

20. R. D. Layman, *Before the Aircraft Carrier: The Development of Aviation Vessels 1849–1922* (London, 1989), 72.

21. Quoted in Stephen Howarth, *To Shining Sea: A History of the United States Navy, 1775–1991* (New York, 1991), 352.

22. Edward Arpee, *From Frigates to Flat-tops: The Story of the Life and Achievements of Rear Admiral William Adger Moffet, U.S.N.* (Lake Forest, Ill., 1953), 99.

Chapter 2: Mobilizing for War

1. Stephen W. Roskill, *The Strategy of Sea Power: Its Development and Application* (London: Collins, 1968), 335 n.1.

2. Samuel Eliot Morison, *History of United States Naval Operations in World War II*, 15 vols. (Edison, N.J., 2001), 15:29. Hereinafter *HUSNO*.

3. Quoted in Coletta, *American Secretaries*, 2:617.

4. Morison, *HUSNO*, 15:29–30.

5. Ibid., 15:30.

6. Montgomery C. Meigs, "... This Must Mean the Philippines," *Proceedings*, 111, no. 8 (August 1985), 73.

7. *Pearl Harbor Attack. Joint Committee on the Investigation of the Pearl Harbor Attack.* 40 parts. (Washington, D.C., 1946), part 13, 1903.

Chapter 3: Flattops in the Atlantic

1. Jack Sweetman, "To Cut a Sleeping Throat," *Proceedings*, 117, no. 3 (December 1991), 31.

2. William H. Garzke, and Robert O. Dulin, "Who Sank the Bismarck," *Proceedings*, 117, no. 6 (June 1991), 50.

3. Quoted in Edwin P. Hoyt, *Carrier Wars: Naval Aviation from World War II to the Persian Gulf* (New York, 1989), 100.

4. Quoted in Howarth, *To Shining Sea*, 382.

5. Morison, *HUSNO*, 15:33–34.

6. Quoted in Walter Karig, et al., *Battle Report: The Atlantic War* (New York, 1946), 190.

Chapter 4: The Rising Sun

1. Paul S. Dull, *A Battle History of the Imperial Japanese Navy (1941–1945)*, (Annapolis, 1978), 3, 4.

2. Quoted in Howarth, *To Shining Sea*, 176.

3. Ibid., 216.

4. Quoted in S. E. Pelz, *Race to Pearl Harbor* (Cambridge, Mass., 1974), 34–35.

5. Ibid., 18.

6. John C. Grew, *Ten Years in Japan* (New York, 1944), 211.

7. Morison, *HUSNO*, 3:16–17.

8. Quoted in Howarth, *To Shining Sea*, 365.

9. Grew, *Ten Years in Japan*, 272.

10. Morison, *HUSNO*, 3:20.

11. Bernard S. Silberman and H. D. Harootian, eds., *Japan in Crisis* (Princeton, 1974), 293.

12. Morison, *HUSNO*, 3:82.

13. Dull, *The Imperial Japanese Navy*, 8.

14. Morison, *HUSNO*, 3:46.

15. Quoted in *Pearl Harbor Attack*, part 13, 516.

16. *Pearl Harbor Attack,* part 13:414, 487–96.

17. Quotes from Wilbur H. Morrison, *Above and Beyond* (New York, 1983), 1.

18. Quoted in Morison, *HUSNO*, 3:79.

19. Quoted in Sweetman, "To Cut a Sleeping Throat," 31.

Chapter 5: Fighting for Time

1. *Pearl Harbor Attack*, part 39, 344.

2. E. B. Potter, "The Command Personality," *Proceedings*, 95, no. 2 (February 1969), 19.

3. Morison, *HUSNO*, 3:256.

4. E. B. Potter, *Bull Halsey* (Annapolis, 1985), 2.

5. Quoted in Patrick Degan, *Flattop Fighting in World War II* (Jefferson, N.C., 2003), 55.

6. Quoted in Morrison, *Above and Beyond*, 15.

7. William F. Halsey and J. H. Walsey, *Admiral Halsey's Story* (New York, 1947), 82.

8. Morison, *HUSNO*, 3:264.

9. Francis L. Loewenheim, et al., eds. *Roosevelt and Churchill: Their Secret Wartime Correspondence* (New York, 1975), 188.

10. Frederick C. Sherman, *Combat Command: The American Aircraft Carriers in the Pacific War* (New York, 1950), 87.

11. Quoted in Ted W. Lawson, *Thirty Seconds over Tokyo* (New York, 1943), 38.

12. Halsey and Halsey, *Admiral Halsey's Story*, 103.

13. Ibid., 104.

14. Quoted in Thomas B. Buell, *Master of Sea Power: A Biography of Fleet Admiral Ernest J. King* (Boston, 1980), 309.

15. Ibid., 310.

Chapter 6: Coral Sea: Battle of Errors

1. Quoted in Morison, *HUSNO*, 4:27.

2. Ibid., 4:31.

3. Stanley P. Johnston, *Queen of the Flattops* (New York, 1942), 181.

4. Quoted in James H. Belote and William M. Belote, *Titans of the Sea* (New York, 1975), 91.

5. Hoyt, *Carrier Wars*, 83.

6. Quoted in S. E. Smith, ed., *The United States Navy in World War II* (New York, 1966), 261.

Chapter 7: Midway: The Turning Point

1. Quoted in Hoyt, *Carrier Wars*, 87.

2. Belote and Belote, *Titans of the Sea*, 102.

3. Ibid., 105.

4. Ibid., 109.

5. Morison, *HUSNO*, 4:107.

6. Ibid., 4:107.

7. Sherman, *Combat Command*, 126.

8. Gordon W. Prange, et al., *Miracle at Midway* (New York, 1982), 388.

Chapter 8: The Eastern Solomons

1. Belote and Belote, *Titans of the Sea*, 140.
2. Flight commander Major Lofton Henderson was shot down during the early action at Midway.

Chapter 9: The Battle for Guadalcanal

1. Quoted in Belote and Belote, *Titans of the Sea*, 187.
2. Ibid., 188.

Chapter 10: Refining Carrier Tactics

1. Morison, *HUSNO*, 5:353.
2. Quoted in E. B. Potter, *Nimitz* (Annapolis, Md., 1976), 233.
3. Quoted in Belote and Belote, *Titans of the Sea*, 196.
4. Quoted in Morison, *HUSNO*, 6:328.
5. Commander James C. Shaw's account in Morison, *HUSNO*, 6:35–36.
6. Halsey and Halsey, *Admiral Halsey's Story*, 183.

Chapter 11: Island-Hopping in the Pacific

1. J. J. Clark, *Carrier Admiral* (New York, 1967), 139–40.
2. Potter, *Nimitz*, 267–68.
3. Quoted in Theodore Taylor, *The Magnificent Mitscher* (New York: W. W. Norton & Company, 1954), 202.
4. Halsey and Halsey, *Admiral Halsey's Story*, 187–88.

Chapter 12: The Marianas Turkey Shoot

1. Quoted in Belote and Belote, *Titans of the Sea*, 292.
2. Quoted in the *New York Times*, June 21, 1944.
3. T. B. Buell, "Battle of the Philippine Sea," *Proceedings*, 100, no. 7 (July 1974), 69.
4. Ibid., 72.
5. Hoyt, *Carrier Wars*, 136.
6. Buell, "Battle of the Philippine Sea," 70.
7. Ibid., 69.
8. Quoted in Belote and Belote, *Titans of the Sea*, 304.
9. Quoted in Morison, *HUSNO*, 8:243.
10. Quoted in Taylor, *Magnificent Mitscher*, 227.
11. Edwin P. Hoyt, *McCampbell's Heroes* (New York, 1983), 61.
12. Quoted in Robert Sherrod, *On to Westward* (New York, 1945), 118.
13. Quoted in Morrison, *HUSNO*, 8:280. *Cavalla's* Action Report, August 3, 1944.
14. Quoted in Philip G. Reed, *Mission Beyond Darkness* (New York, 1945), 15.
15. Carrier TF-58 Action Report, 57.
16. Quoted in Morrison, *HUSNO*, 291.
17. *Hornet* Action Report 0020, July 1, 1944.
18. Montgomery Action Report, July 6, 1944.
19. Mitscher's Action Report, September 11, 1944.
20. E. P. Forrestel, *Admiral Raymond A. Spruance, USN: A Study in Command* (Washington, D.C., 1966), 137.

Chapter 13: The New Air Navy

1. Nimitz to Mitscher in Taylor, *Magnificent Mitscher*, 245.
2. Montgomery Action Report, July 6, 1944.
3. Sherman, *Combat Command*, 243.
4. Quotes from Ernest J. King and Walter M. Whitehill, *Fleet Admiral King: A Naval Record* (New York, 1952), 563.
5. Quotes from Clark G. Reynolds, *The Fast Carriers* (Huntington, N.Y., 1978), 18.
6. Nagano's Statement in U.S. Strategic Bombing Survey, *Air Campaigns of the Pacific War* (Washington, D.C., 1947), 2:356. Hereinafter USSBS.
7. Quoted in Roger Pineau, et al., *The Divine Wind* (Annapolis, 1958), 27.
8. Quoted in Hoyt, *Carrier Wars*, 153.
9. Quoted in Taylor, *Magnificent Mitscher*, 245.
10. Halsey and Halsey, *Admiral Halsey's Story*, 198.
11. Ibid., 194–95.
12. Clark, *Carrier Admiral*, 194–95.
13. A. O. Van Wyen and Lee M. Pearson, *United States Naval Aviation, 1910–1960* (Washington, 1961), 107.

Chapter 14: Prelude to the Philippines

1. Toyoda quoted in USSBS, I:317.
2. Quoted in Morison, *HUSNO*, 12:58.
3. Ozawa's statement, USSBS, 1:219.

Chapter 15: Leyte Gulf

1. Robert B. Carney, "Forum on 'The Command Personality,'" *Proceedings*, 95, no. 6 (June 1969), 98.
2. Quoted in Hoyt, *Carrier Wars*, 186.
3. Halsey and Halsey, *Admiral Halsey's Story*, 214.
4. Quoted in Hoyt, *Carrier Wars*, 190–91.
5. Sherman Action Report, 0090, December 2, 1944.
6. Halsey, *Admiral Halsey's Story*, 217.
7. Hanson Baldwin, *Sea Fights and Shipwrecks: True Tales of the Seven Seas* (New York, 1955), 327.
8. Quoted in Potter, *Bull Halsey*, 297.
9. Ibid., 298.
10. Ibid.
11. Reynolds, *The Fast Carriers*, 272.
12. Quoted in Potter, *Bull Halsey*, 301.
13. Ibid.
14. Clark, *Carrier Admiral*, 201.
15. Quoted in Potter, *Nimitz*, 340.
16. Halsey, *Admiral Halsey's Story*, 220.
17. Ibid., 221.
18. John D. Ahlstrom, "Leyte Gulf Remembered," *Proceedings*, 110, no. 8 (August 1984), 45.
19. Quoted in Reynolds, *The Fast Carriers*, 276.
20. Hoyt, *Carrier Wars*, 202.

21. C. Vann Woodward, *The Battle for Leyte Gulf* (New York, 1947), 185.

22. King and Whitehill, *Fleet Admiral King*, 580.

23. Douglas MacArthur, *Reminiscences* (New York, 1964), 172.

24. Potter, "The Command Personality," 24.

25. Taylor, *Magnificent Mitscher*, 265.

26. Quoted in Buell, *Master of Sea Power*, 479.

Chapter 16: The Setting Sun

1. Toshiyuki Yokoi, "Kamikazes and the Okinawa Campaign," *Proceedings*, 80, no. 5 (May 1954), 507.

2. Toshikazu Kase, *Journey to the Missouri* (New Haven, 1950), 247–48.

3. Halsey and Halsey, *Admiral Halsey's Story*, 236.

4. Hoyt, *Carrier Wars*, 216.

5. Reynolds, *The Fast Carriers*, 338–39.

6. Clark G. Reynolds, "Taps for the Torpecker," *Proceedings*, 112, no. 12 (December 1986), 56.

7. Ibid., 58.

8. Reynolds, *The Fast Carriers*, 341.

9. Quoted in Potter, *Nimitz*, 373.

10. Ibid., 375.

11. Quoted in Hoyt, *Carrier Wars*, 226.

12. Naval Staff History, *War with Japan*, vol. 4 (London: Admiralty, 1957), 202–03.

13. David Hamer, *Bombers versus Battleships: The Struggle between Ships and Aircraft for Control of the Surface of the Sea* (Annapolis, 1998), 324.

14. Quoted in Potter, *Bull Halsey*, 348.

15. USSBS, 3.

16. Morison, *HUSNO*, 12:412.

17. USSBS, 53.

18. Ibid., 57–58.

19. Quoted in Taylor, *Magnificent Mitscher*, 304.

Chapter 17: Korea: Carriers and Politics

1. Hamer, *Bombers versus Battleships*, 366, n4.

2. Quoted in Malcolm W. Cagle and Frank A. Manson, *The Sea War in Korea* (Annapolis, 1957), 71.

3. Ibid., 224.

4. Ibid., 224–25.

5. Ibid., 234.

6. Ibid., 257.

7. Ibid., 267.

8. Ibid., 253–54.

9. Robert Jackson, *Air War in Korea* (Osceola, Wis., 1998), 156–58.

Chapter 18: Vietnam: President Johnson's War

1. Quoted in Allan B. Cole, ed., *Conflict in Indo-China and International Repercussions: A Documented History, 1945–1955* (Ithaca, N.Y., 1956), 18–19.

2. Quoted in U.S. Defense Department, *United States-Vietnam Relations: 1945–1967* (Washington, D.C., 1971), bk. 8, 46–48.

3. Elliott Roosevelt, *As He Saw It* (New York, 1946), 115.

4. Quoted in John T. McAlister, Jr., *Viet Nam: The Origins of Revolution* (New York, 1969), 193.

5. Quoted in Edwin Bickford Hooper, et al., *The United States Navy and the Vietnam Conflict*, vol. 1. (Washington, D.C., 1976), 1:235.

6. Edward J. Marolda and Oscar P. Fitzgerald, *The United States Navy and the Vietnam Conflict,* vol. 2. (Washington, D.C., 1986), 2:36.

7. Quoted in Malcolm W. Cagle, "Task Force 77 in Action off Vietnam," *Proceedings*, vol. 98, no. 831 (May 1972), 71.

8. Ibid., 72.

9. Ibid., 73.

10. Ibid., 74.

11. New York *Times*, April 8, 1965, in ibid., 75.

12. Ibid., 79.

13. Garth L. Pawlowski, *Flat-Tops and Fledglings. A History of American Aircraft Carriers* (New York, 1971), 347, 352.

14. Quoted in Cagle, "Task Force 77," 103.

Chapter 19: Cold Wars and Brush Fires

1. Quoted in Jack Sweetman, *American Naval History: An Illustrated Chronology* (Annapolis, 1984), 217.

2. Ibid., 218.

3. Edward J. Marolda and Oscar P. Fitzgerald. *The United States Navy and the Vietnam Conflict* (Washington, D.C., 1986), 1.

4. Ibid., 20.

5. Quoted in David F. Winkler, *Cold War at Sea* (Annapolis, 2000), 31.

6. Elmo R. Zumwalt, Jr., *On Watch* (New York, 1976), 446–47.

7. A. D. Baker, "Aircraft Carriers in the Falklands," *Proceedings*, vol. 112, no. 2 (February 1984), 102.

8. Quoted in Howarth, *To Shining Sea*, 532.

9. Quoted in J. S. Breemer, *U.S. Naval Developments* (Baltimore, 1983), 30.

10. Robert E. Stumpf, "Air War with Libya," *Proceedings*, vol. 112, no. 8 (August, 1986), 43–44.

11. Ibid., 42.

12. On September 2, 1944, Lieutenant George H. W. Bush flew an Avenger off the USS *San Jacinto* and was shot down and rescued by a submarine off Chichi Jima. See Chester G. Hearn, *Sorties into Hell: The Hidden War on Chichi Jima* (Westport, Conn., 2003), 10–11.

Chapter 20: The Desert Wars

1. Chester G. Hearn, *An Illustrated History of the U.S. Navy* (London, 2002), 195.

2. Quoted in John B. Nathman, "'We Were Great': Navy War in Afghanistan," *Proceedings*, 128, no. 3 (March 2002), 2, in www.usni.org/proceedings/Articles02/PROnathman03.htm.

3. Henry J. Hendrix, "Exploit Sea Basing," *Proceedings*, 129, no. 8 (August 2003), 62.

4. Milan Vego, "What Can We Learn from Enduring Freedom?" *Proceedings*, 128, no. 7 (July 2002), 4, in www.usni.org/proceedings/Articles02/PROvego07.htm.

5. Hearn, *An Illustrated History of the U.S. Navy*, 209.

6. Vego, "What Can We Learn from Enduring Freedom?" *Proceedings*, 128; 7 (July 2002), 5.

7. Quotes from "Operation Iraqi Freedom—March 19/20 Day One," http://globalsecurity.org/military/ops.iraqi_freedom_d1.htm.

8. "US Navy Order of Battle: Operation Iraqi Freedom," http://navysite.de/navy/iraqi-freedom.htm

9. Scott C. Truver, "U.S. Navy in Review," *Proceedings*, 130, no. 5 (May 2004), 81.

10. Cindy Rodriquez, et al, "Harrier Carriers Perform in Iraqi Freedom," *Proceedings*, 130, no. 2 (February 2004), 34–35.

Conclusion

1. J. Michael Johnson and Michael Lobb, "Manned Reconnaissance Must Continue," *Proceedings*, 127, no. 7 (July 2003), 36.

2. Kevin Gross, "Dispelling the Myth of the MV-22," *Proceedings*, 130, no. 9 (September 2004), 38.

Bibliography

OFFICIAL DOCUMENTS

National Archives
World War II Action Reports
Ship/Unit War Diaries
Combat Narratives. Washington, D.C.: Office of Naval Intelligence, 1943.
Investigation of the Pearl Harbor Attack. Report of the Joint Committee. 79th Cong. 2d Sess., Doc. No. 244. Washington, D.C.: Government Printing Office, 1946.
U.S. Defense Department. *United States-Vietnam Relations: 1945–1967*. Washington, D.C.: Government Printing Office, 1971, Book 8.
U.S. Navy. Carrier Air Groups-Korean Combat Action Reports. http://www.history.navy.mil/branches/cvg.htm
U.S. Navy. Korean Combat Action Reports. http://www.history-navy.mil/biblio/biblio6.htm
U.S. Navy. Kosovo: *U.S. Naval Lessons Learned During Operations Allied Force, March–June 1999*. http://www.history.navy.mil/faqs/faq127.htm
U.S. Navy. "*'Thunder and Lightning'—The War with Iraq*." http://www.history.navy.mil/wars/dstrom/ds.htm
U.S. Strategic Bombing Survey. *Air Campaigns of the Pacific War*. Washington: Government Printing Office, 1947.

BOOKS

Ahlstrom, John D. "Leyte Gulf Remembered," *Proceedings*, 110, no. 8 (August 1984), 45–53.
Arpee, Edward. *From Frigates to Flat-tops: The Story of the Life and Achievements of Rear Admiral William Adger Moffet, U.S.N.* Lake Forest, Ill.: Author, 1953.
Astor, Gerald. *Crisis in the Pacific: The Battles for the Philippine Islands by the Men Who Fought Them—An Oral History*. New York: Donald I. Fine Books, 1996.
Baker, A. D. "Aircraft Carriers in the Falklands," *Proceedings*, vol. 112, no. 2 (February, 1984), 102–105.

Baldwin, Hanson. *Sea Fights and Shipwrecks: True Tales of the Seven Seas.* New York: Hanover House, 1955.

Beaver, Paul. *The British Aircraft Carrier.* Wellingborough, U.K.: Patrick Stevens, 1982.

Belote, James H., and William M. Belote. *Titans of the Sea for 1941–1944: The Development and Operations of Japanese and American Task Force during World War II.* New York: Harper and Row, 1975.

Bogan, G. F. *Reminiscences of Vice-Admiral G.F. Bogan.* Annapolis: Naval Institute Press, 1986.

Breemer, J. S. *U.S. Naval Developments.* Baltimore: Nautical & Aviation Publishing Co. of America, 1983.

Brown, David. *Carrier Operations in World War II.* Annapolis: Naval Institute Press, 1974.

Bryan, J., and Philip G. Reed. *Mission Beyond Darkness.* New York: Duell, Sloan, and Pearce, 1945.

Buell, Thomas B. "Battle of the Philippine Sea," *Proceedings,* 100, no. 7 (July 1974), 64–79.

———. *Master of Sea Power: A Biography of Fleet Admiral Ernest J. King.* Boston: Little, Brown and Company, 1980.

———. *The Quiet Warrior: A Biography of Admiral Raymond Spruance.* Boston: Little, Brown and Company, 1974.

Cagle, Malcolm W. "Task Force 77 in Action off Vietnam," *Proceedings,* vol. 98, no. 831 (May 1972), 66–109.

Cagle, Malcolm W., and Frank A. Manson. *The Sea War in Korea.* Annapolis: U.S. Naval Institute, 1957.

Carney, Robert B. "Forum on 'The Command Personality,'" *Proceedings,* 95, no. 6 (June 1969), 98.

Castillo, Edmund L. *Flat-tops: The Story of Aircraft Carriers.* New York: Random House, 1969.

Cavendish, Marshall. *The Vietnam War.* Vols. 7–8. New York: Marshall Cavendish Corporation, 1989.

Chesneau, Roger. *Aircraft Carriers.* Annapolis: Naval Institute Press, 1984.

Clark, Admiral J. J., with Clark G. Reynolds. *Carrier Admiral.* New York: David McKay Company, 1967.

Cole, Allan B., ed. *Conflict in Indo-China and International Repercussions: A Documented History, 1945–1955.* Ithaca, N.Y.: Cornell University Press, 1956.

Coletta, Paolo E. *American Secretaries of the Navy.* 2 vols. Annapolis: Naval Institute Press, 1980.

Cook, Charles O., Jr. "The Pacific Command Divided: The 'Most Unexplainable' Decision," *Proceedings,* 104, no. 9 (September 1978), 55–61.

Degan, Patrick. *Flattop Fighting in World War II.* Jefferson, N.C.: McFarland, 2003.

Dull, Paul S. *A Battle History of the Imperial Japanese Navy (1941–1945).* Annapolis: Naval Institute Press, 1978.

Dunn, Patrick T. *The Advent of Carrier Warfare.* Ann Arbor: University of Michigan Press, 1991.

Field, James A., Jr. *History of United States Naval Operations—Korea.* Washington. D.C.: Government Printing Office, 1962.

Forrestel, E. P. *Admiral Raymond A. Spruance, USN: A Study in Command.* Washington, D.C.: Government Printing Office, 1966.

Friedman, Norman. *British Carrier Aviation: The Evolution of the Ships and their Aircraft.* Annapolis: Naval Institute Press, 1988.

———. *Carrier Air Power.* London: Conway Maritime Press, 1981.

———. *U.S. Aircraft Carriers: An Illustrated Design History.* Annapolis: Naval Institute Press, 1983.

Gailey, Harry A. *The War in the Pacific: From Pearl Harbor to Tokyo Bay.* Novato, Calif.: Presidio Press, 1995.

Garzke, William H., and Robert O. Dulin, "Who Sank the Bismarck," *Proceedings*, 117, no. 6 (June 1991), 48–57.

Gray, James Seton, Jr., "Development of Naval Night Fighters in World War II," *Proceedings*, 74, no. 7 (July 1948), 847–51.

Grew, John C. *Ten Years in Japan.* New York: Hammond, Hammond & Company, 1944.

Gross, Kevin, "Dispelling the Myth of the MV-22," *Proceedings*, 130, no. 9 (September 2004), 38–41.

Hagan, K. J., ed. *In Peace and War: Interpretations of American Naval History 1775–1984.* Westport, Conn.: Greenwood Publishing, 1984.

Halsey, William F., and J. B. Halsey. *Admiral Halsey's Story.* New York: Whittlesey House, 1947.

Hamer, David. *Bombers versus Battleships: The Struggle between Ships and Aircraft for the Control of the Surface of the Sea.* Annapolis: Naval Institute Press, 1998.

Hearn, Chester G. *An Illustrated History of the U.S. Navy.* London: Salamander Books Ltd., 2002.

———. *Sorties into Hell: The Hidden War on Chichi Jima.* Westport, Conn.: Praeger Publishing, 2003.

Hendrix, Henry J., II. "Exploit Sea Basing," *Proceedings*, 129, no. 8 (August 2003), 61–63.

Hessler, William H. "The Carrier Task Force in World War II," *Proceedings*, 71, no. 11 (November, 1945), 1271–81.

Hooper, Edwin Bickford, et al. *The United States Navy and the Vietnam Conflict.* Vol. 1. Washington: Naval History Division, 1976.

Howarth, Stephen. *To Shining Sea: A History of the United States Navy, 1775–1991.* New York: Random House, 1991.

Howse, Derek. *Radar at Sea.* Basingstoke, U.K.: Macmillan, 1993.

Hoyt, Edwin P. *Carrier Wars: Naval Aviation from World War II to the Persian Gulf.* New York: McGraw-Hill, 1989.

———. *McCampbell's Heroes: The Story of the U.S. Navy's Most Celebrated Carrier Fighters of the Pacific War.* New York: Van Nostrand Reinhold Co., 1983.

Hunsaker, J. C. *Forty Years of Aeronautical Research.* Washington, D. C.: Smithysonian, 1956.

Jackson, Robert. *Aircraft of World War II.* Edison, N.J.: Chartwell Books, 2003.

———. *Air War in Korea 1950–1953.* Osceola, Wis.: Motorbooks International, 1998.

Jameson, William. *Ark Royal 1939–1941.* London: Rupert Hart-Davis, 1957.

Johnson, Brian. *Fly Navy: The History of Naval Aviation.* New York: William Morrow, 1981.

Johnson, J. Michael, and Michael Lobb. "Manned Reconnaissance Must Continue," *Proceedings*, 127, no. 7 (July 2003), 36–38.

Johnston, Stanley P. *Queen of the Flattops: The USS Lexington and Coral Sea Battle.* New York: E.P. Dutton & Company, 1942.

Jordan, David. *Firepower: Aircraft Carriers.* Edison, N.J.: Chartwell Books, 2002.

Karig, Walter, and Earl Burton, et al. *Battle Report: The Atlantic War.* New York, Rinehart & Company, 1946.

Kase, Toshikazu. *Journey to the Missouri.* New Haven, Conn.: Yale University Press, 1950.

King, Ernest J., and Walter Muir Whitehill. *Fleet Admiral King: A Naval Record.* New York: W. W. Norton and Co., Inc., 1952.

Lawson, Robert. *Carrier Air Group Commanders: The Men and Their Machines.* Atglen, Pa.: Schiffer Military History, 2000.

Lawson, Ted W. *Thirty Seconds over Tokyo.* New York: Random House, 1943.

Layman, R. D. *Before the Aircraft Carrier: The Development of Aviation Vessels 1849–1922.* London: Conway Maritime Press, 1989.

Layman, R. D., and Boris V. Drashpil. "Early Russian Shipboard Aviation," *Proceedings,* 97, no. 4 (April 1971), 56–63.

Lindley, John M. *Carrier Victory: The Air War in the Pacific.* New York: Elsevier-Dutton, 1978.

Loewenheim, Francis L. et al., eds. *Roosevelt and Churchill: Their Secret Wartime Correspondence.* New York: Saturday Review Press/Dutton, 1975.

MacArthur, Douglas. *Reminiscences.* New York: McGraw-Hill, 1964.

Marolda, Edward J. and Oscar P. Fitzgerald. *The United States Navy and the Vietnam Conflict.* Vol. 2. Washington, D.C.: Naval Historical Center, 1986.

McAlister, John T., Jr. *Viet Nam: The Origins of Revolution.* New York: Alfred A. Knopf, 1969.

McKay, Ernest A. *Carrier Strike Force: Pacific Air Combat in World War II.* New York: Julian Messner, 1981.

Meigs, Montgomery C. " . . . This Must Mean the Philippines," *Proceedings,* 111, no. 8 (August 1985), 72–78.

Mersky, Peter B., and Norman Polmar. *The Naval War in Vietnam.* Annapolis: The Nautical and Aviation Publishing Company, 1981.

Moore, John Hammond. "The Short, Eventful Life of Eugene B. Ely," *Proceedings,* 107, no. 1 (January, 1981), 58–63.

Morison, Samuel Eliot. *History of United States Naval Operations in World War II.* 15 vols. Edison, N.J.: Castle Books, 2001.

Morrison, Wilbur H. *Above and Beyond, 1941–1945.* New York: St. Martin's Press, 1983.

Musciano, Walter A. *Warbirds of the Sea.* Atglen, Pa.: Schiffer Military/Aviation History, 1994.

Nathman, John B. "'We Were Great': Navy War in Afghanistan," *Naval Institute Proceedings,* 128:3 (March 2002), 1–5, in www.usni.org/proceedings/Articles02/PROnathman03.htm.

Naval Staff History. *War with Japan.* vol. 4. London: Admiralty, 1957.

"Operation Iraqi Freedom-March 19/20 Day One," http://globalsecurity.org/military/ops.iraqi_freedom_d1.htm.

O'Toole, G.J.A. *The Spanish War: An American Epic.* New York: W.W. Norton & Co., 1984.

Owsley, Frank L., Jr., and Wesley Phillip Newton. "Eyes in the Sky," *Proceedings* Supplement, 1986, 17–25.

Pawlowski, Garth L. *Flat-Tops and Fledglings. A History of American Aircraft Carriers.* New York: Castle Books, 1971.

Pelz, S. E. *Race to Pearl Harbor.* Cambridge, Mass.: Harvard University Press, 1974.

Pineau, Roger, and Rikihei Inoguchi, et al. *The Divine Wind.* Annapolis: Naval Institute Press, 1958.

Polmar, Norman. *Aircraft Carriers.* London: Macdonald, 1969.

Poolman, Kenneth. *Escort Carrier 1941–1945.* London: Ian Allen, 1972.

Potter, E. B. *Bull Halsey.* Annapolis: Naval Institute Press, 1985.

———. "The Command Personality," *Proceedings*, 95, no. 2 (February 1969), 18–25.

———. *Nimitz.* Annapolis, Md.: Naval Institute Press, 1976

Prange, Gordon W., et al. *Miracle at Midway.* New York: McGraw-Hill, 1982.

Ray, Thomas. "Naval Aviation: The Beginning," *Proceedings*, 97, no. 1 (January 1971), 32–42.

Reed, Philip G. *Mission Beyond Darkness.* New York: St. Martin's Press, 1945.

Reynolds, Clark G. *The Fast Carriers: The Forging of an Air Navy.* Huntington, N.Y.: Robert E. Kreiger, 1978.

———. "Taps for the Torpecker," *Proceedings*, 112, no. 12 (December 1986), 55–61.

Richardson, James D., comp. *Messages and Papers of the Presidents 1789–1905.* vol. 10. Washington, D.C.: Bureau of National Literature and Art, 1907.

Richardson, James O., and George C. Dyer. *On the Treadmill to Pearl Harbor: The Memoirs of Admiral James O. Richardson, USN.* Washington, D.C.: Department of the Navy, 1973.

Rodriquez, Cindy, et al. "Harrier Carriers Perform in Iraqi Freedom," *Proceedings*, 130, no. 2 (February 2004), 32–35.

Roosevelt, Elliott. *As He Saw It.* New York: Duell, Slaon and Pearce, 1946.

Roskill, Stephen W. *The Strategy of Sea Power: Its Development and Application.* London: Collins, 1968.

Scheina, Robert L. "The Malvinas Campaign," *Proceedings Naval Review*, 1983, 98–111.

Sherman, Frederick C. *Combat Command: The American Aircraft Carriers in the Pacific War.* New York: E.P. Dutton & Company, 1950.

Sherrod, Robert. *History of Marine Corps Aviation in World War II.* Washington, D.C.: Combat Forces Press, 1952.

———. *On to Westward.* New York: Duell, Sloan, and Pearce, 1945.

Silberman, Bernard S., and H. D. Harootian, eds. *Japan in Crisis.* Princeton, N.J.: Princeton University Press, 1974.

Smith, S. E., ed. *The United States Navy in World War II.* New York: William Morrow & Company, 1966.

Still, William N. *American Sea Power in the Old World 1865–1917.* Westport, Conn.: Greenwood Publishing, 1980.

Stumpf, Robert E. "Air War with Libya," *Proceedings*, vol. 112, no. 8 (August, 1986), 42–48.

Sweetman, Jack. *American Naval History: An Illustrated Chronology.* Annapolis: Naval Institute Press, 1984.

———. "To Cut a Sleeping Throat," *Proceedings*, 117, no. 3 (December 1991), 30–31.

Taylor, Theodore. *The Magnificent Mitscher.* New York: W. W. Norton & Company, 1954.

Thetford, Owen. *British Naval Aircraft since 1912*. Annapolis: Naval Institute Press, 1991.

Till, Geoffrey. *Air Power and the Royal Navy*. London: Jane's, 1979.

Truver, Scott C. "U.S. Navy in Review, *Proceedings*, 130, no. 5 (May 2004), 80–86.

"US Navy Order of Battle: Operation Iraqi Freedom," http://navysite.de/navy/iraqi-freedom.htm.

Van Wyen, A. O., and Lee M. Pearson. *United States Naval Aviation, 1910–1960*. Washington, D.C.: Government Printing Office, 1961.

Vego, Milan. "What Can We Learn from Enduring Freedom?" *Proceedings*, 128, no. 7 (July 2002), 1–8, in www.usni.org/proceedings/Articles02/PROvego07.htm.

Watts, Anthony J. *Japanese Warships of World War II*. London: Ian Allen, 1966.

Wimmal, Kenneth. *Theodore Roosevelt and the Great White Fleet: American Sea Power Comes of Age*. Washington, D.C.: Brassey's, 1998.

Winkler, David F. *Cold War at Sea: High-Seas Confrontation between the United States and the Soviet Union*. Annapolis: Naval Institute Press, 2000.

Wise, James E., Jr. "Catapult Off-Parachute Back," *Proceedings*, 100, no. 4 (September 1974), 70–77.

Woodward, C. Vann. *The Battle for Leyte Gulf*. New York: The Macmillan Company, 1947

Y'Blood, William. *Hunter-Killer: US Escort Carriers in the Battle of the Atlantic*. Annapolis: Naval Institute Press, 1983.

———. *The Little Giants*. Annapolis: Naval Institute Press, 1987.

Yokoi, Toshiyuki. "Kamikazes and the Okinawa Campaign," *Proceedings*, 80, no. 5 (May 1954), 504–513.

Zumwalt, Elmo R., Jr. *On Watch*. New York: Quadrangle Press, 1976.

Index

ABC-1 Staff Agreement, 25, 35

ABDA fleet, 67

Abe, Hiroaki: at Midway, 99; in Eastern Solomons, 112; at Santa Cruz, 122, 125; in the Solomons, 130,131

Abraham Lincoln (CVN-72), 277, 279; Iraq War, 281–82

Adams, Samuel: at Midway, 100

Admiral Gorshkov, uncompleted Russian carrier, 285

Admiral Kuznetsov, Soviet carrier, 264, 266, 272, 285

Afghanistan operations, 277–79, 280

AF Operation. *See* Midway

Ahlstrom, John D., 209

Aircraft, British carrier: World War I, 11, 13; World War II, 27–28, 30, 35, 38; Korean War, 233, 234, 242; Cold War, 264, 265, 267; Falklands War, 268; Iraq War, 281

Aircraft, Japanese carrier: described, 53, 90, 157, 179, 192, 213

Aircraft, Soviet, 264, 270

Aircraft, United States carrier: World War I, 14; post–World War I, 17, 19–20, 22, 23, 24; World War II, 39, 63–64, 69, 90, 136, 148, 166, 180–81, 215–16, 218; Korean War, 232–33, 235, 237, 240–41, 242; Vietnam War, 245, 247, 250, 251, 252, 253, 255–56, 259; Cold War, 263, 265, 267, 270, 276; Persian Gulf, 278; Balkans, 279; Afghanistan, 280; Iraq War, 282; current designs, 286–87

Aircraft carrier: first used as a word, 16

Akagi, IJN, 17–18, 47; at Pearl Harbor, 51; at Midway, 89, 91, 94, 95, 97, 98, 99, 100

Akers, Frank, 22

Akiyama, Monzo, 148

Akiyama, Teruo, 137

Alabama (BB-60), 166

Albacore (SS-218), 169

Albion, HMS carrier, 262

Aleutian Islands, 87, 88, 90, 101, 103; operations, 136

Algeria. *See* Operation Torch

Almond, Edward M., 235

Alvarez, Everett: Vietnam War, 247

Amagai, Takahisa: at Midway, 99

Amagi, IJN carrier, 179, 194, 211, 213, 219

Amen, William T.: Korean War, 238

America (CVA-66), 277; Libyan incident, 270–71; Persian Gulf operations, 274–75; Balkans operations, 279

Anaya, Jorge, 267

Anderson, Edward L., 62

Andrea Doria, Italian carrier, 286

Antietam (CV-36), 239, 242

Araki, Sadao, 43

Arashi, IJN destroyer, 97

Archer, HMS escort carrier, 34, 36

Archerfish (SS-11), 213

Argus, HMS carrier, 11, 14, 27, 38

Arima, Masafumi: Leyte campaign, 193, 194

Ark Royal, HMS carrier, 27, 28, 29, 287; at Oran, 29–30; attacks *Bismarck*, 32; sinks, 33

Ark Royal (II), HMS carrier, 281

Armistead, Kirk: at Midway, 93

Arms limitations. *See* Washington Treaty

Arnold, Henry H. "Hap," 69; Okinawa campaign, 224

Arnold, J. D.: Marianas campaign, 171

Arromanches, French carrier, 243; in Vietnam War, 244; Suez Canal, 262

Atago, IJN cruiser, 171; Philippine operations, 196

Atlanta (CA-51), 130

Audacity, HMS escort carrier, 34

Ault, William B., 78

Avenger, HMS escort carrier, 36, 38

Badoeng Strait (CVE-116): Korean campaign, 233, 234, 238

Bainbridge (DLGN-25), 263

Bairoko, HMS carrier, 239

Balkans incident, 279

Bang (SS-385), 169

Barnhart, Robert C., 247

Barton, Paul: Falklands war, 268

Bass, Stewart: Okinawa campaign, 224

Bataan (CV-29): Marianas campaign, 172; as night carrier, 180; Okinawa campaign, 218, 219; Korean War, 239

Bataan (LHD-5): Afghanistan operations, 280; Iraq War, 282

Béarn, French carrier, 243

Bebee, M. U.: Korean War, 242

Belleau Wood (CVL-24), 134; Tarawa campaign, 141, 142; Marshall Islands campaign, 147, 149; Marianas campaign, 165, 172; Leyte campaign, 197, 214; Iwo Jima campaign, 216; Okinawa campaign, 221–23; leased to France

Bellinger, Patrick N. L., 10, 60

Belote, James H., 90

Bennington (CV-20), 180, 215; Iwo Jima campaign, 216; Okinawa campaign, 224; Vietnam War, 245

Best, Richard H.: at Midway, 97

Billingsley, W. D., 9

bin Laden, Osama, 277, 278–80

Birmingham (CL-2), 5, 6, 10, 287

Bismarck, German battleship, 31–32

Bismarck Sea (CVE-95), 217

Biter, HMS escort carrier, 36, 38, 243

Blanchard, James W., 169

Blandy, W. H. P., 185

Blick, Robert E., Jr.: Vietnam War, 244

Bogan, Gerald F.: in Palaus, 182, 183, 185; Leyte campaign, 193, 197, 198, 200, 202, 204, 208, 210, 212, 214; Okinawa campaign, 218

Bois Belleau, French carrier, 244

Bon Homme Richard (CV-31), 180, 215; Korean War, 239; Vietnam War, 255, 257

Bon Homme Richard (LHD-6): Afghanistan operations, 280; Iraq War, 282

Bordelon, Guy P., 241

Bowfin (SS-287), 162

Boxer (CV-21): Korean campaign, 233; Vietnam War, 244

Boxer (LHD-6): Iraq War, 281

Boyd, Sir Denis, 231

Bretagne, French battleship, 29

Brett, James H., 81

Bristol, Mark L., 10

British Pacific Fleet, 220, 231; Okinawa campaign, 221, 225, 227

Brown, George P.: Marianas campaign, 172–73

Brown, Wilson, 60–61, 62; commands *Lexington*, 64, 66, 68–69, 73

Browning, Miles, 88; at Midway, 95

Buckmaster, Elliot: in Coral Sea, 74, 82, 88; at Midway, 99, 100, 102

Buckner, Simon Bolivar, Jr., 221, 224–25

Bulwark, HMS carrier, 262

Bunker Hill (CV-17): strikes Rabaul, 143; at Tarawa, 146; Marshall Islands campaign, 150; Marianas campaign, 165, 167, 171, 172; Leyte campaign, 196; Iwo Jima campaign, 216; Okinawa campaign, 219, 225

Burch, William O.: Coral Sea operations, 75, 81

Burke, Arleigh A., 164, 183; Leyte campaign, 202, 204–5; Iwo Jima campaign, 216; as CNO, 269

Burroughs, Sir Harold M., 38

Bush, George H. W., 272–73

Bush, George W., 277; declares war on terrorism, 280

Cabot (CV-11): Marshall Islands campaign, 150; Marianas campaign, 165, 171, 172; Leyte campaign, 193, 197, 200, 214; Iwo Jima campaign, 216; Okinawa campaign, 219

Caldwell, Henry H.: Rabaul air strike, 138

Callaghan, Daniel J., 130, 131

Canberra (CAG-2), 193

Carl, Marion E.: at Midway, 93

Carlson, Harold G.: Korean War, 239

Carl Vinson (CVAN-70), 269; Afghanistan operations, 277, 280

Carney, Robert B. "Mick," 182; Leyte
   campaign, 197; on Vietnam, 244, 245
Caroline Islands. *See* Palau
Carter, Jimmy, 269
Cavalla (SS-244), 162, 169
Cesare, Italian battleship, 30
Chambers, Washington I.: early naval air
   advocate, 5, 7, 8, 9, 10
Chamoun, Camille, 262
Chapin, F. L., 5
Charger (CVE-30), 36
Chenango (CVE-28), 38; specifications, 134;
   operations in South Pacific, 135
Cheney, Richard, 274
Chester W. Nimitz (CVAN-68): specifications,
   269; Libyan incident, 270; Iraq War, 282
Chevalier, Godfrey, 17
Chiang Kai-shek, 187
Chicago (CA-29), 110
Chichi Jima: air strikes against, 160–61, 182,
   183, 217
Chikuma, IJN cruiser, 125, 127, 138; at Leyte
   Gulf, 209
China: Japanese invasion of, 22, 25, 42;
   Doolittle raid, 70
Chitose, IJN seaplane carrier, 117, 154,
   164, 179; in the Philippines, 194, 207
Chiyoda, IJN seaplane carrier, 154, 164, 172,
   179; in the Philippines, 194, 207
Chokai, IJN cruiser, 131; at Leyte Gulf, 209
Churchill, Winston S.: as First Lord of the
   Admiralty, 11; as prime minister, 25; battle
   of the Atlantic, 27–28, 34; relations with
   Franklin Roosevelt, 25, 38, 68
Chuyo, IJN carrier, 134
Clark, J. J. "Jocko," 215; Marshall Islands
   campaign, 148, 149; Marianas campaign,
   160–61, 163; Palau campaign, 182; strikes
   Iwo Jima, 160–61, 182; Leyte operations,
   207; Iwo Jima operations, 216; on carrier
   tactics, 217; Okinawa campaign, 218, 219,
   223, 224; Korean War, 239
Clinton, William J., 277, 279, 280
Code-breakers. *See* Cryptanalysts
Coffin, Al: at Savo Island, 130–31
Collins, J. Lawton: Korea War, 234
Colossus, HMS carrier, 243
Constellation (CVA-64): Vietnam War, 247,
   254; Iraq War, 281, 282
Coolidge, Calvin, 19
Cooper, D. W.: Vietnam War, 245

Coral Sea, 71–85, 87, 89
Coral Sea (CVB-43), 232, 277; Vietnam War,
   248, 249, 259; Libyan incident, 270–71
Courageous, HMS carrier, 19, 27; sunk, 28
Coward, J. G.: Leyte campaign, 203
Cowpens (CVL-25), 134; Tarawa campaign,
   141, 142; Marshall Islands campaign, 147,
   150; Leyte campaign, 193
Crace, J. G.: Coral Sea operations, 75, 76,
   77, 80
Crickett, H. M., 138
Cruzen, Richard H., 206
Cryptanalysts, 73; regarding Midway, 88, 90;
   regarding South Pacific, 121; regarding
   Guadalcanal, 130; regarding Tarawa, 141;
   regarding Rabaul, 142; regarding the
   Marianas, 160
Cuban crisis, 263
Cunningham, Alfred A., 8
Cunningham, Andrew B., 38; at Taranto,
   30–31
Curtiss, Glenn: naval air innovator, 5, 6, 8, 9

Dace (SS-247), 196
Daniels, Josephus, 10
Darter (SS-227), 196
Dasher, HMS escort carrier, 36, 38
Davis, Arthur C., 109, 177
Davison, Ralph E., 183; in Palaus, 182; Leyte
   campaign, 193, 197, 198, 200, 202, 208,
   212; Luzon campaign, 214; Iwo Jima
   campaign, 216, 218; Okinawa campaign,
   224
Denfield, Louis E., 232
Desert Shield/Desert Storm, 273–76, 278–79
Dewey, George, 9
Dickinson, Clarence: at Midway, 97
Diem, Ngo Dinh, 245
Diselrod, J. E., 254
Dixmude, French carrier, 243; in Vietnam
   War, 244
Dixon, Robert E., 78, 80
Dönitz, Karl, 34, 35
Doolittle, James H. "Jimmy": Tokyo raid,
   69–71, 87
Doorman, Karel, 67–68
Doyle, H. R., 17
Doyle, James H.: Korean War, 238, 239
Draemel, Milo F., 62
Dreadnought, HMS battleship, 4
Dull, Paul S., 41, 49

Dulles, John Foster, 261
Duncan, Donald B., 140
Dunkerque, French battleship, 29–30
Durgin, Calvin T., 217; Okinawa campaign,
   221
Dwight D. Eisenhower (CVAN-69), 269;
   Persian Gulf operations, 273

Eagle, HMS, 232; Suez Canal incident, 262
Eagle, HMS carrier, 27, 30; sunk at Malta, 33
Eastern Solomons: battle of, 113–18, 119
Eggert, Joseph R.: Marianas campaign, 166
Eisenhower, Dwight D., 245, 262
Ellis, Earl H. "Pete," 15, 16, 139
Ellyson, Theodore G.: early test pilot,
   5, 8, 9, 10
Ely, Eugene B.: early test pilot, 5, 6, 7, 9, 287
Enola Gay, AAF B-29, 227
Enterprise ("Big E") (CV-6), 44, 57, 59, 73,
   104, 133, 277; authorized, 22;
   specifications, 23; Pearl Harbor attack, 51,
   53; early operations, 61–62, 63, 64, 67;
   Doolittle raid, 70; at Midway, 88, 95, 96, 97,
   98, 99, 100, 101, 103; at Guadalcanal, 108,
   109, 111; in Eastern Solomons, 113, 114,
   115, 117; at Santa Cruz, 120–21, 122, 123,
   125, 127, 128, 129; operations in the
   Solomons, 130, 131, 132; operations in
   the South Pacific, 135; Tarawa campaign,
   142, 146; Marshall Islands campaign,
   147, 149; Marianas campaign, 155, 160,
   164, 171, 172; as night carrier, 180;
   Leyte campaign, 197; Iwo Jima campaign,
   216, 217; Okinawa campaign, 219,
   224, 225
Enterprise (CVAN-65), xiv, 265, 277, 287;
   specifications, 250; Vietnam War, 253, 259,
   263–64; Cuban crisis, 263; Libyan incident,
   271; Persian Gulf operations, 273, 280
Essex (CV-9, CVA-9), 23, 140, 141, 189;
   specifications, 133–34; strikes Rabaul, 143;
   Marshall Islands campaign, 147, 148, 149;
   Marianas campaign, 167; Leyte campaign,
   192, 197: Iwo Jima campaign, 216;
   Okinawa campaign, 219; Korean War, 239,
   240, 242; Vietnam war, 244; at Lebanon,
   262; Cuban crisis, 263

Fabre, M. Henri, 8
Falkland Islands, 267–68, 285
Fanshaw Bay (CVE-70): at Leyte, 208

Felt, Harry Donald: in Eastern Solomons,
   114–15; Vietnam War, 245
Fenton, Charles R.: Coral Sea operations, 75
Finback (SS-230), 169
Fiske, Bradley A., 9
Fitch, Aubrey W. "Jake," 60, 62, 88;
   commands *Lexington*, 73–74; in Coral Sea,
   75, 76, 78, 79, 80, 82, 84
Five-Power Treaty. *See* Washington Treaty
Flatley, James H.: at Leyte, 203
Fleet Problem XVIII, 177
Fleet Problem XIX, 23,
Fletcher, Frank F., 10
Fletcher, Frank Jack, 62, 69; commands
   Saratoga, 63; commands *Yorktown*, 64, 68,
   74; operations in the Carolines, 64–65, 66;
   at Coral Sea, 75–77, 79–82, 84; at Midway,
   88, 90, 91, 93, 95, 99, 100, 101, 102; in
   South Pacific, 107–9; at Guadalcanal, 111,
   112; in Eastern Solomons, 112, 113, 114,
   115, 117–18; relieved, 118, 120
Flying Fish (SS-229), 162
Formidable, HMS carrier, 31; Okinawa
   campaign, 225
Formosa, 191–92, 194
Forrestal, James V., 177, 231, 232
Forrestal (CVA-59), 242, 277; Vietnam War,
   256–57
Forrestel, Emmet P., 174
Franco, Francisco, 29
Frankfort, German light cruiser, 15
Franklin (CV-13), 180; Leyte operations, 193,
   197, 214, Okinawa campaign, 218, 219
Franks, Tommy, 280
French Morocco. *See* Operation Torch
Fuchida, Mitsuo, 53; at Midway, 91
Fukudome, Shigero: Leyte campaign,
   189, 190, 192, 194, 200, 210; Luzon
   campaign, 214
Furious, HMS carrier, 11, 12, 14, 18, 27;
   operations in Norway, 29; at Malta, 33; at
   Oran, 38
Furutaka, IJN cruiser, 81
Fushimi, Hiroyasu, 43
Fuso, IJN battleship, 203

Gaida, Bruno P., 65
Gallaher, W. E.: at Midway, 97, 100
Galtieri, Leopoldo, 267
Gambier Bay (CVE-73): at Leyte, 206,
   208, 211

Garber, Cecil E.: Vietnam War, 250
Gardner, Matthew B.: Iwo Jima campaign, 216
Garibaldi, Italian carrier, 279
Gay, George H.: at Midway, 96
Genda, Minoru: at Midway, 95; at Santa Cruz, 122
Gensoul, Marcel Bruno, 29
George H. W. Bush (CVN-77), 286
George Washington (CVN-73), 277, 283
Ghormley, Robert L., 107, 109, 112, 113, 119; relieved, 120
Giap, Vo Nguyen, 243, 249, 254
Giffen, Robert C. "Ike," 135
Gilbert Islands: strategy, 138, 140; occupied, 145
Ginder, Samuel P., 163; Marshall Islands campaign, 150–52; Marianas campaign, 154
Giuseppe Garibaldi, Italian carrier, 265
Glenn Curtiss Aviation Center, 5
Glorious, HMS carrier, 27; sunk, 29
Gneisenau, German battlecruiser, 29
Goebbels, Josef, 28
Gorbachev, Mikhail, 272
Goto, Aritomo: in Coral Sea, 73, 76–78, 79
Gray, George, 3
Great White Fleet, 4
Grenada incident, 271–72
Grew, Joseph C., 44
Griffin, Virgil C., 17
Guadalcanal, 107, 109, 111–12, 119, 132
Guadalcanal (LPH-7), 271
Guam, 54; attacked, 59. *See also* Mariana Islands
Guam (LPH-9): Grenada incident, 271

Haguro, IJN cruiser, 169–70
Halsey, William F. "Bull," Jr., 75, 107, 229, 258; background, 60, 61; commands *Enterprise*, 63, 64; early operations, 64–65, 66, 67, 68, 73; Doolittle raid, 70–71; falls ill, 88; commands South Pacific Fleet, 120, 133; Santa Cruz operation, 121, 122, 129; on Guadalcanal operations, 130, 132; use of escort carriers, 135; Solomons campaign, 136, 137, 139, 144; strikes Rabaul, 138, 142, 144; island-hopping strategy, 149; two-platoon system, 181–82; commands Third Fleet, 182; relations with Mitscher, 183, 189, 201, 202, 203, 204–5, 212, 228; strikes Philippine airfields, 183–84; regarding Philippine strategy, 184–85; Leyte

campaign, 189, 190, 192–93, 194, 195, 196, 197, 198, 199–200, 201, 202–5, 207–8, 210, 211, 214; regarding TF-34, 201, 206, 207, 208; on kamikazes, 214; on tactics, 228; typhoon disaster, 215, 226; Okinawa campaign, 225–26; Home Islands campaign, 226–27; retires, 231
Hamilton, Weldon L., 78
Hammann (DD-412), 102
Hancock (CV-19, CVA-19), 180, 215; Iwo Jima campaign, 216; Okinawa campaign, 219; 224; Vietnam War, 245, 248, 249, 253, 254, 259
Hara, Chuichi, 153
Hara, Tadaichi: operations in Coral Sea, 73, 76, 77, 79–82; in Eastern Solomons, 112, 114
Harawa, IJN battleship, 154
Harding, Warren, 16
Hardison, Osborne B.: at Santa Cruz, 127, 129; in the Solomons, 130
Harmer, R. E.: at Marianas, 155, 160
Harrill, William K.: Marianas campaign, 160–61, 163
Harris, John R.: Vietnam War, 255
Harry S. Truman, (CVN-75), 277; Iraq War, 281, 283
Haruna, IJN battleship: at Midway, 94, 95; Leyte Gulf, 208
Harwood, B. L.: at Eastern Solomons, 115
Heermann (DD-532): at Leyte Gulf, 209
Helfrich, Conrad E. L., 68
Heller, Roger, 20
Henderson, George: Korean War, 239
Henderson, Lofton: at Midway, 94
Hendrix, Henry J., 278
Henley (DD-391), 77
Hermes, HMS carrier, 11, 16, 27, 269, 287; Falklands war, 268
Hessler, William H, xiii
Hester, John H., 137
Hewitt, H. Kent, 38
Hiei, IJN battleship, 112, 130–31, 132
Hiroshima, 227
Hiryu, IJN carrier, 52, 54; at Midway, 89, 91, 93, 94, 96, 97, 98, 99, 100, 101
Hitler, Adolf, 29, 49
Hiyo, IJN carrier, 120, 122, 179; operations in the Solomons, 130, 131; in Central Pacific, 154, 172–73, 174, 178
Hoel (DD-533), 209

Holden, R. F., 155; at Marianas, 160
Holland, Cedric S., 29
Holland, Lancelot E., 31
Holloway, James L., 265; at Lebanon, 262
Honolulu. *See* Pearl Harbor
Honshu, air attacks, 226–27
Hood, HMS battlecruiser, 31
Hornet (CV-8), 73, 104; specifications, 26;
    Tokyo raid, 69–70; at Midway, 88, 95, 96,
    98, 99, 100, 101, 103; in South Pacific, 112,
    118, 119, 120; at Santa Cruz, 121, 123,
    126–27; sunk, 125, 128–29
Hornet (CV-12): Marianas campaign, 161,
    165, 171, 172, 173; Iwo Jima campaign, 216
Hosho, IJN carrier, 13, 16, 47, 101
Hosogaya, Boshiro, 88: Aleutians campaign,
    136
Houston (CA-30), 193
Hoyt, Edwin P., 163
Hull, Cordell, 26, 54
Hussein, Saddam, 273; Iraq War, 281, 282
Hyuga, IJN half-battleship, 179, 213; in the
    Philippines, 194, 207

I-15, IJN submarine, 119
I-19, IJN submarine, 119
I-22, IJN submarine, 130
I-26, IJN submarine, 118
I-168, IJN submarine, 102
I-175, IJN submarine, 146
Ibuki, IJN carrier, 179
Illustrious, HMS carrier, 30, 40; damaged in
    Mediterranean, 31; Okinawa campaign,
    220, 225
Inchon, 234–35
Inchon (LPH-12), 279
Indefatigable, HMS carrier: Okinawa
    campaign, 221
Independence (CVA-62), 277; Vietnam War,
    250, 251, 255; Cuban crisis, 263; Cold War,
    265; Persian Gulf operations, 273
Independence (CVL-22), 140, 141, 150, 189;
    specifications, 134; strikes Rabaul, 143; at
    Tarawa, 146; as night carrier, 180; Leyte
    Campaign, 197, 205, 210, 212; Okinawa
    campaign, 219; at Bikini Atoll, 232
Indiana (BB-1), 14; (BB-58), 167
Indianapolis (CA-35): Marshall Islands
    campaign, 150
Indomitable, HMS carrier: at Malta, 33;
    Okinawa campaign, 220, 221

Ingalls, David S., 14
Ingersoll, Royal E., 36
Inouye, Shigeyoshi: MO Operation, 73, 76,
    77, 79
Intrepid (CV-11): Marshall Islands campaign,
    150,153; Leyte campaign, 197, 214;
    Okinawa campaign, 218, 219, 224; Vietnam
    War, 253
Invincible, HMS carrier, 268, 268
Iraq War, 281–83
Irvine, Charles B.: Santa Cruz operations, 123
Ise, IJN half-battleship, 179, 213; in the
    Philippines, 194, 207
Isuzu, IJN cruiser, 131, 148
Iwo Jima: air strikes against, 160–61, 182,
    183; campaign, 215, 216, 217
Iwo Jima (LPH-2), 271
Izawa, Ishinosuke, 78

Japan: invades Manchuria, 20; invades China,
    22; invades French Indochina, 26
Jin, Kobayashi, 153
John C. Stennis (CVN-74), 277; Afghanistan
    operations, 280
John F. Kennedy (CV-62): Persian Gulf
    Operations, 274, 275
Johnson, Louis A., 232, 286
Johnson, Lyndon B.: Vietnam War, 247,
    248–49, 252, 253, 254, 255, 257, 258, 259
Johnston, Stanley, 84
Johnston (DD-557), at Leyte Gulf, 208
Johnstone, Ralph, 5
Joy, C. Turner: Korean War, 237
Juneau (CA-52), 130
Junyo, IJN carrier, 88, 101, 104, 179, 213; at
    Santa Cruz, 120, 122, 125, 127, 128; at
    Guadalcanal, 130; in Central Pacific, 154,
    172; in the Philippines, 194
Jupiter, collier, 16, 17
Jyo, Eiichiro, 179

Kaga, IJN, 17–18, 47; at Midway, 89, 91, 97,
    98, 99, 100
Kaiser, Henry J.: on escort carriers, 71
Kakuta, Kakuji, 101; at Santa Cruz, 128; at
    Marianas, 160, 161, 163, 165, 171, 172
Kalinin Bay (CVE-68), 208
Kamikaze (also Kamikaze Corps), 41, 180,
    195, 203, 213, 215, 228; at Leyte Gulf, 209,
    214; Iwo Jima operations, 217; Okinawa
    campaign, 219, 221, 223, 224, 225, 226, 227

Kanawaha (AO-1), 24
Kanno, Kenzo, 80
Kansas (BB-21), 4
Kato, Tadao, 115
Katsuragi, IJN carrier, 179, 211, 213
Kearney (DD-432), 35
Kearsarge (LPD-3): Balkans operations, 279
Kelso, Frank B.: Libyan incident, 270–71
Kennedy, John F., 257; Cuban crisis, 263
Kenny, George C., 138, 155, 189; Leyte
    campaign, 193, 214
Khrushchev, Nikita: Cuban crisis, 263
Kiev-class Russian carriers, 263–64
Kimmel, Husband E., 50, 60; Pearl Harbor
    attack, 53–54, 61, 62, 63; replaced, 57–58
King, Earnest J., 38, 50; background, 57, 58,
    200; relations with Nimitz, 59, 63, 66; on
    Pacific communications, 64; efforts to go on
    the offensive, 69, 107; increases navy
    appropriation, 71; opinion of Fletcher, 74–
    75, 79, 118; on Royal Navy, 135, 220; on
    fleet commanders, 149, 177; on fast carriers,
    178; on night carriers, 180; two-platoon
    system, 181–82, 215; regarding Leyte
    operations, 207, 211; opinion of Halsey,
    212; on kamikazes, 214; Iwo Jima
    campaign, 216; Okinawa campaign, 219;
    retires, 231
King George V, HMS battleship, 31, 32
Kinkaid, Thomas C., 62; in Coral Sea, 84; in
    Eastern Solomons, 109, 114, 117; at Santa
    Cruz, 121, 122, 127, 128, 129; in the
    Solomons, 130, 132, 133; commands North
    Pacific Force, 136; commands Seventh
    Fleet, 185, 189; Leyte operations, 194, 195,
    198–99, 201, 202, 203, 205–7, 208, 209,
    211, 212, 214; regarding TF-34, 201, 206,
    207, 208
Kinugasa, IJN cruiser, 81, 131
Kirishima, IJN battleship, 112, 125, 131, 132
Kitkun Bay (CVE-71): at Leyte, 206, 208
Kitty Hawk (CVA-63), 265; Vietnam War,
    250, 253, 257; Afghanistan operations, 278;
    Iraq War, 281, 282
Kivette, Frederick N.: Vietnam War, 245
Knox, Frank, 71, 178
Koga, Mineichi, 138, 139; replaces
    Yamamoto, 136, 137; operations in South
    Pacific, 142, 143, 144, 145, 146; operations
    in Central Pacific, 153, 154, 157, 158;
    killed, 155, 156

Komura, Keozo, 213
Kondo, Nobutake: at Midway, 90, 91, 93, 94,
    101; in Eastern Solomons, 112, 113, 117; at
    Santa Cruz, 122, 125; operations in the
    Solomons, 130, 131, 132
Kongo, IJN battleship, 154; at Leyte Gulf, 208
Konoye, Fuminaro, 26, 49
Korean War, 232–41
Kosler, Herman J., 169
Kroeger, Edward J.: at Midway, 97
Kurita, Takeo, 142, 285; in East Indies, 68;
    Solomons campaign, 137, 138; Philippines
    campaign, 187; Leyte operations, 194, 195,
    196, 197, 198, 200, 201–2, 203, 206, 208,
    209–10, 211, 212
Kurusu, Saburo, 26
Kusaka, Ryunosuke, 87, 223
Kyushu, air attacks, 218–19, 221, 226

LaFayette, French carrier, 244; Suez Canal
    incident, 262
Langley (CV-1), 16, 17, 21, 22, 149, 177, 283,
    287; sunk, 68
Langley (CVL-28): Marshall Islands
    campaign, 150; Leyte campaign, 197; Iwo
    Jima campaign, 216; Okinawa campaign,
    224; leased to France, 243
League of Nations, 43
Leahy, William D., 36
Leary, Herbert F., 64, 66
Lebanese crisis, 262
Lee, James R.: Santa Cruz operations,
    122–23, 127
Lee, Willis A.: commands battle group, 121,
    181, 212; at Santa Cruz, 122; in the
    Solomons, 130, 132; New Guinea
    campaign, 155; Marianas campaign, 164,
    166, 167
Lehman, John F., 269–70, 271
LeMay, Curtis, 225
Lend-Lease Act, 27, 35
Leslie, Max: at Midway, 97, 98; at Eastern
    Solomons, 117
Lexington "Lady Lex" (CV-2), xiv, 22, 57,
    177, 287; authorized, 17–18; construction
    of, 19–20; Pearl Harbor attack, 51, 53, 60,
    61, 62; early operations, 63, 64, 66; Lae and
    Salamaua strike, 68–69; in Coral Sea,
    73–75, 76, 78–82; scuttled, 84, 86
Lexington (CV-16, CVA-16), 134, 150;
    Tarawa campaign, 141, 142; Marshall

Lexington (*continued*)
  Islands campaign 147, 148, 149; Marianas
  campaign, 154, 166, 167, 171, 172, 173;
  Leyte campaign, 197, 201, 214; Iwo Jima
  campaign, 216; Vietnam War, 245
Leyte (also Leyte Gulf), 285; preliminaries,
  185, 189, 193, 194–98; operations,
  199–203, 202–11, 214
Leyte (CV-32): Korean War, 235, 237, 238,
  239; Vietnam War, 245
Lindbergh, Charles, 20
Lindsey, Eugene E.: at Midway, 96
Lindsey, Robin M.: at Santa Cruz, 128
Liscombe Bay (CVE-16), 146
Lockwood, Charles A., 169
London Conference: arms limitations, 22, 42, 43
Long Beach (CGN-9), 263
Long Island (CVE-1), 36, 112, 113
Louisiana (BB-19), 5
Low, Francis S., 69
Lunga Point (CVE-94), 217
Lütjens, Gunther, 31–32
Lynch, J. J.: at Santa Cruz, 125

MacArthur, Douglas, 68, 75, 158, 179;
  commands Southwest Pacific Area, 107;
  New Guinea campaign, 136, 137, 142, 144,
  155; Philippine strategy, 159, 183, 184–85;
  Leyte campaign, 193–94, 195, 198, 201,
  202, 209, 210, 211, 214; as Supreme
  Commander, 231; Korean War, 233, 234,
  235; relieved, 239
Maddox (DD-731): Vietnam War, 245, 247
Mahan, Alfred Thayer, 42
Makin Islands (CVE-93), 218
Manchuria: Japanese invasion of, 20, 22, 42
Mariana Islands: strategy, 145, 149, 153, 159;
  campaign, 158–74, 177; "Turkey Shoot,"
  165–68; Philippine Sea engagement, 170–
  74, 185
Marshall, George C., 54, 261
Marshall Islands: strategy, 140, 145, 146;
  campaign, 150–53
Marumo, K., 77
Maryland (BB-460): Okinawa campaign, 224
Mason, Charles P.: at Santa Cruz, 125,
  128, 129
Massey, Lem: at Midway, 96, 98
Masuda, Shogo: at Midway, 91; in the
  Philippines, 194
Matsuda, Chiaki, 179

McCain, John S., 107, 113, 117, 163, 181;
  Palau campaign, 182, 183; on Philippine
  strategy, 185, 187, 189, 228; Leyte
  campaign, 193, 196, 197, 207, 210, 212,
  214; kamikaze strikes, 215; Okinawa
  campaign, 226; Home Islands
  campaign, 227
McCampbell, David: Marianas campaign,
  167; Philippine air strikes, 184; Formosa air
  strikes, 190; Leyte campaign, 197, 207
McClusky, Wade: at Midway, 97, 98
McConnell, R. P., 68
McDonnell, E. O., 14
McNamara, Robert S.: Vietnam War, 247,
  248, 249, 250, 252, 253, 254, 255, 257, 258;
  Cold War, 263
McWorter, E. D., 37
Megee, Vernon E., 216
Metcalf, Joseph, Jr.: Grenada incident, 271
Meyer, George, 4–5, 8
Michigan (BB-27), 4
Midway, 70, 73, 86, 87–88, 89; defenses, 90;
  attacked, 93; influence on war, 107
Midway (CVA-41): Vietnam War, 245, 249,
  259; Persian Gulf operations, 274
Mikawa, Gunichi: defense of the Solomons,
  111, 131, 132
Mikuma, IJN cruiser, 101
Miller, Frank B.: Vietnam War, 245, 247,
  250, 252
Milosevic, Slobodan, 279
Minh, Ho Chi: establishes Vietnam, 243, 245;
  Vietnam War, 252
Minneapolis (CA-36), 84, 167
Minnesota (BB-22), 4
Mississippi (BB-23), 10
Missouri (BB-63), 227, 243
Mistral, French carrier, 285
Mitchell, William "Billy," 14–15
Mitscher, Marc A., 227; commands *Hornet*,
  26, 73, 155; Tokyo raid, 69–71; at Midway,
  88; search for Yamamoto, 135; Solomons
  campaign, 136; fleet command, 149;
  Marshall Islands campaign, 150, 152–53;
  Marianas campaign, 154–55, 156, 157–58,
  159–60, 162, 163, 164–67, 168, 177;
  Philippine Sea, 170, 171, 172, 173; opinion
  of Spruance, 174, 178, 228; two-platoon
  system, 181–82; Palau campaign, 182;
  relations with Halsey, 183, 189, 201, 202,
  203, 204–5, 212; Formosa strikes, 190–91,

192; Leyte campaign, 189, 191, 196, 201,
202, 203, 204, 205, 207, 208; on kamikazes,
214; Iwo Jima campaign, 215, 216, 217;
Okinawa campaign, 218–19, 221, 223–24,
225; on tactics, 228; dies, 231
Miura, Kanzo, 161
Moffet, William A., 16
Mogami, IJN cruiser, 101, 138, 139
Monterey (CVL-26), 134; Tarawa campaign,
142; Marshall Islands campaign, 150
Montgomery, Alfred E., 140, 163; strikes
Wake Island, 141, 145; strikes Rabaul, 143,
144; Marshall Islands campaign, 147, 149,
150, 151; Marianas campaign, 154, 165,
172, 177; Palau campaign, 182; relations
with Halsey, 183
MO Operation. *See* Port Moresby
Moore, Carl, 177
Moore, J. H., 249
Moosbrugger, Frederick, 137
Morishita, Nobuei: at Leyte Gulf, 208–9
Morison, Samuel Eliot, xiv, 45, 59, 66, 76
Morris, Steve: Falklands war, 268
Mullinix, Henry, 146
Murphy, Daniel, 267
Murray, George D., 181; commands
Enterprise, 88; commands *Hornet*,
121, 128
Musashi, IJN superbattleship, 153, 154; in the
Philippines, 195, 201
Mustin, Henry C., 10
Myoko, IJN cruiser, 201

Nagano, Osami, 47; on Japanese strategy, 48;
on the Solomons, 112; on carrier losses,
178, 179
Nagasaki, 227
Nagato, IJN battleship, 154; at Leyte Gulf,
203, 208, 210
Nagumo, Chuichi, 26, 46, 63, 71, 158;
background, 50; attacks Pearl Harbor,
50–54; captures Rabaul, 64; at Midway, 89,
90, 91, 93–97, 98–99, 100–101, 103; in
Eastern Solomons, 114, 115, 117–18, 119;
at Santa Cruz, 120, 122, 123, 125, 127, 128;
recalled, 129
Nakajima, Tadashi, 110, 111
Nassau (CVE-16), 136
Nassau (LHA-4): Persian Gulf operations,
278; Balkans operations, 279; Iraq War,
281, 282

Nasser, Gamal Abdel, 262
Nathman, John B., 278; Iraq War, 282
Nautilus (SSN-571): at Midway, 95, 99
Naval (Expansion) Act: of 1916, 10; of 1938,
23; of 1940, 25
Naval War College, 16
Navarre, Henri, 244
Navy Aviation Corps, 9
Nebraska (BB-14), 4
Neches (AO-5), 63
Nelson, R. S.: Marianas campaign, 171
Neosho (AO-23): Coral Sea operation,
77, 78, 79
Neutrality Act of 1939, 24
New Guinea, 68, 73, 144; campaign, 136–37,
142, 155
New Jersey (BB-62), 201
Newton, John H., 60–61
Newton, Wesley, 9
Nimitz, Chester W.: background, 58–59, 133;
relations with King, 59, 66, 67, 107;
commands Pacific Fleet, 59, 60, 63; testing
carrier commanders, 66, 68, 69, 149; orders
Halsey to Coral Sea, 71; opinion of Fletcher,
74–75, 84, 118; involvement with Midway,
88, 90, 91, 103; commands Pacific Ocean
Area, 107; regarding Guadalcanal, 109, 112,
119, 130; on command problems, 129, 135,
149; regard for Royal Navy, 135; search for
Yamamoto, 131, 135; Solomons campaign,
136; Gilbert Islands (Tarawa) campaign,
138, 139, 140, 141–42; island-hopping
strategy, 145, 150, 159, 228; promotes
Mitscher, 150, 153; Mariana Islands
campaign, 158, 160, 163, 169, 174; opinion
of Spruance, 174; fast carrier policy, 178;
two-platoon system, 181–82, 183, 215;
regarding Iwo Jima, 182, 185; opinion
on Philippine assault, 184–85, 189, 195;
regarding Leyte operations, 207, 208,
214; Iwo Jima campaign, 216; Okinawa
campaign, 221, 224–25, 226; replaces
King as CNO, 231
Nishimura, Shoji: Leyte campaign, 187, 195,
197, 198, 201, 202–3, 205, 211
Nomura, Kichisaburo, 26
Norfolk, HMS cruiser, 31
Norris, Benjamin W.: at Midway, 94
Northampton, (CA-26), 128
North Carolina (ACR-12), 10
North Carolina (BB-55), 108, 117, 119

Noshiro, IJN cruiser, 210
Noyes, Leigh, 109, 110, 114, 119

Obayashi, Suemo: Philippine Sea operations,
   161, 164, 167
Ocean, HMS carrier: Suez Canal incident, 262
Office of Aeronautics, 9
Ofstie, Ralph A.: Korean War, 239
Ogier, Herbert L., 247
O'Grady, Scott: Balkans operations, 279
O'Hare, Edward H. "Butch": at Rabaul, 66; at
   Tarawa, 146
Okinawa: air strikes, 215; campaign, 218–19,
   221, 223–26
Okinawa (LPH-3), 271
Oldendorf, Jesse B.: Leyte campaign, 198,
   201, 202–3, 205, 206, 210
Omar, Mohammad, 280
Omark, Warren R.: Marianas campaign, 173
Onishi, Takajiro, 179–80; Leyte campaign,
   189, 194, 195, 200, 209, 210; forms
   Kamikaze Corps, 214
Operation A-Go, 157, 158, 160, 161
Operation Flintlock. *See* Marshall Islands
Operation Forager. *See* Mariana Islands
Operation Galvanic. *See* Tarawa Atoll
Operation Ten-Go, 221, 223
Operation Torch, 38–39
Operation Watchtower. *See* Guadalcanal
Oriskany (CVA-34), 249
Ostfriesland, German battleship, 15
Outlaw, Edward C.: Vietnam War, 249, 250
Owsley, Frank, 9
Ozawa, Jisaburo, 178, 185; commands First
   Mobile Fleet, 158, 159; launches Operation
   A-Go, 160, 161, 162, 163; in the Philippine
   Sea, 164–65, 167, 168, 169, 170–71, 172;
   rebuilding carrier force, 177, 179; on
   kamikazes, 180; Leyte operations, 187, 189,
   191, 194, 195–96, 201, 202, 204, 205, 207,
   208, 210, 211, 212

Pago Pago, Samoa: shelled by Japanese, 64
Palau, 182
Palmer, Frederick F.: Vietnam War, 254
Panama Canal: naval exercises, 20
Panay (PR-5), river gunboat, 44
Parks, Floyd: at Midway, 93
Pearl Harbor, 26, 35, 43, 50; attacked, 51, 52,
   53–54, 58; aftermath of attack, 60
Pegasus, HMS, 13

Peleliu (LHA-5), 279; Afghanistan operations,
   278, 280
Pennoyer, Frederick W., 17
Pennsylvania (ACR-4), 6, 7, 8
Perry, John: Korean War, 240
Perry, Matthew C., 41, 175, 182
Petrof Bay (CVE-80): at Leyte Gulf, 209
Phelps (DD-360), 84
Philippines, 26, 49; as Japanese target, 53;
   attacked, 59; surrendered, 68, 73; plans to
   recapture, 184–85, 228. *See also* Leyte
Philippine Sea. *See* Mariana Islands
Philippine Sea (CV-46): Korean campaign,
   233, 237, 239
Phillips, J. S., 77
Phillips, John L.: at Tarawa, 146
Phillips, William K., 244
Plan Orange, 15, 16, 43, 50; applied to war in
   the Pacific, 139
Pond, Charles F., 7
Port Moresby, New Guinea, 110; shelled by
   Japanese, 68; MO Operation, 73, 75, 76–77,
   79, 84
Potter, Stephen, 13
Pound, Sir Dudley, 135
Power, M. L.: Suez Canal incident, 262
Pownall, Charles, A.: Tarawa campaign, 140,
   141, 142, 144, 145; Marshall Islands
   campaign, 146–47, 148, 149, 150
Prince of Wales, HMS battleship, 31
Prince of Wales, HMS carrier, 285
Princeton (CVL-23), 134, 138; strikes Rabaul,
   143; Marshall Islands campaign, 150;
   Marianas campaign, 161; Leyte campaign,
   197, 201, 211
Princeton (CV-37): Korean War, 232, 239, 241
Principe de Asturias, Spanish carrier, 265
Prinz Eugen, German cruiser, 31
Pusan, 233, 234
Pye, William S., 63

Qadaffi, Muammar, 269–70
Queen Elizabeth, HMS carrier, 285
Quincy (CA-71), 108

Rabaul, 64; as Japanese base, 66, 68, 73, 109,
   111, 119; MO Operation, 75, 76; air strikes
   against, 138–39, 142, 143, 144; elimination
   of; 149
Radford, Arthur W., 163; Tarawa campaign,
   140, 146; Iwo Jima campaign, 216; on

carrier tactics, 217; Okinawa campaign, 219, 224

Rainbow exercises, 50, 54

Ramsey, DeWitt C., 109: commands *Saratoga*, 133

Randolph (CV-15), 180, 215, 217; Iwo Jima campaign, 216; as CVS-15, 262

Ranger (CV-4), 20, 26, 57, 104; specifications, 22; operations in Atlantic, 25, 36, 38, 39

Ranger (CVA-61), 277; Vietnam War, 248, 253, 254, 255, 258; Persian Gulf operations, 274; Somalian operations, 279

Rawlings, Sir H. Bernard: Okinawa operations, 221

Reagan, Ronald, 259, 272, 277; Libyan incident, 270; Grenada incident, 271

Redfin (SS-272), 162

Reedy, James R.: Vietnam War, 250, 253, 255

Reeves, John W.: Marshall Islands campaign, 150–51; Marianas campaign, 154, 155

Reeves, Joseph, 17

Reid, Jack, 91

Renown, HMS battleship, 32

Repulse, HMS battleship, 31

Reuben Jones (DD-245), 35

Reynolds, Clark, 224

Reynolds, F. J.: Korean War, 242

Rice, L. K., 232

Richardson, James O., 50

Ridgeway, Matthew B.: Korean War, 239–40

Ring, Stanhope C.: at Midway, 96

Robbins, Hugh A., 6

Robin, Douglas B., 14

Robinson, Robert G., 14

Rochefort, Joseph: on Midway campaign, 88, 90

Rockets, 216, 217, 241, 254, 259, 274

Rodney, HMS battleship, 32

Ronald Reagan (CVN-76), 286, 287

Roosevelt, Franklin D., 87, 220, 243; as Assistant Secretary of the Navy, 17; National Industrial Recovery Act, 20, 22; on neutrality, 24, 44; expands navy, 25; Japanese embargo, 26, 48; negotiations with Japan, 26; relations with Churchill, 25, 38, 68; on Doolittle raid, 71; advocates more carriers, 71; regarding Philippines, 184–85; death of, 224

Roosevelt, Theodore, 42; on naval power, 3–4

Rowell, Ross E., 20

Rupertus, William H.: regarding Peleliu, 184

Rushing, Roy W.: Leyte campaign, 197

Ryan, John Barry, 5

Ryuho, IJN carrier, 134, 154

Ryujo, IJN carrier, 88, 101, 179, 213; in Eastern Solomons, 112, 114, 115, 117, 118; in Philippine Sea, 172; Philippine campaign, 194; Okinawa campaign, 219

St. Lo (CVE-63), 208, 209, 211

Saipan. *See* Mariana Islands

Saipan (CVL-48), 244

Saipan (LHA-2): Iraq War, 281

Sakai, Saburo, 110, 111

Samejima, Tomoshige, 137, 138, 142, 143

Samuel B. Roberts (DE-413): at Leyte Gulf, 209

Sangamon (CVE-26), 36, 38

San Jacinto (CVL-30): Leyte campaign, 197; Iwo Jima campaign, 216; Okinawa campaign, 219

Santa Cruz: battle of, 121–29

Santee (CVE-29), 38

Saratoga (CV-3), xiv, 22, 23, 47, 51, 57, 59, 73, 90, 104, 120, 133, 177, 287; authorized, 17–18; construction of, 19–20; experiments with, 24; early operations, 63, 64; at Guadalcanal, 108, 109, 111; in Eastern Solomons, 113, 114, 115, 117; operations in South Pacific, 133, 135, 220; Solomons campaign, 137, 138; strikes Rabaul, 143; Iwo Jima campaign, 216, 217; at Bikini Atoll, 232

Saratoga (CVA-60), 277; at Lebanon, 262; Libyan incident, 270; Persian Gulf Operations, 274, 275

Sasaki, Seigo, 117

Saufley, Richard C., 10

Savo Island: naval battle, 111

Scharnhorst, German battlecruiser, 29

Seki, Mamoru: at Santa Cruz, 123–24

Shangri-La (CV-38), 180, 215; Vietnam War, 245

Shark (SS-314), 141

Sharp, Ulysses S. G.: Vietnam War, 249, 250, 252, 254, 257

Sheffield, HMS light cruiser, 32

Sherman, Forrest P.: commands *Wasp*, 109, 119; as aid to Nimitz, 149; Korean campaign, 234

Sherman, Frederick C. "Ted," 231; commands *Lexington*, 69, 163; in Coral Sea, 74, 78, 82,

Sherman (*continued*)
   84; commands *Enterprise*, 133; Rabaul
   strikes, 138–39, 142, 143–44; Marshall
   Islands campaign, 150–52, 153, 174; Palau
   campaign, 182, 183, 185; Leyte campaign,
   193, 196, 197, 198, 200, 201, 202, 204,
   208, 212, 214; Iwo Jima campaign, 216;
   Okinawa campaign, 219, 224; on tactics, 228
Shima, Kiyohide: Philippines campaign, 187,
   193, 195, 196, 201, 202, 203, 211
Shimada, Shigetare, 157
Shimazaki, Shigekazu, 79
Shinano, IJN supercarrier, 179, 213
Shoho, IJN carrier, 55; in Coral Sea, 73, 76, 77;
   sunk, 78, 79, 82
Shokaku, IJN carrier, 87, 89, 103, 104,142; in
   Coral Sea, 73, 76, 79, 80–82, 86; damaged,
   82; at Eastern Solomons, 112, 114, 115,
   117; at Santa Cruz, 120, 122, 123, 125, 127,
   129; in Central Pacific, 154; in the
   Philippine Sea, 165, 169, 172, 174, 178, 185
SHO-Plan, 191, 194, 201, 202, 211
Sicily (CVE-118): Korean campaign, 233, 234,
   238, 240
Sims, Charles A.: Marianas campaign, 167
Sims, William S., 1
Sims (DD-409): Coral Sea operations, 77,
   78, 79
Skon, Warren: Tarawa campaign, 146
Smith, Holland M.: Tarawa campaign, 142
Smith, Homer: Vietnam War, 255
Smith, Joseph G., 80, 81
Snowden, Ernest M.: Marshalls campaign,
   147–48
Sommerville, James, 32, 33
Soryu, IJN carrier, 52, 54, 89; at Midway, 91,
   94, 97, 98, 99, 100
South Dakota (BB-57), 121, 132, 167
Sprague, Clifton A. F.: at Leyte, 206, 208
Sprague, Thomas L.: at Leyte, 189, 195, 202,
   206–7, 209, 214; Okinawa operations, 218
Spruance, Raymond A., 62, 185, 199–200,
   212; at Midway, 88, 90, 91, 93, 95–96, 101,
   102, 104; as Nimitz's chief of staff, 107;
   commands Fifth Fleet, 140; Tarawa
   campaign, 142, 143, 146, 144; fast carrier
   policy; 145–46, 174, 177–78; Marshall
   Islands campaign, 150; Marianas campaign,
   157, 158, 160, 163, 164, 165, 168, 170, 171,
   173, 174, 177; two-platoon system, 181–82;
   Iwo Jima campaign, 214, 216, 217;

Okinawa campaign, 217, 219, 224, 225,
   226; heads Naval War College, 231
Stark, Harold R., 24, 26, 35; on two-ocean
   navy, 25; as CNO, 38, 50, 57
Stather, Richard A.: Vietnam War, 247
Sterling, collier, 9
Stetson, Thomas H., 224
Stingray (SS-186), 169
Strasbourg, French battleship, 30
Strean, B. M.: Marianas campaign, 171, 172
Strong, Stockton: at Santa Cruz, 123
Struble, Arthur D., 232; Korean War, 235–37,
   238, 239
Submarines. *See specific designations*
Suez Canal incident, 262
Suffolk, HMS cruiser, 31
Sullivan, John, 232
Suwanee (CVE-27), 38; specifications, 134;
   operations in the South pacific, 135; Leyte
   campaign, 214

Taft, William Howard, 4
Taiho, IJN carrier, 154, 178–79; in the
   Philippine Sea, 165, 167, 169, 170,
   172, 174
Taiwan. *See* Formosa
Takagi, Takeo, 73, 94; in Coral Sea, 75, 76–78,
   79–82, 84
Talbot, Ralph, 14
Tambor (SS-198), 101
Tanabe, Yahachi: at Midway, 102, 103
Tanaka, Raizo, 112, 131, 132
Taranto, Italy: operations against, 30–31, 35
Tarawa (LHA-1): in Persian Gulf, 278; Iraq
   War, 281
Tarawa Atoll: campaign against, 140, 142,
   145–46
Taylor, Joseph: Coral Sea operations, 75, 81
Taylor, Montgomery M., 15
Teraoka, Kimpei: Leyte campaign, 194
Texas (BB-35), 14
Thach, James: at Midway, 96, 99, 100
Thatcher, Margaret, 273
Theobold, Robert A., 90
Theodore Roosevelt (CVN-71): Persian Gulf
   operations, 274; Balkans operations, 279;
   Iraq War, 281–82
Theseus, HMS carrier: Korean War, 234, 239;
   at Suez Canal, 262
Thetis Bay (CVHA-1): Vietnam War, 245
Thomas, Harry: Vietnam War, 253

Ticonderoga (CV-14, CVA-14), 180, 215;
   Vietnam War, 245, 247, 253
Tillar, Thomas C., 184
Tirpitz, Alfred von, 4
Tojo, Hideki, 26, 48, 71, 103; on Guadalcanal,
   119; removed, 178; on defeat, 227–28
Tokyo, air strikes, 70–71, 217, 226–27
Tomonaga, Joichi: at Midway, 91, 93, 94,
   95, 100
Tone, IJN cruiser: at Midway, 91, 94, 95; at
   Santa Cruz, 127
Tonkin Gulf incident, 245, 247
Torliss, A. D., 232
Tovey, Sir John Cronyn, 31
Towers, John H.: as early aviator, 9, 10; as
   Nimitz advisor, 139–40, 141, 149, 182, 231
Toyoda, Soemu: commands Japanese fleet,
   158, 213; Operation A-Go, 158, 160, 172;
   rebuilding carrier force, 179; Philippines/
   Leyte/SHO-1 campaign, 187, 190, 191–92,
   193, 194, 195, 201, 202, 211, 212
Tracker, HMS escort carrier, 36
Triad hydroplane, 8–9
Triumph, HMS carrier: Korean War, 232, 233,
   234, 238, 239
Trost, Carlisle A. H., 273
Troubridge, Sir Thomas, 38
Truk, 73; strategy to eliminate, 149, 153, 155
Truman, Harry S., 224, 232; Korean War, 233,
   239, 240; Cold War, 261
Turner, Richmond K.: at Guadalcanal, 109,
   111, 119; Solomons campaign, 136, 137;
   Tarawa campaign, 142; Marshall Islands
   campaign, 150, 152; Marianas campaigns,
   160, 163, 174
Turner Joy (DD-951): Vietnam War,
   245, 247

U-29, 28
U-30, 28
U-73, 33
U-81, 32
U-131, 34
U-205, 32
U-336, 38
U-472, 38
U-562, 35
U-572, 34
U-586, 35
U-751, 34
U-973, 38

Ugaki, Matome, 87, 218–19; Okinawa
   campaign, 221, 223, 224; Home Islands
   campaign, 227
United States (CVB-58): cancelled, 232, 242;
   name available, 286
Unryu, IJN carrier, 179, 211, 213

Valley Forge (CG-50), 274
Valley Forge (CV-45), 231; Korean campaign,
   232, 233, 234, 237, 238
Vandegrift, Alexander A., 107, 109; defense of
   Guadalcanal, 119
Varyag, unfinished Russian carrier, 285
Vego, Milan, 281
Vejtasa, Stanley W.: at Santa Cruz, 127
Venerable, HMS carrier, 268
Vermont (BB-20), 4
Vian, Philip: Okinawa campaign, 221, 222,
   225; First Sea Lord, 231
Victorious, HMS carrier, 31, 32; at Malta, 33;
   in South Pacific, 135, 137; Okinawa
   campaign, 220, 221, 225
Vienticinco de Mayo, Argentine carrier, 268
Vinson, Carl, 22
Vose, James E.: at Santa Cruz, 125, 127
Vraciu, Alex: Marianas campaign, 167

Wainwright, Richard, 9
Wake Island: attacked, 54; rescue efforts,
   59, 63, 64; strikes against, 141,
   145, 183
Waldron, John C.: at Midway, 96
Walker, Walton H.: Pusan campaign, 233
Ward, Alfred G.: Cuban crisis, 263
Warspite, HMS battleship, 29
Washington (BB-56), 132
Washington Treaty (also Washington
   Conference): of 1922, 16, 19, 42; of
   1930, 20
Wasp (CV-7), 26, 104; authorized, 22;
   specifications, 25; at Guadalcanal, 108, 109,
   110, 119; in Eastern Solomons, 113, 114,
   115, 118; sunk, 119
Wasp (CV-18, CVA-18): Marianas campaign,
   167, 171, 172; Iwo Jima campaign, 216;
   Okinawa campaign, 218, 219; Vietnam
   War, 244
Wasp (LHD-1): Afghanistan operations, 278
Welch, Vivian W.: at Santa Cruz, 122
Westmoreland, William C., 250
Weymouth, Ralph: Marianas campaign, 172

Whitehead, Richard, 189; Leyte campaign, 195, 205, 206; Iwo Jima campaign, 216; Okinawa campaign, 221
White Plains (CVE-66): Leyte Gulf operations, 206, 208
Whiting, Kenneth, 17
Widhelm, William J.: at Santa Cruz, 125; Marianas campaign, 171
Wilbur, Curtis D., 20
Williams, R. S., 254
Wilson, Woodrow, 15, 23
Winston, R. A.: Marianas campaign, 171
Wright, Carleton H., 133
Wright, Orville, 4
Wright, Wilbur, 9

Yamada, Sadayoshi, 109, 111
Yamamoto, Isoroku: background, 49, 57; on naval strategy, 43–44, 45, 47, 48; on Pearl Harbor, 50–51, 54: MO Operation, 73, 76, 84; plans Midway expedition, 70, 73, 87–88; during Midway operation, 90, 91, 95, 99, 100, 101, 103; in Eastern Solomons, 112, 113–14, 117, 118; on Guadalcanal operations, 120, 121–22, 129–30, 131, 132; relieves Nagumo, 129; search for, 135
Yamagimoto, Ryusaku: at Midway, 98
Yamaguchi, Maseo: at Santa Cruz, 127
Yamaguchi, Tamon: at Midway, 99, 100, 101

Yamashiro, IJN battleship, 203
Yamato, IJN superbattleship, 88, 112, 153, 154, 213; in the Philippines, 195, 208–9, 210; Okinawa campaign, 219, 223, 224
Yonai, Mitsumasa: on naval strategy, 43–44
Yorktown (CV-5), 25, 51, 55, 57; authorized, 22; specifications, 24; early operations, 64–66, 68; at Coral Sea, 73–82, 84; at Midway, 88, 91, 93, 94, 95, 96, 97, 99, 100, 101, 102; sunk, 102, 103, 104
Yorktown (CV-10): Tarawa campaign, 140, 141, 142; Marshall Islands campaign, 147, 148, 149, 150; Marianas campaign, 161, 165, 166, 171, 172; Iwo Jima campaign, 216; Okinawa campaign, 219, 224

Zuiho, IJN carrier, 138, 142, 179; at Midway, 90, 101; at Santa Cruz, 120, 122, 123, 125, 129; in Central Pacific, 154; in the Philippine Sea, 164; in the Philippines, 194, 207
Zuikaku, IJN carrier, 87, 89, 103, 104, 138, 142, 179; in Coral Sea, 73, 76, 79, 80–82, 86; damaged 82; at Eastern Solomons, 112, 114, 115, 117; at Santa Cruz, 120, 122, 123, 125, 127, 128; in Central Pacific, 154; in the Philippine Sea, 165, 169, 171, 172; operations in the Philippines, 194, 207, 211
Zumwalt, Elmo R., 267

ABOUT THE AUTHOR

CHESTER G. HEARN is the author of eighteen books, including *Sorties into Hell: The Hidden War on Chichi Jima* (Praeger, 2003) and *Circuits in the Sea: The Men, the Ships, and the Atlantic Cable* (Praeger, 2004). He has studied naval and maritime history for much of his life, and his works include histories and biographies stretching from the American Revolution to Desert Storm.